Russian–American Relations

Also by Hafeez Malik

CENTRAL ASIA: Its Strategic Importance and Future Prospects

DILEMMAS OF NATIONAL SECURITY AND COOPERATION IN INDIA AND PAKISTAN

DOMESTIC DETERMINANTS OF SOVIET FOREIGN POLICY TOWARDS SOUTH ASIA AND THE MIDDLE EAST

ENCYCLOPEDIA OF CENTRAL ASIA (*editor with Yuri V. Gankovsky and Igor V. Khalevinsky*)

ENCYCLOPEDIA OF PAKISTAN (*editor with Yuri V. Gankovsky and Igor V. Khalevinsky*)

INTERNATIONAL SECURITY IN SOUTHWEST ASIA (*editor*)

IQBAL: Poet-Philosopher of Pakistan (*editor*)

MUSLIM NATIONALISM IN INDIA AND PAKISTAN

POLITICAL PROFILE OF SIR SAYYID AHMED KHAN: A Documentary Record

THE ROLES OF THE UNITED STATES, RUSSIA AND CHINA IN THE NEW WORLD ORDER (*editor*)

SIR SAYYID AHMED KHAN AND MUSLIM MODERNIZATION IN INDIA AND PAKISTAN

SIR SAYYID AHMED KHAN'S HISTORY OF THE BIJNORE REBELLION (*with Morris Dembo*)

SOVIET–AMERICAN RELATIONS WITH PAKISTAN, IRAN AND AFGHANISTAN (*editor*)

SOVIET–PAKISTAN RELATIONS AND CURRENT DYNAMICS

Russian–American Relations

Islamic and Turkic Dimensions in the Volga–Ural Basin

Edited by

Hafeez Malik
Professor of Political Science
Villanova University
Villanova
Pennsylvania

First published in Great Britain 2000 by
MACMILLAN PRESS LTD
Houndmills, Basingstoke, Hampshire RG21 6XS and London
Companies and representatives throughout the world

A catalogue record for this book is available from the British Library.

ISBN 0–333–73389–4

First published in the United States of America 2000 by
ST. MARTIN'S PRESS, INC.,
Scholarly and Reference Division,
175 Fifth Avenue, New York, N.Y. 10010

ISBN 0–312–23168–7

Library of Congress Cataloging-in-Publication Data
Russian–American relations : Islamic and Turkic dimensions in the Volga–Ural basin / edited by Hafeez Malik.
      p.   cm.
Includes bibliographical references and index.
ISBN 0–312–23168–7 (cloth)
1. Muslims—Russia—History. 2. Muslims—Soviet Union—History. 3. Muslims—Russia (Federation)—History. 4. Islam—Russia—History. 5. Islam—Soviet Union—History. 8. Bashkir (Turkic people)—Soviet Union—History. 9. Russia (Federation)—Relations—United States. 10. United States—Relations—Russia (Federation) I. Malik, Hafeez.

DK34.M8 R87   2000
947'.00882971—dc21

                                                                00–021896

This book is printed on paper suitable for recycling and made from fully managed and sustained forest sources.

10   9   8   7   6   5   4   3   2   1
09   08   07   06   05   04   03   02   01   00

Printed and bound in Great Britain by
Antony Rowe Ltd, Chippenham, Wiltshire

This book is dedicated with affection and admiration to the Tatar and Bashkort people, who since 1552 have struggled against all odds to preserve their culture, language and Islamic heritage. May their future be bright. In Allah Ma'a al-Sabirin *(God is with those [who bear their affliction] with fortitude and patience).*

Contents

Preface

This book presents a multidimensional analysis of (1) relations between the United States and Russia; (2) US relations with the former states of the Soviet Union, especially the republics of Central Asia; (3) Russia's endeavour to maintain its influence in (and, if possible, control over) the territory of the former Soviet Union; (4) Russia's futile attempts to crush the Chechen freedom movement in the Caucasus; and (5) Russia's relations with Tatarstan and Bashkortostan in the Volga–Ural basin.

Islam runs as an undercurrent throughout these analyses, a catalytic impulse that has given birth to a cultural and political renaissance in all the areas of study. Slowly and gradually Islam, with its differing interpretations, has emerged at the forefront of Western politics and is perceived as a factor to be reckoned with. Some very influential personages in the United States would like to see Islam replace the defunct Soviet Union as the focal point of international fear. On this score Russia has something in common with the United States: like the United States, Russia had endorsed the Islamic renaissance but condemned 'radical political Islam', or 'Islamic fundamentalism'. In all probability, as Islamic forces assert themselves – both positively and negatively – the term 'fundamentalism' will fade away and 'Islam' alone will remain, delineating what has been euphemistically called 'the fault line' in the projected clash of civilisations. It would be tragic if the legacy of the crusades were revived and poisoned the United States' interaction with the Muslim world.

In the Russian Federation the Muslim population is estimated to be 12–20 million. Most of them are ethnically Turkic and are located in the 21 autonomous republics within Russia; at least half of these republics are Muslims and Turkic.

Historically, Tatars have played a leading role in Eurasia. In the ninth century their ancestors, the Bulgars, established an extensive state whose capital, Bulgar, was located on the Volga river, just a few miles from Tatarstan's capital, Kazan, which historians called, Bulgar al-Jadid (the new Bulgar). Today only its ruins are visible, and an impressive Russian Orthodox Church stands in sharp contrast to the melancholy ruins of a grand mosque, of which only a lonely minaret remains more or less intact.

Flourishing from the ninth to the twelfth century, Volga Bulgaria was conquered in 1236 by the Mongols (the Golden Horde), who established their capital near the mouth of the Caspian Sea at Sarai Batu. The Mongols were succeeded in 1376 by the Kazan khanate, and in 1552 the territory was conquered by Russia. Contemporary Tatarstan was established on 27 May 1920. In 921 Caliph Ja'far al-Muktadir sent Ahmad Ibn-Fadhlan to preach Islam to the Tatars and Bashkorts, who by the end of the tenth century had joined the *umma-al Islamiya¯* (Community of Islamic believers). With the adoption of Islam, Arabic script replaced the Bulgar runes and Tatar literature began to enrich cultural life. According to a Russian historian, S. M. Solov'ev, 'When the Russian slaves had not yet begun to build Christian churches on the Oka, and had not yet occupied these places in the name of the European civilization, the Bulgars were already listening to the Qur'an on the banks of the Volga and Kama.' Since then Islam has remained an inseparable part of the cultural soul of the Tatars and Bashkorts. 'Throughout the ups and downs of history, Islam has been our protective shield' – God alone knows how many times Tatars and Bashkorts have said this to me.

Historically, the Tatar motherland extended from Astrakhan on the Caspian Sea along the River Volga to Kazan, and included the traditional Bashkort lands, which were contiguous to Kazakhstan and stretched onward in the direction of the Muscovite state. The Russian–Tatar conflict started in 1236, when Batu (Genghis Khan's grandson) conquered Volga Bulgaria, inducted the Tatar troops into the vanguard of his army and then conquered Russia. The Mongol rule over the Russian states lasted for 250 years and in Russian historiography is described as the Tatar yoke. Instead of converting to Christianity, Batu's successor, Berke Khan, converted to Islam, leading to the Mongols' assimilation with the Tatars and the Mongol heritage becoming part of the Tatar patrimony.

Berke Khan and his descendants ruled over the Golden Horde and the Russian states from their capital, Sarai Batu, which in the fifteenth century was described by Ibn Batuta as a 'very great, populous and beautiful city, possessing many mosques, fine marketplaces, and broad streets, in which were to be seen merchants from Babylon, Egypt, Syria and other countries'. (During the celebration of the 750th anniversary of the Golden Horde in August 1993, some of my Tatar colleagues, who had travelled on pilgrimage with me from Kazan to the ruins of Sarai Batu, shed tears at the site and picked up pieces of broken pottery and tiles at the ruined central mosque to keep as sacred relics of their bygone glory. This was indeed a vivid demonstration of the strength of modern Tatar nationalism and national identity.)

Finally, in 1552 Ivan the Terrible conquered the Kazan khanate and incorporated the Tatar and Bashkort lands into the Duchy of Moscovy. By 1533 Moscovy's territory had increased from 37 000 square miles to 47 000 square miles, and by 1682 it had expanded to 265 000 square miles, of which about 80 000 were in Europe and about 185 000 in Asia. In the nineteenth century, unified Russia conquered Central Asia.

In the sixteenth century the tsars of Moscovy had clearly understood that by annihilating the successor states of the Golden Horde, including the Nagoi Tatars, the Kazan khanate and the Bashkort lands, they could secure Central Asia and the Muslim-Turkic civilisational strongholds. The definition of Central Asia is problematic, however. Where does it start in regard to Russia, and precisely where are the historical boundaries of Russia itself? The Soviet authorities and Russian scholars (who naturally bowed to the conclusions of the former) excluded Kazakhstan from Central Asia: to them Kazakhstan was neither quite Russia nor quite Asia because it was contiguous to the lands of the Bashkorts and Tatars, who shared their language, culture and Islam with Kazakhs and other Central Asians. Eventually the Tatar and Bashkort lands were designated as Russian and European, and the demographic balance was altered when Russian settlers were brought in. However in 1999 the Russian population was still a minority in the Republic of Tatarstan, and in Bashkortostan the combined population of Tatars and Bashkorts outnumbered the Russians.

The new *oblast* of Orenburg was created to separate so-called Russian territory from West Kazakhstan. The line of separation ran from Karacharyosk to Albulak to Novotriosk. Consisting of land taken from Bashkortostan and Kazakhstan, the *oblasts* of *Chelyabinsk* and *Magnitogorsk* were created in order to flank Tatarstan and Bashkortostan with additional 'Russian territory'. Ironically, still standing to this day is a pillar that was erected on the highway linking Chelyabinsk with Ufa (the capital of Bashkortostan) to indicate the boundary between Asia and Europe, implying that Tatarstan and Bashkortostan are in Europe, while more than half of Chelyabinsk is in Asia. The latter is contiguous to Kazakhstan.

Tatar and Bashkort leaders and scholars reject Russia's demographic and cartographic engineering and look upon the River Volga as Russia's historical boundary, dating back to the national tragedy of 1552. In their perception, despite the penetration of Russian culture and religion the lands stretching from the Ural mountains along the Volga to the Caspian Sea are eternally the lands of Tatars and Bashkorts and part of the Central Asian Islamic civilisation.

In the summer of 1994, while visiting Raphael Khakimov, senior political adviser to President Mintimer Shamayev of Tatarstan at the Kazan kremlin, I broached the subject of holding an international seminar at Villanova University, Pennsylvania, so that Tatar and Bashkort scholars and American specialists could discuss Tatarstan's and Bashkortostan's internal problems and their relations with Russia, as well as Russia's relations with the United States. The following year the subject was discussed again in the office of R. Iskandr Nigmatullin, president of the Bashkortostan Academy of Sciences at Ufa. The governments of both republics blessed the enterprise and the seminar was duly held in October 1996 at Villanova University, where sixteen well-crafted chapters of this volume were presented. Among those attending were US military officers, some members of the State Department and scholars from American universities. For the success of this intellectual enterprise I owe a debt of gratitude to my friends, Raphael Khakimov and Iskandr Nigmatulin, without whose generous support the seminar would not have seen the light of day.

This collective endeavour provides the Western world with its first opportunity to understand the Tatar and Bashkort problems of national survival, self-determination and cooperation with Moscow. Will Russia survive within its present precarious boundaries or revert back to the boundaries of 1552? This is a major question in contemporary world politics. Russian leaders will be called upon to demonstrate a great deal of political sophistication, diplomatic skill and religious tolerance of the Muslim nations that exist uncomfortably in their federation. Under any label or pretext, a crusade against Islamic peoples and their national sovereignty would accelerate the disintegration of the multi-national Russian Federation. On this score, Russia does not have a commonality of strategic interest with the United States, which unlike Russia is not a multinational state. Young America is a breed apart from the old states of the world.

The seminar at Villanova University was organised under the auspices of the Pakistan–American Foundation, in cooperation with the Center for Arabic and Islamic Studies and the Center for Russian Studies. Villanova University has not only been an intellectual haven for me, but for 25 years has also generously supported the *Journal of South Asian and Middle Eastern Studies*, the Pakistan–American Foundation and the American Institute of Pakistan Studies, which have also received generous support from the Pakistani Ministry of Education.

I am equally indebted to Fr Edmund J. Dobbin (President), Jack Johannes (vice President of academic affairs) and Fr Kail C. Ellis (Dean of arts and sciences, and director of the Center for Contemporary Arab and Islamic Studies of Villanova University). Dr Javid Iqbal (former justice of the Supreme Court of Pakistan and until October 1999 a member of Pakistan's senate and a ranking member of its Committee on Foreign Relations) presided over one of the sessions and managed to keep the level of discourse very high in the face of hotly contested political views.

Among my friends I single out Nadia Barsoum, who helped me in many ways to make the seminar a success. Other friends, both in the United States and abroad, have been a source of encouragement and support: Yuri V. Gankovsky, Afaq Haydar, Jack Schrems, Naim Rathore, Lori Kephart, Syed Abid Ali, Zaheer Chaudhry, M. Imtiaz Ali, Riaz Ahmad, Stanley Wolpert, Muhammad Ali Chaudhry, Igor V. Khalevinski, Vyacheslav Ya. Belokrinitsky and (Akhuna) Khalil Ilyas. I value their friendship and cherish their affection. My programme coordinator, Susan K. Hausman, handled the details of the seminar with her usual efficiency and imaginative skills. Last but not least, a colleague at Villanova University, my wife, Lynda P. Malik, a sociologist specialising in Islamic societies, not only participated in the seminar but also acted as a cheerful host.

Villanova University   HAFEEZ MALIK

Notes on the Contributors

Robert V. Barylski is Associate Professor of Government and International Affairs at the University of South Florida in Sarasota. He studies military aspects of political change in the former Soviet Union and relations between Russia and the CIS republics with an Islamic heritage. His recent publications include 'Kazakhstan: Military Dimensions of State Formation over Central Asia's Civilizational Fault Lines' (in C. P. Danopoulos and D. G. Zirker, eds, *Civil–Military Relations in Soviet and Yugoslav Successor States*, and 'The Russian Federation and Eurasia's Islamic Crescent' (*European–Asia Studies*, vol. 46, no. 3, 1994).

Graham E. Fuller is a Senior Political Scientist at the RAND Corporation, Washington, DC. He is former Vice Chairman of the National Intelligence Council at the CIA, where he was responsible for long-range intelligence forecasting. He is the author of *The Democracy Trap: Perils of the Post-Cold War* and several other publications.

M. G. Galeyev is Chairman of the Tatarstan legislature's Commission on Economic Development and Reform.

Makhmud A. Gareyev, an ethnic Tatar from Bashkortostan, is a retired Soviet Army general.

Sergei Gretsky is a faculty member of the Catholic University of America. He was educated in Tajikistan.

M. H. Khasanov is a well-known scholar and President of the Tatarstan Academy of Sciences, Kazan.

Mikhail Konarovsky is a Counsellor at the Embassy of the Russian Federation, Washington, DC.

Rail G. Kuzeyev is an eminent anthropologist and Director of the Bashkort National Museum of Archaeology and Ethnography, Ufa, Bashkortostan.

Hafeez Malik is Professor of Political Science at Villanova University, Pennsylvania. From 1961–63 and 1966–84 he was Visiting Lecturer at the Foreign Service Institute of the US Department of State. An author/editor of 13 books and numerous articles, from 1971–74 he was President of the Pakistan Council of the Asia Society, New York. He also is President of the Pakistan–American Foundation, founding Director (1973–88) of the American Institute of Pakistan Studies, and since 1977, Editor of the *Journal of South Asian and Middle Eastern Studies*, Executive Director of the American Council for the Study of Islamic Societies since 1983, and President of the World Affairs Council of Greater Valley Forge from 1993–95.

Alvin Z. Rubinstein is a Professor of Political Science and Senior Fellow of the Foreign Policy Research Institute at the University of Pennsylvania. An author of several books, Rubinstein has received fellowships from the Ford Foundation, the Rockefeller Foundation and the John Simon Guggenheim Memorial Foundation.

Engel Tagirov is Professor and Dean of History and Law at the Financial and Economic Institute, Kazan, Tatarstan.

Zinnour Uraksin is Director of the Institute of History, Language and Literature, Ufa, Bashkortostan.

D. Zh. Valeyev, a noted Bashkort scholar, is a member of the Bashkortostan Academy of Sciences, Ufa.

Aislu Yunosova is a Bashkort scholar and faculty member at Bashkir University, Ufa, Bashkortostan. She specialises in Islam's social role in her own republic.

Map of Autonomous Areas in Russia

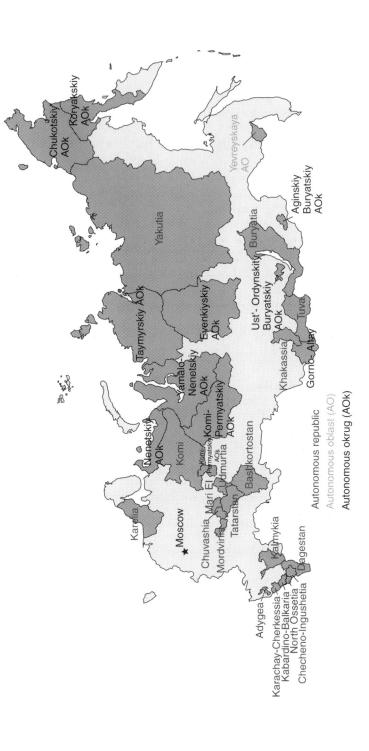

Chukotskiy AOk

Koryakskiy AOk

Yevreyskaya AO

Aginskiy Buryatskiy AOk

Yakutia

Buryatia

Taymyrskiy AOk

Evenkiyskiy AOk

Ust'- Ordynskiy Buryatskiy AOk

Tuva

Khakassia

Gorno-Altay

Yamalo-Nenetskiy AOk

Komi-Permyatskiy AOk

Nenetskiy AOk

Komi

Komi-Permyatskiy AOk

Udmurtia

Bashkortostan

Mari El

Chuvashia

Mordvinia

Tatarstan

Moscow

Karelia

Kalmykia

Dagestan

Adygea

Karachay-Cherkessia
Kabardino-Balkaria
North Ossetia
Checheno-Ingushetia

Autonomous republic

Autonomous oblast (AO)

Autonomous okrug (AOk)

1

Islamic and Turkic Dimensions in Russian–American Relations: An Introduction

Hafeez Malik

In the Preface to my edited volume, *The Roles of the United States, Russia and China in the New World Order* (1997), I highlighted the struggle for power between the three states in the title – all in the name of peace, international cooperation, democracy, trade and human rights. This struggle for power is motivated by the clash of national interests and is likely to remain so in the future. In this volume another dimension of this struggle will be highlighted: the vulnerability of Russia in the Volga–Ural basin and the Caucasus, where the historic clash took place between the Russian slaves and Muslim-Turkic nations. The conquest of the Tatar and Bashkort lands in the middle of the sixteenth century opened the way to the Russian conquest of Kazakhstan, other Central Asian states and the Caucasus. Today another version of the 'great game' is being played out between Russia and the United States, while China remains an active player in the Eurasian land mass.

Since the collapse of the Soviet Union in December 1991 the Russian state has come to look like a 'pitiful giant', while the United States has become the sole superpower, determined to mould the world in its own image. What its specific role should be in regard to Russia and China is the subject of debate in the United States. One school of thought perceives the United States as a 'universal empire' with a messianic mission. All adherents to this view foresee the United States dominating the world in the twenty-first century because it represents the highest form of Western civilisation, having mastered science and technology. Within this school of thought, Samuel P. Huntington has predicted that 'the clash of civilization will dominate global politics. The fault lines between civilizations will be the battle lines of the future.'[1]

In a more thoughtful analysis of the civilisational encounter, Donald J. Puchala describes a pattern of cultural diffusion that has often led to cultural enrichment. 'Most civilizations', according to Puchala, 'have had one core empire within them – the Persian, Macedonian, Roman, Byzantine, Chinese, Gupta, Holy Roman, Arab, Ottoman, etc. – that has assumed the role of protector or extender of the culture'.[2] While he does not say so explicitly, his analysis implicitly points to the United States as the 'protector' and 'extender' of Western civilisation. The twenty-first century, according to him, will usher in 'a global civilization – with universal morality, philosophy, social relations, governance, science, art, and who can say, even religion – may already be congealing in those places where the wires, air routes, sea lanes, markets, marketeers, priests and poets converge'.[3]

Implicit here again is the assertion that the collapse of the Soviet Union has marked the triumph of democracy and the free market economy, as well as the successful mobilisation of technology in the new information age. Who is the leader of this? The United States. Some observers of the contemporary geopolitical situation caution against promoting American culture over others. However a former senior official in the US Department of Commerce during the first term of the Clinton administration and currently the managing director of Kissinger Associates, David Rothkopt, deprecates this as 'relativism [which] is as dangerous as it is wrong'. Rothkopt asserts that

> The United States should not hesitate to promote its values. In an effort to be polite or politic, Americans should not deny the fact that of all the nations in the history of the world, theirs is the most just, the most willing to constantly reassess and improve itself, and the best model for the future. Americans should promote their vision for the world because failing to do so or taking a 'live and let live' stance is ceding the process to the not-always-beneficial actions of others.[4]

Very appropriately, his formulations are entitled 'In Praise of Cultural Imperialism'. Since the United States has more leadership experience 'than any other nation in this new global environment', the United States is the appropriate power to establish *Pax Americana* in the twenty-first century.

In political terms, what does *Pax Americana* mean for Russia and China? Indeed since December 1991 Republican and Democratic administrations alike have urged Russia and China to adopt the main pillars of Western civilisation (including: democracy; the market economy; the capitalist system; human rights with emphasis on the freedom of speech, religion and free association; the opening up of the Russian and Chinese domestic markets to American products; adherence to the American-sponsored rules of conduct in international trade; and nuclear non-proliferation and disarmament), while expecting them to accept the United States' global leadership role.

Sensing a decline or fall in the scale of their power in 1991, the Russian leadership rather naively adopted an orientation of what they called Atlanticism, believing that the United States would extend to Russia an effective partnership in managing world affairs. The euphoria of joining the Western civilisation persisted during 1991–93. In jettisoning communism the Russians believed that they had eliminated the ideological threat to the United States, for which the latter would reward them generously with abundant investment in order to rehabilitate their economy, which would in turn enable them to be equal partners in the G-7. While the West did reluctantly grant Russia membership of the G-7 and accepted it as a successor state to the Soviet Union in the United Nations, the declining power of Russia made it impossible for the West to treat it as an equal partner. Yet the fear of Russia's imperial legacy continued to preoccupy the thinking of US policymakers.

In 1996 former Secretary of Defense Caspar Weinberger (in collaboration with an academic, Peter Schweizer) published his prognostication about the next war, developed 'in the spirit of the Pentagon's computerized scenarios'. He predicted a Russian reconquest of the former Soviet empire in 2006, triggered by nuclear blackmail by an ultranationalist demagogue leader whose antimissile system would be so technologically advanced that American missiles would be rendered useless and American forces would be pushed out of Europe.[5] (In addition to this scenario Weinberger postulated four more deadly scenarios in other parts of the world.)

Despite Weinberger's bone-chilling predictions the fact remains that Russia has been open about the disintegration of its armed forces, the decline in its economy and the reassertion of the Turkic-Islamic peoples in the Volga–Ural basin, and in the Caucasus, where Chechen irregular forces defeated the once powerful Russian army and *de facto* established the sovereignty of Chechnya in 1468.[6]

Economically Russia was (and is) unable to support the 1.8 million members of its armed forces, so in 1997 President Boris Yeltsin decreed that the number would be reduced to 1.2 million. It is estimated that the Russian army could fully supply only one of its divisions for battle; the Russian navy is in a terrible state of decay, and from Murmansk to

Vladivostok its giant ships lie rotting in their berths; and the performance of its air force is no longer credible. Unable to support their families, some Russian officers commit suicide – in 1996 500 Russian
soldiers killed themselves and in 1997 the number rose even higher.
Russian soldiers beg for money in Moscow's subway stations, ostensibly for the families of those soldiers who died in Chechnya.[7] Russia
now spends less than $20 billion a year on defence – about 10 per cent
of the US figure ($250 billion) and a third of that of Britain.[8]

Despite the decline of its armed forces, Russia's imperial ventures in
Central Asia have continued. Speaking of Russia's policy towards the
former Soviet republics the president of Kazakhstan, Nursultan
Nazarbayev, repeatedly highlighted Russia's imperialist 'ambitions
[which] stick out like a sore thumb'.[9] Specifically, he objected to (1) the
presence of Russian troops in Tajikstan, the Donester region and
Armenia; (2) the Russian insistence on having Yeltsin as the chairman
of the Commonwealth of Independent States (CIS); (3) Russia's decision to authorise the Russian Border Service to use Cossacks rather
than regular troops to guard the 5000 km border between Kazakhstan
and Russia; (4) Russia's delayed signing of the agreement on the
Caspian pipeline, which was completed four years ago; and that (5), for
gas extracted in Kazakhstan, Russia has established a natural gas processing plant at Orenburg and a condensate processing plant in the
Bashkortostan city of Salvat Julayev on such disadvantageous terms
that Kazakhstan receives only 13–17 cents in the dollar. To loosen
Russia's economic stranglehold, Kazakhstan and its neighbours created
the community of Central Asian states and joined the larger
Organization for Economic Cooperation and Development (OECD).[10]

Despite its hegemonic policy, Russia is becoming acutely aware of its
demographic vulnerability in the Muslim areas of the federation, especially in the Volga–Ural basin and the Caucasus. Russian demographers
present a rather gloomy picture for ethnic Russians in the twenty-first
century, when they will still be the largest population group in Russia
but not an absolute majority. During 1991–94 the number of Russians
living in Russia decreased by more than two million; their number is
likely to fall to 85 million and will continue to decline thereafter. Some
of the demographic trends which have led to this gloomy prediction
are as follows. First, the population is rapidly aging. Second, people's
health is declining and the mortality rate is increasing. Third, the birth
rate in major cities is as low as six or seven per 1000, and shows a continuing downward trend. Fourth, the fertility index for Russian women
has fallen to one child and is continuing to fall. Finally, close to 50 per

cent of all children are born sick, and about 20 per cent of all new-borns are born out of wedlock to alcoholics or drug addicts.[11]

Against this gloomy picture for ethnic Russians, a substantial increase in the Muslim population is predicted for several reasons. First, the birth rate in Muslim families is significantly higher than the death rate. Second, Muslim families are bigger, stronger and healthier than Russian families. Third, they are generally not addicted to alcohol, and births out of wedlock are rare. In troubled times Muslim families tend to gravitate towards their ancestral regions. Consequently Russian demographers predict that 'some areas in which Muslims predominated up to the middle of sixteenth century (Astrakhan, Chelyabinsk, and Orenburg provinces and the northeastern part of Nizhny Novgorod province) will again become at least half Muslim'.[12] Even today, in the Volga–Ural basin, where Tatarstan is located, the Muslim Tatar population is in the absolute majority. In Bashkortostan the combined Muslim population of Tatars and Bashkorts is about 50 per cent of the total population, and political power is concentrated in the hands of the Bashkorts.

To sum up this part of the discussion, three pronounced trends can be discerned in the Russian situation: (1) despite the decline in its economy and military strength (2) the Russian proclivity for imperialist expansion in both Europe and Central Asia is still intact, and (3) the Volga–Ural basin and the Caucasus have become the soft underbelly of the Russian Federation as Islam is acting as a catalytic force for the resurgence of Tatars, Bashkorts and the Caucasian Muslim peoples.

In order to contain Russian imperialist activity in the post-Soviet environment, the United States and its Western allies have adopted a three-pronged approach: (1) constructive engagement with Russia (as well as with China) while (2) quarantining it behind its existing boundaries through (3) the extension of NATO. Implicit here is the assumption that the members of the Russian Federation will work out their own relationship with Moscow, which has hitherto ranged from varying degrees of autonomy for Tatarstan and Bashkortostan to *de facto* independence for Chechnya. Other Muslim regions are following the same pattern.

Russia mistakenly believes that it can continue to treat the CIS states as being within its own sphere of influence, and that the resources of these states will continue to be subject to its exclusive exploitation. Simultaneously, however, the US policy is to deepen bilateral relations with the CIS states, and especially Ukraine, whose sovereignty and security are *sine qua non* for quarantining Russia. In the Central Asian states, American and European oil companies are investing heavily in the extraction of oil and gas and their distribution to the international

Table 1.1 Planned oil and gas pipelines in the greater Caspian region

Pipeline	Type	Route	Capacity (barrels/day)	Length (miles)	Status
AIOC* Early oil (South–North)	Oil	Baku–Novorossiisk via Groznyi	120 000+	1000	Russian side inoperative
AIOC Early oil (East–West)	Oil	Baku–Supsa via Tbilisi	120 000+	550	Under construction
AIOC Main export Pipeline (MEP)	Oil	Undecided; preferably via Turkey	1 000 000	2000+	Decision pending
Caspian Pipeline Consortium (CPC)	Oil	Kazakstan/Tengiz–Novorossiisk	1 340 000	1500	Contracts signed
Turkmenistan–Afghanistan–Pakistan pipelines	Gas	Dauletabad gas field to central Pakistan	2 billion cubic feet/day	872	The civil war in Afghanistan is stalling construction
Turkmenistan–Afghanistan–Pakistan pipelines	Oil	Chardzhou, Turkmenistan–Gwadar, Pakistan	1 000 000	800+	
Kazakstan–China	Oil	Western Kazakstan–China	TBA	Approx. 3700	Feasibility study pending
Turkmenistan–China	Oil	Chardzhou–China	TBA	Approx. 3700	Feasibility study pending
Central Asia–	Gas	Kazakstan–Turkmenistan–	TBA	Approx.	Pending decision

Table 1.1 Continued

Pipeline	Type	Route	Capacity (barrels/day)	Length (miles)	Status
Turkey		Azerbaijah		1300	on the status of the Caspian Sea
Iran–Turkey	Gas	Northern Iran–eastern Turkey	10 bcm/yr** over 23 years	600	Contract signed; financing unclear

* Azerbaijan International Operating Company.
** billions of cubic meters per year.
Source: U.S. Department of State, 'Caspian Region Energy Development Report', undated report attached to letter from Barbara Larkin, Assistant Secretary for Legislative Affairs, to Senator Robert Byrd, 15 April 1997, p. 3.

markets. Nine pipelines in the greater Caspian region are planned or under construction (Table 1.1), all but two of which will bypass Russian territory. These arrangements will give substance to the sovereign status of the Central Asian states, detach them for Russia and break Russia's economic stranglehold over them.

In the Caucasus the interests of oil companies such as Amoco, Unocal, Exxon and PennZoil have forced the emergence of a US–Turkey–Azerbaijan economic bloc against the Russia–Iran–Armenia 'alliance'. US oil companies are investing billions of dollars to extract the enormous untapped oil deposits in Azerbaijan, and arrangements are underway to establish a 'strong U.S.–Azerbaijan defense cooperation'. Moreover, it is projected that Azerbaijan will act as 'a buffer against its two powerful neighbors, Russia and Iran'. In the US perception this strategy, combining oil with the US-ensured security of Azerbaijan, will further isolate Iran and one more CIS country will slip out of the Russian orbit. Referring to the Caucasus, Yeltsin recently complained that 'Already the United States is declaring that it is in their zone of influence.'[13]

Turning now to the extension of NATO, while this has been extensively debated among the members of the US foreign policy community, the general public has paid no serious attention to the issue. Nevertheless the extension needs to have a rational explanation because a large coalition of states can only come into existence if there is a widespread perception of a common threat to the stability of the balance of power and the survival of the state system. Such was the case with the Soviet Union, and in the past Hitler and Napoleon appeared as destroyers of the European state system. In December 1991 the Soviet 'barbarians' disappeared, yet the NATO coalition, instead of withering away, reasserted its vitality and lurched towards extension!

Lord Ismay, the first secretary general of the NATO, made a waggish statement about the purpose of the alliance, which very substantially explains the nature of the common threat in the post-Soviet environment: 'NATO serves three purposes: Keep the Russians out, keep the Americans in, and keep the Germans down.' Keeping the Russians out is perceived as fundamental to the US intention to prevent any hostile hegemonic power from dominating Europe. Germany is still considered by some Europeans as a potential threat to the stability of Europe, especially if the US nuclear umbrella is withdrawn from NATO and a future generation of German politicians feels the need to develop its own nuclear capability. Consequently the United States is projected as a benign stabiliser of Europe and a guarantee of security.[14]

Before admitting Poland, Hungary and the Czech Republic into NATO in 1997, the United States presented a classical diplomatic pacifier to Russia in the form of the Founding Act between Russia and NATO. The 10-page agreement, signed in Paris on 27 May, established a new NATO–Russia council for consultation on security issues and NATO assured (not guaranteed) that it had 'no plans' to deploy nuclear weapons in the territory of any new members. Also Russia would be unable to exercise a veto over issues brought to the council for determination. At the signing ceremony Yeltsin let out a little theatrical sign of relief,[15] which according to *Izvestia* 'evoked the picture of a country parting with the role of a great power and consciously shifting to a new capacity'.[16] Sadly and reluctantly, Yeltsin accepted this 'new capacity' of subordination. He had no option but to make the best of an adverse situation.

Negotiating from a position of tremendous strategic strength, the United States is able to exercise pressure on a variety of issues related to its vital interests. Against the backdrop of Russia's disintegrating armed forces, the military strength of NATO (Table 1.2) is now in a position effectively to quarantine Russia within its precarious boundaries. Russia planned in 1997 to spend 104 trillion rubles or $18.5 billion) on its armed forces compared with the US allocation of about $250 billion.

Table 1.2   NATO military strength, 1966

	Population	Active armed forces	Defence spending (millions of US dollars)
Belgium	10 082 000	46 300	3230
Britain	58 407 000	226 000	32 462
Canada	28 406 400	70 500	7733
Denmark	5 224 600	32 900	3113
France	58 385 000	398 900	38 454
Germany	81 106 600	358 400	31 945
Greece	10 502 400	168 300	3462
Iceland	272 600	–	–
Italy	57 879 600	325 150	19 951
Luxembourg	409 000	800	121
Netherlands	15 515 600	63 100	8076
Norway	4 371 000	30 000	3711
Portugal	9 870 200	54 200	1728
Spain	39 162 600	206 800	6919
Turkey	62 253 200	639 000	5651
United States	265 622 400	1 483 800	268 843

Source: International Institute for Strategic Studies (London: IISS, 1997).

Clearly, not being able economically to maintain the military establishment it inherited from the Soviet Union, Russia is now under pressure to look favourably upon US proposals for deeper cuts in long-range nuclear arms. In March 1997 Presidents Yeltsin and Clinton agreed in Helsinki to cut the number of long-range warheads on each side to no more than 2000 to 2500 by the end of 2007 in a third strategic arms reduction treaty, Start 3. The two presidents distinguished between *short-range* theatre missile defences, intended to protect troops and ships, from *long-range* strategic missile defences, which are all but banned under the 1972 Anti-Ballistic Missile or ABM Treaty. Washington will continue to pay money-starved Russia for the destruction of the weapons already agreed upon between the two states.[17]

In order to make NATO expansion easier for the Russians to swallow, the United States invited Yeltsin to become a member of the newly renamed 'Summit of the Eight'. At the 23rd summit meeting Russia was 'politely' advised to write off a large part of Soviet-era debt, much of it for military purchases by poor Soviet allies, three of which had recently joined NATO. This diplomatic pacifier, a boost to Yeltsin's ego, proved to be expensive for Russia.

In 1992 Russia, the United States and 27 other countries signed the Open Skies Treaty, which President Eisenhower had proposed to the Soviet Union in Geneva in 1955.[18] The ill-fated U-2 flight in Soviet airspace on 1 May 1960 by Francis Gary Powers had raised a storm of protest from Nikita Khrushchev, but in July 1997 Colonel Mikhail Botvinko's flight across a large swath of the eastern United States, taking photographs of US military bases,[19] was scarcely noticed. Space age spy satellites and US technological superiority over Russia had eliminated the need for aerial reconnaissance and Botvinko's flight was seen as posing no threat to the security of the United States, while the Russian military landscape was an open book to the Pentagon.

Bowing to the US Congress and Department of State, Yeltsin vetoed a bill that would have protected the Russian Orthodox Church from competition by Western churches. Washington commented that 'Yeltsin has done the right thing for freedom of religion in Russia.'[20] The bill, which had been passed by the Duma by an overwhelming majority, had recognised only Russian Christian Orthodoxy, Islam, Judaism and Buddhism as 'Russian' religions. How this issue will eventually be resolved remains to be seen, but the Russian Orthodox Church and the Duma seem determined to protect the religious establishments that existed in the Soviet Union.

In the Soviet era the Middle East in general and the Arab–Israeli conflict in particular were off limits to Russia, and they remain so today. The United States, articulating Israeli security interests, has urged Russia to stop Russian scientists and military institutes from helping Iran to develop a new ballistic missile that could reach Israeli and American troops in the Gulf. (Similarly, questions have been raised in Congress about China's alleged exportation of nuclear and missile technology to Iran and Pakistan.) Congress has also threatened Russia that all aid will be cut off if it does not cease all nuclear and missile cooperation with Iran. Clearly the US strategy is to maintain Israeli technological and military superiority in the Middle East and to keep Russian influence out of the region.[21]

In response to the United States' hegemonial policies, Russia and China have bemoaned the disequilibrium among the three powers. In April 1997 Presidents Yeltsin and Jiang Zemin signed a joint Russian–Chinese declaration on a multipolar world and the formation of a new international order, with emphasis on four points: (1) the two powers would make efforts to further the development of a multipolar world in which 'mutual respect, equality and mutual advantage, not hegemony' would prevail; (2) no one country should strive for hegemony or monopolise international affairs; (3) a comprehensive concept of security should be established, modelled on a regional security arrangement between Russia, Kazakhstan, Kyrgistan, Tajikistan and China and stipulating confidence-building in military affairs and in the border regions; and (4) the role of the United Nations and its Security Council should be strengthened.[22] Clearly the fourth point suggested that NATO should not preempt the international security role of the UN Security Council, where the two powers can exercise their right to veto any military measure.

Indeed, for the first time since 1815 an asymmetrical world system has emerged where the United States remains the only superpower. How long the US dominance will last is anybody's guess, but the prediction is that the post-Cold War world order will not survive into the twenty-first century. According to one European scholar, the world will evolve into four or possibly five political–economic blocs that will be the main actors on the world stage:[23]

1. A European bloc, comprising the European Union and its neighbours.
2. An East Asian bloc comprising 'greater China' and an East Asian economic area.

3. A Pan-American bloc, centred on the United States and with or without a North American free trade agreement.
4. A Moscow-led Slavic and Orthodox Russian bloc.
5. A Japanese-centred economic bloc (although this may find itself in some kind of relationship with the Chinese-led bloc).

Until a multi-bloc state system develops the US superpower will reign supreme.

The geopolitical role of Islam and nationalism

This volume contains a four-dimensional analysis by American, Russian, Tatar and Bashkort scholars who met in a seminar at Villanova University, Pennsylvania, in 1996. The topics include (1) Islam and ethnic diversity in the Commonwealth of Independent States (CIS), with emphasis on Central Asia; (2) mutual adjustment between Russia and Islam in the post-Soviet environment; (3) Tatarstan's quest for autonomy and national reassertion in the Volga–Ural basin and (4) the revival of nationalism in Bashkortostan. Like a symphonic composition, these four subthemes highlight the role of Islam among the Turkic republics that today constitute the soft underbelly of the Russian Federation.

Reflecting the US perspectives on world politics, four well-known and respected American scholars – Graham E. Fuller, Alvin Z. Rubinstein, Sergei Gretsky and Robert V. Barylski – explore the Islamic dimension of ethnic diversity and the problems of national self-determination in the CIS and the states that the Russians like to call the 'near abroad'. Sergei Gretsky's analysis focuses on Central Asia in general and Russia's relations with Afghanistan in particular. In Chapter 2 Fuller explores five US approaches, each of which makes a great deal of sense, despite some degree of mutual contradiction:

1. Some generalised sympathy for self-determination by the peoples of the region.
2. The demands of pragmatic politics, prompting Washington towards a more Russocentric orientation.
3. A concern for regional stability and ambivalence about any Russian role in maintaining regional stability; that is, is Russia an imperialist state or a regional peacekeeper?
4. Anxiety about the potentially destabilising implications of Islamic fundamentalist movements.

5. A discomfort with the realities of political evolution in the region, where both ethnicity and Islam are almost certainly factors of growing importance.

Despite its traditional sympathy for people in search of self-determination, the US government has not supported the Muslim Chechens (who have established their sovereignty *de facto*), neither, for that matter, have the Muslim states openly supported Chechnya's quest for independence because some of them look to Russia for various kinds of diplomatic support. Similarly Western states have been heavily influenced by *raisons d'état* on issues of self-determination in the CIS. This pragmatic approach has indeed led the United States towards a Russocentric orientation. However in order to strengthen the newly independent CIS states, Fuller maintains, the United States 'has sought some UN or OSCE peacekeeping role in the area to avoid difficult questions about Russia's own objectivity and neutrality there'. According to Fuller, the United States 'associates Islamist regimes with nearly automatic anti-American policies and rhetoric and with explicit opposition to the Arab–Israeli peace process – a key US goal in the Middle East … . The US obviously seeks to discourage the spread of Islamist ideology in the region'. This US concern, he believes, is shared by Russia, specifically: 'the potential anti-Russian character of political Islam in the Muslim republics of the former Soviet Union due to the long-term Russian oppression of Islam as a religion; the potential ability of political Islam to stir up negative or separatist views among those Muslims still living inside the Russian Federation such as Tatars, Bashkorts and the Muslims of the northern Caucasus; the ability of foreign Muslim states such as Turkey, Iran, Saudi Arabia and Pakistan to use Islam to increase their own political, cultural and economic influence in the former republics at Russian expense'. Precisely for these reasons, the United States has been 'willing to see Russia take some action, when the threat of political Islam is invoked'.

In chapter 3 Rubinstein focuses on the Turkic peoples of the newly independent states of central Eurasia. He also discusses 'the zone of uncertainty', where Russia and other foreign states – the United States, China, Turkey, Iran, Saudi Arabia and Pakistan – are actively engaged. Russia is no longer a major power in the Arab East, but there still exists an adversarial relationship between Russia and the United States over Transcaucasia and Central Asia, although Moscow's main regional competitors are Turkey, Iran and, to a lesser extent, China and Pakistan.

In 1992, when James Baker was secretary of state, the US approach to the region was to back Turkey against Iran. By 1993 Turkey had signed with the Central Asian states more than 140 bilateral accords on a variety of subjects, but no significant relationship developed because 'Turkey's capabilities were not equal to its ambitions, and the dream of a Pan-Turkic revival quickly vanished'. Furthermore, as Rubinstein points out, Iran enjoys certain advantages over Turkey: (1) Turkey lacks a common border with Central Asia but Iran shares a common border with Azerbaijan, Turkmenistan, Armenia. Afghanistan and Pakistan ('geography does matter'); (2) Iran offers Central Asia access to the sea; and (3) Iran has better relations with Russia than does Turkey.

In addition to problems related to the extraction of oil and natural gas in Eurasia, Rubinstein maintains that the US objectives in Transcaucasia and Central Asia are (1) denuclearisation; (2) recognition of Russia's legitimate security concerns; (3) strengthening the independent character of the newly independent states; (4) dampening regional and intrastate conflicts; (5) promoting market economies, investment and integration into the global economy; and (6) upholding human rights.

In chapter 4 the main thesis of Sergei Gretsky, who was educated in Tajikistan and has maintained a close watch on political developments in Central Asia in general and Tajikistan in particular, is that the Central Asian leaders (former CPSU apparatchiks) were not prepared for the freedom that arrived in December 1991. With the first signs of freedom during the *perestroika* period (1989–91), local democratic and Islamist opposition to their rule emerged and they realised that they were unlikely to survive without Russian assistance. Moreover Russian settlers in Central Asia convinced Moscow that Islamic fundamentalism posed a threat to Russian interests in Central Asia. Against this background, Moscow was invited to intervene in Tajikistan in 1992, which enabled Russians to return to Central Asia to exercise control over independence in the region and absorb Central Asia into Russia's sphere of influence.

Based on these events, Gretsky analyses Russia's recent relations with Turkey, Iran and Afghanistan. He predicts that Russia's close cooperative relations with Turkey and Iran will continue as Turkey is both Eurasian and secular, while the history of Iran and Russia is marked by anti-Western xenophobia. Moreover Russia has revived the 'old Soviet policy of using Islamic countries and groups as a leverage against the West'.

In Chapter 5 Barylski links the Russian war in Chechnya with a larger study of the Russian state's relationship with the Islamic-Turkic peoples. His study is divided into four sections, addressing (1) individual leaders, (2) Russian domestic politics, (3) Russian strategic analysis, and (4) ethnonational factors shaping Chechen and Russian behaviour.

Bold political adventures in the pre- and post-Soviet period, according to Barylski, led Yeltsin to war in Chechnya, where Dzhokhar (Johar) Dudayev, a former major general of the Soviet Air Force turned nationalist, had assumed command of the Chechen national independence movement and organised the Chechen armed forces, which were prepared to take on the ill-prepared Russian army. Very adroitly, Dudayev had persuaded the Russian minister of defence, Pavel Grachev, to transfer about 50 per cent of Soviet military supplies and equipment in Chechnya to the Dudayev administration. Russian intelligence sources also claimed that Dudayev had received additional military supplies from Turkish contacts with links to suppliers in the Federal Republic of Germany who had access to Soviet matériel left over from the days of the German Democratic Republic. Thus while the Yeltsin government was struggling to resolve its systemic weakness, the well-supplied and thoroughly motivated Chechen national forces launched their bid for independence and defeated the Russians in battle. This, according to Barylski's plausible thesis, was the 'secret' of the Chechens' success.

Barylski also raises the fundamental issue of national self-determination in multinational states such as Russia. If national self-determination was allowed everywhere, he asserts 'the number of sovereign states would increase dramatically'. Indeed, this is true, but the same argument could have been used with regard to the preservation of the territorial integrity of the Soviet Union!

Russia and Islam: mutual adjustment and sources of conflict

In Chapters 6–8 three Russian, Tatar and Bashkort scholars – Mikhail Konarovsky, Makhmud A. Gareyev and Aislu Yunusova – examine Islam's role in the Russian Federation and analyse its potential for igniting conflicts within and without the Russian territorial limits.

Konarovsky (Chapter 6) suggests that in respect of Islamic states, two possibilities are seriously entertained by experts on world politics. According to one school of thought, states Konarovsky, 'Muslim nations might secede from the UN in order to set up their own international organisation, with a security council, a common market [and] joint armed forces'. Indeed this paradigm of international relations has remained the Islamic states' aspiration since the founding of the League of Nations. As the internationally known thinker and poet-philosopher of Islam Dr Muhammad Iqbal suggested in the 1930s:

'If Tehran were to become the Geneva of the [Islamic] East, the fate of the nations would certainly change.'

Driven by their national interests and divided by cultural, ethnic and linguistic diversity, the Muslim countries are not likely to create a League of Islamic States. Yet Konarovsky articulates Russian fears about the energy-rich, newly independent states' future orientation and Islam's role: will the latter be moderate, militant or fundamentalist? In the Soviet Union, he concedes, Islam was oppressed in the interest of creating 'an abstract *homo sovieticus*'. Official atheism remained an obstacle against the Soviet Union using Islam in the interests of foreign policy – but Arab socialism was supported. It may be pointed out, however, that from the 1970s to December 1991 the Soviet Union stepped up the exchange of Islamic delegates between the Central Asian republics and the Islamic states. Presumably these exchanges served the Soviet Union's foreign policy interests.

According to Konarovsky the Russian Federation's Muslim population represents about 7 per cent of the total concentrated in 'vulnerable areas' such as the Volga–Ural Basin, the Caucasus and part of Siberia. At present Orthodox Christians and Sunni Muslims are engaged in a 'constructive dialogue' with Moscow, but the picture might change when 'outside Islam' begins to interact with Russian Muslims. Konarovsky explores the current and future prospects of this interaction and what it might entail for Russia's future.

In Chapter 7 Makhmud A. Garayev, retired Soviet Army general and a Tatar by ethnic origin, asserts that nearly 20 million Russian citizens are adherents of Islam, and he expects their numbers to rise to 65 million in the twenty-first century. The Islamic factor, according to Gareyev, will affect the future world order and a new pattern will replace the current one. He discusses the probable emergence of a multipolar world, clustered around such centres of power as the United States, Western Europe, Russia and other countries of the CIS, and China and Japan. A fifth cluster, he speculates, might be found in the Islamic world, even though it is not homogeneous.

The main thrust of Gareyev's analysis is the Islamic factor in Russia's relations with the Central Asian states. In viewing the CIS as a 'living reality' (here one might disagree with him), he supports the continuity of Soviet foreign policy, which can be obtained by coordinating the foreign policies of the individual states in the CIS. Similarly he advocates a single strategic defence system for these countries. One can scarcely view this suggestion as political realism.

Gareyev also deals with Moscow's relations with autonomous republics such as Tatarstan and Bashkortostan. The Muslim-Turkic people in these two republics, he points out, 'share with the Central

Asian republics a common language, culture and religious belief'. Russia cannot afford to adopt a 'careless attitude' towards the sovereignty of these republics. Errors in this respect, he warns, 'may give rise to grave conflicts with serious consequences'.

In Chapter 8 Aislu Yunusova, a Bashkort scholar with a special interest in Islam's social role in her own republic, bemoans the incoherence of views on political Islam. She regrets the fact that Islam is so often associated with fundamentalism and that 'Islamic fundamentalism' is applied to social movements that are presented as anti-Western, anti-Russian and anticommunist. While some movements do use fundamentalist slogans, many others espouse moderate views including Birlik in Uzbekistan, the Party of Islamic Revival in Tajikistan and the late Johar Dudayev's supporters in Chechnya. They appeal to Islam 'in order to gain moral support'.

Islam, according to Yunusova, presents no threat to Russia because Russian Muslims, including Tatars, Bashkorts and Caucasians, constitute less than 10 per cent of the population of the Russian Federation and live in a secular state dominated by Christians. Hence she raises the rhetorical question: how could a minority establish an Islamic state in Russia? Like the Tatars, the Bashkort tribes converted to Islam in the tenth century under Ibn Fadlan's organised missionary activities. (The Bashkorts and their lands were part of the Golden Horde, whose capital was Sarai Batu, 25 miles from Astrakhan.) Yunusova then describes in detail Russia's activities in the Bashkort lands, where Islam was periodically suppressed.

It was not until the twentieth century that Muslims, especially Bashkorts and Tatars, started to play a political role in Russia, but even then the establishment of an Islamic state was not among their aims. Yunusova presents a strong case for the idea that the major powers use the threat of Islam to justify political intervention in Muslim countries, including Afghanistan, Tajikistan, Turkey, Bosnia and Iran, interventions that are usually followed by military actions.

Tatarstan's relations with Russia: the quest for autonomy and cultural renaissance

Tatarstan is the heartland of Islam in the Russian Federation. In Chapters 9–12 four specialists – Hafeez Malik, M. G. Galeyev, M. H. Khasanov and Engel Tagirov – explore the dynamics of Tatarstan's politics since December 1991.

Malik (Chapter 9) analyses the Russia–Tatarstan treaty of February 1994. Tatarstan was seeking independence, but compromised with

Russia and accepted autonomy as a first step towards its goal. This treaty became a model for Russia's negotiations with the twenty other autonomous republics that were clamouring for autonomy or independence, including Chechnya.

Tatars are a great nation whose ancestors, the Bulgars, settled in the middle Volga and lower Kama region during the first half of the eighth century. Islam spread among them in the ninth century. In 1236 Genghis Khan's grandson, Batu, overpowered the Bulgar state and then moved on to conquer Russia, where the Mongol rule lasted for 250 years. The Kazan Khanate, the successor to the Bulgar state and the Golden Horde, was conquered by Ivan the Terrible in 1552 but was resurrected in 1920 by Lenin, who separated the Bashkort lands and established another autonomous republic for the Bashkorts. A wedge was thus driven between the two Islamic-Turkic cousins.

In the wake of Yeltsin's declaration of Russian sovereignty in the Soviet union, Tatarstan declared its independence and sovereignty in 1990. During the next three years four rounds of negotiations were conducted between the two countries, culminating in the granting of autonomy to Tatarstan in 1994. The resulting treaty guaranteed Tatarstan's freedom to conduct foreign economic relations and gave it substantial control over its economic resources. Malik maintains that the treaty was an accomplishment of Tatarstan's President Mintimer Shaymiyev, ably assisted by his political advisor, Raphael Khakimov, and that of President Yeltsin, who sensed that an armed conflict with Tatarstan would involve Russia with other autonomous republics as well, which might break up the Russian Federation.

In Chapter 10, in search of a new and viable paradigm for Russia's economic development and its relations with the autonomous republics, especially Tatarstan, Galeyev (chairman of the Tatarstan legislature's Economic Committee) states categorically that the collapse of the Soviet Union in December 1991 was 'the natural outcome of the perniciousness of the previous system'. He asserts that any attempt by Russia to conduct itself like a great power would have disastrous consequences.

Galeyev suspects that the Russian establishment wants to preserve the military–industrial complex, while placing a maximum burden on regions such as Tatarstan. The Russian economy, according to him, cannot become prosperous by exporting raw materials because the stocks of cheap resources are already exhausted. Russia has to change its technology and do away with giant enterprises with inefficient infrastructures and poor marketing.

In Tatarstan, Galeyev states confidently, 'the process of connecting the civil sector of the economy (mainly the agro-industrial complex) with the large machine building of the military–industrial complex, which for a long time was isolated from the interests of the republic, is now slowing quite rapidly'. Galeyev also highlights the fact that Tatarstan's Law on Investments (which is more liberal than the Russian law) provides foreign investors with more rights and tax privileges, and guarantees accelerated depreciation for enterprises with foreign part-ownership.

In Chapter 11 M. H. Khasanov, a well-known scholar and president of the Academy of Sciences of Tatarstan, considers the Tatar renaissance from the prism of the European Renaissance. While Europe was expanding overseas, the Tatars were conquered by Ivan the Terrible in 1552. Weighed down by the Russian yoke the Tatars struggled to survive over the succeeding centuries. Islam and the feeling of belonging to the Muslim civilisation were their only support in their battle for survival. In the nineteenth century creative thinkers appeared to illuminate Tatarstan's intellectual horizon, including G. Kursavi, Shahab al-Din Mardjani and Kayum Nasiri. Their reformative Islamic reconstruction spread into Central Asia and other Muslim lands. Before Jamal ud-Din Afghani, Kursavi introduced *ijtihad* (innovative thinking) and discouraged *taqlid* (unreserved submission to the *ulama's* views). In Tatar society, according to Khasanov, the principle of *ijtihad* was 'absorbed painlessly and contributed to the formation of the philosophy of *jadidism* (modernism), which was introduced by Ismail Bey Gaspirali (1851–1914), a Crimean Tatar.

In the nineteenth century, Kazan, the capital of Tatarstan, became the centre of oriental studies in Russia and one of the world centres of book printing and publishing. In the twentieth century, Tatar literature was elevated by the appearance of bright 'masters of the pen', including the celebrated poet Gabdullah Tukai (whose statue stands on Kazan's main street, near the shore of Lake Kaban and beside the opera theatre), F. Amirkhan, G. Ibragimov and G. Kamal. These writers tremendously enriched the Tatar literature and language. Professional Tatar musicians and theatrical performers appeared on the cultural scene when in 1906 the first professional theatre company was created. The Tatar national education system developed as well and very largely reflected the philosophy of *jadidism*, which was subsequently destroyed by the communists.

Efforts were made to revive the Tatar national state when Mirsaid Sultangaliev tried to persuade the Bolshevik leaders to agree to the establishment of a Tatar–Bashkort Republic (called Idel-Ural state) with union republic status, which entailed the right to secede from the Soviet Union. Describing the Tatar's existence under communist rule, Khasanov states that the totalitarian regime may have brought the process of Tatar renaissance to a standstill but it failed to eradicate it. In the contemporary setting Tatars do not seek a complete break with Russia; merely the realisation of basic human rights and a free and equal relationship between nations.

In Chapter 12 Engel E. R. Tagirov, a dean and professor at the Faculty of Law and History, Kazan Financial and Economic Institute, reinforces Khasanov's interpretation with a different emphasis. By the end of the twentieth century the Tatars faced national extinction via their assimilation into the dominant Russian culture. The assimilation process, generally associated with the paradigm of *homo sovieticus*, took the form of intermarriage between Russians and Tatars, as encouraged by the CPSU, and the replacement of the Tatar language by Russian in schools, colleges and daily communication. Consequently, according to Tagirov, Tatarstan's 'civilisational revolution' entailed the revival of its culture.

This cultural revival was given political and legal foundation in the declaration of state sovereignty on 30 August 1990, the state constitution of 6 November 1992, and an interstate treaty between Russia and Tatarstan in February 1994, which enabled the state to develop the spiritual aspects of Tatar society. Several noteworthy developments have since taken place, including the establishment of national elementary and high schools, national cultural centres and national holidays.

However, Tagirov suggests that a basic problem with the Tatar national revival is the absence of a national-ideology to mobilise the nation. The Italians, he points out, promoted *Risordgimento* in their quest for unity, the Russians reformulated their national ideology against the background of Orthodox Christianity, autocracy and nationality, and Americans constantly refer to the 'American dream'. Tagirov proposes that a Tatar national ideology could include: (1) Tatarstan's territory is the Tatar Motherland; (2) here, Tatars should play the role of a 'great nation' with emphasis on 'spirit and faith'; (3) Tatar's patrimony is religious tolerance and the co-existence of the mosque with the church; (4) Islam was, and remains today, 'the great power as a culture-making factor', and it contains for the Tatars 'three basic values of originality national spirit and the state'. Finally, Tagirov states categorically that Islam 'is the key to understanding the revival of Tatar culture in the Republic of Tatarstan.

The revival of nationalism in Bashkortostan: ethno-linguistic and political dilemmas

National cultural revival is also underway in Bashkortostan. In Chapters 13–16 four scholars – Hafeez Malik, D. Zh. Valeyev, R. G. Kuzeyev and Zinnur Uraksin – explored in depth the nature of Bashkort nationalism and ethno-linguistic revival since the collapse of the Soviet Union.

In Chapter 13 Malik discusses the proceedings of the Bashkorts National *Kurultai* (National Assembly) held in Ufa, Bashkortostan, on 1–2 June 1995, the first *Kurultai* for 200 years. Two hundred and fifty one delegates from foreign lands, CIS countries, various *oblasts* and autonomous republics of the Russian Federation participated in the deliberations. President Murtaza Rahimov delivered the keynote address and highlighted several themes, in particular Bashkortostan's relations with Russia, the Bashkorts' spiritual revival and their fear of assimilation and the role of autonomy in national rejuvenation.

In his address Rahimov repeatedly professed loyalty to Russia, while at the same time indicting the 'perfidious' policies that Russia had pursued towards the Bashkorts since 1557, when their land had been incorporated into the Russian state. He defined the Bashkort lands for the Russians' benefit as 'stretching from the Ural mountains to the Caspian Sea'. Moreover he asserted that other peoples, including Russians, Udmurts, Chuvashes, Maris and Tatars were merely 'settlers' on Bashkort lands. He forthrightly stated that Bashkortostan was not Russia, despite claims to the contrary. In the Tatar and Bashkort perception the natural boundary of Russia was the pre-1552 line of division, that is, the western bank of the River Volga.

Rahimov also expressed his concern about the Bashkorts' cultural assimilation, not so much with the Russians (which is the problem in Tatarstan), but with fellow Turkic Muslims, the Tatars (in western Bashkortostan 50–55 per cent of all marriages are between Bashkorts and Tatars, while in the republic as a whole intermarriage between Bashkorts and Russians is only about 8–10 per cent).

The Bashkort's fear of assimilation has generated a tacit alliance, Malik points out, between the Bashkorts and the politically and demographically dominant Russians. In Bashkortostan, Russians make up 39.3 of the population, but together the Tatars (28.4 per cent) and Bashkorts (21.9 per cent) constitute a majority of 50.3 per cent, which is by no means in the interest of the Russian state. Consequently divide and rule remains Moscow's strategy.

In Chapter 14 Valeyev, a noted Bashkort scholar and a member of the Academy of Sciences of Bashkortostan, emphasises two basic points. The first of these is a CPSU Executive Committee resolution of January 1934, which improperly and illegally transferred the Bashkort districts of Argayashskiy and Kunashakskiy to the newly created *oblast* of Chelyabinsk, to which neither the inhabitants nor the Bashkortostan administration had given their consent. These two districts were to have been given national autonomy and their own identity, but the decision to do so had been rescinded ten months after it had been taken. When the Bashkorts in these two districts later demanded autonomy, the Russian dominated legislature of Chelyabinsk simply ignored them.

Valeyev's second point concerns the Bashkorts' right to have their republic named after them (Bashkortostan), to have their language as the state language, and for characteristic features of their culture to be included in the design of the national emblem, flag and anthem. But what about the rights of the fourteen other national groups who have settled in Bashkortostan? Valeyev's answer is crystal clear: 'They have no right to national statehood on the territory of Bashkortostan', although they should be able to enjoy the use of their languages in education, broadcasting and publishing, including newspapers and other periodicals.

In Chapter 15 Rail G. Kuzeyev, an eminent anthropologist and director of the Bashkort National Museum of Archaeology and Ethnography in Ufa, takes a long view of the Turkic peoples' encounter with Russia in the Eurasian lands. He points to the existence of a prolonged period of interethnic peace and cooperation, although formidable difficulties remain. Kuzeyev identifies four stages in the Turkic peoples' national liberation movement: the national-democratic stage (from the end of the nineteenth century to the revolution of 1905), the social-democratic stage (1905 to 1912–20), the Bolshevik stage (1919/20 to the 1980s) and the present stage, which is more or less a revival of the second (social democratic) stage.

The Bolsheviks, Kuzeyev asserts, halted the disintegration of the Russian Empire, but 'the forcible assimilation [of ethnic cultures] into the Russian culture contained the seeds of the national liberation movements we are witnessing today'. The CPSU ideologists promoted the ideas of ethnic subordination and Russia as the 'elder brother' in a concord of nations. The tragedy of the current stage, according to Kuzeyev, is that the policy of establishing a unitarian statehood, which is opposed to the principle of democratic federation has reappeared, which expresses itself in slogans like 'elder brothers', and 'little nations'. The Russian state is now beleaguered by conflicts in the Caucasus, the Middle Volga, the Urals and southern Siberia.

The solution to Russia's problem is, according to Kuzeyev, none other than democratic federalism, which should include power-sharing between the federal government and the republics within the Russian Federation; extensive rights for the subjects of the Federation; acceptance of a plurality of views; and representation of the people at all levels of government.

Finally, in Chapter 16 Zinnur Uraksin (director of the Bashkortostan Institute of History and Language) analyses the ethno-linguistic scene in the republic. He highlights the basic Bashkort dilemma: demographically, Bashkorts rank third in number after Russians and Tatars, yet they have the strongest political power. Uraksin offers a detailed review of the ethnic–linguistic composition of Bashkortostan and addresses the following issues: (1) how the Bashkorts fell from first to third position in terms of numbers; (2) the similarities and differences between the Bashkort and Tatar languages; and (3) the Bashkort's need to preserve their ethnic identity in their own republic, where they are outnumbered by Russians and Tatars.

Uraksin bemoans the fact that 24 per cent of the Bashkorts living in north-western Bashkortostan have adopted the Tatar language. In a sense they have been Tatarised and lost from the Bashkort nation. The language problem, according to him, can be resolved by giving Bashkort the status of state language, the idea of which is resisted by Russians and Tatars. With regard to the question of whether Bashkort and Tatar are different languages, he argues that all Kypchaq languages, including Bashkort, Tatar, Kazakh, Kara Kalpak, Balkar, Nagoi, Kumyk, Karachai and to a certain extent Uzbek and Kirgiz, are so close to each other that their speakers have no major difficulty conversing. While Bashkort and Tatar have their own dialects and differ phonetically, they share a common grammatical structure and are lexically very similar. Nonetheless Uraksin insists that they are two different languages.

Uraksin also highlights a major dilemma that all Turkic languages confront, not only in Central Asia but also in the Russian Federation. Bashkorts, like Tatars, have changed the script of their language three times, each time under pressure from Moscow. The historical Arabic script of their language, which was used for a millennium, was changed in 1928 to Latin and in 1939 to Cyrillac. The discarding of the Arabic script, Uraksin rightly points out, caused a serious break with the nation's cultural and historical heritage. Changing it back to Arabic would again result in cultural dissonance. So the linguistic dilemma continues to trouble the Bashkorts, as well as the Tatars.

Notes and references

1. Samuel P. Huntington, 'The Clash of Civilization', *Foreign Affairs*, Summer 1993, pp. 22–49.
2. Donald J. Puchala, 'International Encounters of Another Kind', *Global Society*, vol. II, no. 1 (January 1997), pp. 5–29.
3. Ibid., p. 29.
4. David Rothkopf, 'In Praise of Cultural Imperialism', *Foreign Policy*, Summer 1997, pp. 38–53.
5. Caspar Weinberger and Peter Schweizer, *The Next War* (Washington, DC: Regnery Publishing, 1996), ch. 20, p. 217 ff.
6. Alessandra Stanley, 'Yeltsin Signs Peace Treaty with Chechnya', *New York Times*, 13 May 1997; for the text of the treaty and its implications see Veronika Kutsyllo, 'Russia Recognizes Chechnya's Independence', *Kommersant-Daily*, 13 May 1997, pp. 1, 4.
7. For the picture of Russian soldiers begging for the families of fallen comrades, see *New York Times*, 28 July 1997, p. 1.
8. For the catastrophic state of the Russian armed forces see Igor Korstchenko, 'The Minister of Defense asserts that soon Russia will have no defense', *Nezavisimaya Gazeta*, 8 February 1997, pp. 1–2.
9. George Bovt and Stanislav Tarasov, 'CIS Presidents' Rebellion Against Moscow Could Begin in Alma-Ata', *Savodnya*, 20 May 1997, p. 9.
10. Ibid.
11. Yury Kobishchanov, 'Who Will Be Living in Russia in the 21st Century', *Nevavisimaya Gazeta*, 10 February 1995, pp. 1–2.
12. Ibid., p. 2.
13. Stephen Kinzer, 'Azerbaijan Has Reason to Swagger: Oil Deposits', *New York Times*, 14 September 1997.
14. For a debate on NATO, see *The New Shape of World Politics: Contending Paradigms in International Relations* (New York: W. W. Norton, 1997); Kenneth W. Thompson (ed.), *NATO Another Changing World Order: An Appraisal by Scholars and Policymakers* (New York: University Press of America, 1996).
15. Craig R. Whitney, 'Russia and West Sign Cooperation Pact', *New York Times*, 28 May 1997, p. 1.
16. Boris Vinogradov and Yuri Kovalenko, 'The Signatures are in Place: NATO moves East', *Izvestia*, 28 May 1991, p. 7.
17. *New York Times*, 24 March 1997.
18. For the effect of the U-2 flight on Pakistan's relations with the Soviet Union see Hafeez Malik, *Soviet–Pakistan Relations and Post-Soviet Dynamics* (London: Macmillan, 1994), pp. 166–72.
19. Philip Taubman, 'Sky Wars: Dangerous Encounters of the Cold War', *New York Times*, 10 August 1997.
20. Ibid.

21. Steven Erlanger, 'U.S. Telling Russia to Bar Aid to Iran By Arms Experts', *New York Times*, 22 August 1997, p. 1.

22. 'A Breakthrough for Russian Policy on the Asian Front', *Rossiiskiya vesti*, 24–25 April 1970, pp. 1–2; Sergei Makarov, 'Russia and China Warn the U.S.', *Kommersant Daily*, 24 April 1972, p. 1; Aleksandr Chudodeyev, 'Russian–Chinese Songs on the Essence of the Universe', *Sevodnya*, 24 April 1997, pp. 1, 4; Natalia Pulina and Aleksandr Reutov, 'An Agreement Whose Preparation Began in the Time of the USSR was Concluded with the PRC Yesterday', *Nezavisimaya Gazeta*, 25 April 1997, p. 1.

23. Alpo M. Rusi, *Dangerous Peace: New Rivalry in World Politics* (Boulder, CO: Westview Press, 1997), p. 4.

2
Islam and Ethnicity in the CIS: The American Perspective

Graham E. Fuller

The problems of nationalism and ethnicity in the former Soviet Union in the American perspective evoke at least five diverse approaches – partially contradictory among themselves:

- Broader issues of principle suggesting some generalised sympathy – especially at the popular level – for the self-determination of the peoples of the region.
- The demands of pragmatic politics, prompting Washington towards a more Russocentric orientation.
- A concern for regional stability and ambivalence about any Russian role in maintaining regional stability, that is, imperialist or regional peacekeeper?
- Anxiety about the potentially destabilising implications of Islamic fundamentalist movements.
- A discomfort with the realities of political evolution in the region, where both ethnicity and Islam – like it or not – will almost certainly be growing factors in the future.

Sympathy in principle for national self-determination

American history demonstrates strong popular trends towards some instinctive sympathy for people in search of self-determination. Such sympathies at the policy level go back most vividly to the Wilsonian days after the First World War – if indeed not back to the American Revolution itself – and sympathy for independence struggles in Latin America. With the break-up of empires there has been a natural assumption in the West that some degree of national self-determination would emerge in the process. As such, most Americans, indeed most

Westerners, most recently have had an inherent sympathy and interest in the Chechen cause. Another well-known case evoking Western sympathy would be the Tibetans in China. And it goes without saying that nearly all of the Muslim world at the popular level strongly sympathises with the plight of the Muslim Chechens; for *raisons d'état*, however, many of their governments do not, since they look to Russia for various kinds of diplomatic support. As we shall see below, Western states are also heavily influenced by *raisons d'état* on these issues.

Pragmatic Russocentric politics

The Cold War was the commanding feature of the second half of the twentieth century for US policies; the end of that war was therefore the most important event of that entire period. The collapse of the Soviet Union and its ideology has transformed the world; clearly few people, especially in the West, want to go back to the geopolitical certitudes of mutually assured destruction as a way of international life. So not surprisingly, the United States places its highest priority on the development of good working relations with Russia to try to ensure that the latter will be stable, ideologically moderate, moving towards membership of a broader international community sharing the values of democratic governance, a free market economy and partnership in a broader UN Security Council 'management' of the world order.

This approach has meant active US support for whomever the most pragmatic and democratic candidate in Russia has appeared to be over the past six years – first Gorbachev, then Yeltsin. US policies have aimed at strengthening those leaders against more radical internal opposition. Throughout the post-Soviet period Washington has sought to avoid policies that would inflame the internal situation in Russia or the CIS. In particular this has meant avoidance, where at all possible, of issues that might inflame Russian radical nationalists or communists and play into their anti-Western rhetoric. The actual break-up of the Soviet Union was of course an event in which the United States had little direct role; indeed it was initially slow to embrace the independence of the new states. But their independent existence is by now a fact of international law, and as such will be firmly upheld by Washington. When it comes to separatism within the Russian Federation itself, however, Washington will understandably be very conservative – first to avoid exacerbating relations with Moscow, and second because Washington is, very uncomfortable – as indeed are most great powers – with the idea of ethnic separatism in principle.

As a result of the centrality of Russia in American policy thinking, the United States has clearly withheld support, for example, for the Chechens' struggle for independence. To be sure, most Western countries, including the United States have criticised the brutal military approach and violation of human rights by the Russian army in Chechnya, but there has been no suggestion of support for Chechen independence *per se*, despite sympathy in principle for 'brave peoples seeking self-determination'.

In all likelihood this Russocentric orientation of the United States towards most developments in the Russian Federation, and even in some parts of the CIS, will last for a long time. As Russia moves towards becoming a more 'normal' state on the international scene, however, Washington may grow more relaxed about general stability and Russia's moderation and will perhaps feel less need to sacrifice so much to the maintenance of a stable Russia. By 'normal' state one particularly has in mind a state that has come to terms with loss of empire, that does not have neo-imperialist ambitions in the region, that is fairly steady and predictable in its behaviour, pursues the rule of law and is willing to work with the West on a range of international security issues.

Regional stability and Russia's regional role

The United States, as the preeminent great power in the world, has a broad interest in global stability, which includes the areas of the former Soviet Union and their impact on the broader international order. The emergence of ethnicity in this region has sparked a number of conflicts of concern to the West: the fighting in Georgia, Armenia, Azerbaijan and Moldova in particular. The West is also quite ambivalent about what to do about these conflicts. They could conceivably spread beyond their current borders, affecting the interests of the West and its various allies. Yet who should be the main arbiter of such situations? In many ways Russia is ideally suited to play the role of policeman in troubled areas, yet concern arises as to what kind of Russia: a democratic Russia, or an authoritarian Russia that will use regional conflict in the CIS as a pretext for extending neo-imperial control over these now independent states? To bolster the independence of the new successor states in the CIS, Washington has sought some UN or OSCE peacekeeping role in the area to avoid difficult questions about Russia's own objectivity and neutrality there. This has also been the desire of the states themselves who share uncertainty and even anxiety about Russia's intentions towards them.

Major ambivalence thus remains in US policy towards Russian peace-keeping roles in the CIS. It has become a major interest of the United States in the former states of the Soviet Union to see the new republics maintain their freedom and independence in accordance with their wishes as sovereign states. If unrest occurs in the CIS there is only a small likelihood that the United States would itself become involved in peacekeeping efforts there. The normal preference would be for either international forces or Russia itself to take the action, depending on the character of Russia governance.

Islamic Fundamentalist movements in the region

The United States devotes particular concern to the question of the role of Islamic politics in the Muslim states of the former Soviet Union. The United States has unfortunately had a number of very bad experiences with Islamic 'fundamentalism' (Islamism or political Islam) in the past two decades, starting with the Iranian Revolution and the hostage crisis and extending to the large number of American deaths from bombings and kidnappings in Lebanon and numerous smaller terrorist incidents. Washington's close ties with Israel have tended to link the United States (inaccurately) to broader 'anti-Muslim' policies; in reality this represents contradiction rather than consistency in the US view. The United States as a global power, has also attracted the attention of radical groups of all stripes – including Islamists – as the leading representative of the 'new world order' and all its ills. US policy makers have made it explicitly clear that the United States has no problems with or hostility towards Islam as a religion; its sole problem is with extremism of any origin – religious, nationalist, leftist or rightist.

The United States is also concerned with limiting the ability of the Islamic Republic of Iran to export its own revolutionary ideology. (In fact Washington's statements about Iran's terrorist activities and its overall regional threat are considerably exaggerated.) Nonetheless the experience with the world's first two Islamist regimes – Iran and Sudan – are not encouraging since neither can be considered moderate and both are destabilising factors in their respective regions. Washington associates Islamist regimes with nearly automatic anti-American policies and rhetoric, with explicit opposition to the Arab–Israeli peace process – a key US goal in the Middle East – and with strong hostility towards a number of regimes that are allied with the United States. As a result the United States obviously seeks to discourage the spread of Islamist ideology in the region.

Interestingly this US concern is shared by Russia which is itself worried about several aspects of political Islam, including:

- the potential anti-Russian character of political Islam in the Muslim republics of the former Soviet Union due to the long-term Russian oppression of Islam as a religion;
- the potential ability of political Islam to stir up negative or separatist views among those Muslims still living inside the Russian Federation, such as Tatars, Bashkorts and the Muslims of the northern Caucasus;
- the ability of foreign Muslim states such as Turkey, Iran, Saudi Arabia and Pakistan to use Islam to increase their own political, cultural and economic influence in the former republics at Russian expense.

Because of this shared concern for radical Islam, the United States has seemingly been more willing to see Russia take some action when the threat of political Islam is invoked: the Tajik civil war is the best case in point, where Russia has stationed troops to protect the Tajik borders with Afghanistan with little objection from the United States which also did not strongly oppose the Russian troop action in Azerbaijan in 1989. But while the United States opposes the influence of Iran anywhere outside its borders, it is important to remember that Turkey – a close ally of the United States and a challenger for influence in the Caucasus and Central Asia – is also unofficially a purveyor of Islam. While Iran is Shi'ite, most of Central Asia and the Caucasus is Sunni (with the partial exception of Azerbaijan); Turkish Islam, including Turkish political Islam, is therefore in a more advantageous position than even Iran is to promote the ideology. Several hundred Muslim schools in the Muslim republics of the CIS are already funded and administered by rather moderate Islamist movements in Turkey. The United States is naturally less concerned than Russia is about these activities emerging from Turkey, especially since Russia perceives Turkey as a geopolitical rival.

Future realities of nationalism and Islam in the region

Whatever preferences the United States and Russia may pursue in relation to nationalism and Islam in the region, the reality that confronts both is the increasing growth of national and ethnic consciousness in the world, the quest for ethnic identification and the desire to express ethnicity in political terms. Coupled with this is the rise of religion as a factor in politics, not just in Islam but also in Christianity, Buddhism and other religions; indeed some scholars speak of the phenomenon of 'religious nationalism' – a highly relevant term.

In the twenty-first century we are bound to witness the continuing rise and expression of nationalist and religious sentiments affecting nearly all states. Nationalism and religion will be key vehicles of grievances, frustrations and discontent. Where governments are not able to manage their minority populations in a satisfactory way, these governments will face severe challenges, the threat of separatist movements, civil war and possible break-up. International forces of democracy, human rights, spread of communications and global travel, education and economic aspirations – all work to fortify the desire for self- determination among ethnic groups to some extent. Former communist states such as the Soviet Union present the most drastic cases of ethnic discontent and separatism, including in Yugoslavia and Ethiopia. But nearly all states of the world present the prospect of dissatisfied minorities seeking change. Only in those parts of the West where nationalist instincts have been 'satisfied' is there an opposite move towards federalism and cooperation; that is not the case in most of the rest of the world. The challenge lies in the demand for good governance: if minorities cannot find good governance they will seek their own autonomy or independence from oppressive, incompetent or unenlightened regimes.

This is not a happy picture, since the prevalence of bad governance suggests a considerable amount of future instability in much of the world. Great powers that tend to prefer the *status quo* may resist these trends, but they cannot be fully resisted. If governments cannot satisfy minority demands they are doomed to internal instability, disorder, riots, violence and potential civil war. Such states can always choose to use force to suppress such movements for a certain period of time, but in the end, force cannot settle the problem. If the conditions are bad enough, minorities will seek to leave the state to which they have been arbitrarily and forcefully assigned by history. States that are required to engage in heavy repression in order to keep order or prevent separatism are doomed to become garrison or pariah states that cannot readily join the international community of respected, prosperous and democratic nations. To succeed, societies will need to be open and democratic, possessing free markets, open communications, liberal laws that are attractive to outside investment, and closely linked to other successful societies of the world,. Thus the 'Saddam Hussein solution' to maintaining territorial integrity is destined to fail in the long run.

In many parts of Russia and the former Soviet Union, national feelings have not yet fully reached fruition. Nationalism, especially in the southern republics, is still a growing force, with important future consequences. Borders drawn by Soviet authorities often represent 'time bombs' where peoples are divided, or else subordinated to larger groups whom they distrust. The Caucasus is especially afflicted by this problem. In Central Asia as well we are likely to witness a certain process of ethic homogenisation in which minorities will come to feel uncomfortable – or will be made to feel uncomfortable – with their titular nationality and opt to leave for their 'home' ethnic region. Russians are already in the process of leaving Central Asia, as are many other nationalities there. Even Kazaks in Uzbekistan and Uzbeks in Tajikistan may eventually opt to return to their ethnic homeland because of ethnic tensions in the region. Hopefully this more modest form of 'ethnic cleansing' will not take on the characteristics of former Yugoslavia, but the process is nonetheless under way even now on a semivoluntary basis. This is regretable, since multiethnic societies are probably a more tolerant and rich form of social organisation – but events in most regions are moving the other way.

The Russian federation itself has probably not yet reached the 'final resolution' of its ethnic problems. There are minorities that will probably demand a greater degree of autonomy, as the Chechens have, although they may not resort to the same degree of violence. The northern Caucasus is particularly unsettled, and saddled with deliberately drawn volatile borders with divided peoples, such as the Cherkess–Karachai versus the Kabardin–Balkar autonomous regions, in which both the Cherkess peoples and the Turkic (Karachai and Balkars) peoples are deliberately divided.

The future role of the Tatars and the Bashkorts is of particular importance. The Tatars were the single most important Muslim nationality in the days of the tsarist empire; they led the reform movements in the late nineteenth century (Jadidism) and were highly active in cultural and political spheres, heavily influencing the political consciousness of the Turks of Central Asia as well. A nationality that has played such a major role is not likely to lose its historical importance among today's Turkic population. One is therefore inclined to speculate about what the Tatar role will be in the development of a broader Turkic national self-consciousness in the Caucasus, Central Asia and Crimea. While neither Tatarstan or Bashkortistan are likely to seek total independence from Russia, they will probably seek a greater degree of autonomy and will encourage policies that lead to greater concentration of the Tatar and Bashkort populations within their republics. The complex legacy of Russian and Soviet history simply cannot all be unravelled and resolved in the first few years after the break-up of the Soviet Union; this process is likely to go on for a generation or more as both the Tatars and Bashkorts on the one hand and the Russians on the other evolve in new political directions.

This is the probable future reality, irrespective of how good it may or may not be for all the peoples involved. Russians in particular are likely to be extremely anguished at the prospect of yet further change in the make-up of the Russian republic. It is to be hoped that any further change will be peaceful, but it is hard to imagine that such change will not occur, given that so many dynamic ethnic factors in the region are still emerging from the communist deepfreeze.

Islam, too, will grow in the former Soviet Union; it was artificially suppressed for a very long time, under both tsarist and communist rule. Islam is not simply a religion, but a vital element of community and personal identity. It is one of the defining elements that distinguishes an Uzbek or Tatar from a Chechen or a Russian – that is, it is not simply a linguistic difference, but also a religious and social one. Islam also functions as a form of nationalism when it is directed against non-Muslims. However much Islam was weakened during the long Soviet night of official atheism, it is rapidly recovering. Former Soviet Muslims are relearning their Islamic rites, rituals, lore, traditions and customs. It is helping to fill out their identities. Indeed nationalists in Central Asia see positive value in stressing Muslim traditions as a way of strengthening national identity, particularly *vis-à-vis* Russia. Paradoxically Islam is of particular interest and value to nationalists where Islam has historically been weak, such as among the more nomadically oriented of Kazaks and Kyrgyz.

Finally, it is important to recognise that Islam is entering the political order throughout the Muslim world. It is a vehicle for political and economic discontent. Islamist political parties are usually the strongest political movements in many of these countries, with more deeply developed grass-roots institutions responsive to the economic and social needs of the poor. Where the state is repressive and inhibits the growth of political parties that rival state control, the Islamist parties, built up around the institution of the mosque, usually survive far better than other political organisations. To the extent that political and economic conditions deteriorate in Central Asia, or that political parties are discouraged, Islamist parties will be the political movements of default. There is no reason why the Muslim areas of the former Soviet Union should be exempt from those classic preconditions that strengthen political Islam elsewhere in the Muslim world.

The Muslim states and regions of the former Soviet Union will also be courted by Muslim states and movements outside the country. The rest of the Muslim world is only now beginning to recognise that a major demographic, geopolitical and cultural resource from the Muslim past has reentered the Muslim world as an active force. Other Muslim states will seek new ties in the region, may show special economic and cultural interest there, and may be in a position to offer various kinds of aid. They will seek to reorient many of the former Soviet states and regions towards concerns that matter to other Muslim states. They are bound to introduce new ideas and a new world outlook into the region in ways that may seem 'foreign' or 'imported' to some at the moment, but in reality represent a restoration of the 'normal' Muslim past. Russia may fear and resent such interlopers, but it will not be able to stop the process in the long run.

For all these reasons, then, Islam is destined to attain a greater role in these societies and become a more significant political force. It will not necessarily become the dominant political force in the region, but it will remain a permanent factor in political life, its strength and vigour differing from country to country according to circumstances. But Russia – and other concerned countries – must be prepared to live with this reality. Oppression of political Islam will in all likelihood only strengthen it in the longer term. And oppression of other political parties by authoritarian regimes will only serve to strengthen Islamist parties as the natural beneficiaries.

These two realities – growing nationalist–separatist movements and political Islam – are certain to be part of the evolving political scene in the former Soviet Union. The states of the former Soviet Union are just beginning to grope towards new political identities, to decide who they are, what their goals are, what their place in the world is, and who their allies and adversaries are. Given the degree of displacement that occurred during the Soviet period, the process of recovering from the long period of isolation will take a very long time. States may break up or regroup, and populations may recombine in new forms that we cannot yet anticipate. Russia itself faces a quite uncertain future as it struggles to define new relationships among its various component peoples, between Moscow and regional power, and new constitutional arrangements. The consequences are unknown.

Conclusion

The United States has a complex task in front of it in determining its policies towards the region. Concern for the nature of Russian politics and rule are likely to remain a dominant consideration for the foreseeable future. The course of those politics will influence how the United States will tactically view the nature of struggle or conflict within the former Soviet Union.

Political stability is of course desired by nearly everyone. The question is, at what price is it purchased? Regional stability that rests on authoritarianism and repression does not represent true stability and ultimately can be an unreliable factor in international politics. Like it or not, nationalism and religion are growing factors in international politics, and will almost surely be a feature of international life over which few states will have control. The United States, as well as most of the rest of the world, must recognise that lack of good governance will be the single most important factor in strengthening nationalist-separatist movements and Islamist politics. We will have to be prepared to face the consequences if good governance remains absent in many parts of the world.

3
Turkic and Islamic Dimensions of Russian-American Relations

Alvin Z. Rubinstein

The dramatic dissolution of the Soviet Union on 25 December 1991 transformed the geopolitics of the Eurasian land mass. In Transcaucasia and Central Asia, it ended Russian imperial rule over most of the Islamic peoples whom Moscow had conquered over a period of more than 400 years. The six Muslim entities that emerged to independence – Azerbaijan, Kazakhstan, Kyrgyzstan, Tajikistan, Turkmenistan and Uzbekistan – had been created by Stalin in the 1920s and 1930s as tactical nation-states in order to strengthen the administration of a polyglot imperial system; to give form (but not substance) to the Bolshevik espousal of the principle of national self-determination; and to enable Moscow to pursue a policy of divide and rule by separating ethnolinguistic groups across two or more union-republics. Most of the Muslims in these republics are Sunni by religion and ethnically Turks, the exception being those in Tajikistan, two thirds of whose six million inhabitants are Tajik or Indo-Iranians, with the remaining one third mostly Turkic-speaking Uzbeks.[1] There are another estimated ten to twelve million Muslims living in postcommunist Russia, the overwhelming majority of whom are ethnic Turks and live mainly in the autonomous republics of Tatarstan (six million), Chuvashia (two million), and Bashkortostan (1.5 million). However, only the situation of the Turkic and Islamic peoples of the former Soviet Union living in the newly independent states of central Eurasia will be considered here.[2]

Another geopolitical development occasioned by the end of the Soviet Union inheres in the quest for influence in the zone of uncertainty between the Russian Federation on the one hand and Turkey and Iran on the other, by not only Russia but also Turkey, Iran, the United States, Saudi Arabia, China and Pakistan. No longer being contiguous to Turkey, Iran and Afghanistan, Russia has also lost a good deal of its former importance as a major power in the Arab East. Currently its Islamic interest is primarily with the newly independent states of the former Soviet Union, plus Iran and Turkey. This vast region, with its new Muslim republics, has become an arena of international rivalry. Russian–American relations are far less adversarial than during the Cold War; however a certain competitive tension is evident in their pursuit of national objectives in Transcaucasia and Central Asia. But it is Turkey and Iran, and to a lesser extent China and Pakistan, who are Moscow's main regional competitors. Of these, Turkey was initially considered the leading candidate for influence by virtue of its ethnolinguistic and religious affinity with most of the newly independent states of Eurasia.

The emergence of eight independent countries on the southern flank of Russia's new border was a geopolitical development that brought a surge of US interest. Washington was interested in influencing what happened in the states of the region and in the nature of Russia's policy. New circumstances dictated reassessment of the old assumptions and adaptation to a changed strategic environment and unforeseen economic opportunities.

Washington's initial response

In his autobiography, former Secretary of State James Baker tells of his visit to Russia, Transcaucasia and Central Asia in mid February 1992. The first stop on his packed itinerary was Chelyabinsk-70 (Russia), the centre of Russian nuclear weapons research and the equivalent of the Los Alamos or Lawrence Livermore laboratories in the United States. Baker's main purpose was to further Washington's paramount policy priority, namely to establish a comprehensive and cooperative relationship that would stabilise their nuclear relationship and push ahead with the arms control treaties concluded during the Reagan/Bush and Gorbachev periods. He sought to ensure that nuclear weapons controlled by Belarus, Kazakhstan and Ukraine were placed under sole Russian control, on the assumption that this would enhance strategic stability between the United States and Russia and prevent, or at least reduce the risk of, any possible diversion of nuclear weapons or weapons-grade nuclear material to other parties. The visit to Chelyabinsk-70 symbolised the commitment of Moscow and Washington to continuity in nuclear matters. This centrality of the nuclear problem in Russian–American thinking goes a long way towards explaining Washington's minimalist approach to events in Transcaucasia and Central Asia: once diplomatic ties were established, US policy relegated them to subsidiary importance in the overall scheme of Russian–American relations.

Baker's visit to Transcaucasia and Central Asia was intended 'to show the flag' and demonstrate US interest in the independence of the new states. He stopped briefly in Transcaucasia and then having been to Kazakhstan and Kyrgyzstan the previous August, moved on to Turkmenistan, Uzbekistan and Tajikistan, eager to see the strategically important area 'where the British and other European powers had played "the Great Game" of high-stakes diplomacy in the nineteenth century'.[3] Because of his concern about Iran, he took every opportunity to express support for 'Turkey's efforts to bring Central Asia more into its sphere of influence'.[4] Along the way he left model trade and economic agreements to acquaint the indigenous, ex-communist leaderships with procedures that underlay the workings of the market-oriented economy, and he encouraged them in their efforts to promote democracy and free markets. Unfortunately the substantive follow-up left much to be desired. Finally, Baker stressed Washington's interest in strengthening secular, Western-oriented states and countering Iranian-financed Islamist regimes. According to one Russian journalist, in his talks in Ashkhabad (Turkmenistan), Tashkent (Uzbekistan) and Dushanbe (Tajikistan) he did not 'put too much emphasis' on the usual package of democratic principles that Washington insists on as a condition for recognition of new states, such as human rights, protection of minorities, private enterprise and so on; instead he hit hard at the importance of building a secular society and 'pointed persistently to the need for those states to take the West as their example, rather than the theocratic Middle East'.[5] Washington understood, in a basic way, that the political–military situation in the Middle East, the Gulf region and Southern Asia would be profoundly affected by the outcome of the various unfolding regional rivalries in the new Eurasia, and it was clearly trying to back Turkey's hand against Iran.

The limits of influence: Turkey's experience

As the only Turkic-speaking country, Turkey had long felt the absence of a congenial cultural–linguistic ally in international organisations and forums. Imagine then the euphoria that swept its elites with the advent to independence of Azerbaijan, Kazakhstan, Kyrgyzstan, Turkmenistan and Uzbekistan. Patricia Carley described the mood well:

> After decades of the humiliation of running after others, pleading for acceptance, here was a region where Turks were welcomed as

kin, as brothers, by people who looked up to them. Central Asia was a region so obviously meant for them to lead. For many Turks, it represented a chance to recapture the greatness of their past, and could perhaps lead to a time when the 'Turks' of the world would once again be a force not to be dismissed, a force with Turkey at the helm.[6]

By 1993 Turkey had signed numerous economic cooperation agreements, instituted frequent political, military and cultural exchanges, and brought thousands of students from Central Asia to study at Turkish universities. Its political model, introduced by Kemal Ataturk, the founder of modern Turkey, was a mixture of secularism, statism and market economy, for the most part congenial to the Muslim oligarches of the new Eurasia reared under Soviet communism. Its media offensive included leasing time on Russian television for broadcasting to Uzbekistan, which was an early recipient of more than $600 million in low-interest credits.[7] And diplomats from Azerbaijan and the Central Asian Turkic republics started training at the Turkish foreign ministry. Indeed by February, 'Turkey and the five Turkic republics had signed more than 140 bilateral accords on a variety of different subjects, adding to the impression that formalities were increasingly a substitute for substance.'[8] These measures of alleged influence were misleading: being present was not enough.

Turkey's capabilities were not equal to its ambitions, and the dream of a Pan-Turkic revival quickly vanished. By the end of 1993 Azerbaijan and the states of Central Asia had become disillusioned. So too had the United States and the Arab Gulf states, who feared that Iran's theocratic model, with its emphasis on Islam, would be an inadvertent beneficiary. For one, Ankara's lack of the necessary military power to act as a regional patron–protector was clearly demonstrated in Azerbaijan: after courting the Turkic-speaking Azeris, Turkey was unable to prevent neighbouring Armenia from seizing the historically Armenian enclave of Nagorno-Karabakh from Azerbaijan, to which it had been attached by the Soviet leadership in 1921–22. To Armenia it is liberated land; but to Azerbaijan, which has seen hundreds of thousands of Azeris displaced by Armenian 'ethnic cleansing', Nagorno-Karabakh has been a victim of aggression. Unwilling to polarise the tension between Turkey and Russia any further on this issue, Washington has generally kept a low profile. It condemned the use of force, pressed for negotiations under the auspices of the 52-member Organization for Security and Cooperation in Europe (OSCE), and occasionally undertook tentative initiatives. Basically, however, the

United States has been content to allow Russia to restrain the fighting and maintain the uneasy ceasefire. For its part, with Russia playing the major intrusive role in managing the conflicts in Azerbaijan, Armenia and Georgia, Turkey is cautious, refraining, for example, from sending Turkish troops to help the Azeris.

Another disappointment for Turkey's supporters was the discovery that Turkey found the Turkic Eurasian hinterland more difficult to penetrate than it had supposed. On the leadership level, the death of President Turgut Ozal in April 1993 deprived it of a staunch advocate of Pan-Turkism. Coming two days after a strenuous twelve-day trip to the five Central Asian countries, his death removed a champion of activism, secularism, modernisation and a market-oriented economy. He had also been outspoken in upholding 'the cause of Turkey's Muslim allies in regional disputes from the Caucasus to the Balkans'; on one occasion he was quoted as saying that 'Turkey must show its teeth to Armenia. What harm would it do if a few bombs were dropped on the Armenian side by Turkish troops holding maneuvers on the border?'[9] Quite a bit, apparently, according to the risk-averse approach of his successor, the durable political figure, Suleyman Demirel.

As if all of this were not frustrating enough, the Turks even found speech with their 'Turkish brothers' difficult. Language was not the self-evident natural bridge that Turkey had expected. One Indian observer noted that, 'unlike Arabic, there is no classical Turkish language intelligible to all [Turkic-speaking] communities'. As a result Pan-Turkism has even less chance of success than Pan-Arabism.[10] To its disappointment, Turkey attracted few listeners to its broadcasts: quite the contrary, 'Central Asians have generally remained tuned in to Russian TV for the plain reason that they can understand it more readily'.[11] Among the thousands of students brought by Turkey from Central Asia there was little gratitude: inadequately financed, lacking language skills and socially isolated, many, ironically, gravitated toward Islamist organisations, and might well have returned home opponents of the very regimes they were intended to serve. For all the similarities, the differences between the Turks and the Turkic-speaking Kazakhs, Uzbeks, Tatars, Turkmens, Azeris and so on are extensive, as the United States has discovered. Far from being a natural leader of the newly independent Turkic peoples of the former Soviet Union, Turkey finds itself in stiff competition for influence with Russia and other regional powers.

Turkey is arguably the United States' most important strategic ally in the Islamic world. Yet tension is growing between them over the

Kurdish issue and the human rights questions that raises, over Turkey's widespread corruption and unresolved economic policy dilemmas, and over efforts in the US Congress to put pressure on the Turkish government by withholding economic and military assistance unless it acknowledges responsibility for the massacre of Armenians in 1915–16 by the former Ottoman Empire.

Kurdish nationalism, long dormant and long suppressed, has become an increasingly serious problem, especially since the 1991 Gulf War, when the Iraqi Kurds gained newfound Western sympathy and support in their struggle against Saddam Hussein. As Turkey's largest minority, the Kurds comprise about 20 per cent of the population, numbering between 10 and 12 million, most of whom live in the south-eastern part of the country, where they are contiguous with the Kurdish groups in Iraq, Iran and Syria. A non-Arab, non-Turkic people, the Kurds have endured countless conquerors. Since the end of the First World War, when the Ottoman Empire was divided into new nation-states, they have found themselves separated among the four aforementioned countries and used as pawns in international politics. In 1972, for example, the Nixon administration acceded to pressure from the Shah of Iran and agreed to help Iraqi Kurds in their struggle for autonomy against the then pro-Soviet Iraqi government. The Iraqi Kurds fought well, but in 1975 Iran and Iraq reached an accommodation. As a result they were abruptly left high and dry by the United States and Iran to face Baghdad's revenge alone.

The Turkish government refuses to make the political concessions that might end the bitter insurgency. The struggle is led for the most part by the Kurdish Workers Party (PKK), which was created in 1974 by Abdullah Ocalan, who later fled to Syria. Ocalan apparently 'recently dropped Marxism–Leninism and demands for independence', and in November 1995 he called for a ceasefire and talks with the government in Ankara.[12] Henri Barkey, an American specialist, is pessimistic, however, seeing little prospect of a solution in the foreseeable future:

> Ankara fears that the creation of an independent Kurdish state or even a federated entity within a reconstituted Iraq would fuel the fires of Kurdish autonomy in Turkey. Turkey's preoccupation with the Kurds eclipses all of its other regional concerns, including the potential danger that an Iraq, ruled by an erratic regime armed to the teeth, possibly with nuclear weapons, in control of 20 per cent of the world's known oil reserves, could pose to Turkish security.[13]

Ever since the Cold War ended and the Soviet Union collapsed, Washington's quandary has deepened. Although mindful of Turkey's geostrategic position at the hub of the Middle East and its value as a strategic ally – witness Ankara's crucial rule in the Gulf War and in sustaining the United Nations' humanitarian and economic support for the Kurdish enclave in northern Iraq – the US government is pressed by Congress and various special interest groups to protest against Turkey's human rights abuses and use its influence to urge a settlement of the Kurdish issue. Growing corruption has also tarnished Turkey's economic image and raised questions about the durability of its modernisation and its prospects for admission to the European Union. This has resulted in a surge of popular support for the Islamic Welfare Party of Necmettin Erbakan, whose Islamist agenda would reverse Turkey's secular, pro-American, pro-West European and pro-Israeli orientation. The last thing Washington wants to see is a Turkish equivalent of Iran's Islamic Republic. A parliamentary compromise between Erbakan's Welfare Party and former Prime Minister Tansu Ciller's True Path Party led to Erbakan assuming the post of prime minister in late June 1996 for two years, after which Ciller will serve for a similar period. This is the first time in modern Turkish history that an avowed 'Islamist' was permitted by the military to assume the post of prime minister. In the background is the Turkish military, which is prepared to intervene, as it has several times before, to preserve Ataturk's legacy against perceived threats. A US government on the defensive in the face of rising anti-Turkish groups and views at home may find military–economic support for Turkey no easy matter to negotiate, especially in light of growing tension elsewhere in the Middle East. Turkey must be mulling, these days, over the adage about having the United States as ally: 'Being with the United States is like being on the bank of a river; sometimes very rich, sometimes very dry.' And to add to the growing strains in the US – Turkish relationship, in mid August 1996 Turkey's prime minister signed a long-term oil and natural gas agreement with Iran. The agreement, which looks to greatly expanded economic links between Turkey and Iran, further undermines Washington's 'dual containment' policy of trying to isolate Iran and Iraq (like Turkey, West European allies are making their own deals with Iran); and it could occasion various sanctions, depending on how the recently passed Iran–Libya Sanctions Act is interpreted by the Clinton administration.

The Iranian factor

Any consideration of US policy towards the Turkic and Islamic world has to keep in mind Washington's anti-Iranian animus, which dates from the 444-day incarceration of American diplomatic personnel by Ayatollah Khomeini's militants between November 1979 and January 1981. Washington and Tehran have been adversaries on a wide range of issues: conceptions about security in the Gulf, settlement of the Arab–Israeli conflict, nuclear technology, international terrorism, economic development in Central Asia, and secular versus theocratic states. Aware now of Turkey's limitations in the struggle for Central Asia, Washington seeks other ways to counter Iran's ambitions.

Though Iran too is constrained by cultural, economic, military and political conditions from playing a prominent role in the new Eurasia, it does have important advantages over Turkey. First, whereas Turkey lacks a common border with any of the new Turkic republics, Iran borders Azerbaijan and Turkmenistan, as well as Armenia in the Caucasus and Afghanistan and Pakistan in South-West Asia. Geography does matter in the nuclear and cybernetic age.

Second, Iran offers Central Asia access to the sea, a land corridor for commerce and contacts that can greatly enhance the independent character of the Muslim republics, lessen their dependence on Russia and, in the process, help secure its own northern borders as well. Just as railroads were essential for the development of the west in the United States, they can serve the same function in Central Asia. In 1995 Iran and Turkmenistan completed a trunk line at Serakhs in north-east Iran, which enables goods to be shipped by rail to Turkmenistan and from there to Kazakhstan and east to Uzbekistan. With a few hundred miles of additional track, Iran could become a bridge to Central Asia. Looking ahead a decade or more, trains will be the 'camels' that resurrect the Silk Road, linking Beijing with Central Asia, the Gulf and the Mediterranean via Turkey. 'Twixt design and creation much needs to be done, but the dream is not an impossible one.'

Finally, Iran has a more friendly Russia to contend with than Turkey. Not only has it been respectful of Russian interests in regional conflicts in Azerbaijan, Tajikistan and Afghanistan and shown a readiness to work with Moscow to dampen civil strife there, it has also become a major customer for Russian arms and nuclear technology. The US hostility and roadblocks that hamper its economic development have had the unwitting effect of pushing Iran and Russia closer together, and of exacerbating the tension between Washington and Moscow.

An ailing Russia and a pariah Iran have been prompted into cooperation by calculations of mutual economic advantage, by an interest in stability on their borders and by a desire to limit US influence in the region. These convergent aims portend a lengthy period of high-profile political accommodation. Each expects to derive benefits from, among other things, the exchange of Russian arms for Iranian oil and natural gas. For Iran, Russia's key commodity is weapons. The only great power that is able and willing to provide the wherewithal Iran seeks to overcome its military weakness is Russia, which has signed agreements for arms sales that go far beyond those concluded in the late Gorbachev period. Russia is selling a wide range of weapons, including multirole combat aircraft, air defence missile batteries, T-72 battle tanks and surface-to-surface missiles. However it is the sale of Kilo-class submarines and a nuclear infrastructure capable of producing nuclear weapons that has provoked the strongest objections and remains a stumbling block to better US–Russian relations.

In addition Moscow tends not to share Washington's view that Iran is an active promoter of radical Islam and terrorist movements. Moscow may be correct with respect to Central Asia, its primary region of concern. Iran's hand is more obvious in Lebanon and Sudan. Regrettably Washington is silent on the larger amount of Saudi money that is funnelled into Central Asia for investment in mosques, religious schools and Korans, and into Afghanistan in support of Islamist groups such as the Sunni Taliban, an ultra religious 'student' militia that has emerged as the major force in the factional struggle for dominance.[14] As America's closest partner in the Arab world, Saudi Arabia complicates and in some places undermines Washington's position by financing militant Islamic groups. The terrorism that struck directly at US personnel twice in one year in Saudi Arabia, most recently in Dhahran on 25 June 1996, when 19 servicemen were killed, ironically appears to have had a Saudi, not an Iranian signature.

Energy and Eurasia

Another factor affecting US–Russian relations in the region is the prevalence of energy sources, particularly oil. The Eurasian land mass of the former Soviet Union is potentially the world's richest source of oil and natural gas. Some speculate that Russia alone may have reserves that approximate those of the Arabian peninsula; however its oil is trapped deep in the frozen tundra of the arctic north and will require massive investment in costly extractive technology and thousands of miles of new pipelines from the oilfields to ports or markets. Such undertakings presuppose extensive commercial arrangements, political stability and US government guarantees: in the absence of the last, the first will not be forthcoming.

Since the late Gorbachev period, when the government began to woo foreign capital, US companies have shown keen interest in investing. After the demise of the USSR they moved quickly to renegotiate agreements originally made with the Soviet regime. In Kazakhstan the Chevron Corporation arranged to exploit the Tengiz oil field on the north-eastern littoral of the Caspian Sea. Others became involved in Azerbaijan's three giant oil fields off the Caspian's western shore. How to tap into this wealth is one of the great political–diplomatic games of the decade:

> It involves calculations about Chechnya, Georgia and the rest of the turbulent Caucasus; Turkey's war against the Kurds; the future of Iran; and, above all, Russia's relations with its former empire, including the unfortunate Azerbaijan. When a key is found, it could well turn out to be in Russian hands.[15]

To the list of Turkic republics with oil should be added Turkmenistan. Each of the three – Kazakhstan, Azerbaijan and Turkmenistan – poses particular problems, the first *vis-à-vis* Russia, the third mainly with the United States.

Having oil is a blessing, but controlling the pipelines is power. A number of competing interests and conflicting proposals cloud the commercial and diplomatic environment. Two important ones are the status of the Caspian Sea and the route of the proposed pipelines. The issue of ownership of the Caspian Sea oil arose with the emergence of Azerbaijan, Russia, Kazakhstan and Turkmenistan as sovereign states. With Iran they comprise the five riparian powers. Russia and Iran, joined by Turkmenistan, argue that, based on the Soviet–Iranian treaty of 1940, the Caspian Sea is a lake, not a sea, and as such international maritime law does not apply to it. Under this interpretation, any decisions regarding the use of the Caspian's resources must be made on the basis of consensus by all the parties. Azerbaijan and Kazakhstan, on the other hand, insist that the Caspian is a sea, and accordingly each state has a right to exclusive jurisdiction and control of the resources out to a distance of twelve miles. In their view they 'are deprived of the right to independent exploitation of those deposits to which their jurisdiction extends at the present time'.[16] Washington has come out in favour of this position. For the moment the drilling and pumping of oil are proceeding, with Azerbaijan setting up its rigs far out to sea.[17]

The second major oil problem relates to pipelines. In September 1994 a number of Western oil companies (including Exxon, Unocal and Amoco) signed an agreement with Azerbaijan, estimated at $8 billion, to develop the oil fields off Baku over the next thirty years. At issue were the number and location of the pipelines to be built. Thirteen months later President Clinton intervened and persuaded Azerbaijan's President Haidar Aliev to accept two pipelines: one from Komsomolskaya in Russia (which is at the terminus of a line from the Tengiz oil fields in Kazakhstan) across the northern Caucasus to Novorossiysk on the Black Sea; the other from Baku (Azerbaijan) on the Caspian Sea to Tbilisi in Georgia, then (probably skirting Armenia because of Armenia's occupation of Nagorno-Karabakh) down to Midyat in south-eastern Turkey and west to the port of Ceyhan. The Russian pipeline was scheduled to be built first.

An agreement signed on 27 April 1996 between President Boris Yeltsin of Russia and President Nursultan Nazarbaev of Kazakhstan, calling for a Caspian pipeline consortium to invest $1.5 billion, may accelerate development of the region's oil fields:

> Western oil companies, particularly American ones, plan to sink billions of dollars into Kazakhstan and Azerbaijan. American oil production is declining and, though American firms would prefer to replenish reserves by investing in friendly countries in the Middle East, Saudi Arabia and Kuwait refuse to countenance foreigners running their oil industries. Iraq and Iran are out of bounds because of UN and American sanctions respectively. So several American firms are pinning great hopes on Caspian oil. In 1993, Chevron, an American oil company, signed a deal worth $20 billion [since scaled down to allow for other participants] over 40 years to develop the Tengiz oil field on the north-eastern shore of the Caspian. Such a deal expanded Chevron's reserves by a third. But the exploitation of these reserves is crucially dependent on developing a pipeline and thus on the region's murky politics.[18]

If anything in Central Asia can be said to be a done deal, the pipeline seems to be it.[19]

Dealing with Russia

Given geographic and military realities, Washington's relations with Russia must affect its approach to the Turkic and Islamic republics of the former Soviet Union. As on almost any policy issue, analysts disagree on what importance to assign the various considerations. Any line of analysis or advocacy ought to be explicit about its criteria and aims. The position of this chapter is that the current priorities of the US objectives in Transcaucasia and Central Asia – essentially accepted by the leaderships of both political parties – are as follows:

- Denuclearisation.
- Recognition of Russia's legitimate security concerns.
- Strengthening the independent character of the newly independent states.
- Dampening regional and intrastate conflicts.
- Promoting market economies, investment and integration in the global economy.
- Upholding human rights.

Denuclearisation

A prime objective of the Bush and Clinton administrations was to work with Russia on the dismantling of the nuclear weapons and delivery systems that came under the control of Kazakhstan, Ukraine and Belarus when the Soviet Union collapsed and Russia inherited the bulk, though not all, of the Soviet Union's nuclear weapons. For a few months the new Kazakh leadership acted as if it were seriously considering remaining nuclear in order to ensure its independence. After all, with a nuclear arsenal of 1400 long-range missiles, including 104 SS-18 multiple warhead missiles, Kazakhstan was the world's fourth largest nuclear power.

However Nursultan Nazarbaev, Kazakhstan's astute president, exacted concessions from the United States, even as he succumbed to pressure from Washington and Moscow and signed the Lisbon Protocol to the Strategic Arms Reduction Treaty (START I) and the Nuclear Non-Proliferation Treaty (NPT), which committed Kazakhstan to accept the status of a non-nuclear state. During Secretary of State Warren Christopher's visit in Almaty in late October 1993, he agreed to provide about $200 million in aid for various projects and to arrange a

White House meeting with President Clinton in early 1994 in return for ratification of the NPT before the end of the year.[20] On 13 December 1993, with Vice-President Al Gore on hand for the occasion, the Kazakh parliament ratified the treaty. Gore's presence was symbolically important, satisfying Nazarbaev's need for recognition of his accommodation on the nuclear issue, for US attention and for encouragement of his alignment with NATO's 'Partnership for Peace'. These are integral to Nazarbaev's cultivating an international – and especially a US and Russian – commitment to Kazakhstan's independence and territorial integrity.[21] If being highly visible and welcoming to US investors are ways of surviving in an uncertain neighbourhood, Kazakhstan is doing well so far.

Recognition of Russia's legitimate security concerns

The United States recognises the special circumstances under which Russia must operate in fashioning its security with the newly independent states along its southern flank. Russia shares 4600 miles of undemarcated border with Kazakhstan. Moreover its space centre at Baikonur, the largest in the world, and its former nuclear weapons testing site at Semipalatinsk are both located in Kazakhstan. In 1994 the two countries agreed to a twenty-year extension of Russia's operation of the cosmodrome. In return Russia pays $115 million annually. Baikonur is to be regarded as 'Russian territory for the duration of the lease period where all Russian laws will have equal force as in the rest of Russia'. Another significant and related agreement covered the dismantling, protection and removal of strategic nuclear forces temporarily stationed in Kazakhstan, and Kazakhstan's accession to the nuclear non-proliferation treaty. For the time being the two countries find it in their mutual interest to develop a strategic relationship that is stable, consistent and transparent. Whether Russia is interested in doing this on a permanent basis is the big question – and the source of endless debate among analysts in all concerned countries.

Shortly after the Soviet Union was abolished the leaders of the new republics realised that some institutional cooperation was essential for the continued functioning of the assets they shared, such as railroads, pipelines, roads, factory materials and so on. Thus was created the Commonwealth of Independent States (CIS) (Estonia, Latvia and Lithuania stayed out). The dominant actor seeking to foster military and economic integration is Russia. The key mechanism is a series of interstate and inter-ministerial treaties. By late 1993 the CIS was showing signs of life. In the Caucasus this coincided with the pressured membership of Georgia and Armenia, both of which have become increasingly dependent on Russian favour and arms. Exploiting their internal weakness and vulnerability to opposition groups (whom Moscow encourages with calculated supplies of weapons), Russia has pushed bilateral military pacts on them. It has also signed pacts with Tajikistan, Azerbaijan and Kyrgyzstan for combinations of reasons, all related to upholding the independence of the newly independent states, but in a dependent relationship with Moscow. These linkages give Russia military privileges. However, as in the Third World during the heyday of the Soviet era when Soviet troops came at the invitation of beleaguered client governments (except in Afghanistan in December 1979), Moscow's contingents have thus far been committed for limited aims and come only when invited by governments that are internationally recognised. Moreover their presence is maintained against the continuing emigration of Russians from Central Asian countries. Moscow has used its leverage in a limited fashion; it does not seem bent on a neo-imperial course, though admittedly it may be too soon to discount this possibility. The inept performance of its army in the bitter struggle being waged in Russia's separatist-minded autonomous republic of Chechnya since December 1994 attenuates the credibility of 'the empire is preparing to strike back' scenario positing a Russian takeover of independent Muslim republics of the former Soviet Union. To date there are grounds for cautious optimism about the limited nature of Russia's intentions in the region.

The United States may be uneasy about Russia's influence in Armenia, Georgia and Azerbaijan, but not enough to condemn the major course of developments or oppose Russian peacekeeping operations in Georgia and Tajikistan (in Russian, peacekeeping – *mirotvorchestvo*, creation of peace – includes the ideas of peacekeeping, peacemaking and conflict management, and is therefore far broader than Western terminology implies). In judging the intentions of Russian forces, it relies on criteria laid down in the Helsinki Agreement: respect for human rights, no use of force to suppress peoples or alter recognised borders, and due regard for the rights of minorities. As Deputy Secretary of State Strobe Talbott, President Clinton's point man on Russia and Eurasia, wrote, 'we will endorse regional cooperation only so long as it is truly and totally voluntary and only if it opens doors to the outside world'.[22]

Strengthening the independent character of the newly independent states

Through a mixture of diplomatic, political and economic carrots, the United States provides what it can to strengthen the independence of each republic, while at the same time trying to convince Moscow that it is not out to exploit anti-Russian sentiments or undermine legitimate Russian interests. In Azerbaijan, Clinton supported a two-pipeline solution that Moscow liked; in Kazakhstan he pushed the Tengiz project, though he came out against Moscow's interpretation that the Caspian Sea is a lake rather than a sea; and in Uzbekistan he has encouraged American investment, even though President Islam Karimov has a poor human rights record and on one occasion said that stability in Central Asia 'can be assured only by the presence of Russia as a guarantor'.[23]

Dampening regional and intrastate conflicts

It is to the present interest of both the United States and Russia to find political settlements to the conflicts in the Turkic and Islamic parts of the former Soviet Union. The United States closely follows the Armenian–Azerbaijanian struggle in the Caucasus. In 1988, at the end of the Gorbachev era, Armenia raised the question of the status of Nagorno-Karabakh, a predominantly Armenian enclave Moscow had arbitrarily joined to the Azerbaijan SSR in 1921. When Azerbaijan declared its independence from the Soviet Union after the attempted coup against Gorbachev in August 1991, Armenia's President Levon Ter-Petrossian took advantage of the Russian military's displeasure with Azerbaijan to obtain weapons and take military action to support the Armenians in the Nagorno-Karabakh enclave who had risen against the Azeris and, with help from Armenia, drove them out by the end of 1992. A narrow corridor is Nagorno-Karabakh's lifeline to Armenia. In the process of aiding the liberation of Nagorno-Karabakh, Ter-Petrossian seriously weakened Armenia's economy and, in the face of a possible intervention by Turkey on behalf of Azerbaijan, fell into heavy dependence on Russia.

Moscow, eager to keep Azerbaijan in the CIS, has been trying to find some resolution of the conflict.[24] Having been instrumental in the overthrow of the pro-Turkish, more nationalistic government of Abulfaiz Elchibey and his replacement with the former Soviet Politburo member, Haidar Aliev, it would like to fashion a settlement that would leave it with good relations with both Armenia and Azerbaijan. The

United States supports a negotiated settlement episodically: though not happy to have Moscow dominate the field, it is not really equipped to deal vigorously with the issue.

Turkey and Iran are also interested parties. Given Turkish–Armenian hostility from the First World War, Ankara's strongly pro-Azerbaijani orientation led Armenia to look primarily to Russia for support, despite this meaning a heavy degree of dependency. Iran too has ethnic, economic and strategic concerns in Azerbaijan. Like Iran, Azerbaijan is Shiite, though ethnically and linguistically the Azeris are a Turkic people. Iran fears that too nationalistic an Azerbaijan might be tempted to encourage secessionist moves among the approximately seven million Iranian Azeris: Tehran has not forgotten that Moscow tried under Stalin to exploit Azerbaijani nationalism and detach the Azeri region of north-western Iran in 1945–46. Though economically Azerbaijan and Iran could be good trading partners, with Iran offering an alternative route to ship Azeri oil to the outside world, trade is not a major consideration in this relationship. What is important is that Azerbaijan remains independent enough to be able to keep the Russian military presence to a minimum. Strategically therefore, Iran accepts Russian influence in Azerbaijan as inevitable for the moment, but hopes through a cooperative policy on Azerbaijan and elsewhere to convince Moscow that minimalist military involvement will foster regional stability and rebound to their mutual advantage.

In Tajikistan also, where a civil war once raged, Russia is the principal great power actor. Its support is crucial for the survival of the government of Imomali Rahmonov. The United States lacks geographic, economic and military reasons for direct involvement, and is generally in favour of Moscow's aim of seeking a political settlement, opposing the triumph of a coalition that includes groups considered as Islamist, and containing the spread of Iran's influence.

Promoting market economies, investment and integration in the global economy

The Turkic areas of the former Soviet Union are rich in resources, especially oil. The oil fields of Kazakhstan and Azerbaijan are already major areas of investment for US companies, though American entrepreneurs are virtually invisible in other commercial ventures. The Clinton administration advocates open access for private capital, but not if Iran is a potential beneficiary. Thus in effect, it has placed Turkmenistan off limits because of the joint Turkmen–Iranian construction of railroads and pipelines. The inherent contradiction between assumptions of commercialism and containment leads to a certain confusion in US policy, as critics have pointed out.

Human rights

Regardless of their parliaments, judiciaries and other accoutrements of democratic practices, the Turkic and Islamic regimes of the former Soviet Union are run with a tight hand and by a small, autocratic elite. Violations of human rights – jailed dissidents, limited freedom of the press, stringent military and police controls – are regularly reported by Western observers. For the moment the official commitment of the various Islamic leaders to market-oriented and secular societies is enough of an inducement for Washington to put an optimistic face on the slow progress towards more open and democratic societies.

A policy for Washington

The path followed in the name of national interest is a function of capability and context – and, of course, domestic determinants. What makes political sense in one set of circumstances may not in another. Thus when the United States argued that strategic stability would best be maintained if Russia were the only member of the former Soviet Union to possess nuclear weapons, Kazakhstan accepted the logic underlying the American position and agreed to denuclearise. However, when the United States argued for Iran's isolation on the grounds that it was a terrorist state and a threat to the region, Kazakhstan and the other Central Asian states stood out against Washington; on the contrary, for them friendship with Iran was a valuable alternative to overdependence on Russia. Indeed the dire US warnings about Iran and Islamic fundamentalism can, it turns out, legitimate as well as motivate a line of policy. In 1992 Russia intervened militarily to restore power to a pro-Moscow coalition dominated by former Communist Party bosses on the ground of thwarting the entrenchment of an Islamist regime. Some in the West suggest that at the time Russia played upon Washington's fears of radical Islam 'to promote its regional interests – all the while working to strengthen its influence among renegade [that is, Iran, for one], as well as respectable, Middle Eastern and western Asian state'.[25] At the end of 1996, however, the notion that Iran was in a position to do very much to advance Islamist agendas was regarded with far less concern, even in

Turkey, where popular support for the Islamist Welfare Party was growing and Necmettin Erbakan, the long-time advocate of militant Islam, was approved by the Turkish parliament in June 1996 as prime minister.

It is to be hoped that the United States has learned more in recent years about the countries and cultures it would like to help, and perhaps also about the hazards of relying on packaged advice and agendas for action. Its difficult, tragic, costly and largely unsuccessful experience with helping to promote nation building and democratic development in the Middle East, Africa and Central America may not be a bad source from which to glean a few relevant operational principles to guide US foreign policy towards the Turkic and Islamic countries of Transcaucasia and Central Asia.

First, do not discount the hurdles to change presented by historical memory, geography and political culture. Even a prolonged conquest, a conscious effort at socio-political transformation and massive investments cannot ensure an outcome deemed successful by the conquerors – as the Soviet era attests. The United States can look back with satisfaction on its achievements in West Germany and Japan, but there it took over totally destroyed and defeated societies that willingly accepted a generation or so of imposed tutelage. None of the countries we have been discussing are in this category.

Nor is the United States' own experience of much use in Transcaucasia or Central Asia: not its legal system, its institutional arrangement of checks and balances, its concept of individual rights, its system of political parties, or even its concept of private property and civic society. Attempts, therefore, to micromanage their domestic political situations in this early stage of their independence are doomed to fail. The advice offered, sound for those in the United States, may not accord with the views and values of those they seek to help. Turkey, the United States' most important strategic ally in the Middle East, faces a 'no end in sight' conflict with its Kurdish population unless it is prepared to make what are now considered unthinkable concessions by the ruling military–political elite. What, then, can the United States do? For the moment, probably nothing. Discuss its views of the problem discreetly and at the same time reassure the leadership of its readiness to assist diplomatically in ways they think useful, but make clear the limits applying to any predominately military approach. Implicit in this assessment and approach is a sense that Turkey will not be in a position to play a major role in Transcaucasia or Central Asia for a long time to come.

Second, think in terms of strategic denial rather than strategic advantage in Eurasia. Concretely, this entails using all the levers of diplomacy and political influence available to the US government to strengthen the independence of the newly independent states. Their emergence as sovereign actors on the international stage was a regional windfall for the United States. Individually they may be of marginal interest, but collectively they provide a defensive buffer for the Middle East – Turkey, Iran, Afghanistan and the oil-rich Arab East – against an expansionist-minded Russia, or, looking to the long term, China. The territorial *status quo* in the new Eurasia is geopolitically the strongest assurance of US military preeminence in the Middle East well into the next century. Moreover, in the future Azerbaijan and Central Asia may well be a major source of energy for the West.

Third, the time has come in Central Asia for the United States to practice what it preaches, namely to give commerce a chance to counter and meliorate conflict. Presidents Reagan, Bush and Clinton have extolled free markets and open trade as a way of promoting democracy and building security in an interdependent world. With the end of the Cold War and in the absence of serious military threats to international stability, the time for commercial and entrepreneurial risk taking has arrived. No US professions of support mean very much if they do not encourage Central Asian countries to explore alternatives to permanent dependency on Russia.

The Turkmenistan–Iran connection is the key to a trading–commercial grid that can link all of landlocked Central Asia to the outside world. In late 1993 the two countries opened a bridge across the Tedzhen (Tedjen or Tajan) River at the town of Serakhs (Siraks); it has two crossings – one for rail traffic, one for regular traffic. And in October 1995 they began to construct a transcontinental natural gas pipeline. Iran in particular has given priority to the construction of a railway network that could be the 'Silk Road' of the next century. It has already built 'a 440-mile railway line from its warm-water Gulf port of Bandar Abbas to join the national railway network at Bafg'.[26] In March 1996 Iranian President Hashemi Rafsanjani officially opened the 100-mile extension from Meshed (Mashhad) to Serakhs; this new line gives the Central Asian rail network access to the rail lines of Iran and Turkey. A planned 1100 mile shortcut from the Iranian port of Chah Bahar to Serakhs would reduce the time and cost of transporting goods even further, and it would permit Pakistan to use Iran as an alternative to Afghanistan for trade with Central Asia.

All of this is proceeding without the participation of US companies and in the face of opposition by the US government. Washington's suspicion of Iran has left it pretty much odd capital out on this issue. Its NATO allies and Japan are ignoring its call for sanctions against Iran. During a visit to the United States in February 1994, Kazakhstan's President Nazarbaev commented on Washington's anti-Iranian views, rejecting allegations of a threat from Islamic fundamentalism in Central Asia and stressing the special significance (an alternative to Russia) of the role played by Iran in Central and Southern Asia.[27] The least Washington can do is refrain from hawking the NATO Partnership for Peace programme in Central Asia, as if this contributes anything positive towards building a sound security system in the region.

Fourth, the Transcaucasian and Central Asian countries should be encouraged to be active in international governmental and non-governmental organisations as one way of affirming their sovereignty and discouraging possible Russian adventurism in the 'near abroad' (those areas of the former Soviet Union with Russian minorities). Forums such as the United Nations, the Organization for Security and Cooperation in Europe (OSCE) and the World Bank, and non-governmental organisations dealing with economic development, human rights and the environment are all building blocks for security and survival. Helping them to consolidate their independence reinforces the position of those in Russia who favour acceptance of the new states of Eurasia.

An essential complement to this process is regionalism, economic collaboration, cooperation in matters of security, water conservation, food production and saving the environment. Kazakhstan's Nazarbaev has been a crucial and indefatigable actor in all these endeavours. His aim has been to internationalise Central Asia's circumstances. Aware of his country's expanse and extreme vulnerability, he strives to shore up ties as much with the Pacific Rim states as with Europe and the Middle East. In March 1994 he proposed a Eurasian union, at the heart of which would be institutionalised cooperation in the space of the former Soviet Union towards the creation of an economic union, regularisation of citizenship throughout the CIS and mutual security. On 7 February 1996 he convened a meeting in Almaty of 16 Asian countries to discuss the creation of a regional security forum modelled on the OSCE, which would be 'capable of preventing conflicts in Asia through creating "a preventive diplomatic mechanism"':

Among the countries that took part in the forum were Pakistan, Iran, India, Israel, and China. It was the first time that Pakistan had taken part in a forum where both Israel and India participated. However, at the outset, Kazakhstan made it clear that 'human rights issues will not be discussed.'

This is the first such initiative for regional security in Asia after the end of the Cold War, and it is the first such forum which is not explicitly ideological in character, unlike the past when ideology was the principal motivating factor for such initiatives.[28]

Finally, the United States should be as sparing of advice as it is of aid. The foreign leaders of the countries we have been discussing are shrewd and sophisticated when it comes to their security and political survival. What they lack is power. Their problem then, is how to play a weak hand in the big game of nations.

The Turkic/Islamic world of Eurasia is no threat to vital US interests. On the contrary, by their very independence these countries are doing at least as much for the United States as the United States can or should do for them. Enormous reserves of petroleum and natural gas are a prize worth seeking. But economic considerations aside, Transcaucasian and Central Asian interests in forestalling any reemergence of Russian imperialism coincide not only with those of Turkey and Iran but also of the United States.

All of this boils down to a situation of uncertainty in politically unstable and economically troubled circumstances. In such an environment the United States should proceed with due regard for the limited impact it can have on most of the problems, sensitivity for the differences between cultures and traditions, and recognition of Russia's legitimate interests. Above all, *Surtout, pas de zèle.*

Notes and references

1. See Charles Warren Hostler, *The Turks of Central Asia* (Westport, CT: Praeger, 1993).
2. For relations between, on the one hand, Tatarstan and Bashkortostan, and, on the other, the Russian Federation, of which they are a part, from the perspective of international law, see the relevant essays in this volume.
3. James A. Baker, III, *The Politics of Diplomacy: Revolution, War & Peace, 1989–1992* (New York: G. P. Putnam's Sons, 1995), p. 629.
4. Ibid.
5. For example, Aleksandr Golts in *Krasnaya Zvezda*, 22 February 22 1992, p. 2, as cited in Foreign Broadcast Information Service (hereafter referred to as FBIS/International Affairs), 26 February 1992, p. 10.
6. Patricia M. Carley, 'Turkey and Central Asia; Reality Comes Calling', in Alvin Z. Rubinstein and Oles M. Smolansky (eds), *Regional Power Rivalries in the New Eurasia: Russia, Turkey and Iran* (Armonk, NY: M. E. Sharpe, 1995),

p. 187. For a Turkish perspective that cautioned against trying to play an ambitious role as a regional power on the ground that it would be detrimental to Turkey's own economy and security, see Ziya Onis, 'Turkey in the Post-Cold War Era: In Search of Identity', *Middle East Journal*, vol. 49, no. 1 (Winter 1995), pp. 48–68.

7. Semyon Novoprudskii, 'Uzbekistan', *Nezavisimaya gazeta*, 22 July 1992, pp. 1, 3.

8. Philip Robins, 'Between Sentiment and Self-Interest: Turkey's Policy Toward Azerbaijan and the Central Asian States', *Middle East Journal*, vol. 47, no. 4 (Autumn 1993), p. 603.

9. Alan Cowell, 'Turgut Ozal, 66, Dies in Ankara', *New York Times,* 18 April 1993.

10. Ramesh Chandran, 'Quest For a Modern Islamic Turkey', *The Times of India* 12 March 1993.

11. Carley, 'Turkey and Central Asia', op. cit., pp. 189–90.

12. 'Turkey Survey', *The Economist*, 8 June 1996, p. 15 (of special survey).

13. Henri J. Barkey, 'Turkey's Kurdish Dilemma', *Survival*, vol. 35, no. 4 (Winter 1993), p. 64; see also Henri J. Barkey, 'Iran and Turkey', in *Regional Power Rivalries in the New Eurasia*, op. cit., pp. 159–61.

14. After the Soviet withdrawal from Afghanistan in 1989, Iran promoted a four-party alliance of Shiite groups, especially the Hezb al-Wahdat militia. In early 1995 this coalition was defeated by the Taliban, whose militancy and puritanical agenda exceeded its own. Accordingly Iran offered to work with Pakistan towards a political settlement that would bring an end to the sectarian and personal wars that were serving to keep Afghanistan destabilised and divided.

15. 'Of Pipedreams and Hubble-Bubbles', *The Economist*, 25 March 1995, p. 59.

16. Aydyn Mekhtiyev, 'Opinion', Moscow *Nezavisimaya/gazeta*, 15 June 1994, pp. 1, 3, in FBIS/USR/Russia, 7 July 1994, p. 34.

17. Yuriy Kirinitsianov, 'The Caspian Cannot Divide Us', *Rossivskaya gazeta*, 24 February 1996, p. 7, as translated in FBIS/Russian International Affairs, 27 February 1996, p. 14.

18. 'Pipe Dreams in Central Asia', *The Economist*, 4 May 1996, p. 37.

19. See the coverage of the Russian and regional press in *Commonwealth of Independent States and the Middle East*, vol. XXI, nos 1–2 (1996), pp. 1–11.

20. Thomas W. Lippman, 'Harried Christopher Finds Respite, Reassurance in Kazakhstan', *Washington Post*, 25 October 1993, p. 14.

21. For details of the evolution of Nazarbaev's foreign policy, see Murat Laumulin, 'Kazakhstan's Nuclear Policy and the Control of Nuclear Weapons', in George Quester (ed.), *The Nuclear Challenge in Russia and the New States of Eurasia* (Armonk, NY: M. E. Sharpe, 1995), pp. 181–211. Mr Laumulin is a member of the Kazak Ministry of Foreign Affairs.

22. Strobe Talbott, 'Terms of Engagement', *New York Times*, 4 February 1996, p. E 13.

23. 'Karimov: Russian Presence Guarantees Stability', Moscow Interfax in English, 22 February 1994, in FBIS/SOV/Central Asia, 25 February 1994.

24. See Oles M. Smolansky, 'Russia and Transcaucasia: The Case of Nagorno-Karabakh', in Rubinstein and Smolansky, *Regional Power Rivalries in the New Eurasia*, op. cit. ch. 8.
25. For example Lowell Bezinis, 'Exploiting the Fear of Militant Islam', *Transition*, vol. 1, no. 24 (29 December 1995), p. 6.
26. Cohn Barraclough, 'Will New Railway Open Door to Central Asia?', *Insight*, 25 December 1995, p. 14.
27. FBIS/SOV/Central Asia, 18 February 1994, p. 37.
28. Mushahid Hussain, 'Central Asia's Quest for Security', *Middle East International*, no. 524 (26 April 1996), pp. 18–19.

4
Russia, Central Asia and Central Asia's Neighbours

Sergei Gretsky

The break-up of the Soviet Union in December 1991 necessitated the formulation of a Russian policy towards the former Soviet republics, twelve of which eventually joined the Commonwealth of Independent States (CIS). Despite its professed espousal of democratisation and adherence to international law, the Russian government embraced the term 'near abroad' *vis-à-vis* the newly independent states – an early sign that Russia was not going to treat them in the same way as it treated other foreign countries. By default, it meant that the declared policy of cooperation with Western democracies in the post-Soviet space, especially Central Asia, would not last. And it did not – Russia moved to restore its domination over Central Asia in December 1992 when it intervened in the civil conflict in Tajikistan. Its penchant for picking up the pieces of the old Soviet empire under the guise of integrating the CIS countries changed its initial policy towards its Central Asia's neighbours from cooperation with Turkey (viewed as a model of a Westernised, secular Muslim state) and wariness and containment of Iran (viewed as a model and exporter of Islamism) to apprehension of Turkish intentions and strategic partnership with Iran. Likewise Russia's relations with Afghanistan came to reflect the twists and turns of Moscow's policy towards the newly independent states of Central Asia.

Central Asia in the context of the near abroad policy

The blueprint of the near abroad policy was shaped by the discussion of Russia's foreign policy concept, launched in March–April 1992 by Sergei Stankevich, political counsellor to President Boris Yeltsin, and Foreign Minister Andrei Kozyrev. The two presented what became known in the West as the 'Eurasian' and 'Atlanticist' approaches to Russian foreign policy. For all their differences, both camps never questioned Russia's Eurasian nature, nor did they differ in their views *vis-à-vis* Russia's role in the post-Soviet space.

Kozyrev declared that the new Russian foreign policy would be driven by national interests understandable to other world democracies and not by a messianic belief in its special mission, as characterised by tsarist Russia and the Soviet Union.[1] He described the basic concept of Russian foreign policy as gravitation towards the most dynamic democratic states – the United States, Japan and Western Europe – in order to build an alliance with them.[2] However he fell short of defining Russia as a European country. Like the Eurasians, who spoke of a mission for Russia and its right to be a moral policeman in the post-Soviet space, Kozyrev spoke of Russia as a great Eurasian power and espoused Russia's special responsibility in the Eurasian geopolitical space.[3] He did not favour the creation of a separate CIS ministry, arguing that such a step 'might suggest to these countries that they were treated as less sovereign than other foreign countries'.[4] Yet in contradiction with that statement, Kozyrev and the Russian government officially embraced the term 'near abroad' as a geographical and political description of the newly independent states, indicating that Russia viewed these countries as less than sovereign and was going to treat them in ways that diverged from the principles of international law and respect for their independence.

The results of the Atlantisist/Eurasian debate were reflected in the 'Concept of the Foreign Policy of the Russian Federation' (CFPRF),[5] which was adopted at the end of 1992. Among its goals in the near abroad the CFPRF specified the deepening of political, economic and military cooperation with the newly independent states within the framework of the CIS as well as on bilateral basis; broadening and strengthening the CIS infrastructure; bilateral agreements on protecting the rights of Russian citizens in each of the newly independent states; collective protection of the CIS borders; and the formation of CIS peacekeeping forces. Without declaring the region a zone of Russian vital interests, the CFPRF warned any third country against building up a political or military presence in the newly independent states, pledging to resist such attempts with the help of leading democratic countries and international law.[6] Without mentioning Central Asia by name, the latter warning mirrored Russia's alarm about developments in the area, particularly the increased role of Islam in political life, and fear that these developments were being inspired by countries seeking to replace Russia's influence in the region with their own. At the same time the CFPRF did not differentiate Russian policy in the CIS by country, nor did it mention any specific goals or special interests Russia had in Central Asia.

Though the break-up of the Soviet Union caught Central Asians unawares, it did not cause an identity crisis. Despite more than a century of incorporation into first the Russian empire and then the Soviet Union, Kazakhstan, Kyrgyzstan, Tajikistan, Turkmenistan and Uzbekistan had lost neither their Asian nor their Islamic identities. Perestroika and then independence gave a remarkable boost to the revival and cultivation of these identities through the restoration of close links with the Islamic world, where they belonged civilisationally. It was a natural process, and Russia saw 'no unequivocally negative orientation' in it.[7] Yet the abovementioned warning demonstrated that for all the pledges to abrogate its 'big brother' role, psychologically Russia was not ready to act on it nor let Central Asians determine their own destiny.

Perhaps with the exception of President Askar Akaev of Kyrgyzstan, neither were the Central Asian leaders. They felt that their sudden independence was premature and left them alone to face the forces that were seriously contesting their rule. So it was not Russia but Kazakhstan and other Central Asian states that initiated the formation of the Commonwealth of Independent States in its present form. Russia was so absorbed with its 'thrust to the West' and by the complexities of the post-Soviet transitional period that initially it displayed little interest in instituting the CIS in any other way than a loose union. The Russians even suggested that the CIS headquarters should be located somewhere other than Moscow.

The forces that were challenging Central Asian communist party *apparatchiks* were Islamic and nascent national democrats. Both groups championed real independence and political and economic reforms, and the Islamists wanted a greater role for religion in public affairs. The success of such forces in Tajikistan – where Islamists, in alliance with secular protodemocratic and nationalist parties and groups, won almost 40 per cent of the votes in the November 1991 presidential election, secured the legalisation of the Islamic Renaissance party in October 1991, and formed the Government of National Reconciliation in May 1992 – necessitated a concerted effort on the part of the Central Asian leaders to stymie opposition forces in their own countries and survive the transition to a post-Soviet existence. Against the backdrop of growing regional cooperation among the opposition forces, Central

Asian political elites realised that without Russian assistance their chance of survival was poor. They drew Moscow's attention to the threat that Islamic fundamentalism allegedly posed to regional and Russian stability. Also, the Central Asian Russian population's genuine anxiety about their future was used to convince Russia actively to support the Soviet-era political elites, who portrayed themselves as the only guarantors of the resident Russians' interests. After the formation of the CIS the Central Asian leaders signed a host of agreements designed to guarantee a measure of their own security.

By inviting Moscow to intervene in Tajikistan in December 1992, the Central Asian leaders, with the exception of President Saparmurad Niyazov of Turkmenistan, were effectively inviting the Russians to return to Central Asia and exercise control over their countries' independence. This intervention, with the active participation of Uzbekistan, was designed to ward off what was described as the spread of 'Islamic fundamentalism' from Iran and Afghanistan, and in the West their actions were met with understanding.

It was a time of unprecedented US–Russian rapprochement, and the two countries seemed to coordinate their polices towards the Islamic world. Russia backed the US-led Operation Desert Storm against Iraq, its former ally. It severed relations with Libya and the PLO, pressured Syria to negotiate with Israel and shared the US concern about Iran's ideological expansionism. In 1992 this common approach was reflected in the CFPRF, which proclaimed Moscow's intention to pursue a differentiated approach towards Muslim countries bordering the southern edge of the former Soviet Union, favouring those with which Russia could cooperate in preventing the spread of Islamic fundamentalism and promoting secularism in Central Asia.[8] In this respect, relations with Turkey were prioritised. Turkey – as a member of NATO, 'susceptible to Western values' and with a state-controlled Islamic infrastructure – was seen as a role model for Central Asians, to whom, with the exception of the Tajiks, the Turks were ethnically and culturally related. Russia's intention to work with Turkey – viewed by some in the United States as the only Muslim democracy – in Central Asia was a clear reflection of the US–Russian partnership. For its part Turkey was very enthusiastic to seize this window of opportunity.

Russia and Turkey

Perestroika in the Soviet Union coincided with major changes in Turkey. Turgut Özal, first as prime minister (1983–89) and later as president (1989–93), initiated a departure from the Kemalist principles of laicism and disengagement in foreign policy ('Peace at home, peace abroad') that included abrogation of any plans to restore the empire. Despite the warning by President Kenan Evren in 1987 that the major source of danger for Turkey was not communism but Islamic fundamentalism, Özal became the first Turkish prime minister to state that Islam was the main bond uniting the Turkish nation. He performed hajj and launched an unprecedented programme of mosque and madrassah construction that has brought their number to 70 000 and 60 000 respectively.

Gorbachev's opening up of the Soviet Union to the outside world and improved Turkish–Soviet relations provided an opportunity for Turks to revive their ties with ethnic kin in the Transcaucasus and Central Asia. In March 1991, on his second visit to the Soviet Union, President Özal visited Azerbaijan and Kazakhstan, and this was followed by the opening of a Turkish consulate in Baku. Envoys of the National Action Party, which espouses nationalist and pan-Turkist ideology, travelled to Turkic republics in the Soviet Union to bolster the sense of common identity and destiny. The break-up of the Soviet Union boosted the international aspirations of Turkey, which found itself in a unique position as all regional players – with the exception of Iran, Turkey's competitor for influence in Central Asia and the Transcaucasus – sought Turkey's active involvement in regional affairs. The United States and other Western countries wanted Turkey to represent their interests in the southern part of the former Soviet Union, while Russia wanted Turkey to pass on its experience to Azerbaijan and the Central Asian countries in building a secular society. For their part, these countries expected Turkey to become their main economic and commercial partner, and their window on the West, all of which would sustain their independence and reduce their economic and political dependence on Russia. With such a large and promising opportunity, Özal had every right to declare the next century the 'Century of the Turk' and herald the creation of a Turkish economic and cultural zone running from the Adriatic Sea to the Great Wall of China.

Russia sought to build its relations with Turkey on the progress made in the *perestroika* years in reducing tension between the two countries. This included an end to broadcasts by Bizim Radyo, the mouthpiece of the Turkish Communist Party, pressure on the Bulgarian government to soften its policy towards ethnic Turks, and cooperation during Operation Desert Storm. Moscow appreciated the policy of restraint that Turkey had pursued *vis-à-vis* the Armenian–Azerbaijani conflict over

Nagorno-Karabakh since its onset in 1988. Despite growing domestic pressure, Özal refused to provide any assistance to the Azeris without Moscow's consent, stating that his country had no interest in the conflict since the Azeris were Shiites and thus were oriented towards Iran.[9] When the Turkish prime minister, Süleyman Demirel, paid a visit to Moscow in May 1992 a joint statement was issued that the two countries would coordinate their policies towards regional conflicts. At the same time they denounced Armenian bellicosity. Russia and Turkey also sponsored the establishment of the Black Sea Economic Cooperation Zone Organization, headquartered in Istanbul. While in 1992–93 it repeatedly voiced alarm about the perceived Iranian intention to export Islamic fundamentalism to Central Asia, the Kremlin ignored, if not endorsed, the steps taken by Turkish leaders to create an association or union of Turkic-speaking states from the Mediterranean to China, and turned a blind eye to the activities of the National Action Party of Alparslan Turkes and the Islamist Welfare (Refah) Party of Necmettin Erbakan, which established dozens of middle schools in Central Asia and Azerbaijan. To bring these states closer together, Prime Minister Demirel came up with the idea of annual summits of Turkic-speaking countries, thus bringing together Azerbaijan, Kazakhstan, Kyrgyzstan, Turkey, Turkmenistan and Uzbekistan. The first such summit was held in Ankara in October 1992 and was not regarded by Moscow as a threat to its interests in the region.

The mood in the Kremlin changed after it began to gravitate towards a more assertive role in the post-Soviet space, and when in October 1994 Ankara hosted the second Turkophone summit, the Russian Foreign Ministry issued an official statement expressing the Kremlin's opposition to what was termed the 'seclusion of Turkic-speaking countries on ethnic grounds'. The new Russian military doctrine, adopted in late 1993, was the first official document to identify the near abroad as a sphere of vital Russian interests, which Moscow pledged to protect by use of force if necessary.

The change in the near abroad policy towards what was called integration or reintegration of the former Soviet republics was followed by the calibration of Russian policy towards the Muslim 'far abroad'. First, Moscow aspired to minimise whatever influence other countries had gained in the newly independent states after the breakup of the Soviet Union. Second, modifications in the near abroad policy reflected broader changes in Russian foreign policy: the honeymoon with the United States and the West was over and the Kremlin opted for a more balanced foreign policy. In part this meant greater independence from the United States in terms of relations with the Islamic world, which for a long time had had its advocates among the Russian political elites, including Yevgeny Primakov, then director of the Russian Foreign Intelligence Service. By default, these changes had a negative effect on Russian–Turkish relations, dampening the initial welcome extended to Turkey and making Russia 'increasingly concerned about the expansion of Turkish influence in its former possessions' which had already spread into some parts of Russia itself – Tatarstan and Chechnya.[10] They also obliged Russia to find a new regional ally, especially when Uzbekistan, Moscow's traditional ally in Central Asia, clearly showed it had regional aspirations of its own. This ally would not be closely tied to the West and would be less forthright in pursuing its own agenda in the region.

Reaching the first goal – curtailing foreign influence – was facilitated in Turkey's case by Ankara's inability in 1991–92 to deliver on its promises and match the hopes that the Central Asian countries and Azerbaijan had pinned on their Turkish brethren.[11] In addition the sentiments about a common bond that dominated both official and unofficial discourses were quickly shattered by reality. Turks and Central Asians very soon realised that they were ethnically, linguistically and culturally different from each other. In what was an open affront to the Kyrgyz people, the Turkish Education Ministry blacklisted the Manas epic, the 1000-year-old history of the Kyrgyz, for its 'orthographic errors and immoral language'.[12] Largely because of language differences, Turkish satellite TV failed to draw meaningful number of viewers, the lower standard of Turkish education precluded an exodus of Central Asian students from Turkish universities and, above all, Central Asians were put off by the explicit intention on the part of the Turks to play a 'big brother' role. These factors played into the hands of the Russians, facilitating their comeback and further confounding Turkey's plans to make its political and economic presence in the region more visible.

Moscow seemed to take every opportunity to vex Ankara. In the spring of 1994, as a protest against Johar Dudaev's unofficial visit to Turkey in 1993, Moscow hosted a conference of the Workers' Party of Kurdistan (PKK), followed by the establishment of a confederation of CIS Kurdish organisations in the autumn of that year, again in Moscow. In a gesture of open hostility, on 14 April 1995 the Duma passed a bill that established 24 April as a day of commemoration for what the Armenians call the genocide against their compatriots by the Turks in 1915.

For her part Tansu Çiller, who as Turkish prime minister was touring Central Asia and holding discussions with regional leaders at the time, concentrated on the Turkic identity as a stimulant to regional cooperation aimed at reducing Russia's influence and curtailing Islamic revival.[13] The influential Turkish military establishment labelled the provisions of the new Russian military doctrine on the 'new abroad' as the revival of Russian imperialism and a threat to Turkey. Though such tough language *vis-à-vis* Russia is rare, Turkey remains deeply committed to the idea of Turkic unity and uses every Turkophone summit as an opportunity to promote it and to draw the five leaders into closer regional cooperation.

The war in Chechnya has put an enormous strain on Russian–Turkish relations. Despite the presence of a sizeable and influential Circassian community in the country, the Turkish government has generally avoided any confrontation with Russia, stressing that the conflict must be resolved by political means. This can be partially explained by Turkey's own intervention in northern Iraq to quash Kurdish rebels operating in Turkey from bases in that neighbouring country. At the time Russia and Turkey were reported to have agreed on a *quid pro quo* – Moscow would not voice opposition to Turkish actions in Iraqi Kurdistan, and in return Ankara would keep silent about Chechnya.[14] But the presence in Turkey of such NGOs as the North Caucasus Solidarity Committee and the National View Organization (Refah Party), which raised money and recruited mujahiddin for the Chechen war, and reports in the Turkish press that around 2000 Turkish mujahiddin were fighting in Chechnya and other north Caucasian republics with another 7000 ready to join them, generated a number of official Russian protests.[15] In July 1995 it was reported that Armenian villagers had caught two unknown persons and handed them over to the Russian border guards, who had declared them Turkish spies.[16] As soon as the military actions in Chechnya scaled down and political negotiations began, Russia felt free to castigate Turkey for a new incursion into Iraq in July 1995, demonstrating the fragility of political deals between the two countries. Grigoriy Karasin, a Foreign Ministry spokesman, described it as 'unacceptable' because it violated the 'territory of an independent state'.[17] Turkish leaders answered in kind, occasionally abandoning the official 'no comment' line. On a visit to Tashkent in May 1996 President Demirel called Russia an oppressor of the Chechens, and that by organising bloodshed in Chechnya, Russia was trying to prevent the Chechens and others from gaining independence.[18]

At the same time it is interesting to note that Russian–Turkish rivalry in Central Asia has never motivated Turkey to take sides or become an active player in the civil war in Tajikistan, or to capitalise on the difficulties Russia faces there. This can be explained by the lack of ethnic and cultural bonds between Turks and Tajiks, though Turkey may be content with the fact that all the other Central Asian countries, particularly Uzbekistan, are involved as observers in the UN-mediated intra-Tajik peace talks and that President Islam Karimov is talking to the United Tajik Opposition in an attempt to involve it in his efforts to abate Russian influence in Tajikistan and the region. The issue of Russian control over Tajikistan and its massive military build-up there may prove pivotal in determining the future of the region and change Turkey's inactivity in respect of the ongoing Tajik drama. In fact the civil wars in Tajikistan and Afghanistan were at the top of the agenda of the October 1996 Turcophone summit in Tashkent.

The debate over oil and gas routes from Azerbaijan and Central Asia, and the related issue of the status of the Caspian Sea is another thorn in Russian–Turkish relations. To preserve its control over the oil and gas resources of these countries, Russia wants the pipelines either to be joined to the ones it already has or to build new ones to the Black Sea port of Novorossiisk, to be transported to Europe by Russian tankers. Turkey, however, would like the pipelines to run through Turkish territory to its Mediterranean ports. Aside from economic benefits, this would give Turkey an excellent opportunity to support Azerbaijan and Central Asia in their struggle for political and economic independence from Russia. In a clear move to force the pipelines to be routed to the south-west, Turkey decided to limit supertanker movement through the Dardanelles as of 1 July 1994. Azerbaijan and the Central Asian countries hope that the alternative route will attract foreign investment, especially by Western oil companies, and contribute to their economic recovery and transition to a market economy. Russia well understands the political significance of the pipeline routing, and is evidently ready to use all possible means to impose its will. Albert Chernyshev, deputy foreign minister of the Russian Federation in charge of relations with Turkey, Iran, Central Asia, Afghanistan and Pakistan, made the following comments on the chance of a pipeline going through Turkey: 'There is a great amount of oil and no one denies that part of it might be transported through Turkey. But neither the political situation nor economic expediency should be neglected.' Russia, said Chernyshev, 'has certain doubts about Turkey in terms of stability'.[19]

What complicates matters for Azerbaijan and Kazakhstan is the unresolved status of the Caspian Sea, where a number of their oil and gas fields are located. Their attempts to divide the sea into national sectors have been obstructed by Russia and Iran, which favour the joint exploitation of Caspian resources. In an attempt to discourage the West from participating in the oil and gas projects of the Caspian littoral states, Moscow warned the West that any deals not coordinated with Russia would have no legal force. On the eve of the signing of an agreement between Azerbaijan and a British Petroleum-led consortium of Western companies to develop Azeri and Chyrag oil fields and transport the oil to the West via Turkey, Brian Fall, British ambassador to Russia, was handed a letter from the Russian Foreign Ministry claiming Russia's right to the oil fields and emphasising that the consent of all Caspian littoral states was required to begin implementation of the project.[20] The deadlock over the status of the Caspian Sea gives substance to Chernyshev's reasoning: 'Who will invest in a project which has no juridical footing?'[21] The fact that Azerbaijan has repeatedly raised the stake of the Russian LUKoil company in all sorts of oil consortia has yet to change Russian policy.

However it should be noted that political competition between Russia and Turkey and their attempts to dominate Central Asia and the Transcaucasus at the expense of each other have been inconsequential for the development of fruitful economic relations between the two countries. In fact in the mid 1990s Turkey ranked second after the United States in investments in the Russian economy – around $2 billion, while 'brotherly' Azerbaijan received just $120 million. Turkish construction companies alone had contracts worth $5.5 billion underway in Russia, and the annual volume of Russian 'shuttle' trade (*chelnochnaya torgovlya*) with Turkey was estimated at $5 billion, whereas Turkish exports to Uzbekistan dropped in the first half of 1995 by 95.7 per cent compared with the same period in 1993.[22] As Thomas Goltz sums it up, 'For Turkey the real money is in doing business within Russia,'[23] Turkey is also interested in acquiring Russian arms and ammunition, and the value of existing contracts is estimated at $130 million. Turkey currently buys armoured vehicles, helicopters, firearms and military equipment, and intends to expand its military–technical cooperation with Russia, though NATO standards, under which the country operates, pose some complications.

In summary, for the time being it is highly unlikely that Russian and Turkish interest will peacefully coexist in Central Asia and the Transcaucasus. Both countries, in a drive to restore their imperial grandeur, have focused on the same part of the world as their best bet. The other reason why a partnership with Turkey could not work out is the same reason why Russia pursued it in the first place. Because of its desire to reassert its influence over Central Asia and other parts of the former Soviet Union, Russia no longer wishes the West and NATO, to which Turkey belongs, to spread their influence in what Russia considers to be its backyard. The same reasons explain why Russia chose Iran as a substitute for Turkey as its regional partner.

Russia and Iran

For Iran – a centuries-old rival of the Ottoman Empire and republican Turkey – Russia's change of heart *vis-à-vis* the West and in its near abroad policy was the best news possible. Iran was delighted when Russia finally accepted Ayatollah Khomeini's call on Gorbachev to turn Russia's face to the Muslim world and to avoid falling into the net of the United States and the West.

After the collapse of the Soviet Union, containment became the key element in Russian policy towards Iran. It was a departure from the intentions outlined in a memorandum on the principles of political, economic and cultural cooperation that Ali Akbar Velayati (Iranian foreign minister) signed with Yegor Gaidar (deputy prime minister of the Russian Federation) in November 1991 when the Soviet Union was still in existence. The CFPRF identified Iran as a source of regional instability and hinted at its direct involvement in the civil war in Tajikistan.[24] Russia also warned Iran against any attempt at political and military expansionism and vowed to stymie it by enlisting Western assistance. As Russian policy in Central Asia was losing its benign character and cooperation with the West (Turkey included) in the post-Soviet space was dropped from the agenda, Russia had to find a new regional ally that would pose no immediate threat to its drive to restore regional domination. This need became critical after Russia broke up with Uzbekistan, its historical ally which emerged as its adversary in the bid for Central Asia. It was under these circumstances that Russia directed its attention to Iran. By the middle of 1993 it had become evident that Iran, despite its ethno-linguistic (though not geographic) links to Tajikistan, was not playing active role in Tajik developments nor was it openly threatening Russia's geopolitical interests.[25] Quite the opposite, Iran never forgot that 'the way to Central Asia lies through Russia', as an Iranian diplomat from President Hashemi-Rafsanjani's entourage stated.[26] For Iran, relegated to the status of

international pariah, stable relations with Russia were of greater importance than being a defender of the rights of Muslims in Tajikistan and
Central Asia as a whole.

Once all that became clear to Russia, rapprochement with Iran was
pursued at full speed. The first area of cooperation was trade and economic relations. Attempts by the United States to shut off Iran completely from the outside world for its alleged support of international
terrorism adversely affected the Iranian economy and seriously curtailed Iran's access to arms markets. The latter fact explains the quick
resolution of the problem of unsettled Iranian payments to Russia and
became the basis for a boost in Russian–Iranian trade and economic
cooperation, though Iran's chronic insolvency continues to be a major
impediment to further cooperation. At the same time the trade and
economic ties between the two countries acquired a rather unidimen-
sional character. First and foremost, Iran needed Russia to fill the void
in military products and services denied to Iran by others. Russia, on
the other hand, having lost the Soviet share of the world arms market
and being pressed for foreign currency, was looking for new opportunities and new markets. Military supplies and related technical services
thus came to account for more than 85 per cent of total Russian
exports to Iran and in 1994 amounted to $437 million. Iran expressed
its readiness to increase its military purchases to $1 billion in
1997–98.[27] Another area of bilateral cooperation, a cause of concern in
the West and the United States in particular, is nuclear power engineering. By the turn of the century Russia will complete the construction of
a nuclear power station in Bushehr, begun by Germany, and talks are
being held on the construction of another nuclear power station in
southern Iran. Some analysts believe that Russian nuclear physicists
and technicians working on the project may pass on nuclear technology and contribute to the development of an Iranian A-bomb. Should
this happen, they argue, Iran will pose a real threat to regional stability
and American interests. Despite numerous attempts by the Clinton
administration to talk Russia into reversing its decision on the reactors,
Russia has remained intractable.

To all appearances the Russians seem not to be worried about Iran's
nuclear aspirations or that Russian-supplied arms will turn up in the
hands of United Tajik Opposition (UTO) combatants, who are fighting
the Moscow-backed Tajik government of Imomali Rahmonov and the
Russian border guards stationed on the Tajik–Afghan border. Russia's
confidence rests on significant headway in Russian–Iranian regional
cooperation, the second and most important dimension of their

relations. As Russia expected, partnership with Iran in managing regional affairs proved to be beneficial. There has been a surprising lack of official Iranian concern for the plight of their Tajik brethren and an equally unorthodox silence about the Russian military's brutality in Chechnya. Iran was the only foreign country, apart from Afghanistan, to send observers to the February 1995 parliamentary elections in Tajikistan, which were generally, perceived as undemocratic and unfair. In a clear bid to please Russia, the Iranians, who among others act as intermediaries at the UN-mediated intra-Tajik talks, exerted pressure on the Tajik opposition to agree to hold the first round of talks in Moscow in April 1994. Since these talks began they have continued to encourage the UTO delegation to be more receptive of Russia's proposals for a peace settlement in Tajikistan, which the UTO find unacceptable because of their pro-Rahmonov thrust. The generally helpful stance of Iran in its intermediary role was repeatedly praised by Ramiro Piriz-Ballon, the UN secretary-general's special envoy to Tajikistan.[28] Iran's policy of keeping a low profile in Tajikistan caused Akbar Turajonzoda, head of the UTO's negotiating team, in a rare display of disappointment, publicly to accuse Iran of indifference and inaction in its capacity as an observer at the talks to ensure the implementation of the signed agreements.[29] The Russian leadership reciprocated Iran's ideological self-restraint by declaring that it regarded Central Asia as a region of partnership with Iran.[30] Iran validated this statement by confirming that there were no 'serious problems' with the two countries' approaches to regional affairs and by avowing not only to continue their cooperation, but also not to let others decide regional issues.[31] The latter pronouncement clearly indicates that Russia had not miscalculated when it invited Iran to jump on its bandwagon. Iran is as interested as Russia in minimising the Turkish and Western impact on the political and economic evolution of Central Asia and Azerbaijan, if not excluding such influence altogether.

Among other pivotal regional issues on which Russia and Iran have a common line are the Armenian–Azerbaijani conflict, where Iran supports the idea of Russian peacekeeping force, and the Caspian Sea, which both countries consider to be a lake whose natural resources should be developed by all littoral states. The two countries have coordinated their policies towards Afghanistan, where they support the Afghan Tajiks – headed by Burhanuddin Rabbani and Ahmad Shah Massoud – and to a lesser extent Uzbek General Abdurashid Dostam – whose primary mentor is President Karimov of Uzbekistan – against the Taliban, who, as they suspect, are supported not only by Pakistan but

also by the United States in its drive to provide the Central Asian countries with alternative pipelines through Afghanistan to Pakistan.

The third and equally important area of Russian–Iranian relations is
anti-Westernism. For Iran, Russia is not just an important economic
partner and supplier of arms and 'dual use' technology. By supporting
Russian policy in Central Asia, Iran is trying to win Russia's support in its
confrontation with the West, specifically the United States, at a time
when anti-Western and anti-American sentiment appears to be on the
rise in Russia. One of the ways in which this sentiment is exhibited is the
policy of collaborating with Islamic countries and movements whose
attitude towards the United States and the West is expressly hostile.

Such an ideologically driven approach mirrors the old Soviet policy
and was revived by Primakov after he took over the Russian Foreign
Ministry. One of his first acts was to write off half of the $16 billion
Libyan debt as a friendly gesture and to allow more arms sales to that
country, which was viewed by the United States as a terrorist state.
Primakov's political credo was best described by the foreign minister of
a gulf country who, citing the example of policy towards Iran and Iraq,
said, 'If the U.S. sees two co-equal enemies, then Mr. Primakov, you
can be sure, will see two co-equal potential friends.'[32] Russian politicians from across the political spectrum spoke in support of the
nuclear reactor deal with Iran. Reflecting the view of many of them,
Vladimir Zhirinovsky, leader of the Russian Liberal Democrats, during
a visit to Baghdad called upon Russia and the Orthodox and Muslim
worlds to create an anti-Western coalition. 'We have one common
enemy – the West', he told journalists after meeting President Saddam
Hussein.[33] The same conviction is held by Russian Islamic activists,
many of whom support the Russian government, keep silent about the
government-organised bloody massacre of fellow Muslims in
Chechnya, and are close with the Iranians.[34]

For its part Iran seems to have offered to act as an intercessor within
the Russian Islamist community. In 1994 Teheran advised the Russian
leadership not to cooperate with the West even in Bosnia and
Herzegovina, notwithstanding the fact that it would suit the cause of
their fellow Muslims, whom Iran itself was trying to help. Iran offered
Russia a 'comradely' caution that if it associated itself too closely with
the West, the latter would put all the blame on Russia if it failed in
Bosnia. This would do irreparable damage to Russia's 'already fragile
relations with Muslim countries', asserted an editorial in the *Tehran
Times*.[35] That the Russian campaign in Chechnya in 1995–96 did not
cause an outcry in the Muslim world, unlike the Soviet invasion of

Afghanistan in 1979 and despite the most graphic pictures in the mass media, is another manifestation of the ayatollahs' realpolitik.

Russian–Iranian relations seemed to be evolving just as Moscow had planned, and Russia assured the Iranian leaders that it was 'ready to provide *any* help for promoting Teheran–Moscow ties'.[36] Happy with the progress made so far, Russia decided to bring relations with Iran to a higher level. At a meeting with Iranian Foreign Minister, Ali Akbar Velayati, in January 1996, Boris Yeltsin announced that the two countries had become strategic partners. The Iranians took a more cautious approach, but did not deny such possibility.[37] To all appearances Russia and Iran have entered into a happy marriage of convenience, but whether it will hold is a moot point.

Russia and Afghanistan

Russia's relations with Afghanistan, torn apart by its own civil war, are of critical importance for the success of its endeavour to tame the United Tajik Opposition and bring Tajikistan and the other Central Asian states back into its orbit. In handling the Afghans, Moscow has employed the same principles used by the Russians and Soviets *vis-à-vis* other Central Asians, that is, promoting ethnic and regional divisions, and backing of one group against another. The overall Russian strategy in Afghanistan has always been to keep the Afghan Tajiks and Uzbeks out of power and out of contact with their kin in Tajikistan and Uzbekistan, and to stymie the dissemination of Islamic ideas and unity across the border into Soviet and post-Soviet Central Asia – all in its drive to keep the region under Russian domination.

From the time of the invasion in 1979 until the fall of the communist regime in 1991, Russia supported the Pashtuns who, numbering eight million, made up the majority of the Afghan population prior to the intervention. Subsequently, however, some three million Pashtuns migrated to neighbouring Pakistan, balancing the remaining Pashtuns with the five million Tajiks. The Uzbek population numbered around 1.2 million. From 1992 Russia masterminded a number of unthinkable coalitions, which emerged and collapsed frequently as Russia changed its policy towards Central Asia, Tajikistan specifically. This policy largely contributed to the fragmentation of Afghanistan along ethnic lines, notwithstanding the logic of domestic developments in the country that contributed to it capitalised on it.

After the outbreak of the Tajik civil war Afghanistan sheltered around 150 000 Tajik refugees, UTO fighters included, mainly in the northern provinces of Balkh – controlled by General Abdurashid Dostam, an Uzbek faction leader – and Qunduz and Tahor – controlled by forces loyal to President Burhanuddin Rabbani and Ahmad Shah Massoud, the former minister of defence. Such a high number of refugees disturbed the Russians, who feared that the former would become a source of manpower for the UTO. Indeed at the beginning of 1993, from its bases in Afghanistan the opposition resumed its armed struggle against the Rahmonov regime and against the Russian forces along the Tajik–Afghan border and inside Tajikistan.

Alliance with the Uzbeks and old ties with Dostam helped Russia and Tajikistan to repatriate around 20 000 refugees in 1993 to early 1994 from areas controlled by the general. Dostam, an ethic Uzbek, had acted as a Kremlin stooge when he was commander of the *Tsarandoi* (the Afghan police) under President Najibullah. After the break-up of the Soviet Union, President Karimov of Uzbekistan had recruited him into his coterie, but Dostam's office in Moscow had kept functioning. The UTO contended that the general used material assistance provided by the UNHCR to encourage would-be repatriates to return home, and that some local UNHCR employees had been paid to persuade the refugees to leave, often against their will.[38] At the same time Dostam prevented international help from reaching the Tajik refugee camps in Qunduz and Tahor.

Dostam's participation in the repatriation of the refugees showed that his political links with Moscow and the ethnic bonds that connected him with President Karimov were more important than loyalty to his formal allies: President Rabbani and Massoud, both of whom were ethnic Tajik and reported to be the principal backers of the UTO.[39] In fact the Rabbani–Dostam alliance was ethnically motivated as well. Najibullah, a Pashtun, who with Russia's blessing kept the reigns of government firmly in the hands of fellow Pashtuns, for a long time disregarded Dostam's request for promotion and inclusion in the inner ruling circle. Only after the withdrawal of Soviet troops in 1989, when Najibullah's position became shaky, did he confer the rank of general on Dostam as a result of pressure from Moscow, generated by General Makhmut A. Gareyev, chief Soviet military advisor to Najibullah.[40] Yet Dostam's relations with Najibullah remained strained, and when the circumstances changed the Uzbek faction leader switched sides to support the Afghan mujahiddin in their struggle against Najibullah's communist regime.

Dostam's alliance with Rabbani and Massoud continued until late 1993, when he switched sides yet again and formed an alliance with

Gulbeddin Hekmatyar, a Pashtun mujahiddin leader and opponent of Rabbani and Massoud. The much publicised repatriation of the Tajik refugees had not brought the expected results, the fighting had continued and the unlikely coalition of Dostam and Hekmatyar had been conceived by Moscow to undermine Rabbani and Massoud's strength, if not defeat them. The Russians needed that badly as it would reduce the fighting potential of the UTO, or even extinguish it.

For the sake of truth it should be put on record that Russia was never keen on the idea of Tajik or Uzbek rule in Afghanistan. In 1929, Habibullah, generally called Bachai Sako, a non-commissioned officer of Tajik origin,[41] toppled the Russian-backed Amir Amanullah, a Pashtun, and governed the country for nine months. The Russians did everything they could to reinstate Amanullah, including providing him with military assistance, but failed. Yet, Bachai Sako's reign did not continue long either – after nine months in power he was deposed and Pashtun rule was restored. For more than seventy years Russia feared that the ascension to power of Tajiks or Uzbeks in Afghanistan – mostly refugees and their descendants who had fled Turkestan and the Emirates of Bukhara and Khiva in the 1920s after the imposition of the Soviet rule by the Bolsheviks – would inspire national liberation movements in Soviet Central Asia. Indeed the victory of the Islamic resistance fighters in Afghanistan in April 1992 was greeted with enthusiasm by many in the region and coincided with their own independence as a result of the break-up of the Soviet Union in December 1991. Yet this victory and the emergence of Rabbani as Afghan president were regarded as a threat by Russia once the Kremlin opted to reassert its power in the region. Nonetheless the Moscow mint continued to print Afghan currency for Rabbani's government.

Russia's hopes *vis-à-vis* the Dostam–Hekmatyar alliance were not realised as Rabbani survived numerous offensives on Kabul and refused to resign as president. Then came another shift in Russia's relations with Afghanistan, which, in a 'join up the dots' fashion, followed the change in Russian domestic politics towards a more nationalistic and imperialist foreign and near abroad policy, a chill in its relations with the West, rapprochement with Iran and rivalry with Uzbekistan. The latter necessitated a choice of new allies in Afghanistan because it put General Dostam clearly in Karimov's camp.

The only option that Russia had not tried was an alliance with Rabbani and Massoud. This eventually took place after the emergence at the end of 1994 of the Taliban, a conservative Islamic militia of Afghan Pashtuns. The Taliban's rapid advancement through the southern and central provinces of the country threatened Rabbani's presidency and alarmed Russia, which suspected that Pakistan and the United States were trying, with the Taliban's help, to bring Afghanistan completely under their control and taper off Russia's influence in Central Asia. This suspicion was reinforced when the Pakistani press reported that two oil companies, one American (Unocal) and one Saudi-based (Delta), had signed an agreement to build a gas pipeline from Turkmenistan to Pakistan to provide Ashgabat with an alternative means of selling its gas, independent of Russia.

As in the case of Iran, Russia demonstrated pragmatism, abandoned its confrontational posture and toned down its rhetoric on the support the Afghan government was giving to the UTO. Determined to thwart the Taliban's rise to power and remain a player in Afghan affairs, Russia quickly found a common language with Rabbani and Massoud, thus closing a chapter on a relationship based on mutual annihilation. As a result of the deal, Russian military advisers and technicians were dispatched to Afghanistan in 1995 to buttress Rabbani's regime. Two of their major tasks were to upgrade the Bagram airbase near Kabul, and to build a new road and a bridge to connect the autonomous province of Gorno-Badakhshan (Tajikistan) with the Badakhshan province of Afghanistan, thus enabling a steady supply of Russian arms and ammunition.[42] This was necessary because the traditional route used by Moscow in the 1980s – via Termez (Uzbekistan) and the Salang highway – was now controlled by Uzbeks and General Dostam. It should be noted that Dostam and Rabbani always kept their channels of communication open and eventually came together in the face of the Taliban advance on Kabul in August 1996. The Russians also built an airport near the town of Taliqon, which hosted the headquarters of the UTO and was developed as an alternative command centre in case Rabbani had to flee Kabul, which is exactly what happened in September 1996.

Russian military aid to the Rabbani government became an open secret when the Taliban forced a Russian cargo plane to land in Kandahar in August 1995 – the 'humanitarian aid' it was carrying to Kabul turned out to be Chinese-made ammunition. Revising its Afghan policy, Iran, now an ally of Russia, also began to provide assistance to the Rabbani regime.

As Russia expected, the pact with the Rabbani government allowed it to make some headway in limiting support for the Tajik opposition and, as a result, restricting its activities in Afghanistan and on the Afghan–Tajik border. In April 1996 Rabbani signed an agreement with the Moscow-backed government of Imomali Rahmonov that stipulated the establishment of a 25-kilometer security zone along the border. That move considerably restricted the movement of the UTO fighters and their ability to make inroads into Tajikistan. As a result, according to UTO sources, 59 UTO fighters died in clashes with Rabbani government troops. The government also put direct pressure on the leaders of the UTO and appealed to them to refrain from violating the Afghan–Tajik border.

In the last attempt to prop up Rabbani, Russia masterminded his 'reunion' with Hekmatyar in July 1996 and with Dostam in August that year. All the parties involved loathed the idea of a Taliban-governed country. The union with Dostam reopened the Salang highway to Russian and Iranian military convoys, but it was too late and on September 25 1996 Kabul fell to the Taliban.

The fall of Kabul both sent jitters through the Russians and provided them with an opportunity to consolidate and expand their military presence in Central Asia under the familiar pretext of the imminent threat for stability of the CIS borders and a need to foil the spread of Islamic fundamentalism. Inside Afghanistan, the Russians moved to consolidate the Rabbani–Hekmatyar–Dostam alliance by mediating an agreement on the military cooperation between Massoud and Dostam.

Highly dependent on Russia for his survival, Rabbani may be forced by Moscow further to obstruct the UTO's fight against the Rahmonov government, and even to conduct a forced repatriation of the remaining Tajik refugees in northern Afghanistan, close down the camps of the Tajik opposition and expand their military presence in Central Asia under the familiar pretexts of an imminent threat to stability of the CIS borders and the need to foil the spread of Islamic fundamentalism. In any event, Russia stands to gain from the Taliban's advancement. It has already provided an excuse for a military buildup in Tajikistan and it is certain to tie Rabbani closer to Moscow, thus giving it more clout in any future decision making in Afghanistan. For that reason Russia is likely to continue its support of the Rabbani–Massoud–Hekmatyar–Dostam alliance for the foreseeable future. Yet as history shows, there are no stable alliances or allegiances in Afghanistan, and in the long run Russia may go back to its traditional policy of supporting the Pashtun rule. After all, it is doubtful that Russia is seriously alarmed about the prospect of the Taliban crossing the CIS borders to spread the Quranic word – they appeared on the Afghan–Turkmen border in September 1995 and nothing transpired.

Conclusion

The future of Russia's relations with its Central Asian neighbours will depend on its Central Asian policy. Many suspect that the current thrust of its near abroad policy, 'integration' of the post-Soviet space, is an attempt to reunify the former Soviet republics into a confederation, if not a Russian empire. Whether or not this is its ultimate goal, Russia clearly wants to reassert its control over the newly independent states in one form or another. Thus we may expect it to be very wary of Central Asia's other neighbours – Turkey, Iran and Afghanistan – and keep a close watch on their movements.

At the same time Russia has limited resources to implement its near abroad policy, and it also has to deal with the crusade being waged by autonomous republics and regions for decentralisation and greater sovereignty. The Chechen debacle put the territorial integrity of the Russian Federation into question and will inevitably force Russia to delegate more powers to the regions. The fact that Tatarstan and Bashkortostan, both Muslim-Turkic republics, are striving for a greater say in their own affairs makes the Turkic dimension in Russia's near abroad and foreign policy critically important.

For eighty years Russia's policy was to promote a measure of national identity among the Soviet and post-Soviet Muslims, as opposed to a religious identity. This kept the Muslims divided by mutual suspicion and mistrust, rather than developing a sense of unity and of belonging to a shared culture. This policy continues today in Russia and has been embraced by those Central Asian leaders whose power is an extension of their Soviet-era legitimacy. Fearful for their survival, they too promote a national identity rather than a Muslim one, and suppress Islamist movements and groups that, together with prodemocracy forces, question their rule.

In view of all this in the long run Russia may opt for Turkey as its regional partner rather than Iran. This projection is based on the fact that Russia has historically favoured close relations with republican Turkey over relations with any of its southern neighbours, and on a number of factors that draw the two countries together. First, Turkey is a secular state, ideologically based on nationalism, while Iran has historically been a centre of Islamism. Second, Turkey, like Russia, is a Eurasian state – not only geographically, but also politically and culturally – while Iran belongs to the Islamic and Oriental world. Third, Turkey is a much more viable economic partner than Iran. Fourth, it is already clear that Turkey will be in no position to supplant Russia's influence with its own in Central Asia and the Transcaucasus and that there are no grounds for pan-Turkic unity, much feared by Russia in the early post-Soviet years. Once this is understood at the official level the major obstacle to Russian–Turkish rapprochement will be removed.

As for relations with Iran, they are likely to remain on the same track and stay friendly in the future, if only for one reason – both countries have a history of anti-Western xenophobia. Russia is seemingly reviving an old Soviet policy of using Islamic countries and groups as a leverage against the West, Iran is interested in enlisting Russia to the same end. Whether anti-Western sentiments in Russia will become deeply rooted depends on the success or failure of the democratic reforms. The longevity of the present Islamic regime in Iran is also questionable.

Notes and references

1. Andrei Kozyrev, 'Russia: A Chance for Survival', *Foreign Affairs*, Spring 1992, pp. 2, 10.
2. Andrei Kozyrev 'Union Left Russia a Bad Foreign Policy Legacy', interview with the Russian foreign minister', *Nezavisimaya gazeta*, 1 April 1992.
3. *Washington Post*, 10 October 1992. On the Eurasians, see Sergei Stankevich, 'State in Search of Itself', *Nezavisimaya gazeta*, 28 March 1992, and Vladimr Lukin, 'Our Security predicament', *Foreign Policy*, no. 88 (Fall 1992).
4. *Izvestiya*, 16 July 1992, in Suzanne Crow, 'Russia Prepares to Take a Hard Line on "Near Abroad"', RFE/RL Research Report, vol. 1, no. 32 (14 August 1992), p. 21.
5. This document will be cited throughout this chapter as the concept of the Foreign Policy of the Russian Federation (CFPRF).
6. CFPRF, pp. 10–16.
7. Ibid., p. 15.
8. Ibid., p. 45.
9. George S. Harris, 'The Russian Federation and Turkey', in Alvin Z. Rubinstein and Oles M. Smolansky (eds), *Regional Power Rivalries in the New Eurasia: Russia, Turkey, and Iran* (Armonk, NY: M. E. Sharpe, 1995), p. 12.
10. Shireen Hunter, *The Transcaucasus in Transition* (Washington, DC: CSIS Press, 1994), p. 46.
11. On Turkey's relations with Central Asia and Azerbaijan see ibid., pp. 161–70; Patricia M. Carley, 'Turkey and Central Asia', in Rubinstein and Smolansky *Regional Power Rivalries*, op. Cit., pp. 169–97; Daniel Pipes, 'The Event of Our Era: Former Soviet Muslim Republics Change the Middle East', in Michael Mandelbaum (ed.), *Central Asia and the World* (New York: Council on Foreign Relations Press, 1994), pp. 71–82.
12. OMRI report, 27 June 1995.
13. OMRI report, 11 July 1995.

14. Thomas Goltz, 'The Turkish Carpet Frays', *Washington Post*, 28 January 1996; Konstantin Eggert, 'Russia–Turkey: Arguments, Weapons, Money', *Izvestiya*, 9 June 1995.
15. Interfax Agency, Moscow, 1 June 1995; Andrei Palariya, 'Brothers-in-Islam Fly to Chechnya', *Trud*, 7 March 1995.
16. Aragil Electronic news bulletin, 12 July 1995.
17. OMRI report, 12 July 1995.
18. Interview with President Demirel on Turkish television, *FBIS-SOV-96-092*, p. 61.
19. Interfax Agency, Moscow, 16 July 1995.
20. Aidyn Mekhtiev, 'Who Will Get First Oil Rights? The Smell of Caspian Fuel Is Exciting World', *Nezavisimaya gazeta*, 2 June 1995.
21. Interfax Agency, Moscow, 16 July 1995.
22. Gabriel Namtalashvili, 'Sarp Checkpoint Stimulated an Increase in Turkey's Trade with the CIS', *Finansovye Izvestiya*, 15 June 1995.
23. Goltz, 'The Turkish Carpet Frays', op. cit.
24. CFPRF, op. cit., p. 42.
25. See Graham Fuller, 'Central Asia, The Quest for Identity', *Current History*, vol. 93, no. 582, pp. 145–9; Sergei Gretsky, 'Civil War in Tajikistan and its International Repercussions', *Critique*, no. 6 (Spring 1995), pp. 3–24; Martha B. Olcott, 'Central Asia's Islamic Awakening', *Current History*, vol. 93, no. 582, pp. 150–4; Barnett Rubin, 'The Fragmentation of Tajikistan', *Survival*, vol. 35, no. 4 (Winter 1993), pp. 71–91.
26. *New Times International* no. 44, 1993, p. 24.
27. *FBIS-SOV-96-032*, 15 February 1996, p. 14.
28. Piriz-Ballon made one such statement at the Tajikistan Open Forum held by the Soros Foundation in Washington, DC, on 8 March 1994.
29. Akbar Turajonzoda, 'Tajikistan – Politics, Religion, and Peace', *Problems of Post-Communism*, July/August 1995, p. 28.
30. *New Times International*, no. 44, 1993, p. 24.
31. *FBIS-SOV-96-003*, p. 8; *FBIS-SOV-95-088*, p. 17.
32. Arnaud de Borchgrave, 'Moscow Writes Off Half of Libya's Debt', *Washington Times*, 22 January 1996, pp. A1, 12.
33. *FBIS-SOV-95-039*, 28 February 1995, p. 9.
34. Alexei Chelnokov, 'Muezzin on the Spasskaya Tower', *Izvestiya*, 20 December 1995; Ilya Maksakov, 'The "Union of Muslims" Supported the "Our House is Russia" Movement', *Nezavisimaya gazeta*, 9 December 1995.
35. *FBIS-NES-94-084*, p. 97.
36. *FBIS-SOV-95-051*, 16 March 1995, p. 5, emphasis added.
37. *FBIS-SOV-96-003*, 4 January 1996, p. 8.
38. Statement by Akbar Turajonzoda at a briefing in the US Congress on 10 February 1995. Turajonzoda asserted that the opposition had written testimonies by Afghan employees of the UNHCR in the Mazori-Sharif area that they had been paid by Dostam for every refugee they had helped to return.
39. Davlat Usmon, deputy chairman of the MIRT, acknowledged that the UTO received financial support, arms and ammunition from sympathetic Afghan Tajik mujahiddin commanders.
40. Statement by General Gareev to the author at a West Point conference, June 1995.

41. An interesting historical parallel can be drawn between the then Tajik leader and Ahmad Shah Massoud – both come from the same district of Panjshir, near Kabul.
42. 'Russian Advisers Back in Afghanistan', *Washington Times*, 27 January 1996, p. A8.

5

National Self-Determination, Russian State Unity and the Chechen Conflict

Robert V. Barylski

If politics were completely rational the president of the Russian Federation would not have launched a war against the president of one of its federal subjects, the Chechen autonomous republic, and Chechen rebels would not have adopted extreme positions on national self-determination. This chapter explains why ostensibly rational leaders engaged in self-destructive behaviour in the name of higher values such as state integrity, rule of law, general security and national self-determination. It uses a four-dimensional analysis to link the Chechen conflict to the larger study of the Russian state's relationship with the Turkic and Islamic peoples. The chapter is divided into four sections addressing individual leaders, Russian domestic politics, Russian strategic analysis, and ethno-national factors shaping Chechen and Russian behaviour.

The first section focuses on Boris Yeltsin and Dzhokhar Dudayev and explains how their patterns of behaviour, experience and leadership styles shaped history. It argues that Dudayev and allied Chechen military professionals quickly 'militarised' the Chechen drive for national self-determination and created an armed political force that was far more powerful than civilian leaders such as Boris Yeltsin expected to confront. The second and third sections address the Chechen conflict's domestic and international context. Since individuals operate within larger political structures, the struggle between Yeltsin and Dudayev has to be examined as part of Russian domestic politics. Since Russia exists within a regional system of states, its conflict with Chechen separatists has to be studied as part of a larger strategic competition for power and influence.

The fourth section discusses civilisational ideologies or ethno-national world views that influence political behaviour and give leaders a sense of place in the grand sweep of history. Leading politicians and strategic advisers develop broad overviews that tie all four levels together. Such world views influence behaviour on all levels and are themselves influenced by national tradition and memory. Tradition teaches Chechens to regard Russians and the Russian state as threats to their very existence, rather than as natural protectors and allies. Traditional civilisational ideology teaches ethnic Russians that they are in permanent competition with Turkic and Islamic peoples for control over the Black Sea, the Caucasus, parts of the Volga region and the greater Caspian Sea region. President Yeltsin's decision to use war to block the Chechen drive for national independence was influenced by geopolitical strategic thinking that warned him that Chechen independence was the first step in a grand scheme to force the Russian state to withdraw into the Eurasian heartland. The four dimensions can be summarised and restated as four perceived threats that drove Kremlin policy: Boris Yeltsin came to see the Chechen rebellion, led by Dzhokhar Dudayev, as a threat to his personal power, to the Russian state's political integrity, to Russia's interests in the greater Caucasus and to Christian–Slavic Russia's place in Eurasia.

Individual leaders: Yeltsin and Dudayev

Boris Yeltsin

Boris Yeltsin viewed himself as a courageous leader who was able to break through one political impasse after another. Less flattering evaluations attribute his cycles of manic offensive and withdrawn defensive behaviour to a combination of psychological and physiological problems. Common among the Russian people was the image of Yeltsin as a combination of communist bossism and athletic coaching skills and habits.[1]

Boldness had paid off for Yeltsin. Instead of accepting political disgrace in the autumn of 1987 when Mikhail Gorbachev fired him from the prestigious Politburo of the Communist Party and from his political base as boss over the Moscow political machine, he fought his way back and triumphed over the August 1991 coup, pushed Gorbachev aside, outlawed the Communist Party and closed down the Soviet state. As the leader of sovereign democratic Russia, he competed with parliament for control over policy. After some eighteen months dominated by repeated cycles of confrontation and compromise, Yeltsin took the offensive and ordered parliament to disband. He ended this impasse by ordering tanks to fire on parliament building on 3 October 1993. That episode had a high cost. The official government report states that there were 878 casualties. A total of 145 people were killed by both sides on 3–4 October. About 100 died in and around parliament and 40 at Ostankino. There were 121 civilians killed. The MVD lost 18 personnel and the Ministry of Defence lost six. Sixty-two MVD and 42 military personnel were hospitalised.[2]

As the crisis with parliament matured, serious and respected leaders emerged from Russian society and attempted to mediate a peaceful settlement, but Yeltsin refused to compromise and permitted the situation to fester until he had the excuses he needed to use overwhelming coercion to get his way. He put a new constitution before the public and it was approved in the December 1993 referendum, at the same time as a new State Duma was elected. The new constitution made Yeltsin the direct manager of all the military, police and security forces of Russia. The people in charge of these 'power ministries' reported directly to him, not to the prime minister. Furthermore the new constitution granted the president exclusive power to appoint and to remove all officers in the Russian armed forces. There is no provision for State Duma review of such appointments, no direct legislative check on presidential control.

Yeltsin was in the habit of making key national security decisions within his presidential branch of government through formal and informal consultations with his power ministers and key advisers. He used the Security Council, a body under his control, to formalise such actions. Since the State Duma was dominated by opposition parties, he did his best to avoid sharing power with it. Russia's armed and security forces ministries did not give their respective parliamentary committees detailed information on their budgets and operations.

The December 1993 constitution reaffirmed Russia's territorial and political integrity and provided no mechanism for any of its 91 subjects to move towards secession. Yeltsin felt personally accountable for the preservation of the Russian Federation's integrity. He was willing to enter into special agreements with each entity to achieve that goal. For example he signed treaties with Tatarstan that gave Tatarstan special status within the Russian Federation. This resulted in a patchwork of agreements affecting tax collection and revenue sharing.[3] By the summer of 1994 Yeltsin had agreements with 90 subjects; only Chechnya continued to defy him. Yeltsin decided that it was time to complete the process of rebuilding the Russian Federation's political integrity. Given his previous behaviour and the absence of any effective institutional and societal checks on his power, he could have been expected to order a bold breakthrough after his first unsuccessful attempts to get his way.

Yeltsin was patient with Chechnya, devoting three years to various overt and covert efforts to reach a settlement. However he had very little personal experience of dealing with the ethno-national politics of the northern Caucasus, so when experts urged restraint he followed their advice, with a few notable exceptions, until November 1994.

Dzhokhar Dudayev

The person leading the drive for Chechen national independence had something that Yeltsin lacked, a thorough knowledge of the military profession. Yeltsin had never served in the armed forces and he mishandled his own Chechen war policy. But Dudayev was a Soviet military professional, a Chechen nationalist and a natural expert on his homeland's political culture. Dudayev had become a major general in the Soviet Air Force at a time when it was very rare for military officers of Islamic heritage to be promoted beyond the rank of colonel. When the Soviet regime began unravelling in 1989–90, Dudayev was commanding a division of long-range nuclear bombers stationed in the Baltic region. He observed the Baltic nationalists as they organised their national independence movement and began to arm in anticipation of an eventual attack by federal forces.

In the autumn of 1991, when Dudayev emerged as leader of the Chechen national independence movement, he demanded independence from Russia but was willing to discuss Chechen membership of post-Soviet, multinational organisations and treaty arrangements that would guarantee Russia that little Chechnya would not pose a threat to big Russia's security. However he insisted that Chechnya should maintain a monopoly on all armed and security forces within its territory, a fundamental element of state viability. The Russian Ministry of Defence's military press initially described Dudayev in quite favourable terms when he bested the federal politicians.[4] When he made his first dramatic moves to lead the Chechens towards independence he was still a major general in the Soviet Air Force reserves! Dudayev had passed through the entire programme of advanced officer training and had been screened by the usual Communist Party officers as he moved up the career ladder. He was a Soviet officer and had been a member of the Communist Party, a typical Soviet professional, neither an Islamic extremist nor a Caucasian 'bandit'. For this reason the Chechen National Congress recruited him to lead their struggle for national independence and self-determination in 1990–91. To be sure, he was a Chechen and felt deeply about the Chechen cause.

Dudayev was born in 1944, just before Joseph Stalin ordered the immediate arrest and deportation of the Chechen and Ingush people – entire families, clans, villages and towns. In February 1944 Stalin mobilised a force of 200 000 armed personnel – composed of regular Red Army forces and militarised security police (NKVD armies) – for the task. Stalin's forces moved systematically from village to village and block to block, uprooting virtually the entire Chechen and Ingush population of some 500 000 people, including the infant Dudayev. The Chechens and Ingush were deported to Kazakhstan under harsh conditions and about 30 per cent of the deportees perished. In 1957 Nikita Khrushchev granted Chechen and Ingush requests to return to the Caucasus and he restored the Chechen–Ingush Autonomous Soviet Socialist Republic to the official roster of basic Soviet administrative-political units within the Russian Federation.[5] The lessons of history were clear. On the one hand, if the Chechens expected to exercise sovereignty in their traditional homeland they had to arm. On the other hand, they were a small people of some 900 000 and could not expect to win a war against the rest of the Russian Federation, which had a population of 150 000 000. For this reason Dudayev insisted on independence but repeatedly stated his willingness to enter into special security agreements with the Russian Federation. He hoped that a democratic Russia would agree to this compromise.

As a military professional and a strategic organiser, Dudayev knew that the independence movement had no chance of winning unless it immediately began dismantling the Soviet and Russian state security forces in Chechnya and replacing them with the loyal Chechen armed forces. He accomplished this in less than three months – between 19 August 1991, while the coup was still in progress in Moscow, and 8 November 1991, the day that Yeltsin ordered him to disarm or face armed forces flying in from Moscow. The Chechen National Congress met in Grozny on 1–2 September 1991 and proclaimed its Executive Committee as the only legitimate expression of Chechen sovereignty.[6] On 5–6 September their armed forces seized key government buildings in Grozny and evicted the regime headed by Doku Zavgayev. Dudayev and every Soviet officer knew by heart the Leninist dictum that 'no revolution is worthy of the name unless it is capable of defending itself' and he began implementing it from the day the Chechen

National Congress made him its leader. Other Soviet-trained Chechen military professionals joined him. Colonel Aslan Maskhadov, who became his chief of general staff, had broad experience, including service with the Soviet forces in Hungary.

Dudayev defied Yeltsin's decrees and pushed ahead with elections to validate his claim to the presidency and legitimise the Chechen declaration of independence. Federal military, police and security forces, in alliance with Chechens who opposed Dudayev, held more than one third of Chechnya and did their best to undermine the elections.[7] They prevented Dudayev from being able to claim that all Chechens had voted and gave Moscow the opportunity to insist that Dudayev did not represent all the Chechen people. Moscow refused to recognise the validity of the elections, but Dudayev had himself sworn in as president of free Chechnya on 27 October 1991. This precipitated a crisis. However the Russian military press reported that the people in Chechnya were rallying to Dudayev.[8]

Yeltsin wavered back and forth and finally yielded to Vice President Aleksandr Rutskoi's advice that an immediate show of armed force was required. Rutskoi believed he had Yeltsin's firm backing for direct talks, backed by federal troop deployments. He flew to confront Dudayev in person in the Chechen capital, Grozny. Thus the face-to-face negotiations were led by two Soviet Air Force officers, Dzhokhar Dudayev and Colonel General Aleksandr Rutskoi. Although both shared a common experience as Soviet officers and politicians, there are important differences between the skills required of jet fighter pilots and those required of strategic nuclear force commanders. Rutskoi was a fighter pilot, a colonel who had been shot down, taken prisoner and ransomed out of Afghanistan. He had a pilot's quick reactions and fight or die mentality. He was an ethno-Russian nationalist with only the vaguest understanding of political life in the northern Caucasus, or for that matter of Kremlin politics.[9]

Dudayev's revel fighters took up position and stated that although they did not want violence, they were nonetheless prepared to attack the troops that Rutskoi had flown to Grozny. The federal troops also hoped to avoid conflict and the two sides managed to keep things under control while the rebel and federal officers talked things over.[10] In Moscow the political leadership, led by Ruslan Khasbulatov and other parliamentarians, insisted that Yeltsin withdraw the troops and seek a peaceful solution to the crisis. Rutskoi quite rightly felt that his mission had been undermined and complained bitterly about it after returning to Moscow, where he propagated extremely negative assessments of the 'bandit' Chechen regime and its threat to Russian security and integrity. This image fed upon extremely negative stereotypes of Chechens as 'criminals' and became the basis of the Yeltsin administration's propaganda.

Federal politicians organised a rump parliament of anti-Dudayev deputies from the Soviet-era parliament he had overthrown. This body, called the 'Temporary Higher Soviet of Chechnya' claimed the status of successor to the last, legitimately constituted political authority. In addition the federal security agencies made certain that there were several armed factions contending for power in Chechnya. Moscow's goal was to prevent Dudayev from achieving national Chechen unity under his independence banner, and to make the conflict a fratricidal struggle among Chechens rather than a war between Chechens and the Russian Federation. Yeltsin's political strategy needed such factions – without them he would have to face Dudayev alone and confront the independence issue head on.

The fact that military professionals such as Dudayev and Maskhadov had taken command of the Chechen independence movement led to the militarisation of the drive for national self-determination. The Chechen military nationalists created an armed political force capable of resisting significantly larger numbers of Russian federal troops. This was partially understood by Boris Yeltsin and helps explain why he waited three years to launch the final effort to topple Dudayev. But it was only during the fighting that the federal government and the rebels themselves fully realised the power of their military–political invention. The Chechens' experience of deportation, exile and return was also a contributing factor. With little prodding the population armed itself and prepared to defend its homeland.

The Chechen armed forces

Dudayev's military skills made possible the Chechen National Congress's rapid transformation into an effective state. As soon as the Congress armed it was on its way to statehood. The process started with its seizure of Soviet weapons from Soviet police and security forces in Grozny immediately after proclaiming itself the only legitimate government of Chechnya in early September 1991. Over the next nine months the Dudayev regime continued to purchase or seize weapons, primarily from Soviet units still stationed in areas under his control. Chechnya claimed the right to nationalise the Soviet weapons on its territory, even though Dudayev's proto-state was never recognised as a Soviet successor state. However in 1992, as the Soviet armed forces were being divided among the 15 former Soviet republics, the Russian Federation made a special side deal with Chechnya whereby Russia claimed ownership of all Soviet military personnel, installations and equipment in Chechnya. On 28 May 1992, however, the Russian Federation through Minister of Defence Pavel Grachev, agreed to transfer about 50 per cent of the Soviet military inventory in Chechnya to the Dudayev regime. Russian military forces withdrew from territory held by Dudayev on 6 June 1996 and left behind substantially more than the 50 per cent agreed to, a highly controversial decision in light of the subsequent events.

Russian intelligence sources also claimed that the Dudayev regime had received additional Soviet military supplies through Turkish connections with links to suppliers in the Federal Republic of Germany who had access to matériel left behind by the Soviet and allied German Democratic Republic forces. They claimed that this flow had began in autumn 1991.[11] Dudayev instituted a Chechen military draft and mobilisation programme in October 1991 in response to Russian Federation demands that he cancel his plans for a presidential election and some indication that Moscow might try to enforce its decrees by sending special MVD forces into Grozny. Dudayev also declared the Soviet military draft invalid. By June 1992 the Chechen statelet had some 10 000–15 000 fighters in its full-time national armed forces and a larger number in the militias.[12] Federal sources regularly charged that Dudayev was hiring mercenaries and accepting volunteers from Abkhazia, Afghanistan, Azerbaijan, the Baltic republics, Egypt, Iran, Jordan, Turkey, Ukraine and elsewhere. The Chechen diaspora in Turkey and Jordan raised funds and carried out political activities in support of the Chechen war for independence. The news media in the Islamic countries covered the conflict in detail.

Chechen revenues

The federal propaganda campaign against Dudayev claimed that his primary sources of income were criminal activities based upon an organised international network engaged in narcotics trafficking, counterfeiting and piracy. Yeltsin regularly repeated that litany when defending his Chechen policies. The rebels were called 'bandits' and 'gangsters' and the Dudayev government was called a 'criminal' regime. However the truth was far more complex and pointed towards several years of Russian cooperation with Chechnya.

States need funds to hire and hold military professionals and to equip and maintain their armed forces. Chechnya's petroleum production, refining and transportation industries were Dudayev's main source of income. This revenue-producing machine could not operate without the cooperation of Russian federal authorities and entrepreneurs. Dudayev's Grozny refineries processed oil from Chechnya and the Russian Federation, some from as far away as western Siberia. He exported product through the Russian Federation and continued to supply petroleum products to consumers in the north Caucasian region of the Russian Federation. It is estimated that he earned over $1 000 000 from oil and refined product sales in 1992–93.[13] The break-away regime continued to receive some federal transfers to cover various social welfare programmes, including pensions, into 1994.[14] Moscow began to cut off these sources of income in summer 1994 as part of its drive to force Dudayev to agree to a compromise agreement that recognised the Russian Federation's claim to Chechnya.

Systemic factors: Russian domestic politics

Dudayev took advantage of the confusion that reigned from August to December 1991. Yeltsin's political battle with Gorbachev immobilised the Soviet state's military, security and police forces. The rising Russian team, headed by Yeltsin and Rutskoi, was inclined to take action against Dudayev. The declining Soviet team, headed by President Mikhail Gorbachev, Defence Minister Yevgeny Shaposhnikov and Interior Barannikov, was inclined to negotiate and work towards a compromise with Dudayev. Military, security and police professionals located in Chechnya were confused about the chains of command and authority. What powers did Yeltsin have as the head of Russia, of which they were part? What powers did Gorbachev have as head of the Soviet Union of which they were also part? And what about Dudayev's Chechnya? Was it outside Russia but inside the Soviet Union, or outside both?

Prior to Gorbachev's reforms of 1988–89 the Soviet political system had the necessary military–political capacity to maintain the state's political integrity. It raised, equipped and maintained the administrative, police and military apparatus required to enforce its laws and defend its borders. The Soviet Union was a viable state until Gorbachev's political and economic reforms shattered the integrity of these institutions.

The political leaders of the fifteen republics that constituted the Soviet Union undermined its political effectiveness through such acts as refusing to send revenues to the central treasury, seizing political control of all the major economic assets within their borders, and placing restrictions on where the Soviet armed forces could send draftees from their republics. Boris Yeltsin – president of Russia, the largest of the fifteen republics – delivered the main shocks to President Gorbachev's sources of power. Yeltsin argued that the governments of the fifteen republics were the natural successors to the Soviet Union and that they could achieve political viability relatively quickly after the union's demise, especially if they cooperated in economic and military affairs. He and they dispensed with the union state and President Gorbachev rather quickly over a six-month period, beginning with Yeltsin's victory in Russia's first democratic election (June 1991) and ending with the Belovezhskaya and Almaty accords of December 1991. The Soviet Union's last cabinet – the Gorbachev team without Gorbachev – made a weak and poorly organised attempt to halt the Soviet Union's disintegration in August 1991. But Yeltsin quickly converted that pro-union coup into a decisive victory against the unionists and Gorbachev and then went on to dismantle the union state.

Yeltsin argued that bold, decisive leadership – his leadership – could restore the Russian state's viability and create a Commonwealth of Independent States, which would enhance all the former Soviet republics' prospects of successful political and economic reform. The assumption that the Soviet state's administrative, law enforcement and military organisations could be converted quickly and successfully into fifteen separate administrations, law enforcement agencies and armed forces turned out to be naive. All fifteen post-Soviet states experienced systemic problems. They also found it difficult to organise their new interstate relations in a rational and complementary manner, and this damaged each state's ability to make authoritative decisions, raise revenues and support effective administrative, police and military operations.

The fifteen republics justified their decision to destroy the Soviet Union by pointing to the doctrines of national self-determination and popular sovereignty. However they were unwilling to extend the same rights to the ethno-national minorities living within their republics. Nevertheless some national minorities rose to the challenge and even resorted to armed struggle to achieve their political goals. There were also intra-ethnic political struggles between different elements of the same ethnic group. The governments of Georgia, Tajikistan and Azerbaijan were toppled by armed coups and/or civil war.

Assertive national minorities were not the only problem the fifteen new central governments had to face. Each had to resolve institutional

balances of power between the various branches and levels of government and among the various departments of government. For example
President Yeltsin clashed with his own federal parliament over basic
policy directions and political authority. Yeltsin defeated parliament in
a brief armed confrontation in early October 1993. However defeating
the old parliament and persuading the voters to endorse a new constitution that made the presidency, on paper, the dominant power in the
federal government did not end the competition with city and regional
politicians for control over taxation and revenues. Yeltsin handled this
problem by negotiating a myriad tax and revenue-sharing agreements
between the federal and regional authorities. This created a general situation in which the federal government lacked the capacity to enforce
tax laws evenly and failed to collect enough revenue properly to
finance the public administrative institutions police and armed forces.

The Chechen nationalists launched their drive for national independence while the Russian federal government was struggling to resolve its
systemic weaknesses, but in November–December 1994, after some
four years of Chechen rebellion against federal authority, the Yeltsin
administration struck back. However, because it launched the war
without first resolving its chronic command, control, financial and
moral problems, the federal forces did not do well.

From November 1991 to November 1994 Boris Yeltsin had more
pressing problems than the Chechens. He devoted 1991 and 1992 to
dismantling the Soviet Union and to only partially successful efforts at
forming a Commonwealth of Independent States. During 1993 he concentrated on his struggle with parliament and on getting a new constitution approved and implemented. In 1994 he focused on making the
new system work and on completing his patchwork of treaties and
agreements with the 91 federal units. He returned to the Chechen
problem as part of a larger Russian diplomatic, economic and military
effort to bring the greater Caspian region and its oil wealth into the
Russian sphere of influence.[15]

The fact that Boris Yeltsin believed in dramatic breakthroughs and
had shed blood in Moscow to get his way in his confrontation with
parliament was not encouraging to those who hoped for a peaceful resolution of the Chechen problem. His leadership style was confrontational and the Chechen national movement was militarised. This
combination pointed towards war unless other societal and political
forces could intervene.

On 26 November 1994 the federal side made its play and sent some
26 tanks and 75 Russian military personnel into the Chechen capital,

Grozny. These troops were on temporary leave from the Russian Ministry of Defence and were being paid by the federal secret services to pose as anti-Dudayev Chechen rebels. They were supposed to hold part of Grozny long enough for anti-Dudayev politicians to set up operations there. Yeltsin's next move would have been to insist that Dudayev and all the other Chechen factions form a new coalition government and recognise that Chechnya was part of the Russian Federation. However Dudayev captured them all, they confessed and Yeltsin was deeply humiliated. Now Yeltsin's personal prestige was on the line as well as his ability to demonstrate that he could defend Russia's political integrity.

In November and December 1994 Dudayev demanded face-to-face negotiations with Boris Yeltsin and offered to sign agreements with Russia that satisfied Russian national security concerns in exchange for Russian recognition of Chechen national independence. Yeltsin refused several such offers[16] and instead sent Defence Minister Pavel Grachev to negotiate with Dudayev. Dudayev called for direct discussions with Yeltsin and asked Grachev to convey this request to Yeltsin. Again Yeltsin refused and insisted that Dudayev accept the Kremlin's position that he was but one of several competing for power in Chechnya, and that he should sit down at a roundtable with the other Chechen leaders under the aegis of Russian federal authorities.

On 9 December 1994 Yeltsin issued a presidential *ukaz* that in effect was a declaration of war on the Dudayev regime. He ordered Dudayev to surrender all arms to federal authorities within three days and simultaneously authorised the federal military, police and security forces to use all means necessary to ensure that this orders was followed. Yeltsin ignored all calls from members of parliament and other civic and political organisations to withdraw the ultimatum, and he pushed the federal power ministries into action despite the objections of some prominent, competent, high-ranking officers, who resigned in protest. Yeltsin threw 24 000 federal troops into action without proper preparation or training. Within days it became clear that the Chechen population and other peoples in neighbouring Dagestan and Ingushetia were confronting the federal troops and demanding that they disobey Yeltsin's orders. Yeltsin gave them no way out and insisted that they obey. After a week of slow progress and heavy casualties, Yeltsin fired off new orders and doubled the number of troops committed to the war, which rapidly took on the character of a national liberation struggle. The armed movement for national self-determination, led by experienced military professionals who were determined to win at almost any cost, resisted successfully and adapted to all new political and military circumstances more ably than the Yeltsin administration.

From December 1994 to March 1996 Yeltsin refused to yield to Dudayev's demands for direct negotiations. Finally, on 31 March 1996, with the presidential election approaching and the war extremely unpopular with voters, Yeltsin shifted his position and told Moscow reporters that he was prepared to talk directly to Dudayev, much as Israel – after many years of refusing to talk with the PLO – had finally reached an agreement and started to work towards a final settlement.[17] Yeltsin apparently found the Israeli strategy attractive since it allowed Palestinian autonomy but stopped short of recognising an independent state of Palestine. He said that he was prepared to meet with Dudayev and was willing to talk without preconditions. But he stressed that he was aiming for a treaty between the Russian Federation and Chechnya in which the Chechens would recognise their membership of the federation in exchange for substantial autonomy up to but not including formal independence.[18] However, before this new peace process could get under way Dudayev was killed by Russian military forces on the night of 21–22 April 1996.[19] Zelimkhan Yandarbiyev emerged as the leader of the Chechen regime, with Aslan Maskhadov, an experienced Soviet military officer, serving as its supreme military commander. Dudayev duly became a *shahid*, or martyr, for Chechen independence.

On 2 May 1996 Yeltsin offered to go to Chechnya for talks if the Chechens would not go to Moscow.[20] Yandarbiyev eventually agreed to talks and was received in the Kremlin on 27 May 1996. Yeltsin opened the discussion but soon left and turned the work over to Prime Minister Viktor Chernomyrdin. The federal side included Doku Zavgayev, a pro-Moscow Chechen. The rebels were highly suspicious of Yeltsin's true intentions. They knew that the Chechen war had been highly unpopular with the Russian public and that Yeltsin was anxious to present himself as a victor and a peacemaker in time for the presidential election in June 1996. While the Chechens were travelling home from Moscow, Yeltsin staged a quick visit to federal controlled territory in Chechnya and declared that the federal troops had won a victory and prevented secession.[21] This confirmed Chechen fears that Yeltsin was more interested in winning votes than in making a settlement with them. He had not changed his basic pattern of behaviour and still refused to engage in face-to-face talks with them. The Chechens took advantage of the pre-election ceasefire and moved fighters into place in all the key urban centres that the Kremlin claimed were under federal control. During the first week of August

1996, as Yeltsin was having himself sworn into office, the rebels launched a bold offensive.

Russian military analysts had been warning that the rebels were preparing for action ever since Yeltsin had imposed his pre-election ceasefire on 31 March 1996. The federal troops were aware that the rebels were reinforcing their positions and were in fact surrounding them. When the rebels launched their post-election offensive the federal troops were already demoralised and in no mood to fight. Yeltsin's controversial new Security Council chief, Lieutenant General (Retired) Aleksandr Lebed, stopped the fighting by negotiating with Aslan Maskhadov and treating him as a fellow officer rather than a bandit. Lebed, Maskhadov and Yandarbiyev agreed to end the war and to postpone the final resolution of Chechnya's status until December 2001. But Lebed had presidential ambitions and could not disguise his disgust for the Kremlin civilian leaders, including Boris Yeltsin, whom he held accountable for the disaster in Chechnya. On 17 October 1996 Yeltsin fired Lebed for engaging in self-promotion and maverick behaviour instead of working as a member of the Yeltsin team. Nevertheless Yeltsin accepted the framework agreements that Lebed had worked out with the Chechens and slowly withdrew most of the federal troops. This withdrawal gave the Chechens *de facto* military and political control over their statelet.

Presidential power to use armed force in Russia

The Russian constitution includes provisions for states of emergency, during which the president can suspend normal governmental operations within a region and impose martial law, backed by federal armed forces. The constitution requires the president to take such actions to the Duma and the Federal Council for review and approval in a timely manner. Although the constitution's intentions seem implicitly clear in this regard, it does not specifically prohibit the president from using armed force. Yeltsin should have proclaimed a state of emergency and sought legislative approval. Initially it appeared that he intended to take that step – in his address to the citizens of Russia on the situation he said that a state of emergency had become necessary. However, over the next few days he issued presidential decrees which authorised a special committee, headed by Defence Minister Grachev, to use 'all measures necessary' to restore constitutional rule in Chechnya, but no specific references were made to any state of emergency.

Yeltsin emphasised efficiency over legality and set a poor precedent for the future. He deliberately circumvented constitutional provisions that were designed to prevent presidents from using armed force to impose their will inside Russia. This was the second time he had used his direct authority over Russia's armed forces to resolve a political crisis in his favour. The first time had been in September–October 1993, when he had used force to dissolve parliament. At that time he had also suspended the Constitutional Court in order to prevent it from proclaiming his actions in violation of the constitution. He had justified those actions in terms of the Russian national interest, a higher 'constitutional' obligation than respect for every detail of the existing constitution.

Critics of the war repeatedly complained that the manner in which Yeltsin had launched it had placed every member of the armed forces serving there in jeopardy. Yeltsin had to reassure the federal armed forces repeatedly that they would not be prosecuted for using lethal force in Chechnya. Various protest groups tried to get the Russian Constitutional Court to rule on the war's constitutionality, but the court failed to take up this highly sensitive issue until July 1995, when the conflict appeared to be coming to an end.

Vice-premier Sergei Shakhrai presented the Yeltsin administration's case. Yelena Mizulina (Federal Council) and Anatoly Lukyanov (State Duma) argued for the opposition. They argued that a ruling against the presidency was required to prevent future presidents from using their power over the armed forces to impose dictatorship on Russia. They insisted that court action was required to strengthen the legislative branch of government and enable it to act as an effective check on presidential power. Shakhrai cited Russian federal legislation and parts of the constitution that require the president to defend law and order and recited the familiar litany of Dudayev's violations of federal law.[22]

Because the case had enormous implications for the Chechen rebels and the federal forces alike, the talks in Grozny went into recess to await the court's ruling. On 1 August 1995 it ruled that the use of armed force in Chechnya was legal and constitutional and that President Yeltsin had acted in keeping with his authority and responsibility.[23] There were dissenting opinions, which were partly reflected in the court's 45-minute opinion. The court explained that the fact that the war itself was constitutionally legitimate did not absolve those fighting from legal responsibility for their actions. This was a bow towards human rights activists who were deeply concerned about civilian casualties. By refusing to rule against the Yeltsin administration the court may have averted a major national political crisis but it also set a dangerous precedent. The first president of post-Soviet Russia had fought a civil war without obtaining proper authorisation from the Russian legislature. The Yeltsin administration continued to manage the Chechen affair as an executive branch operation.

Systemic factors: Russian strategic interests

The Russian state faced serious problems because large stretches of its southern frontier were neither properly demarcated nor fortified. Russia's first line of defence was the southern border of the former Soviet Union which after the collapse of the Soviet Union became the external borders of eight sovereign states: Georgia, Armenia, Azerbaijan, Turkmenistan, Uzbekistan, Tajikistan, Kyrgyzstan and Kazakhstan. Furthermore, six of those states were of Islamic heritage and all six had coreligionists and members of their respective titular nationalities across the border. Hence it was natural for them to begin to develop relations with the greater Islamic world to the south. Since they also maintained ties with Russia, they became Russia's links to the Islamic world and opened Russia to influences from that region.

There are two ways of evaluating this development. If Russia adopts a positive attitude towards the Islamic world and maintains positive relations with peoples of Islamic heritage within the former Soviet republics and the Russian Federation, the opening to the south could enhance economic prosperity and regional security. However if Russia adopts a negative attitude and falls into conflictual relations with these peoples the opening to the south could pose a serious threat to Russian state security. It is in Russia's national interest to build positive relations, but Russian culturalism makes this difficult. Russian policy makers are aware of the problem but find it difficult to overcome. It is difficult for the former overlord and those subjugated to form egalitarian working relations and avoid emotion-driven politics.

National self-determination and regional stability

The international system of states is composed of a mixture of nation states and multinational states. It is based upon the conservative principle of regime sovereignty, not the democratic principle of national self-determination. It assumes that most national minorities will never obtain sovereign states of their own. Nevertheless the international community encourages multinational states to grant minority peoples a reasonable opportunity for national development, short of statehood.

If national self-determination was given free reign everywhere and every ethnic group was given its own sovereign state, the number of sovereign states would increase dramatically. Some states would increase in size; others would decrease. Such changes would damage the viability of major states and the stability of the international order. The international system of states in the broad swath of territory stretching between the Balkans and north-west China is particularly vulnerable to such destabilisation.[24]

For this reason the international consensus is statist and conservative on the question of national self-determination. Neither the great powers nor the United Nations insist upon the right of every people to self-determination. Instead they emphasise steps that will preserve the existing state system, current state borders, and the principle of non-interference in the internal affairs of states. The great multinational states of central Eurasia have maintained their integrity and viability by relying upon authoritarian political systems and a combination of persuasion and coercion to prevent national minorities from organising effective independence movements and/or from attempting to improve their status by realigning themselves with another state. Nevertheless borders change, peoples break out of multinational states and new states form. Wars of state formation and reformation are part of that process.

When challenged by a national independence movement, the multinational state's central political leadership has three main policy options. First, it can try to defeat the movement. Second, it can renegotiate its status in order to retain it within the multinational state under new arrangements acceptable to both sides. Third, it can grant the subject people national independence. The national minority has three similar options. It can adopt a military strategy, buildup its military—political capability and wage war. Alternatively it can use the threat of war to renegotiate its status and agree to remain in the multinational state. Or it can accept the *status quo*.

Oil and geopolitical strategic factors

Russia needed to control Chechnya in order to dominate the oil pipeline routes from the greater Caspian region to Russia's primary oil export terminals near Novorossiisk on the Black Sea coast.[25] Chechnya's domestic oil production was comparatively small, about 1.5 million metric tons per year, compared with the Russian Federation's total annual output of some 600 million tons.[26] Russian industry did not need Chechen oil but the Russian strategic planners were convinced that they needed to control Chechnya and the adjacent regions in order to dominate the main rail, highway and pipeline routes linking

Georgia, Armenia and Azerbaijan to Russia. Moscow wanted to prevent the three Caucasian republics from pulling out of its sphere of influence. Russian Foreign Ministry leaders made no secret of this, and they were certain that rivals, including the United States and Turkey, were working to push Russia out of the Caspian oil industry and deprive it of future income flows. They saw this as a natural product of interstate competition, one that Russian weakness encouraged.[27]

The pipeline issue was linked to Russian–Turkish rivalry for influence over the greater Caspian region and billions of dollars of income from the oil transportation business. Turkey wanted Turkic-speaking Azerbaijan, Kazakhstan and Turkmenistan to export oil to the world markets from Turkish ports on the Mediterranean. Russia tried to block that development and insisted that the cheapest and most immediate route was through Novorossiisk. The Chechen rebellion was damaging Russia's ability to get its way in this matter, much as the war between Armenia and Azerbaijan and the Kurdish rebellion against Turkey combined to undermine Turkey's ability to guarantee the safety of the pipeline route it wanted to develop. Because Russia, Turkey and Iran competed instead of cooperating, the entire region suffered and millions of people were deprived of the benefits that the Caspian Sea oil could have brought.

Ethno-national world views and lessons of history

The military evidence suggests that the post-communist Russian leaders assumed that it was natural to return to the past for inspiration instead of pressing ahead with new forms of patriotism based upon liberal political ideology. Instead of adopting new and original regalia, post-Soviet Russia revived the imperial czarist crest as its official national emblem: a double-headed eagle embellished with St George and other Christian symbols. These old imperial symbols were at least mildly provocative to ethnic groups within the Russian state who were not of Russian Orthodox cultural descent. Russian military uniforms were stripped of their red stars and hammers and sickles and gained refurbished imperial eagles. This process started in the 1980s or even earlier.[28]

As early as 1988 the Soviet Ministry of Defence issued a new military history, under Defence Minister Yazov's signature, which restored traditional Russian Orthodox Christian warriors to a place of honour and celebrated every major Russian victory over non-Christian, primarily Islamic rivals for wealth and power in Eurasia. It began with Prince

Svyatoslav's defeat in 956 of Khazar, a Jewish state north of the Caspian Sea, and extended all the way to the Russian–Turkish wars of 1877–78, which were described as Russian support for Bulgaria's liberation from the Turkish 'yoke'.[29] The Russian state's struggle against the Mongol–Tatar khans and Turkish sultans was well on its way to becoming part of the official curriculum for Soviet officers before the collapse of the Soviet Union and the revival of ethnic Russian culturalism. (In 1990, when Colonel Aleksandr Rutskoi campaigned for a seat in the Russian Parliament, he pledged to defend Russia and to preserve its territorial integrity. He conjured up images of great military heroes in Russian history such as Aleksandr Nevsky, Dmitry Donskoi and Peter the Great.)[30]

Post-communist Russia's national parliament – the State Duma – addressed the military holiday problem in 1994–95. On 15 February 1995 it adopted an official list of 'military days of glory', which President Yeltsin signed into law in March even though Ministry of Defence experts pointed out that the Duma committee had failed to adjust the dates of prerevolutionary holidays for post-imperial calendar reforms. The Duma's list of 15 special days included nine traditional czarist military holidays and six Soviet victories. Even though political instructors were supposed to teach officers to respect and value the peoples of Islamic heritage, in history lessons they taught that Russia's rivals in the south had been the Mongol–Tatar khans and Turkic empires – precisely the states and leaders who were heroes to many Russian Muslims. This made the post-Soviet Russian military officer the successor to imperial czarist military traditions. The old was being revived to fill the ideological vacuum and this included an open door policy towards the Russian Orthodox Church. The patriarch made the rounds of important military institutions, blessed them, and placed icons in them. For example he made St Barbara the protector of Russia's Strategic Rocket Forces and blessed their command and control centre near Moscow. On 1 December 1995 he dedicated a chapel inside the prestigious General Staff Academy. The Church also erected a large memorial chapel on Poklonnaya hill outside Moscow to commemorate the fiftieth anniversary and honour the veterans of the Great Patriotic War. Islamic clergy placed a small memorial on the site and waited for a permit to build a mosque dedicated to those who had given their lives in that war. Meanwhile one of Russia's leading politicians, Moscow mayor Luzhkov, took personal responsibility for the reconstruction of the Church of Christ the Saviour in central Moscow, an imperial cathedral dedicated to military–patriotic themes that had been demolished by Stalin. Luzhkov also made certain that the Russian state memorial and Orthodox chapel on Poklonnaya hill were completed on time.

Meanwhile the Islamic clergy and faithful not only had difficulty obtaining building permits, they were also subjected to unpleasant treatment. For example Moscow's special OMON police invaded an historic Tatar mosque, where they roughed up and hauled off all the worshippers without bothering first to check their residence papers.[31] This was typical of the manner in which Muslims were being treated during the mayor's drive to rid the capital of criminals and illegal residents. Although the worshippers were released, the authorities had made their impression.

Officially Russia was multiconfessional, but in practice it was Russian Orthodox clergy who offered the blessings at public events such as Boris Yeltsin's first and second inaugurations. Muslims existed inside a state which rested upon an Orthodox Christian heritage, even though this was not formal state policy. It was only natural for Muslims to revive their own national traditions and religious and historical perspectives in those regions where they lived in significant numbers: the southern band of the North Caucasus, Tatarstan and Bashkortostan. Russian federalism created the constitutional foundations for the development of distinctive ethno-national cultures in such minority regions once the unitary communist dictatorship had been dismantled.

The Soviet state's military–political intervention and bitter experience in Afghanistan from 1978 to 1989 must have reinforced the negative Islamic stereotypes. Gorbachev's military suppression of the developing national rebellion in Azerbaijan in January 1990, the greatest use of Soviet military power against civilians inside the Soviet Union since the death of Stalin, seemed to confirm that the Muscovite state was less concerned about the life of Islamic peoples than it was about that of Christians. Furthermore, from 1988 onwards the Russian public was treated to images of brutality arising from communal violence in parts of Central Asia and the Caucasus. And by the mid 1990s Caucasian nationality had become synonymous with criminality due to the spectacular success Caucasian syndicates had in the struggle to take control of significant parts of the public vegetable market, and various black markets in key Russian cities such as Moscow. By summer 1993 Russian soldiers were standing guard on the border between Afghanistan and Tajikistan and being told that their presence was required to prevent the Islamic jihad from spreading into Central Asia and moving up the Volga through Tatarstan towards Moscow.

Chechen history and the Russian threat

Of the 31 ethnic groups with special administrative–political home-lands within the Russian Federation, only the Chechens adopted a militant strategy and opted for war. There are two basic schools of thought on why the Chechen nationalists and Russian federal authorities went to war. The first school points to Chechen history and a political culture which creates the expectation that Chechens have to fight repeatedly to win and preserve basic national rights. The second school recognises the political cultural problem but holds specific politicians responsible for the war and denies the fatalistic inevitability of the war between the Chechens and Russians. The first school argues that history demonstrates that Chechens will not be able to develop their national culture as long as they are forced to remain within a Russian-dominated state. The second argues that new political arrangements are possible to guarantee the necessary conditions for Chechnya to prosper within the Russian Federation.

The Nokhchy people lived in the northern Caucasus long before the Russian empire began pushing southward into the Caucasus. Chechen and Chechnya, the names the Russians applied to them, have their origin in Nokhchin names for the region where the Russians first encountered them. They are part of the indigenous mountain peoples and are not related to the Slavic, Turkic or Iranian linguistic groups. The Chechens converted to Sunni Islam.

In the mid nineteenth century the Chechens and other Islamic peoples in the northern Caucasus fought to block aggressive Russian expansion into their land. They were led by the legendary Imam Shamil, who made peace in 1859 and went into internal exile in Russia after decades of fighting. Moscow broke Chechen resistance by sending a large military force capable of overwhelming that resistance. Thereafter the conquered Chechens were governed by imperial administrators. As Imperial Russia expanded at the expense of the Turkic empire, Islamic peoples took refuge in what later became modern day Turkey, Jordan and other countries. Some sources place the number of their descendants now living in Turkey at around 6 000 000.[32] Consequently any north Caucasian rebellion has implications for Russian–Turkish relations and natural links to public opinion and sources of support in the Near and Middle East. Furthermore the czars encouraged Slavic Christian Cossacks to settle in the north Caucasian frontier regions in order to create a living and loyal defence perimeter. Their descendants still occupy parts of the territory that Chechen nationalists claim as their homeland. Since 1992 Cossacks have demanded and received the right to bear arms under the control of the Russian Ministry of Defence. However, informal militarised organisations also exist.

Chechens, like most Caucasian peoples, tried to establish national independence when the Russian empire collapsed in 1917 but were coerced into the new Russian Soviet Socialist Federation by the Red Army. The Soviet regime slapped two key restrictions on the national self-determination it promised the peoples. First, no political movement other than the Communist Party would be tolerated. Second, membership of the Soviet Union would be permanent, in spite of pledges made and enshrined in the union treaty and the Soviet constitution. Nevertheless sporadic armed resistance to the Soviet authorities continued in remote areas since the Chechens had retained their weapons. Trouble erupted during Stalin's collectivisation drive and was brutally suppressed. Rebellion revived when Nazi legions fought their way into the Caucasus and threatened to cut off Stalin's Red Army from Caucasian oil and wartime aid routes through Iran. However, when Stalin defeated Hitler's multinational forces at Stalingrad, hopes for a German-backed general Islamic uprising evaporated.

During the Chechens' absence, Stalin moved ethnic Russians and others into Chechnya, developed the petrochemical industry and made Grozny – the main city – into a typical Russian-speaking regional centre. When the Chechens returned they revived abandoned villages and reoccupied the rural areas, while the ethnic Russians remained the dominant group in the city. In 1959 the region's total population was 710 000, of which the Chechen and Ingush component was only 292 000. By 1989 the balance had shifted in favour of the titular nationalities, which accounted for 898 000 of the total population of 1 270 000 in the Chechen-Ingush republic.[33] The ethnographic trend that favoured Chechen domination of politics intensified after 1990–91 as some 250 000 ethnic Russians moved out of the region and ceded their economic, social and political space to Chechens.

Chechnya's immediate neighbour to the east, Dagestan, has a population of some 1 800 000 diverse peoples of Islamic heritage and a very small Russian minority of 8–9 per cent.[34] The prospect of building a compact alliance of north Caucasian mountain peoples of Islamic heritage hinges upon Chechen–Dagestanian cooperation. If all the ethno-political units named after Muslim peoples from Abkhazia on the Black Sea coast to Dagestan on the Caspian were to unite, the federation would have some 5 000 000 people. Such ideas have been floated in the past and continue to be promoted.

There are 32 special ethnic political–administrative regions inside the Russian Federation. Apart from the cluster of north Caucasian mountain peoples around Chechnya, titular nationals make up less than 50 per cent of the population of these regions, and in most cases Russians are the largest ethnic group. Furthermore most of the ethno-political units have comparatively small populations. Only two – Tatarstan and Bashkortostan – have populations greater than 2 000 000; seven have between 1 000 000 and 2 000 000; and 23 have fewer than 1 000 000 inhabitants.[35] Tatarstan and Bashkortostan are special cases because Tatars comprise about 50 per cent of the population in Tatarstan, and if the figures for Bashkorts and Tatars are combined for neighbouring Bashkortostan they make up slightly more than 50 per cent of the population and ethnic Russians drop to 40 per cent. This means that the demographic balance in the general area of the old Golden Horde is tipping towards peoples of Islamic-Turkic heritage.[36]

Russian history and the Islamic threat

The Islamic threat has two dimensions. One is internal to the Russian Federation and is seen as a national self-determination problem. The other is external but contiguous to the Russian Federation and is normally seen as political change and reorientation towards the Islamic world at the expense of Russian economic, political and security interests. Do the Muslim peoples living within the borders of the Russian Federation pose a serious threat to Russia's territorial integrity? Is a general threat to Russia's national interests and security brewing in the 'Islamic crescent', the band of states along both sides of the former southern border of the Soviet Union?

In order to envisage an Islamic threat to the Russian state's integrity, it is necessary to imagine a situation in which vast numbers of ethnic Russians are driven out of southern Russia and the middle Volga region. The main political units that occupy the political space between Tatarstan and Bashkortostan and the north Caucasian mountain belt are dominated by ethnic Russians.[37] Moving from north to south, the following demographic facts are noted. Saratov province is 85 per cent Russian, the Volgograd region is 90 per cent Russian, the Astrakhan region is 73 per cent Russian, the Rostov region is 90 per cent and the Krasnodar and Stavropol regions which are closest to the mountain trouble spots are 85 per cent Russian (and 2–5 per cent Ukrainian). The only exception to this is Kalmykia, where Russians comprise some 37 per cent of the population. However the Kalmyks are Buddhists of Mongol stock, not Turkic Muslims. Ethnic Russians make up 81 per cent of the Russian Federation's population. When the closely related Ukrainians and Belarussians are added, the Eastern Slavic, Orthodox Christian component is 85 per cent. This is a formidable ethnic foundation and not one that will produce massive fragmentation along ethnic lines. Some 18–20 million Russians are living in well-developed, deeply rooted towns and cities that form a permanent ethnographic barrier between the northern Caucasus and greater Tatarstan.

In the eighteenth and nineteenth centuries the czarist empire conquered the northern shores of the Black Sea and the Caucasus from the Turkic sultans and their local allies, such as the Crimean Tatars. Two hundred years of Muscovite policies that encouraged Russians and Ukrainians to settle in southern Ukraine and southern Russia tipped the ethnographic balance decisively against the peoples of Islamic heritage. The latter retained strong positions in the historical centre of the Golden Horde – Tatarstan and Bashkortostan to the north and in the northern foothills of the Caucasian mountains. The region in between became 'Russian' in the broadest sense of the term. It includes descendants of the military settlers – the Cossacks, who defended the Orthodox czar's southern frontiers. As the Chechen war developed and particularly after the Chechen rebels staged a dramatic terrorist and hostage-taking show of force in the town of Budyennovsk, Cossacks in the north Caucasian region began to demand the right to bear arms for Russia again. Yeltsin played on those sentiments during his 1996 presidential campaign and signed orders creating a special presidential department of Cossack armies (*Glavnoe unpravlenie kazachyikh voisk pri Prezidente Rossiiskoi Federatsii*). Cossack military – political leaders or *atamany*, representing some 300 000 Cossacks, met with him and urged large crowds to cheer him on. But the regular, mainline military, not the Cossack irregulars, were to be the backbone of Russia's defences in southern Russia.[38]

In the Caucasus as a whole, the president noted that forces were working to partition Russia. He also noted that there had been tragic and dark episodes in Russian history in the region. However he emphasised that only Russia had created the conditions under which all the peoples of the Caucasus were able to live together in one unified socio-economic complex.[39] It seemed natural for Yeltsin to reach out to Cossack militiamen, just as Muscovite Christian rulers had done for centuries. Such political behaviour certainly made it easier for Chechen separatists to argue that this new Russia could not serve as a reliable guarantor of the conditions that Muslim peoples needed to rebuild their national cultures.

Russia had more than enough military power in the north Caucasian military district to liquidate the Chechen rebellion, and ethnic Russians dominated the geographical space and politics of southern Russia. Therefore it was ridiculous to stir up fears of a grand Islamic sweep from the mountain regions, where Muslim peoples predominated up to Tatarstan and Bashkortostan. The ethnographic balance was in favour of ethnic Russians in southern Russia and the Russian state reinforced that ethnographic reality with military power. Russia's main challenge in the south is its relationship with Ukraine, which has sovereignty over the former Soviet Union's most important Black Sea naval bases and coastal defences.

Moscow identified the northern Caucasus as one of its most important strategic regions. In effect, strategic thinkers replaced the NATO threat with the new threat from the south, mainly Turkey. Moscow's military planners developed a grand design that included the Black Sea, the north Caucasian military district (NCMD) and the Caspian Sea. Russian leaders informed the European powers that the flank agreements included in the conventional forces in Europe (CFE) arms reductions agreements were no longer acceptable. Russia announced that it would increase its military presence in the NCMD beyond the levels provided by the flank agreements, and it duly did so. Russia also pressed Georgia, Armenia and Azerbaijan to accept Russian troops on their respective borders with Turkey and Iran. Russia saw Turkey as its permanent rival in the region and Iran as its natural ally against Turkic expansion. Yeltsin toured the NCMD during his 1996 presidential campaign and reaffirmed the district's central role in defending Russia's position in the Black Sea, the Caucasus and the Caspian. He boasted that the Chechen rebellion had been crushed.[40]

Conventional military power, additional bases and Russian–Iranian cooperation improved Russia's strategic position. However, conventional military power cannot resolve every conflict. The Chechen rebellion's non-conventional and terrorist component was a warning that Russian majority regions could face bombings, hostage taking and other deliberate acts of political violence. Conditions were ripe for the development of protracted conflict by hardcore rebel extremists acting in the name of national self-determination, much as IRA militants have fought against the Protestant majority and Britain in Northern Ireland. Russia has internal ethno-political problems that can be solved by granting maximum autonomy to three regions of Islamic heritage – the northern Caucasus, Tatarstan and Bashkortostan. It will, however, be difficult for the ethnic Russian majority to build a new world view for a multiconfessional Russian state.

The near-abroad problem

The former Soviet republic with the greatest ethno-national problem is Kazakhstan, not Russia. Some 40 per cent of its population is Russian. Turkic Kazakhs account for somewhat more than 40 per cent.[41] Kazakhstanians of Turkic and Slavic ancestry have a common interest in preventing radical Islam from taking root in Central Asia. If that happened, Russians would demand the right to national self-determination and unification with the Russian Federation. Therefore Kazakhstan's president, Nursultan Nazarbayev, adopted policies aimed at preventing Kazakh and Russian ethno-national extremists from operating openly in his country. He argued for close cooperation with Russia but insisted that Russians needed to adjust to new political realities and to make way for more Kazakhs in leadership positions at all levels of government and industry. 'Our future was determined in the past. Slavs and Turks have always been together.'[42]

Russians comprise 5.5 per cent of Azerbaijan's population, 6.5 per cent of Tajikistan's, 8.35 per cent of Uzbekistan's, 9.5 per cent of Turkmenistan's, 21.5 per cent of Kyrgyzstan's and 37.8 per cent of Kazakhstan's.[43] The largest group of Russians outside Russia is in Ukraine – 11 350 000 or 22 per cent of Ukraine's total population.[44] As an ethno-political problem, the Russians in Latvia and Estonia attracted the greatest attention during the first five years of post-Soviet existence (1991–96). They accounted for 34 per cent and 30 per cent of their respective country's populations but did not receive full rights of citizenship. Since those countries had small populations, the 34 per cent only amounted to about 900 000 and the 30 per cent to 344 000 people.

These numbers suggest that relations between Russia and Ukraine and between Russia and Kazakhstan will have the greatest influence on the greatest number of Russians living outside the Russian Federation. Of the 25 000 000 Russians outside the Russian Federation, 11.3 million are in Ukraine and 6.2 million are in Kazakhstan. No more than 4 000 000 Russians live in the other five Muslim republics combined. Furthermore Ukraine and Kazakhstan are Russia's primary security buffers. Kazakhstan buffers Russia's southern border from Mongolia to Astrakhan by occupying three quarters of Central Asia, and Ukraine buffers Russia from Turkey by occupying the northern shore of the Black Sea. The region between Ukraine and Kazakhstan is Russia's heavily defended north Caucasian military district. Neither

Ukraine nor Kazakhstan is likely to demand any Russian Federation territory in the name of national self-determination. To the contrary, Russian nationalists regularly demand parts of Ukraine and Kazakhstan. Ukraine and Kazakhstan are Russia's first line of defence and there are Russians living in the border regions inside Ukraine and Kazakhstan.

Russian actions demonstrate that Kremlin strategic thinkers see no great threat from the south's Islamic radicals.[45] Instability and local wars, yes. Massive invasions, no. Only 25 000 Russian border forces are committed to the defence of the Tajik–Afghan border, the most valuable sector in Central Asia. There are another 5000 Russian troops – the 201st Motorised Infantry Brigade – in Tajikistan. If Russia expected a major invasion from the south it would have more than 25 000 troops there. Russia's real first line of defence was inside Afghanistan with the armed forces of Afghan-Uzbek General Dostum and Afghan-Tajik General Akhmed Shah Masoud. What about the Chechen rebellion? Here the evidence also points to a rather casual attitude towards the rebels, and towards the fate of the federal troops and the local population. Moscow did little to restrain Dudayev for three years; and even after the fighting began, Kremlin politicians were unable to give steady, high-level attention either to winning the war or ending it. They treated the war like a manageable, unpleasant but necessary policing operation even though it cost them some 5000 soldiers, ruined Chechnya's towns and cities, and probably killed some 50 000 civilians, who with few exceptions were citizens of the Russian Federation.

Conclusion

The Chechen rebellion represented a real but limited threat to post-Soviet Russia's political integrity and security. It could and should have been handled differently. Boris Yeltsin and Dzhokhar Dudayev bear responsibility for the war, although they were propelled by broader forces deeply rooted in Russian and Chechen historical memory. Chechnya's national self-determination quickly acquired ethno-religious dimensions. This came naturally as Dudayev sought ways to rally his people and draw support from the greater Islamic world. The federal troops bore the insignia of the imperial double-headed eagle, proof that the new Russian state viewed itself as part of the European Christian world and regarded its Muslim minorities as remnants of rival states and empires that Russia had conquered. The rebels bore Islamic prayers and the green flags of *jihad*. Modern communication systems and the general international climate meant that the Chechen rebellion was watched throughout the Muslim world. This made the small conflict into a major issue, part of the new 'clash of civilisations', in the post-Cold War world view.

Nevertheless the Russian Federation's ethnographic structure and military system have prevented Islamic rebellions from linking Tatarstan and Bashkortostan with the northern Caucasus and Turkey. Russia may have made the north Caucasian military district into a military machine capable of obliterating the Islamic statelets, but that was not its purpose. It was developed to counterbalance major Islamic states such as Turkey, not statelets such as Chechnya. It was ineffective against the modern terrorist tactics that Chechen extremists employed to great political advantage. First the czars and then the general secretaries converted southern Russia into solid ethnic Russian country. They also left a legacy of distrust and ethnic prejudice that still influences behaviour and makes it difficult for Russian policy makers and aspiring ethno-national leaders in the Islamic statelets within the Russian Federation to strike the right balance, reach agreements and cooperate for the common good. Eastern Slavs of Orthodox Christian heritage and diverse peoples of Islamic heritage have been living together in both war and peace for one thousand years – it is the general weakening of the Russian state that has invited challenges to the Russian position.

This weakening of the Russian state is the greatest contributor to Eurasian systemic instability. The civilian politicians who have led Russia since 1990–91 must take responsibility for their own failures. Using Muslims and the Islamic threat as a scapegoat will not stand up to careful analysis. Poor relations with Ukraine and the Baltic states have done more to damage Russian interests than all the Islamic nationalists in the Caucasus, the Middle Volga region and Central Asia combined. The Muslims in the south are not likely to pull together into one grand anti-Russian alliance. There are too many natural, deeply rooted, cross-cutting cleavages in the broad Muslim zone from Turkey to Xinjiang. The very cleavages that keep this zone divided will produce regional conflicts and insurrections. Conflicts between peoples of Islamic heritage are as likely as conflicts across religious–civilisation lines. In the past czars and shahs competed and had both Christian and Muslim allies.

The Russian Federation made a mistake in November 1994. Yeltsin miscalculated and probably bullied his ministers into accepting the war plan as an extension of his domestic policies. He believed that he could blast down the Chechen rebels the way he had blasted down the Russian parliament a year earlier. Yeltsin captured Dudayev's presidential palace but Dudayev refused to yield and his rebels used partisan warfare tactics, periodic ceasefires and several nasty terrorist strikes to destroy Russians will to fight. Although Dudayev was killed and his country was wrecked, in the end the rebels won a major military – political victory. The average Russian did not want to fight that war. From the outset the Russian military saw no great strategic threat from Dudayev and resented Yeltsin's mismanagement of the crisis. It took a maverick general turned politician – Aleksandr Lebed – to sit down with the Chechen commanders and find a way to stop the fighting. This sordid affair was the result of mediocre Russian national leadership and regional great power cynicism.

The regional system is inherently competitive and driven by competition between Russia, Turkey and Iran. For several hundred years Russia and Iran have cooperated against Turkish interests. A change in Turkish policy could produce major positive shifts, assuming that Turkey could convince Russia and Iran that it was not moving to undermine their national interests in the greater Caspian region.

Pipelines are the touchstone issue and the economic cause of the Russian military move against Chechnya. A tripartite agreement between Russia, Iran and Turkey, linked to agreements with the oil- and gas-producing states of the Caspian region, would provide the economic foundation required to build regional peace and prosperity.

Notes and references

1. Yeltsin played volley ball and coached teams. He loved competition and bold offensive breakthroughs. He made his career in the Sverdlovsk party machine as an innovative boss whom Gorbachev brought to Moscow in order to shock the 1 000 000 strong Moscow Communist Party organisation into accepting perestroika. See Boris Yeltsin, *Against the Grain* (New York: Summit Books, 1990), and *The Struggle for Russia* (New York: Times Books/Random House, 1994). Russian edition: *Zapiski prezidenta* (Presidential diary) (Moscow: *Ogonek*, 1994).
2. Valery Yakov, 'Number of Casualties During Events of Oct. 3–4 in Moscow Has Been Established', *Izvestiya*, 25 December 1993; *CDSP*, vol. XLV, no. 52 (1993), pp. 20–1.
3. See Alexandar Morozov, 'Tax Administration in Russia', *The East European Constitutional Review*, Spring/Summer 1996, pp. 34–47.
4. For example, see the interview by Major A. Petrov, 'General Dudayev: Eto Vse Rossiya', *Krasnaya zvezda*, 26 October 1991.
5. See V. A. Tishkov (ed, *Narody Rossii: Entsiklopeidya* (Peoples of Russia: An Encyclopedia) (Moscow: Bol'shaya Rossiiskaya Entsiklopediya Press, 1994), p. 399 ff.

6. The Chechen National Congress was a cultural and political organisation, not a governmental institution. It included representatives from Chechen diaspora communities in the Middle East as well throughout the former Soviet Union.

7. The Russian military were informed of this dispute and the federal parliament's claims that only 200 000 out of 1 500 000 Chechen–Ingush citizens voted. See Captain Vladimir Ermolin, 'S. V. Vneocherednogo Syezda narodnykh deputatov RSFS' (Extraordinary session of the RSFSR Supreme Soviet), *Krasnaya zvezda*, 30 October 1991.

8. See Major A. Petrov, 'Baudin Bakhmadov: Poka lyudi idut za Dudayevym' (For now the people are going with Dudayev), *Krasnaya zvezda*, 26 October 1991.

9. See Nikolai Gul'binskii and Marina Shakina, *Afghanistan Kreml' Lefortovo: Epizody politicheskoi biografii Aleksandra Rutskogo* (Afghanistan, the Kremlin, Lefortovo: Episodes from Aleksandr Rutskoi's Political Biography) (Moscow: Lada, 1994), p. 141 ff. The authors provide an excellent summary of the first confrontations between Yeltsin and Dudayev in autumn 1991.

10. The central military press called this rebel action 'armed picketing', a form of militarised political action. See Major A. Ivanov, 'Vooruzhennoe piketirovanie voinskoi chasti', *Krasnaya zvezda*, 30 October 1991.

11. See G. Anishchenko, A. Vaslievskaya, O. Krugusheva and O. Mramornov (eds, *Kommissiya Govorukhina* (Moscow: Laventa, 1995), p. 41 (hereafter, *Govorukhin Commission Report*). State Duma deputy Stanislav Govorukhin held a controversial inquiry into the Chechen affair, beginning in January 1995.

12. *Govorukhin Commission Report*, p. 43.

13. Ibid., pp. 29–30.

14. Ibid., p. 29.

15. See Robert V. Barylski, 'Russia, the West, and the Caspian Energy Hub', *The Middle East Journal*, vol. 49, no. 2 (1995), pp. 217–32.

16. See, for example, the interview conducted immediately after the November events by Alexei Venedikov, 'Dzhokhar Dudayev: "This Is Intervention, Pure and Simple"', *Moscow News*, no. 48, 1994.

17. See Boris Yeltsin, 'Mir, spokoistvie i bezopasnost' nuzhny chechenskomu narodu, vsem narodam Rossii: Zayavlenie Prezidenta Rossiiskoi Federatsii Borisa Yeltsina', *Krasnaya zvezda*, 2 April 1996.

18. Boris Yeltsin, press conference of 31 March 1996, *Golos Rossii*; personal notes.

19. See 'Izvestii o smerti Dudayeva', *Krasnaya zvezda*, 25 April 1996.

20. *Golos Rossii*, 2 May 1996.

21. Anatoly Stasovskii, 'Na peregovorakh v Moskve dostignut progress. Boris Yeltsin pribyl v Chechnya s mirom', *Krasnaya zvezda*, 29 May 1996.

22. See Aleksei Kirpichnikov's reports in *Sevodnya*, 18 and 19 July 1995. *CDSP*, vol. 47, no. 29, pp. 10–11.

23. Aleksandr Pel'ts, 'Konstitutsionnyi sud priznal: prezident deistvoval v grankakh Konstitutsii Rossiii' (Constitutional court ruled the president acted within the bounds of the constitution of the Russian federation), *Krasnaya zvezda*, 2 August 1995.

24. See Robert V. Barylski, 'The Russian Federation and Eurasia's Islamic Crescent', *Europe–Asia Studies*, vol. 46, no. 3 (1994), pp. 389–416.
25. See Robert V. Barylski, 'Russia, the West, and the Caspian Energy Hub', *Middle East Journal*, vol. 49, no. 2 (1995), pp. 217–32.
26. *Govorukhin Commission Report*, op. cit., p. 31.
27. See First Deputy Foreign Minister Igor Ivanov's strategic analysis, 'Faktor cily' (The power factor), *Krasnaya zvezda*, 19 November 1996.
28. Stalin began to revive Russian military nationalism during the war against Nazi Germany (1941–45).
29. See Army General Dmitry T. Yazov's *Verny otchizne* (Loyal to the Fatherland) (Moscow: Voennoe Izdatel'stvo, 1988), pp. 18–64.
30. See Gul'binskii and Shakhina, *Afghanistan, Kreml', Lefortovo*, op. cit., p. 143.
31. *Moscow News*, no. 40, 1996, p. 14.
32. See John Colarusso, 'Chechen: The War Without Winners', *Current History*, October 1995, pp. 329–36.
33. Tishkov, *Narody Rossii*, op. cit., p. 33.
34. Ibid., p. 34.
35. See ibid., p. 19. In 1993 the Chechen–Ingush unit was divided into separate Chechen and Ingush autonomous republics. Thereafter, each had fewer than 1 000 000 people. The numbers have been adjusted accordingly.
36. See Hafeez Malik, 'Tatarstan's Treaty with Russia: Autonomy or Independence', *Journal of South Asian and Middle Eastern Studies*, vol. XVIII, no. 2 (winter 1994), and 'Bashkort National Kurultai and Revival of Nationalism', ibid., vol. XVIX, no. 2, (winter 1995), pp. 1–37. These articles discuss the ethnographic and political issues in detail and over time.
37. Ibid.
38. See Anatoly Borovkov, 'Kazaki otveitli: 'Lyubo!', *Krasnaya zvezda*, 18 April 1996, and Sergei Knyaz'kov, 'Severnyi Kavkaz–forpost Rossii', *Krasnaya zvezda*, 19 April 1996.
39. Ibid.
40. Ibid.
41. According to the 1989 Soviet census, Kazakhstan's 6 227 549 Russians made up 37.82 per cent of the republic's population. See Tishkov, *Narody Rossii*, pp. 48–50 for tables showing the relative proportion of ethnic Russians in the other 14 former Soviet republics.
42. Nursultan Nazarbayev, cited by N. Zhelnorova, 'Mirotvorets Nazarbayev' (Nazarbayev the peacemaker), *Argumenty i fakty*, nos. 51–2, 1992.
43. Tishkov, *Narody Rossii*, op. cit., pp. 448–50.
44. Ibid., p. 448.
45. See the interesting analysis by Vitaly Strugovets and Anatoly Ladin, 'Naskol'ko seryezna ugroza s yuga?' (How serious is the threat from the south?), *Krasnaya zvezda*, 8 October 1996.

6

Russia and Islam: Mutual Adjustment in the New World

Mikhail Konarovsky

There is significant evidence that the next millennium will be marked by the rise of Islam as a global political phenomenon, exerting a growing influence on both regional and international affairs. Some experts even argue that many Muslim nations might secede from the UN in order to set up their own international organisation, with a security council, a common market, joint armed forces and so on. Consequently the world of Islam is seen by these as experts becoming a completely self-contained segment of the international community.

Such a scenario is probably not very realistic as the world of Islam is highly heterogeneous and politically dissimilar, with a broad diversity of opinion even within single regions.[1] Nevertheless, the more than 500 Muslim nations – with a total population of about one billion and increasing rapidly – have common historical and cultural roots. They control enormous mineral resources, with oil as the principal resource. The Muslim nations' economic and political ties likewise offer a significant integrative potential. Structural geopolitical changes after the Cold War resulted in the emergence of a number of newly independent Muslim nations in the post-Soviet space (such as oil- and gas-rich Azerbaijan, Kazakhstan, Uzbekistan and Turkmenistan) fueléing predictions of Islam turning into one of the most dynamic and turbulent political forces in the world. Common stands on a number of pressing regional and global issues – Bosnia, Chechnya, the world population, human rights, the role of women in society – are cementing mutual cooperation in the Muslims' leading international body – the Organisation of Islam Conference (OIC) – in order to urge the world community to adopt a sympathetic approach to Muslim views and demands.

At the same time many Muslim nations are suffering from severe economic stagnation and an ever growing identity crisis, and this will probably continue in the foreseeable future. Outbursts of fundamentalist activities indicate a tough domestic struggle to set up specific social institutions to resolve the current economic and political dilemmas.[2] Another reason for the Muslim's desire to return to their roots stems from the ideological vacuum that appeared after the cessation of East–West rivalry. The psychological shock consequent on direct contact between Western (Christian) and Eastern (Muslim) values and traditions against the background of the information revolution and world-wide economic integration is also playing a significant role.[3] Shaky democratic movements in parts of the world that are not consolidated enough to introduce a real alternative to assertive, fundamentalist, political Islam is no doubt a factor in its rise.

However, the main challenge to the interests of other nations, including Russia, which might be posed by an 'Islamic choice' will not emanate from fundamentalism. The issue is whether Islam will be a moderate movement or a radical political force, with extremism and terrorism being used to obtain political objectives, both inside and outside the Muslim world. It is an increase in militancy that in the long run may challenge the new democratic trends in international affairs.

Political Islam is a formal ideological doctrine in Iran and Sudan. The rise of domestic terrorism has already affected a number of Muslim nations, the best known examples being Algeria and to a certain extent Egypt. Future developments in those countries could influence the political landscape of North Africa, setting off a chain reaction that would stimulate instability in the Gulf region. The gradual spread of militant Islam in that area has caused grave concern not only to the Gulf Cooperative Council (GCC) (as indicated at the December 1995 Summit in Muscat), but also in the West because of its vital interest in long-term stability in the region, which is regarded as the principal oil reservoir for the developed world. Radicals are seeking to reinforce their political positions in Turkey and Pakistan. Intolerance and religious radicalism among Israelis and Palestinians are still putting obstacles in the way of the Middle East peace process. Intolerance and radicalism are also stirring up domestic conflict in India and South-West Asia.

The developments in Afghanistan in the late 1970s and mid 1980s, inflamed by the Soviet invasion of that country, served as 'a lighting rod for Islamic zealotry'.[4] After the Najibullah regime collapsed, mujahiddin from a number of Arab nations were not accepted back in their countries so they scattered across the Muslim and non-Muslim world, promoting religious militancy and intolerance.[5] Their influence has been apparent in Algeria, Egypt, Bosnia and Chechnya, as well as in the bombings in Saudi Arabia in 1995–96 and in Islambad, with dozens injured as a result of a blast at the Egyptian Embassy. Despite the November 1995 Dayton Accords on Bosnia, calling on all foreign fighters to leave the country, it seems unrealistic to believe that the thousands of mujahiddin from Algeria, Afghanistan, Iran, Pakistan and Saudi Arabia who were welcomed by the Bosnian government to fight against the Serbs would immediately depart from Bosnia.[6]

According to NATO, 'since the collapse of communism, Islamic militancy has emerged as the most serious threat to Western security.'[7] The OIC Summit in December 1994 acknowledged that this militancy also poses a threat to the Muslim nations themselves, damaging the image of Islam as an influential world religion. Simultaneously the Islamic world has expressed growing concern about the rise of intolerance towards Muslims in Europe and other parts of the world. In this connection the European Union (EU) proposed a security conference to discuss with the North African and Middle Eastern nations a joint strategy to tackle the problem. The Euro-Mediterranean conference, held in Barcelona in November 1995 with delegates from the EU nations and eight North African Arab states, focused on drawing up a partnership for economic development in the Mediterranean Muslim regions in order, among other things, to slow the massive immigration of Arabs to prosperous West European countries. More than five billion ECUs were targeted for development projects to promote European investments, a free trade zone and the exchange of goods and services. While Russia welcomed Euro-Mediterranean cooperation, it favoured a 'greater Mediterranean' strategy, based on a cooperative partnership of nations in the Mediterranean and Black Sea basins and the Middle East region, since in Russia's view those areas are historically linked by mutual interests and ties in politics, economies, ecology and culture.[8]

On the eve of the collapse of the Soviet Union and immediately after it, militant Islam appeared in Central Asia and the Caucasus, as well as in Russia's northern Caucasus and other Muslim regions of the country. As a result one can not rule out the possibility that in Russia's immediate proximity as well as in the Russian Federation's current territory an assertive bloc of nations may emerge, whose policies might bring about a complex challenge to Russia's stability and security.

The former Soviet Union and Islam

In general the Soviet attitude towards the Muslim world was not very sophisticated, and was predominantly theoretical rather than pragmatic. The Islamic factor did not exert much influence on either external or internal Soviet policies. Domestic ideological patterns were based on official atheism and the intention to create an abstract *'Homo Sovieticus'*. In spite of formally declared freedom of conscience, integrated actions were taken to curtail the influence of both Christian Orthodox and Muslim religious institutions. Nevertheless their role, particularly in everyday life and culture, was significantly unchanged. Religion kept its place in maintaining specific features of the life of individual Soviet republics from generation to generation. The phenomenon was more deep-rooted in predominantly Muslim Central Asia and the Caucasus, where the formal Communist Party of the Soviet Union (CPSU) and governmental structures were not able to replace the peculiarity of relations among local clans and different segments of society.

Official atheism was a principal obstacle against the Soviet Union using Islam in the interests of foreign policy. Broad ties with a number of Muslim nations were based mostly on Soviet support for 'Arab socialism' and on countering the West's influence in the Middle East and South-West Asia. The Arab–Israeli conflict was mainly viewed through the same prism. Moscow's 'infidelity' and atheistic policy significantly hampered the mutual ties, despite many Arabs' keen interest in expanding their relations with the Soviet Union, predominantly as a lever to obtain their own objectives when bargaining with the United States and Israel. Arab disillusionment with socialist slogans, which were unable to challenge nationalism and Islam as a driving force for their economic and social development, had an additional negative impact on their approach to Moscow. Muslim 'frontliners' such as Saudi Arabia, Pakistan and Iran after the Islamic regime had been established in Tehran, were particularly suspicious of the Soviet Union. Their anxiety found new ground in the late 1970s when the Soviet Union invaded neighbouring Afghanistan. That badly calculated step was the first and highly controversial experience of the Soviet Union after the Second World War in dealing with Islam. This misguided adventure indicated how gravely the Islamic factor was underestimated in Moscow's external policy.

Although developments in Afghanistan and the Islamic revolution in Iran, which caused an eruption of Muslim activity in the southern enclaves of the Soviet Union, at last put the issue on the domestic agenda, the gradual move towards the dissolution of the union gave Moscow no chance to work out a new vision and policy in this respect. With the collapse of communism an ideological vacuum developed. In the absence of new integrative ideas, a trend towards the revival of specific historical and cultural identities grew in each of the Soviet republics. Since the middle of the 1980s nationalism, significantly backed by the rise of religious consciousness, has turned into a driving force. Similar moves have taken place in the Russian Federation, since its ethnic and administrative make-up is much like that of the former Soviet Union. Both the old and the newly emerging national elites have contributed to the development of national and religious movements.

Dilemmas inside Russia

Balanced options with respect to Islam seem to be of vital importance to Moscow, which after the breakup of the Soviet Union found itself in a completely new external and domestic environment. A number of independent, predominantly Muslim nations have emerged in Russia's southern 'near abroad'. The need to adjust itself to new geopolitical realities has obliged Russia to draw up a new conceptual vision of its place in the world, with relations with the near abroad as its central point. On the other hand, dramatic domestic reconstruction is necessitating broad economic, political and cultural self-sufficiency on the part of autonomous republics and territories (*oblasts*), but not necessarily strengthening the country's political indivisibility. Markedly increased tensions and the war in Chechnya in 1994 made it quite clear that the Russian assessment that 'the support for slogans about the secession of that or another territory from the Russian Federation has considerably weakened'[9] was premature. However it might become more realistic if the present stand-off between the central authorities and those in Chechnya who advocate complete independence from the Federation is successfully resolved by political means. Russia's political integrity will remain seriously challenged until nationalism and the different religious activities (let alone the excessive power ambitions of the local elites) are placed by the government into a constructive channel to resolve nationwide economic, social and cultural dilemmas.[10]

Though Russia's Muslims are estimated at just 7 per cent of the total population,[11] they are concentrated in such vulnerable areas for the country's economy and political integrity as Central Volga, the northern Caucasus and part of Siberia, and represent a dynamic and enterprising section of society. Gambling with religious forces is a time bomb in the hands of a number of nationalistic and chauvinistic movements in both Christian and Islamic parts of Russia. The government itself, by drawing attention to the Christian Orthodox Church as a principal ally in building a new system of national values, is wittingly or unwittingly playing into the hands of radicals on all sides.[12]

For the time being the leaders of the main confessions (Orthodox Christianity and Sunni Islam) are speaking in favour of a constructive dialogue with the state and with each other. Each urgently needs to obtain the government's moral and financial support for the revival of religious beliefs and increased influence on the part of its institutions. As a result most far-seeing clerics do not show disloyalty to the central government – this is an important trump card in Moscow's hands, and if it is played wisely Moscow may gain many advantages. The approach of both Muslim and Orthodox institutions to Russia's domestic policies was tested in late 1994 during the ambiguous events in Chechnya.[13] Being highly critical of military options, Russia's Islamic leaders did not call into question the legitimacy of the Dudayev regime but did favour the maintenance of Chechnya within the framework of the Russian Federation. Their mediatory initiatives, though timid, were the first attempt by Russia's Islamic community to introduce itself as an independent and authoritive domestic political force.

The expansion of ties with 'outside Islam' has not yet influenced Russia's Muslims to the extent that they contradict Moscow's basic views on developments in specific Islamic regions in the near and far abroad. An obvious example of this was their approach to the Bosnian crisis. Muslim leaders in Russia showed great restraint in echoing the view of a number of Islamic countries that the conflict was a clash between Christianity and Islam. On the other hand an incident with a cargo plane from Tatarstan, which in August 1995 was forced by the Taliban (one of the most fundamentalist Afghan factions) to land in Kandahar,[14] prompted President Mintimer Shaymiyev of Tatarstan to call on Mufti Galiullah (Tatarstan's top Sunni leader) to join the mediation process.[15] His visit to Kandahar to meet with the Taliban was the first attempt by Russia's Muslim authorities to reach an understanding with a radical Islamic movement on a disputed issue. The Taliban's political demands on Russia[16] and their attempts to convert the detained crew members to Islam caused the Russian Orthodox Church serious concern. According to the Patriarch, Aleksii II, such efforts could have ended the 'confessional coexistence that now exists in Russia' and had a negative impact on Russian Muslims.[17]

In the Russian Federation both Christianity and Islam are going through a complicated process of seeking new identities while struggling with the different spheres of influence among their respective followers. The moderate wing of the Russian Orthodox Church is led by the patriarch. A more fundamentalist wing, until his death in early November 1995, headed by the Metropolitan of St Petersburg is particularly resistant to any outside influence. The increased desire on the part of a number of regional Muslim communities to obtain greater flexibility and autonomy for themselves resulted in a split of the Spiritual Body of Muslims of Russia, the European part of the CIS and Siberia (DUMEC).[18] Under the pressure of young dissident mullahs, DUMEC was broken up. Separate institutions have been set up in Tatarstan and Bashkortostan. Being opposed to DUMEC, they focus their attention on the ethnic and national consolidation of Tatars and Bashkorts, including those who live outside the two autonomous republics.

Against that background, new political institutions that gave prominence to Russian Muslims have emerged, including the Union of Russian Muslims (URM), with 50 branches all over the country, and the All-Russia Muslim Movement, 'Noor' (light), with 47 branches. Having established close ties with many intellectuals and a number of prominent figures in both the executive and the legislative branches of the Russian Federation, they launched an impressive campaign to unite Muslims on the eve of the December 1995 parliamentary elections in order to encourage them to vote solely for Islamic party nominees.[19]

Their main objective was to protect the political interests of the country's Muslims. That goal was announced at a URM congress held in late August 1995, when the intention was declared to seek ministerial portfolios in order to protect Muslims' interests and curb anti-Islamic sentiments. Another task was to absorb into the movement other religions and ethnic minorities.[20] This turn of events caused concern in the Orthodox Church's liberal branch. It had supported the view that the parliament should not be used to champion confessional or ethnic interests, and also distanced itself from a number of Christian-oriented political movements. The patriarch had warned that such attempts would only aggravate relations between Christianity and Islam in Russia.[21] Despite strong efforts, the URM was unable to collect the number of signatures necessary to register as an electoral movement; however, Noor was able to participate in the elections. The irony is that many leaders of the URM and Noor were dissidents who had split away from Zhirinovsky's ultranationalistic Liberal Democratic Party.[22] This indicates the radicals' deep interdependence. On the eve of the break-up of the Soviet Union, Russian nationalism was impugned and attracted an accusation by other ethnic groups that Russians alone were responsible for the ideological, political, economic and social decline of the country. Now it is the LDP's neoimperialist slogans that are tilting ethnic and religious minorities towards greater political separatism.

Undoubtedly, politically oriented Islamic movements in Russia will affect trends in Central Asia and the Caucasus, and *vice versa*, since the attempt to create an All-Union Islamic Renaissance Party (IRP) to protect the interests of Muslims has been gaining momentum since as long ago as the mid 1980s. Although with the collapse of Soviet Union the IRP lost its initial role, its branches have continued to operate illegally, promoting Muslim political movements in Uzbekistan, Tajikistan and elsewhere.

The Muslim communities, identity crisis and their intention to obtain a free hand in dealing not only with each other, but also with the local and central authorities mirrors Russia's decentralisation in general. Against this background, further shifts will gain momentum in the Muslim communities, and a new generation of Islamic leaders (both religious and secular) will try to exert more pressure on 'the old guard'. The prospects for further developments remain uncertain. Much will depend on the options chosen by the new Islamic elites as they try to secure their ultimate objectives, and on the policies of the central government and local authorities. The spread of democratic institutions in Russia, together with increasing contact between Russian Muslims and the larger Islamic world, will inevitably lead to Islamic institutions having a greater influence on the country's domestic affairs.[23]

Such a trend is already apparent with respect to the Christian Orthodox Church, which nevertheless does not intend to encourage the emergence of political parties representing only the interests of Russia's Orthodox Christians. But activities by the URM and Noor might cause it to revise this basic stand, which would create further splits in Russian society. Unlike the Russian Muslim communities, the Orthodox Church cannot expect to be backed by a massive inflow of donations from abroad; especially in the light of its poor relations with other branches of the Orthodox Church and its ill-concealed mistrust of the Vatican. This may encourage the Church to strengthen its relations with the government, Russian-oriented nationalist organisations and the new capitalist and business classes in order to obtain financial support. Consequently the central and local authorities would become involved in confessional and ethnic disputes.

Creating a new and vibrant economy is Russia's number one priority for the foreseeable future. At the same time domestic developments in the country increasingly indicate that Russia has an urgent need to formulate a new ideological system that will enable it to shore up its new market-oriented identity. In this endeavour, unilateral appeal to any religion, though important, is unlikely to close the ideological gaps in society. The only way to unite the multinational and multiconfessional state in the long run may be full adherence to basic democratic values held in common by all wings of the political elites.

The central government will inevitably be urged to take new developments seriously, and to work out a balanced policy towards the country's religious communities. While supporting efforts for the cultural and spiritual revival of the nations of the Russian Federation, Moscow should try to avert any increase in the politicisation of and polarisation between Church and Mosque. The government is probably already aware of the necessity of this. In mid 1994 a Commission on Religious Associations was formed by the Russian government. In mid 1995 an analogous body was established within the framework of the presidential administration.[24] At the first congress of the World Russian People, Sobor (Convent), Prime Minister Chernomyrdin spoke of growing cooperation between the state authorities and the Orthodox Church. Such cooperation, in the government's view, is of special importance for the establishment of an order where commitment to civil rights and the law will block out evil and harm. Chernomyrdin met separately with the URM leaders, who expressed their readiness to support his bloc in the parliamentary elections. Having emphasised the multinational nature of the country, the prime minister stressed the unacceptability of any community predominating over another. Nevertheless a long-term approach to world religions in general and Islam in particular has not yet been comprehensively articulated.

Dilemmas in the near abroad

Good relations with its immediate neighbours is of paramount importance to Russia since the nation's basic economic and defence interests are focused on its CIS neighbours. Good relations with them will play a significant role in its efforts to achieve an equal place in world markets and international economic and political institutions. The state of affairs in neighbouring states and their policies towards Russia will inevitably affect Russia's domestic developments and foreign policy. On September 1995 Russia's strategy in relation to the other CIS nations was reaffirmed in an executive order by President Yeltsin. The document confirmed the strategic importance of promoting comprehensive ties with the CIS member states and outlined Moscow's objectives as follows: to promote mutual cooperation in economic, cultural and defence matters; to create grounds for the CIS countries to cultivate cordial and friendly policies towards Russia; and to turn the CIS into a fully integrated regional organisation similar to the EU.[25]

The status of Russians in the CIS countries is of permanent concern to Moscow and has caused friction in Russia's relations with the bulk of the CIS nations, including those in Central Asia and the Caucasus. Russia favours either dual-citizenship agreements or comprehensive human rights accords with the CIS that nations will guarantee full equality of rights for Russians and other non-titular nationalities. So far only Turkmenistan and Tajikistan have concluded dual-citizenship agreements with Russia. Central Asian nations such as Kazakhstan and Uzbekistan are strongly opposed to such accords.

Developments in the southern CIS countries indicate that the 'Muslim north' might remain a source of regional instability. Political differences among the Central Asian states may cause unpleasant fluctuations in their bilateral relations. Regionalism and nationalism are driving forces in the construction of new identities in Central Asia and the Caucasus. Regional leaders' support for moderate Islam is viewed by them as complementary to their nations' quest for a new political identity. In keeping an eye on their Muslim institutions, the Central Asian authorities banned the Islamic Renaissance Party and adopted a tough policy on radicals. For the time being, religious radicalism in the region has significantly less influence than in the rest of the Muslim world. This is not only a result of the lack of religious freedom in the former Soviet Union; an additional and important factor restraining fundamentalism in Central Asia is the continuing impact of nomadic traditions on everyday life. The Turkic identity of the majority of the population (with the exception of Tajikistan) is counteracting the spread of fundamentalist movements. Common Turkic values, bolstered by Turkey itself, have always been hostile to religious fundamentalism. Turkey's plan to enlarge its political and economic presence in Central Asia (and Azerbaijan in the Caucasus) by introducing liberal Islam is more acceptable to regional leaders than

Iran's efforts in this respect. In order to strengthen and foster ties among the formal Islamic institutions in Central Asia and Turkic-speaking regions of the Russian Federation, the Caucasus and the Balkans under its auspices, in October 1995 Turkey established the Eurasian Islamic Council Organisation, and Diyanet Vakfi intends to open offices in the region to enhance Turkish religious influence in Eurasia.

Appeal to Islam is on the rise in Central Asia and the Muslim autonomous republics of the Caucasus, and governments in these regions will be urged to take this development seriously. Though Islamic militancy has yet to pose a direct threat to regional regimes, the situation may change if they fail to resolve their basic problems. As in Russia, the economy is the most pressing of these problems. In many of the traditional Islamic countries in the Middle East and North Africa, the ruling elites' inability to meet economic and social challenges is throwing the younger generation into the arms of radicals. Economic stagnation, unemployment, corruption and a high birth rate are pressing issues in Central Asia, as in the entire Islamic world.

It is important for Russia to prevent developments in Central Asia and the Caucasus from becoming religiously coloured, while backing their leaders' support for liberal and non-militant Islam. A clash between Islam and Christianity may be envisaged for Nagorno Karabakh in particular. While such a conflict would probably be ethno-political in nature, Islam and Christianity are already a factor in the motivations of local elites. External involvement could easily give a stronger religious hue to these political conflicts. There are challenges in Georgia too. If the current centrifugal tendency came to involve that country's Muslims, the prospect of an intraconfessional conflict might turn into reality. These developments would jeopardise the very shaky peace in the Muslim areas of the northern Caucasus, including Chechnya, Ingushetiya and Dagestan.

The dangers of Tajikistan splitting up have not been removed either. The political dynamics in that country present the possibility of instability spreading across the whole of Central Asia, especially to Uzbekistan and Kyrgyzstan. Continuation of the stand-off between Tajikistan and its mainly Islamic opposition against the backdrop of the ongoing domestic conflict in Afghanistan may eventually embrace South-West and South Asia too. There is little doubt that whoever is in power in Tajikistan will be interested in Moscow's support and in maintaining comprehensive relations with Russia. On the other hand, any prospect of Russia taking unilateral action in Tajikistan would play into the hands of those who stress Russia's 'neoimperialist ambitions' and its collision with Islam. Russia's efforts to assist reconciliation in Tajikistan will be trusted only if there is agreement between all parties and close cooperation with regional nations, as well as the United Nations and the OSCE.

The situation in the Caucasus and Central Asia might also be aggravated by competition between Turkey and Iran. If Turkey becomes suspicious of Moscow's intentions it may manipulate the 'Turkic factor' (which is also of an Islamic hue), both in Russia's near abroad and in Russia itself. If Iran grows more hostile towards Moscow, it might increase its efforts to erect an aggressive Islamic fundamentalist tier alongside Russia's southern borders.

Dilemmas in the far abroad

Ties with the far abroad are of great importance as Russia strives for a new status in the world and improvement of its relations with the international community. To meet these objectives, Moscow's policy 'inevitably has to be of an independent and assertive nature'.[26] This also applies to its policy towards the Middle East and South-West Asia, which during the Soviet era were traditional spheres of Russian political and economic interest. The opportunity to introduce flexibility in the region is dependent on the deideologisation of Russia's international policy and a balanced and rational approach to all countries in the region.

Durable peace in the Middle East and peaceful resolution of the Arab–Israeli conflict is in Russia's long-term interests.[27] Without stability in the Middle East Russia will not be able to prevent the spread of instability to the Caucasus and Central Asia, or attract financial resources from the Middle East to aid its economic development and strengthen its position in world markets. Russia is interested in close cooperation with the United States to prevent any form of regional terrorism. Despite serious domestic economic challenges, Russia is strategically positioned to participate in the newly emerging trade and economic environment in the region. Its concept of the 'greater Mediterranean' (stemming from a proposal made in the mid 1980s by the last Soviet leader, Mikhail Gorbachev) substantiates this desire.

Expanding ties not only with traditional partners in the Middle East such as Syria and Egypt, but also with nations that until recently had little interest in a dialogue with Russia, is of particular interest to

Moscow. Its policy toward the Gulf region is focused on its recent 'discovery' of the GCC nations; stable relations with them are seen as a significant factor in attracting investment in the Russian economy and counterbalancing its ties with Tehran, which is a cause of concern in both the Arab world and the United States. The Islamic factor in regional relations is also of great significance. In the long run relations between Russia and the Islamic world will depend on how well Russia stage-manages a balanced coexistence between the government and Orthodox Christian citizens on the one hand and religious and ethnic minorities on the other. Reaching an understanding with Saudi Arabia and other influential conservative regional Muslim states, which have already established broad ties with Muslims in Russia and its near abroad, is especially relevant. Stable and predictable relations with them would give Moscow a real chance to avoid outside support being given to Islamic political radicals in Russia.[28]

In November 1994 Prime Minister Chernomyrdin visited Saudi Arabia, Oman, Kuwait and the United Arab Emirates, the first state visit to these countries in Soviet and Russian history. Moscow's relations with the two latter states have progressed further than with other GCC nations. Nevertheless these new horizons are not cloudless, and to promote further ties, bilateral economic exchanges must be based on currency transactions, and Russia's foreign investment legislation will need to be adjusted to international standards. Having reviewed the prospects for foreign investment and promised to lift all hurdles in this respect, Chernomyrdin called on the Arabs to cooperate with Russia in the production of oil, steel and aluminum.[29]

Even after the dissolution of the Soviet Union, Russia remained one of the world's principal arms producers. Moscow intends to regain the international trade it lost in the late 1980s and early 1990s.[30] Revenues are badly needed for reconstruction and conversion of the military complex, and for Russia's market-oriented economy. A limited partnership with Kuwait and the UAE[31] is not enough for Russia, which is interested in increasing its presence in local arms markets traditionally dependent on the United States and Western Europe.[32] However the arrival of massive investment from the Gulf nations is doubtful because the GCC (Gulf Cooperation Council) economies are not yet on the mend, and it is highly unlikely that Washington while selling its arms abroad will relinquish lucrative business, especially in strategically important markets. Indeed the expansion of military and security ties with the Gulf states is a top policy priority in Washington.

Iraq may also remain an obstacle to Russia's relations with the Gulf nations, despite the fact that there is no basic discord between Russia's approaches to Iraq, the GCC and the United States. During the Gulf War Russia favoured Iraq's full compliance with UN Security Council resolutions and urged it to cooperate fully with the United Nations. In October 1994 Russia played a leading role in pressing Iraq to recognise Kuwait's sovereignty and independence. When General Hussayn Kamel defected in August 1995 to Jordan, highly significant data was obtained about Iraq's weapons of mass destruction. Russia called for Iraq to cooperate fully with the UN Special Commission in order to resolve the issue of Kuwait's missing in action personnel (MIAs) and then played down its backing of Iraq in the UN Security Council. Despite delays and obstructions, Iraq has moved towards compliance with the international demands. International pressure has also mounted for the UN to lift the oil embargo. Economic sanctions are causing suffering among the Iraqi people and seen as a matter of grave concern in many Muslim nations. The early implementation of UN Resolution 986, which allows Iraq to export limited amounts of oil, is of great importance to the Iraqis. The situation has aggravated the economic problems of a number of other states, including Russia,[33] Turkey and Jordan. Several countries already plan commercial ties with Iraq after the sanctions are lifted. According to the press, a number of American companies are keeping an eye on developments as well.

The events in Chechnya have revived Arabs' (especially Saudis' and Jordanians') concerns about Russia's behaviour with respect to Islam, though the majority of Muslim nations do not see the war as an indication of religious conflict between Moscow and Islam.[34] However if Russia fails to reach a settlement that is honourable for both itself and Chechnya, its relations with the Islamic world will suffer.

Relations with Iran are a special case in Russia's foreign policy. The two countries understand that their mutual hostility in the past was counterproductive to their vital interests in the region. Even during the Cold War, when the shah was a principal ally of Washington, Tehran and Moscow sought a smoother political dialogue and broader economic ties. The Soviet Union's balanced approach to the 1979 Islamic revolution, even though the Soviet Union was castigated by Tehran as the second 'great Satan' after the United States, was mostly designed to avoid an open breach with its neighbour. In 1989 Speaker Rafsanjani (later president) visited the Soviet Union and bilateral meetings in Moscow produced a Soviet–Iranian rapprochement. The two sides concluded a number of economic agreements that included cooperation in matters of space, defence and nuclear power for peaceful purposes. They also signed a new memorandum on the principles of bilateral relations.

Having inherited the Soviet pledges in relation to Tehran, Russia's approach to Iran is determined by (1) their geographical proximity on the Caspian sea, (2) deep-rooted historical and economic ties, (3) Iran's potential ability to influence developments in the Caucasus and Central Asia,[35] and (4) the state of affairs of Muslim communities in the Russian Federation. Both states have an interest in resolving the political and economic challenges in the Caspian Sea region.[36] Energy resources in the Caspian Sea are a crucial issue. Russia, Iran and Turkmenistan share the view that the Caspian mineral resources should be used jointly by the five coastal countries, and they favour a high-level conference to determine the legal status of the Caspian Sea without outside pressure. The oil reserves of the Caspian Sea – a probable annual output of 140 million tons – are second only to those of the Gulf region. Revenues are expected to play a key role in the economy of the littoral states and influence the geopolitical environment of the entire region. Consequently the issue of Caspian oil is of not only economic but also political significance. Much is at stake for several littoral states, including Azerbaijan, Kazakhstan, Turkmenistan, Russia and Iran, and outsiders, such as the United States, Turkey, Britain and Georgia, which pay particular attention to the pipeline issue. Some experts suggest that the outcome of the dispute on the pipeline routes will show 'who has control of much of the world's new industrial order in the foreseeable future'.[37]

This assessment is realistic since the United States and West European states are seeking ways to reduce their dependence on Gulf oil. Azerbaijan and to a certain extent Georgia are looking at the proposed pipeline as an opportunity to become more flexible and independent in their relations with Russia, favouring the main route to the Mediterranean via Turkey (under US political pressure its transit through Iran was blocked). Their wish is likely to have the Unites States' full support because it would like to see the Caucasus and Central Asia further dissociated from Russia not only politically, but also economically. After extensive bargaining in the autumn of 1995 the parties came to an understanding on the pipeline. The small (Russian) pipeline, carrying 'early oil', would go across Chechnya to Novorossiysk on the Black Sea. The larger (Georgian) one would carry oil from Baku to the Black Sea and then out through Turkey.

Iran is sensitive to developments in Central Asia too, especially in Tajikistan. Russia has no reason to prevent Iran from taking part in resolving the dispute between Tajikistan and its opponents. Undoubtedly Tajikistan, which is the only Central Asian nation with strong cultural and linguistic ties with Iran, will have a particular interest in maintaining relations with the latter, and will also view it as a partner in restricting Turkic regional predominance. Aware of this, Iran uses a great deal of sophistication in managing smooth relations with the Tajiki government and its political opposition, which is allowed to maintain its headquarters in Iran. After 1995, when the United States implemented the trade embargo against Iran, and after the D'Amato Bill was signed by President Clinton in 1996, Tehran doubled its effort to expand its relations with Asian and African countries and CIS nations such as Georgia and Turkmenistan. This expansion of relations is also significant for Moscow.

Common grounds and differences with the United States

Political activism by Muslims in Russia and the United States is gaining momentum, but the governments of both countries are interested in maintaining good relations with their religious communities, in line with their broader domestic and foreign policies. But Russia's coexistence with Islam is quite different from the US experience. Over the centuries Russia has had encounters with Islam in the Volga region, Siberia, the Caucasus and Central Asia. A number of Muslim nations were absorbed into the Russian empire and later into the Soviet Union. Such coexistence has always been highly controversial and is still burdened by suspicion and mistrust. Much effort will have to be made to overcome the mutual prejudice that arose during the Soviet ideological experiment (first as 'proletarianism' and later as 'socialist internationalism').

The bulk of Muslim migrants to the United States only arrived in recent decades. They moved to the United States to seek a better life, and the majority of the 2.5 million Arab-Americans now feel quite comfortable, both economically and politically, and want to deepen their roots in American society. They welcome the Middle East peace process and favour increased ties between the United States and the Arab and Muslim world. They call on Washington to take more seriously specific features of Muslim civilisation. Supporting the administration's tough stand on regional and international terrorism, they reject violence and religious extremism as means of obtaining political ends.[38] Thus it seems that building harmonious relations with domestic Islam is a less difficult task for Washington than it is for Moscow. (The issue of the Nation of Islam in the United States is a special case.) Russia is more sensitive and vulnerable to 'political Islam', especially since 1991, as the country is suffering from a deep identity crisis and economic hardship. Any radical movement that is nurtured by a sense of religious or ethnic superiority (or inferiority) could affect Russia's stability. The United States does not face this challenge. The historical and traditionalist belt of Islam is geographically and psychologically much closer to Russia than it is to the United States. This means that any development in the external Muslim world will inexorably impinge on Russia, so it has to be particularly cautious in its dealings with Islamic movements both inside and outside the country.

Any new alignment of political forces in the Kremlin and the Russian parliament will not mean renunciation of the indivisibility of the Russian Federation. All in Russia's political spectrum, from liberal democrats to former communists, stand for an indivisible state. The manifestos issued by the country's leading parties – Russia is Our Home, Yabloko, Russia's Choice, the Communist Party, the LDP and the Congress of Russia's Communities – on the eve of the December 1995 parliamentary elections bore testimony to this fact. The West should show an interest in Russia's political integrity because the break-up of the Federation would bring further regional chaos. A chain reaction would destablilise a number of the newly independent states, as well as the traditional belt of Islamic states, which would in turn affect Europe and ultimately damage US interests in the Middle East and the Gulf.

The West's condemnation of Russian human rights violations in Chechnya is undoubtedly justifiable. But violations have been committed by both sides in the conflict, a fact that has been largely ignored by the Western media. Moscow is keen to avoid any new political and moral costs being incurred in Chechnya and is striving to bring the situation back to normal by peaceful means. Russia is ready to provide Chechnya with maximum autonomy, similar to that enjoyed by Tatarstan, Bashkortostan, North Ossetia, Saha (Yakutiya), Buryatia and the other (seventeen) autonomous republics. On 8 December 1995 an agreement on the basic principles of relations between the Russian Federation and the Chechen Republic was signed in Moscow. It provided for Chechen participation in international economic ties, its own constitution, budget, taxation system and local authorities.[39] Agreements concluded in autumn 1996 had a similar focus. The expectation that Moscow might retreat from its basic stand (no secession from the federation) is not realistic. In this respect the wisest course of action for the West would be to support the current Russian policy. Much patience should be shown, since the situation in the northern Caucasus is not amenable to immediate conciliation and rapid results. Should the West show extreme irritability, paving the way to a multilateral reproach, it may cause a knee-jerk reaction in Moscow and complicate East–West relations.

Russia's strategy in the CIS is aimed at strengthening the common economic, political and defence institutions in order to turn the CIS into a valuable regional organisation. This approach was underlined by Foreign Minister Primakov in January 1996 during a visit to Uzbekistan and Tajikistan. Moscow has neither the power nor the political and economic will to restore the Russian empire. Those in Moscow – both in and out of power – who advocate the revival of the Soviet Union would sober up if they confronted the political realities inside and outside Russia. New elites in Central Asia and the Caucasus, having fully adjusted to the advantages of political and economic independence, are already aware of these realities. Their loud speculations about Russia's imperial ambitions are mainly played to domestic audiences, or to obtain specific concessions and benefits from Russia and the West.

Until late 1992 the United States paid little attention to Central Asia as it was not among its political and economic priorities.[40] (Kazakhstan was an exception to this rule because when the Soviet Union broke up it retained its nuclear capability, and Chevron had shown great interest in investing in Kazakhstan's huge Tengiz oil fields since the 1980s) Eventually, however, the newly emerged republics' interest in establishing international contacts encouraged Washington to take a greater interest in them. Moreover there was a shift in the general priorities of the United States away from Russia and towards other nations of the former Soviet Union. In addition to Kazakhstan, Washington has paid special attention to Kyrgyzstan, which is today regarded by the West as the most democratically advanced nation in Central Asia. Despite being politically allergic to Tashkent and its leadership's ambitions to play a leading role in the region, the United States decided to pursue relations with that country. Though Washington has a low economic and political profile in Turkmenistan, the latter's relations with Iran as a railroad partner,[41] as well as the US interest in assisting with the construction of a gas pipeline from Turkmenistan via Afghanistan to Pakistan, has persuaded the United States to keep an eye on Turkmenistan. The US interest in Tajikistan stems from its anxiety about Russian influence, the possible reemergence of communist-style politics, the lack of Western-style democracy, and the government's slow progress in resolving its dispute with the Islamic opposition. The United States is also keen to contain Iran's influence on developments in the region.

The alarmist approach adopted by the Republican-dominated 104th Congress towards Russia in general and its policy on the near abroad in particular, is causing the administration to become more skeptical about Russia's activities in the southern belt of the CIS. But the tendency to evaluate Moscow's actions in domestic and external affairs through the prism of the traditional Western attitude towards the former Soviet Union is politically counterproductive. Ironically, calls to make assistance to Russia conditional on its behaviour in Chechnya, Iran, Iraq and former Yugoslavia have an 'Islamic colouring'. The US administration's approach seems to be more realistic than that of the congress. The former is critical of 'neo-isolationists' and all those who argue that Russia is inevitably imperialist and undemocratic.[42] However a few still consider that Russia should not be entitled to have vital interests alongside its borders. But Russia and the CIS nations need stability in Eurasia and comprehensive mutual ties. Russia's need for stable and predictable relations with its southern neighbours is comparable to the US need for similar relations with Latin America and the Caribbean.

The OSCE members and a number of other countries, including the United States, criticise the current political and legal institutions in Tajikistan. Undoubtedly this is of concern to Moscow too. At the same time the contention that Tajikistan (along with other Central Asian countries)[23] is undemocratic and totalitarian is simplistic and faulty. It is true that modern democratic (Westernised) practices do not exist there, but there are deep-rooted traditional institutions, including those linked to Islam, and these should be taken into consideration when observing domestic developments.

Moves towards strong presidential authoritarian rule is the dominant trend in the Central Asian republics. If the suggestion that the traditional Islamic world should move only slowly towards Western-style democracy and that this movement should be rooted in national values and traditions is acceptable to the United States,[44] especially in respect of the Arabian peninsula, then why should such an approach not be acceptable with regard to the post-Soviet Muslim nations? The effort to build a civil society is hampered in Central Asia by intraregional differences, as well as economic and political dilemmas. Any expectation that general or local elections in the near future will be absolutely democratic and fair is shortsighted, although the outside world should by all means encourage progress in that direction. The 1994–95 parliamentary and presidential elections in Tajikistan did not resolve the country's problems. Hostility between the government and the Islamic opposition is the most difficult factor. Political reforms and dialogue must continue.

Russia is interested in progress being made in relations between Central Asia and the Caucasus on the one hand, and the West and the United States on the other, but not at the expense of its own ties with its neighbours. Broader relations with the West will mean not only economic benefits for the region's nations, but also support for their gradual democratisation and adjustment to a market-oriented economy. Ties with the democratic world might encourage the Central Asian elites to introduce a more broad-minded approach to their domestic politics as well. Coincidence of regional goals between Moscow and Washington is evident in this respect. The two sides should favour such a trend. But attempts to 'squeeze' Russia out of the region might be viewed by Moscow as aimed at encouraging the neighbouring countries to the south to cool their relations with Russia. Such a perception would only generate further unease in Moscow about the West's policy towards Russia. The argument that Russia has imperialist ambitions should not be taken seriously by the West as it could result in a new Cold War.

Deliberation on the impact of Islam on international politics occurred earlier in Washington than in Moscow. It started in the United States in the 1960s as a result of the deep US involvement in the Middle East and gained momentum in the late 1970s after the fall of the shah of Iran. The Soviet Union encountered political Islam only in the mid 1980s in Afghanistan. Obstacles to the Middle East peace process and the eruption of Islamic terrorism, including on American soil, prompted Washington to adopt a formal approach towards Islam.[45] This includes respect for Islam and its ethical system as one of the principal world religions, but insists on the separation of religion from militancy and extremism. Indeed this is fully in accord with Russia's interests, and hence provides common ground for mutual efforts in the Middle East as well as in Central and South-West Asia. There are common goals to be pursued in the maintenance of balance to prevent the region from sinking into permanent instability and becoming a source of political extremism, including the spread of weapons of mass destruction. At the same time differences over concrete interests, stemming from the different geopolitical locations of Russia and the United States, will influence each country's dealings with individual Muslim nations.[46]

Iran is the most obvious case. Washington's 'dual containment' policy, seeking Iran's isolation within the region, is unlikely to be acceptable to Moscow. Russia's interests require it to avoid a tough posture on Iran, and in this sense Moscow's views are similar to those of Western Europe and Japan. Expanding economic ties with Iran and not labelling it as an international outcast would in Moscow's view be the best way of keeping an eye on Iran's behaviour.

When in late 1994 it signed an agreement on the construction of an atomic power station,[47] Russia was not in violation of the Nuclear Non-proliferation Treaty since Iran, like any other country, is entitled to use nuclear energy for peaceful purposes. According to the IAEA, there is also no evidence of Iran violating the treaty.[48] The fact that the Russian-designed reactor cannot produce plutonium for military purposes has been repeatedly confirmed by Moscow and foreign experts. However, bearing in mind the United States' anxiety about Iran's nuclear ambitions, Russia should make it clear to Iran that any shift in that direction will be unacceptable. Simultaneously, strict control should be imposed on Iran's use of Russian high technology. Likewise, conventional arms supplies should be carefully monitored so that new imbalances in the Gulf region do not emerge. At the 1994 US – Russia Summit in Washington, the two sides reached an understanding that after the current Russian–Iranian defence contracts had been fulfilled the Russian Federation would not conclude any new ones with Iran. That Moscow decision, together with its commitment not to supply a gas centrifuge to Iran, should be regarded as a significant concession to the United States in the light of its anxiety about the 'Iranian threat' to the region. For its part the United States should adopt a similar approach to its sales to the Gulf countries, and the competition for arms sales to the Gulf should be prevented from growing into political rivalry.[49]

It is particularly important for Moscow and Washington to avoid any temptation to manipulate Islam against each other in order to seek unilateral advantages.[50] Such an approach would only lead to dead-lock, confirming Samuel Huntingdon's pessimistic scenario of a clash of civilisations. On the other hand, influential Arab nations such as Egypt, Saudi Arabia, Jordan, Tunisia, Morocco and others, as well as Muslim Turkey and Pakistan, the South-East Asian Islamic belt, India and China would welcome US – Russian cooperation to prevent regional terrorism and extremism. Ironically, even Iraq and Syria, despite being viewed by the United States as international outlaws, may in the long run be very supportive of measures to contain political militancy based on religious radicalism.

Notes and references

1. Greg Noakes, 'Moderates, Radicals Drifting Apart as Islamism Enters New Phase', *Washington Report on Middle East Affairs*, October/November 1995, p. 17.
2. John Battershy, 'Arab Leaders Stumped by Rise of Militant Islam', *Christian Science Monitor*, 7 March 1995.
3. L. Polonskaya, 'Modern Islamic fundamentalism: political deadlock or an alternative for development?', *Asia and Africa Today*, 0.11 (1994), pp. 22–29; 'US emphasizes it isn't anti-Muslim', *Washington Times*, 8 March 1995. According to Graham Fuller 'the next ideology a challenge the West is likely to represent an amalgam of opposition to its values and institutions'. Graham Fuller, 'The Next Ideology', *Foreign Policy*, Spring 1995, p. 145.
4. B. Netanyahu, 'The Likud's approach to Peace and Security'. *Peacewatch*, Washington Institute for Near East Policy, no. 65 (1 November 1995).
5. Ibid.
6. Washington Post, 30 November 1995. *New York Times*, 3 December 1995.
7. Christian Science Monitor, 7 March 1995.
8. 'Memorandum on Russian Policy in the Mediterranean'. Press release no. 39, Embassy of the Russian Federation, Washington, DC, 30 November 1995.
9. President Yeltsin's address to the Federal Assembly of the Russian Federation, 16 February 1995.
10. According to Susan Clark and David Graham, there are three possible scenarios for the future of Russia: maintain once of the Federation's territorial integrity, as the centre works out *ad hoc* arrangements with its various constituent components; the emergence of a nationalistic, authoritarian regime that seeks to recentralise virtually all power back into the hands of Moscow; or a much looser, confederal relationship leading to the disintegration of the state into several new areas. The latter scenario, the authors suggest, would be the most desirable for Western interests and 'also the most likely for the foreseeable future'. Susan L. Clark and David R. Graham, 'The Russian Federation Fights for Survival', *ORBIS.*, Summer 1995 pp. 347–48.
11. By the end of the 1980s the Muslim-Turkic population was estimated at nine million, including 6.6 million Volga Tatars, 1.4 million Bashkirs and one million in the northern Caucasus. Compiled from 'Natsionalniy Sostav Naseleniya', Chast 2, Informatsionno-izdatelskyi Tsentre Moskva, 1989 pp. 3–5.
12. ITAR-TASS, 5, 7 December 1995.
13. As far back as 1992 General Dudayev proclaimed a jihad against the central authorities, having sought support from Islamic movements in Azerbayjan, Tatarstan and Bashkortostan. In 1993 Islam was proclaimed as Chechnya's state religion. Assertive calls for Islamic solidarity worldwide continued after Moscow had made the risky decision to resolve the long-term crisis by the use of force.

14. *Izvestiya*, 10 August 1995.
15. 'Trud', ITAR-TASS, 23 August 1995.
16. The Taliban refused to release the crew until about 60 000 Afghans, who supposedly had been interned in the USSR in the mid 1980s, were released. Both the former Soviet Union and now the Russian authorities repeatedly denied that these Afghans were being held. (ITAR-TASS, 15, 17, 24 August 1995; *Izvestiya*, 17 August 1995). Realising that their demands were not realistic, the Taliban argued that the UN and OIC should be involved in negotiations on the fate of the crew. Later the Taliban provided a list of about 7000 Afghans and demanded that the Soviet Union confirm its non-involvement in the domestic affairs of Afghanistan.
17. *Monitor* (a daily chronicle of the Post Soviet states), 28 August 1995 vol. 1, no. 83 (Washington, DC The Jamestown Foundation).
18. DUMEC was founded in 1788 by the decree of Empress Catherine the Great. DUMEC's head mufti, Talgat Tajuddin, was born in 1949, educated in Bokhara (Uzbekistan) and at Al-Ahzar University in Cairo. He was elected as mufti in 1981 and a Muslim convention in 1990 reelected him for life.
19. S. Shermatova, 'Islamic Factor in the future Duma', *Moscow News*, no. 53 6–13 August 1995.
20. Russian public TV, 1 September 1995.
21. ITAR-TASS, 1 September 1995.
22. Shermatova, 'Islamic Factor', op. cit.
23. Under the auspices of the URM, a conference of Russian Muslims was held in Moscow in August 1995 to consider how to increase contacts with each other and with Muslims living abroad. The participants were especially eager to develop ties with Islamic educational centres abroad so that Russian Muslims could attend them in greater numbers and obtain more foreign financing for the construction of new mosques in Russia. *Monitor*, vol. 1, no. 86 (31 august 1995).
24. ITAR-TASS, 4 August 1995.
25. *Rossiyskiye vesti*, 24 September 1995.
26. A. Kozyrev (foreign minister of Russia), 'The Lagging Partnership', *Foreign Affairs*, May–June 1994, p. 67.
27. V. Gudev, director of the Middle East and Northern Africa Department, Foreign Ministry of Russia. With interview. Interfax Diplomatic Panorama, 20 February 1995, p. 3.
28. Stephen Grummon, 'Russia, the "Near Abroad", and the Persian Gulf', *Policy Watch*, no. 128 (6 October 1994). (Washington Institute for Near East Policy). p. 2; Prince Turki, the Saudi minister for Islamic affairs, while in Moscow to attend the conference of Russian Muslims in August 1995, met with the first deputy foreign minister, I. Ivanov. The two sides stated that contacts between Muslims of Russia and Saudi Arabia to promote better understanding between the peoples of the two countries were of great importance. (ITAR-TASS, 31 August 1995). Earlier Saudi Arabia had called for Russia's support for its plan on Afghanistan's reconciliation. On Bosnia, Russia favoured the Saudi proposal for a meeting to be arranged between 'contact group' and the OIC team.
29. Interfax business report, 24 November 1994.

30. Russian arms transfer agreements with developing nations dropped from 57.7 per cent in 1987 to 18.1 per cent in 1994 (expressed as a percentage of total transfers by the principal world suppliers: the United States, Russia, France, Britain, China, Germany and Italy). In the same period the US share increased from 11.8 per cent to 24 per cent. Major West European nations, mainly France increased their sales accordingly, from 13.3 per cent to 48 per cent. For more details see 'Conventional Arms Transfers to Developing Nations, 1987–1994', CRS report for Congress, 4 August 1995, table 1B, CRS-51.

31. Russia supplied Kuwait with 60 BMP-3 armoured personnel carriers, 27 multiple rocket launchers ('Smersh') and five SS-30 missile systems. A number of Kuwaiti cadets and officers received military training in Russia. The UAE spent $200 million on Russian personnel carriers, jet fighters, tanks and anti-aircraft systems. *Washington Times*, 22 February 1994; Interfax business report, 15 September 1994; *Christian Science Monitor*, 23 November 1994.

32. In 1991–94 the percentage of total agreements between the United States and the Near East nations was estimated at 55.9 per cent. The percentages for the major West European suppliers and Russia were 32.2 per cent and 5.7 per cent respectively. CRS report for Congress, 'Conventional Arms Transfers', op. cit., table 1E CRS-54.

33. Iraq's debt to Russia was estimated at $7–9 billion, but according to some experts it was as much as $30–45 billion. ITAR-TASS, 13 March 1995; *Rossiyskaya gazeta*. 15 March 1995.

34. Deputy Foreign Minister V. Posuvalyuk, press conference in Moscow, Interfax, Diplomatic Panorama, 9 March 1995.

35. Cyrus Bina, 'Towards a New World Order; US Hegemony, Client-States and Islamic Alternative', in Hussin Mutalib and Taj-Islam Hashmi (eds), *Islam, Muslims and the Modern State. Case Studies of Muslims in Thirteen Countries.* (London: Macmillan, 1994), p. 12.

36. In late October 1995, when Russia's deputy prime minister, A. Bolshakov, was on a visit to Tehran, the two sides confirmed that all types of economic activity on the Caspian littoral must be approved by the five coastal states; that before the Caspian's legal status was defined, any unilateral action to develop its resources would not be allowed; and that defining the status of the Caspian was strictly a matter for the five regional states without outside interference. *Monitor*, 31 October 1995; ITAR-TASS, 31 October, 2 November 1995. However the coastal nations remain divided on the issue. Russia and Iran are supported by Turkmenistan, with Azerbazjan and Kazakhstan opposing the approach. The stand of the latter two is favoured by Turkey and the West.

37. George Anne Geyer, 'Oil pipelines Russia wants to control', *Washington Times*, 5 September 1995. For more on the issue see G. Robbins, 'The geopolitics of oil in the Caspian', *Washington Times*, 21 August 1995; 'Caspian Oil Pipelines – Will the Oil Barons Eat Caviar?', special bulletin, C & O Resources, Inc., 27 July 1995; *Christian Science Monitor,* 8 June 1995; 'Caspian Crossroads', US – Azerbaijan Council, issue no. 1 (Winter 1995); *Financial Times*, 5 September 1995.

38. Martin Sief, 'Benchmark gathering of Arab-Americans', *Washington Times*, 26 November 1995.

39. ITAR-TASS, 8 December 1995.
40. M. Konarovsky, 'Russia and the Muslim States of Central Asia and Afghanistan', in Mutalib and Hashmi, *Islam, Muslims and the Modern State*, op. cit., p. 242.
41. Turkmenistan inherited from the former Soviet Union the understanding that a railroad would be constructed through Iran to give Turkmenistan access to the Persian Gulf. Turkmenistan designed a multinational project to deliver Turkmeni gas to Europe via Iran. An alternative route, backed by the United States and Turkey, would be via Afghanistan to South Asia.
42. Warren Christopher (US secretary of state), 'America's Leadership, America's Opportunity', *Foreign Policy*, Spring 1995, p. 11.
43. The West and international human rights organisations were highly critical of violations during elections in Kazakhstan, Uzbekistan and Kyrgyzstan, let alone Turkmenistan.
44. Edward P. Djerejan, 'A Five-Step Plan for Working with Islam', *Christian Science Monitor*, 17 March 17 1995.
45. This was articulated by the assistant secretary of state for near eastern affairs, R. Pelletreau, and the national security adviser, A. Lake, in late spring 1994. Pelletreau spoke on the issue at the Middle East Policy Council conference on 'Resurgent Islam in the Middle East' on 26 May 1994. (*Middle East Policy*, vol. iii no. 2, 1994), and in testimonies before Congressional committees. President Clinton made remarks about Islam during his November 1994 visit to Indonesia. On 15 March 1995, during King Hassan of Morocco's visit to Washington, he said that the United States had 'great respect' for Islam and intended 'to work with its followers throughout the world to secure peace and a better future'.
46. Dimitri Simes, 'Yeltsin Runs the Kremlin: Get Over It', *Washington Post*, 12 March 1995.
47. Iran had two research reactors and number of nuclear facilities, constructed by Western countries and staffed by people trained in the United States and Western Europe. In addition, in the 1970s Germany and France began construction of two nuclear power plants in Busher and Karune. Cooperation between Russia and Iran in the peaceful use of nuclear energy is based on a long-term program use for commercial economic, science and technology cooperation between Russia and Iran until 2000, signed on 22 June 1989; an agreement between the government of the Russian Federation (RF) and the Islamic Republic of Iran (IRI) on cooperation in the peaceful use of nuclear energy, signed on 25 August 1992; and an agreement between the two governments on cooperation in the construction of a nuclear power station in Iran, signed on 25 august 1992.

Pursuant to the agreement on construction of nuclear power plants in Iran, a contract worth about $800 million was signed in January 1995 to complete the construction of the first nuclear unit in the Busher region. Under this contract a light water reactor type VVER with an electrical capacity of 1000 MW would be constructed. The reactor design would be submitted to the IAEA in due course. In 1993, after the Iranian proposal to finalise the construction of the plant in Busher, Minatom of Russia had asked the German Ministry of Economy and Trade to participate in the project, but Germany had rejected the request. In September 1995 a new contract was signed to ship in two newer light water reactors (VVER-440). Iran guaranteed to pay for the work according to the signed contract. There about 300 Russian specialists in Iran. Their main task is to review building designs and equipment for the Busher-1 unit. The total number of Russian experts may rise to about 500 persons. Depending on problems arising during the construction the specialisations of the Russian staff may change. Upon completion Iranian personnel will take over.

48. Interfax, Diplomatic Panorama, 15, 16, 23 February 1995; *Izvestiya*, 15 February 1995; *OMRI Daily Digest*, 28 February 1995.
49. Kozyrev, 'The Lagging Partnership', op. cit., p. 67.
50. While in Bagdad in February 1995 the LDP leader, V. Zhirinovsky, called for an anti-West coalition between Russia, Orthodox Christians and the Muslim world. ITAR-TASS, 27 February 1995. On the other hand, a transparent hint for the United States to cooperate closely with the Islamic World against 'fascist Russia' was made by Robert D. Grane in 'Islam and US: New Directions?', American Muslim Council Report, autumn 1994, pp. 11–12.

7

Russia and the Islamic Factor: Possible Sources of Military Conflicts and Their Prevention

Makhmud A. Gareyev

Islam is one of the leading religions and the basis of entire civilisations. Almost one billion believers profess Islam. There are more than 50 Muslim countries in the world, and there are Muslim communities of varying sizes in 120 countries. Nearly 20 million people in Russia belong to the Islamic world and their number is expected to rise to more than 65 million in the twenty-first century. The Islamic factor exerts a considerable influence on international affairs and the global military and political situation. Islam is also used by leading world powers for political and strategic purposes.

The Islamic factor in the new multipolar world

During the Cold War Islamic countries were spheres of conflict between the Soviet Union and the United States. Now that the Cold War is over the struggle for influence over the Islamic world is intensifying and is impinging on Russia's national interests. The struggle for power has been particularly evident in former Yugoslavia, where the Bosnian Muslims (as well as Croatians) have been used to strengthen the US position in the area. The role and significance of the Islamic factor, including its military aspects, can be properly understood only by considering the tendencies and processes of world political development as a whole.

The manifestation of the Islamic factor will to a great extent depend on the future political order of the world, on the pattern that replaces the current bipolar configuration based on two opposing superpowers. Some political scientists, statesmen and public figures maintain that the world will inevitably become unipolar under US leadership. This view is unrealistic – as Manfred Werner has emphasised, 'if the United States tries to act on its own, it will exceed its capabilities'.[1] The current allies of the United States, such as Germany, Japan, France, China and other great powers, are unlikely to tolerate a situation in which one country is superior to others and rules the world. For one thing they would not be able to realise their economic potential. Generally speaking, as historical events show, if countries strive for absolute security, especially by escalating their military capabilities, they are seen as a threat to others and thus rivalry intensifies.

Another group of scientists and political figures consider it possible to resurrect the bipolar world by consolidating some South-East Asian countries, Euroasia and the Middle East around China in order to oppose the political and economic expansion of leading Western countries, headed by the United States. If this were to develop into political reality, then rivalry rather than cooperation between the highly developed industrial countries would cause the group of challenger countries to lag behind in technology and lead to a new spiral of cold war and military confrontation. All things considered, most realistic and appropriate to the long-term interests of the world community would be the appearance of a multipolar world, clustered around such centres of power and political and economic influence as the United States, Western Europe, Russia and other countries of the CIS, China and Japan. Though not homogeneous, the Islamic world could form a relatively self-sufficient centre.

It should be kept in mind that the balance of interests and power was formerly based on five or six equally powerful countries. Nowadays the economic and military power of the leading states is extremely unequal. The United States, Western Europe and Japan produce two thirds of the world output. As Joseph Nigh, president of the Harvard Centre for International Affairs, states: 'The disposition of power in world politics has become similar to puff pastry. The upper military layer is basically unipolar, because there are no countries comparable with the USA in military potential. The middle economic layer has been for about twenty years made of three strips. The lower layer of transnational interdependence is characterized by diffusion of power'.[2]

Considering all these factors, one should not exclude the possibility that before the majority of leading states ultimately come to the conclusion that transition to a multipolar world is essential, attempts might be made to establish a unipolar or a new version of the bipolar world pattern, which would worsen the international situation and adversely affect strategic stability.

The multipolar world would be characterised by a greater variety of national interests; and it would be more complex than the unipolar or bipolar world. It might also be relatively stable if it were based on a balance of interests between the various states. Some strategic thinkers regard peace and stability 'the result of balance of power, set into motion by the states' own interests'.[3] But a balance of interests could only be attained by restructuring the entire system of international relations, which seems problematic in the near future.

One of the most important factors, especially in respect of the Islamic world, may be a rise of national self-awareness that could not be confined to a narrowly understood concept of nationalism. Only 10 per cent of countries are ethnically homogeneous. Everywhere in Europe (not only in former Yugoslavia and Russia but also in such relatively politically stable countries as Belgium and Spain), in the Middle East and in Asia (Pakistan, India, Afghanistan and regions inhabited by Kurds) movements for national self-determination are flourishing. The desire for national self-determination is present in Muslim countries too, and the struggle for sovereignty and independence on a national and ethnic basis is generating a great number of interethnic conflicts. Because of growing antagonism between leading and backward countries, the previous confrontation between East and West may be transformed into a confrontation between North and South. In the Cold War period many countries deliberately put themselves under the influence and protection of the superpowers. While to a certain extent this limited their ability to pursue their national interests, they considered it appropriate to their security to remain within the structure of major state formations. However this possibility has now disappeared. During the first half of the 1990s 23 new states were formed and the number of peoples and nations aspiring to gain independence and statehood increased. On the territory of Russia the struggle for independence is taking place in areas with Muslim populations, especially Chechnya, Tatarstan and Bashkortostan.

What is the attitude of the United Nations and the world community in general towards this phenomenon? Taking into account the realities under which nations should be given the right to national self-determination, what kind of scientific criteria should be applied? Why, for instance, was Slavonia's and Croatia's sovereignty acknowledged while the 30 million Kurdish people have been denied this right? Why was Georgia granted the right to secede from the Soviet Union but not

Abkhazia, where half the population is Muslim? What are the limits of this permissiveness or non-permissiveness? It is not intended here to judge who is right and who is wrong, nor to take anyone's side. But it is stressed that United Nations bodies must work out acceptable ways of solving this acute problem. Otherwise the spontaneous and uncontrolled processes of confrontation among various peoples will continue and could involve larger nations in national strife, with all the grave consequences that implies.

In the case of Russia, some political thinkers and public figures insist that for the time being there is no external threat to Russia, that all threats and conflicts will come from within. However this will depend on the policy that Russia pursues. If it accepts all the claims of other countries, no one will threaten it. But if it strives to uphold its own interests and these interests clash with the interests of other countries, then a threat might arise and even aggression could not be excluded. It is no secret that the conflicts in Yugoslavia, Nagorno-Karabakh, Chechnya and Tajikistan were stirred up from outside.

Most dangerous to international stability might be attempts to change the existing frontiers. There are smouldering territorial conflicts in various areas, and in recent decades they have broken out on the Eastern and Western frontiers of Germany, between Balkan countries, between Arab countries and Israel, Iraq and Iran, Afghanistan and Pakistan, China and India, India and Pakistan, China and Japan, Argentina and Britain. Six states – China, Taiwan, the Philippines, Malaysia, Brunei and Vietnam – contest the right to sovereignty over the Spratly Islands, and there are many other disputed territories. Especially dangerous is a policy to revise borders established after the Second World War, especially the boundaries of Poland, the Czech Republic, the Kaliningrad region and the Kurile Islands. Revision of the postwar borders even by one or two states might prompt a chain of territorial claims by one nation against another, which would aggravate the political and military situation.

Radical military and political changes in Russia during the early 1990s, following the disintegration of the Soviet Union and the liquidation of the defensive alliance of socialist countries (the Warsaw Pact), brought about considerable changes in the global geopolitical sphere. As a consequence, the arrangement of strategic forces also underwent change. The majority of the newly formed sovereign states in Eastern Europe and on the Western frontier of Russia are orientating themselves towards military and political relations with or membership of NATO. Also evident is the aspiration of Muslim countries for closer contact with Turkey, Pakistan, Saudi Arabia and other Arab States. The Soviet Union's loss of the former union republics and its socialist allies has negatively affected the equilibrium of the strategic forces and geopolitical situation of contemporary Russia.

In the near future the most acute sociopolitical and economic contradictions in the world might be directly related to the socioeconomic development of mankind. Recent developments illuminate thinking on these difficult issues. The majority of states are developing along capitalist lines. Even the majority of the former socialist countries have adopted the capitalist market economy. There is ample factual evidence to demonstrate that the steady increase in the rate of production and the unlimited exploitation of natural resources cannot last much longer. If Russia, China, India and other countries started to consume as many resources as the United States, the resources of the planet would be exhausted in no time and the world would face an ecological catastrophe.

In 25–30 years the world community will face the problem of limiting, regulating and qualitatively transforming the volume and nature of production. If the United Nations (especially the major powers) and the giant transnational corporations fail to find ways and methods of coordinating and regulating production and consumption, the struggle for natural resources will become extremely intense. While certain officials in the West cooperate with Russia and the Muslim countries, objectively speaking the West is not interested in the improvement of their technological power. That is why the political and economic efforts of the West, and especially the United States, will be mainly directed at gaining access to the natural resources of Russia and the Muslim countries. Even military confrontation cannot be ruled out in this respect. In light of these possibilities, preserving and protecting its natural resources remains one of the most important political, economic and military tasks for Russia and the Muslim countries.

Russia, being the second largest nuclear power after the United States, will retain its influence over the military–political situation in Europe and to a certain extent Asia. Many countries in the Asia-Pacific region and South Asia have lost much of their former influence over the military–political situation in the Third World. Moreover some of the Muslim states that in the Cold War period acted as a buffer between East and West lost this political advantage as the major powers' need to recruit allies from these countries disappeared. Yet at the same time the attitudes adopted by major regional powers – especially Iraq, Iran, India and Pakistan – during the Cold War period have generated a range of territorial, national, religious and other problems, causing instability in this region. The fact that India, Pakistan and Israel refused to sign the Nuclear Non-proliferation treaty is indicative of their intention to retain their nuclear weapons.

In order to reinforce its influence in the Islamic World, the United States intends to strengthen its military connections with the countries of Near and Middle East. Its aim is to influence the military–political capability of these countries and to stockpile armaments and military equipment for military use by American troops if the need arises. Washington officials designate Iran and Iraq as potential enemies.

Instability in the Near and Middle East has set off an arms race, in contrast with the process of disarmament in Europe. Hence there is a need to strengthen international controls over the exportation of most types of destructive armaments and technologies.

The military–political situation in South Asia is likely to remain complicated and unstable for the foreseeable future. A considerable influence on the military–political situation in this region is the historically established arrangement of forces. The regional centre of power, India, has traditionally held the dominant place in the region. Disagreements and territorial disputes between India and Pakistan have led to a nuclear arms race between the two countries.

Possessing the strongest economic and scientific–technological potential, Japan is likely to continue to work towards its main long-term goal of becoming a great power in the twenty-first century, securing its leadership in the Asia-Pacific region and strengthening its political influence in the world, especially with regard to those Muslim countries which supply Japan with oil.

China's main aims are to create a favourable domestic environment for economic development programmes and to increase its economic and political influence in the Asia-Pacific region, and then at the global level. Its recent economic achievements have enabled it to spare no effort in modernising its armed forces. The independence of Kazakhastan, Kirgizia and other Asian republics provoked separatist activity in the Sinjan–Uigur region, which is one of the reasons why China is striving to reinforce its influence in the Muslim countries.

Turkey has stepped up its activities in the south-west of the former Soviet Union, openly trying to oust Russia from the Caucasus and ignoring Russia's vital interests. Turkey has also made political and economic attempts to draw some Central Asian Turkic republics into its zone of influence. Turkist Islamists regard a large part of Russian Territory as belonging to the so-called 'Great Turan', stretching from the Bosphorous to the Pacific Ocean and embracing settlements of Tatars, Chuvashes and even Yakuts.

By drawing Tajikistan into their zone of interest, Afghanistan, Iran and Pakistan have caused a real threat to Russia's national interests. In Tajikistan, Afghan mujahiddins and Arab and Pakistani 'volunteers' are taking an active part in the military operations of the Tajik Muslim opposition. If developments in Tajikistan prove unfavourable for Russia, then Uzbekistan and the southern (Muslim) regions of Kazakhstan may be drawn into the resulting confrontation, providing a vast springboard for extensive mujahiddin operations in Russian territory.

If Russia does not take suitable measures, it is possible that powerful vectors of Islamic force, coming via Transcaucasia, the northern Caucasus and Central Asia, might converge in the Lower Volga Basin and spread further upstream, eventually dividing Russia into two parts. The western part would be incapable of sustaining itself as it would be deprived of the powerful industrial and natural resources of the Urals, Siberia and the Far East, while the eastern part would not be able to develop to its full potential due to insufficient manpower. The greatest danger to Russia comes from the direction of Afghanistan, where a number of leading Muslim countries are involved.

Afghan problem and relations between Russia, Kazakhstan and the republics of Central Asia

One of the complex foreign policy problems of the CIS is that of Afghanistan, which is affecting the interests of the Central Asian republics to varying degrees. Millions of Turkmen, Uzbeks, Tajiks and other kindred peoples of the Central Asian nations live in northern areas of Afghanistan. Although many years have elapsed since the withdrawal of Soviet troops from Afghanistan, the Afghan problem remains unsettled and armed opposition and bloodshed persist. How can it be resolved? The answer seems to be a simple one: the participants in the conflict must closely adhere to the Generva Accords of 1988. These accords were respected by the Soviet Union and the Kabul governments, but the United States, Pakistan and the mujahiddin leaders failed to adhere to a single point of the accords. For instance Article 7 forbids direct and indirect support of separatist activities, as well as the training, financing and recruiting of volunteers of any origin, but detachments of Talibans were nonetheless trained on Pakistani territory. Interference in Afghanistan's affairs goes on, but there are wider implications – with such a 'liberal' attitude towards agreements the question arises: what guarantee is there that other international agreements will be respected?

Moreover, the Afghan opposition leaders stated that after seizing power in Afghanistan they would not stop at its northern frontiers but would take measures to destabilise the Central Asian republics and expand their realm of influence. Even now the danger exists of illegal weapons being carried to Central Asia via Afghanistan. Sovereign CIS states bordering on Afghanistan should watch closely for such developments. Other republics obviously will not wait until danger approaches their borders. They will come to a preliminary agreement on preventive measures and take mutual action to defend their southern frontiers.

With the emergence of a hostile state on the CIS's southern borders, security expenditure would increase tenfold. That is why not only the Central Asian republics but also the CIS as a whole would like Afghanistan to be, if not friendly, then at least a good neighbour. The efforts of the whole of the CIS should be directed towards this end. It is necessary to reject a simplified and unilateral approach to the solution of the Afghan problem, which in fact is nothing but a recurrence of the former class approach from a different angle. Under the present circumstances, efforts should concentrate on finding a political settlement of the problem, preferably in cooperation with all the states concerned and the opposing factions. However political parties and foreign powers should also give the Afghan people the chance to decide their own fate.

The Islamic factor in Russia's relations with other countries of the CIS

The Central Asian republics are mainly Muslim and their relations with Russia are of paramount importance. Although the disintegration of the Soviet Union presented the possibility of the successor states pursuing independent foreign policies, the stability of the commonwealth depends on foreign policy coordination. The founders of the CIS provided for continuity of the foreign policy pursued by the former Soviet Union, which can be attained only by coordinating the foreign policies of the CIS countries.

Under the Soviet Union, federal interests dominated and the specific interests of the republics were ignored, but nowadays the national interests of each independent state has become predominant. If their foreign policies are not coordinated at least on vital issues, embracing mutual interests, then it is easy to imagine the complications this will create. On the whole, international agreements signed by the Soviet Union should not be totally rejected. If all the CIS countries were to start their political life anew and ignore all the international treaties signed by the Soviet Union, this would destabilise the international situation and undermine the security of each and every republic. The United States and other NATO states trying to influence these countries and separate them from Russia do not take this aspect of the problem into account.

An integrated strategic defence system for the CIS countries needs to be planned, which will require a concerted foreign policy effort. To this end it is imperative to establish a coordinative body under the leadership of the council of Heads of State. Once founded, representative bodies dealing with domestic and foreign affairs should concentrate on their designated activities rather than on the ideological and scientific aspects of solving federal problems. The sovereign republics have to be really interested in this task and be convinced that it is beneficial as well as necessary.

Interrepublican bodies should promote most comprehensive regional interests and objectively determine the interests of the sovereign republics in vital areas of foreign policy, comparing different views and working out optimum conceptual (including alternative) ways of implementing them. Without representative interstate bodies the 500 or 50 agreements signed in recent years will never be realised.

In the political sphere, further democratisation of federal and social relations must be conducted to complete the social–political reforms. Russia should provide a positive approach to political and economic problem solving. Central Asia's most authoritative figures may claim that Russian society is not ready for democracy, but they themselves are even less prepared for the so-called 'rash' democratic reforms. There is no point in imposing on them everything that is being done in Russia. The specific nature of their social and political life should be considered. Moreover one cannot say with certainty that everything in Russia is being done correctly and is well-founded.

Of vital importance for the new Russia is a balanced policy towards the autonomous republics within the Russian Federation, especially with regard to the Turkic peoples, who share with people in the Central Asian republics a common language, culture and religious belief. A careless attitude towards internal ethnic issues, especially in the sphere of culture in Tatarstan, Bashkortostan and other Russian Federation republics, will not only complicate interstate relations but also have a profound effect on Russian-speaking residents of the Central Asian republics. Errors in this respect may give rise to grave conflicts with serious consequences.

Moscow's signing of treaties with Bashkortostan, Tatarstan and the Russian Federation was unprecedented and unique. The judicial background of this experiment should be thoroughly investigated as it is being conducted not only in Russia but also in other areas of the world. In order to avoid conflicts the Russian government must work out and pursue a well-considered national policy. In the absence of such a policy, no concerted action could be taken to prevent the outbreak of conflicts. At the moment things seem topsy-turvy. On the one hand, government officials express their wish to sign a treaty with Chechnya, similar to the one signed with Tatarstan, but on the other hand the same officials suggest that all republics should be abolished and that Russia should be a unitarian state, consisting of provinces. With such a confused approach it will not only be impossible to prevent conflicts, but the whole country runs the risk of turning into a big Chechnya. All references to the unitarian statehood of tsarist Russia are without foundation: Poland was not a province, Finland had its own constitution and in Central Asia the emir continued to rule in Bukhara. In addition many political peculiarities prevailed in the Caucasus. Contemporary Russia is also a multinational state and its future stability depends on the principle of federalism.

There are other demographic issues awaiting clarification and the adoption of long-term decisions. Solzhenitsin and other political figures are acting counterproductively when they call upon the so-called Russian-speaking peoples (there are Ukranians, Tatars, Bashkorts, Belorussians and other peoples among them) to move from the Central Asian republics and settle in Russian territory, following the example of the Russian troops' withdrawal from Germany and Poland. This approach is unrealistic for the time being at least, if we consider the economic aspects and the additional cost of providing them with decent accommodation. Rising unemployment, the housing shortage, the high criminal rate, the existence of ethnically mixed families, the fact that Russians who were born in other republics and have lived there for their whole lives have a somewhat different mentality – all these factors indicate that moving 25 million Russian-speaking people to 'promised lands' would be fraught with conflict and could be calamitous.

The Caucasus is a very difficult region for Russia. The difficulties in Russia's relations with the newly independent states of Transcaucasia are in many respects due to the ethnopolitical conflicts in Nagorny Karabakh and Abkhazia, which aggravated relations between Armenia and Azerbaijan brought them to war, sparked the civil war in Georgia and threatened Russia's national security in the region.

The proximity of this unrest to the 'hot spots' of the Russian northern Caucasus (Chechnya, Ingushetia and Ossetia), and the involvement of contiguous countries (Turkey and Iran) in the conflicts, present the grave possibility of their becoming internationalised and spreading to neighbouring regions and deep into Russia itself. All of the Russian northern Caucasus, Stavropol, Kuban and other areas of Russia might be drawn into the conflict.

In these circumstances Russian national security interests do not require resident Russians to leave the Caucasian region, the solution suggested by some analysts. Rather Russia should act as a mediator to resolve the conflicts and bring peace to Transcaucasia. President Yeltsin's meeting with the Presidents of Azerbaijan, Georgia and Armenia and the top figures of the northern Caucasus in May 1996 was of great significance. In the immediate future the most important task for Russia is peaceful resolution of the conflict in Chechnya because the Chechen people's struggle is supported by many Muslim countries. Consequently the conflict has the potential to lead to serious complications in Russian – Muslim relations. Also , taking into consideration the multinational nature of the Russian Federation, it would not be desirable (even covertly) to adopt Orthodox Christianity as Russia's official state religion as this would aggravate interdenominational relations.

There is also an urgent need to take steps to counteract the negative attitude towards the central representative bodies. First, this negativity is hindering the formation of interstate representative bodies to coordinate defence, economic and foreign policies. Second, it causes doubt about the need for central representative bodies in Russia and other sovereign republics. If the independent states, as is sometimes maintained, can come to agreements with each other in the absence of any coordinating body, then the autonomous republics, provinces and regions in all states of the CIS should be able to do likewise.

The desire for national isolation in some republics and the rejection of any form of unification within the CIS has gone to such ridiculous lengths that it has caused widespread indignation. Why has it been possible to form international social and sports organisations and teams representing Asia, America and other territories (FRG and GDR sportsmen and women sometimes appeared in the same team), but it is not considered possible within the CIS. In this respect the NATO countries may serve as an example.

In the sphere of economics it is imperative to preserve a single economic space. Transformation to the market economy is inconceivable in a country characterised by complex cooperation and interdependence among industrial enterprises without preserving industrial ties and free trade. Not a single republic, including the Baltic states, can transform itself into a market economy in economic isolation. It is also the case that Kazakhstan and the Central Asian republics, having acquired national sovereignty, would not be able to bring about the necessary structural changes to their economy, especially as some republics produce only raw materials while others only process them. Especially painful for Kazakhstan and other republics was severing of the economic ties between them. The arbitrary raising of prices on industrial products, along with the maintenance of low prices on raw materials and the absence of an interrepublic stabilisation fund, caused an abrupt fall in living standards in these republics and brought their economies to the brink of crisis. If CIS-wide coordinative measures are not taken and if Russia does not promote such cooperation, Kazakhstan and the republics of Central Asia will be compelled to sell their raw materials to other countries at the considerably higher world prices.

For international relations with the Islamic world, settlement of the political situation in Tajikistan is imperative. According to the Russian and foreign press the abrupt destabilisation of the area was a natural consequence of the failure to implement political and economic reforms. A catastrophic situation in the sphere of economics has developed there. In 1995 industrial output fell by 30 per cent in comparison with 1993, the yield of cotton went down and the value of the national currency fell sevenfold in a few months. According to international experts, Tajikistan faces famine and about 400 000 people are already starving. Bread distribution – no more than 100 grams a day per person – has been introduced in some rural areas. The strategically important region of Gorny Badakhshan actually depends for its maintenance on Agha Khan IV, the head of the World Ismailis, as the government is neglecting this region as well as others. In the Leninabad region about 80 per cent of the 100 000 remaining Russian and Russian-speaking people live in poverty: in February 1996 the average salary of a teacher was equal to nine loaves of bread!

But how are things with integration? Here Russia faces the most acute competition with Western countries. While voicing its economic orientation towards Russia, the Tajik Leadership has turned over the most strategically significant enterprises to Western companies. In Darvaza the right to extract the biggest deposits of gold on the territory of the former Soviet Union, plus a big deposit in Penjikent, was passed to British companies, which are planning to extract 10–12 tons of gold a year. During 1995 the Tajik government had negotiations with an Israeli company on transferring its biggest deposits of silver and non-ferrous metals to that company for their exploitation.

So, the anomalous situation has developed in Tajikistan of Russian troops (frontier troops in the Collective Peacemaking Forces, the core of which consists of Russians) defending Western property. Hence all the assurances that Russian troops are in Tajikistan to defend the Russian frontier mean nothing and obscure the heart of the matter. Russians are constantly told that if the troups were withdrawn Mujahiddins would immediately appear in the vicinity of Moscow. But they are already in Russia, in Chechnya for instance, and the Tajik knot is still not resolved. If the political situation in Tajikistan spins out of control it would have an immediate impact on the other Central Asian republics. Another mistake made by the Russian authorities and the mass media is to use Islam, and especially Islamic fundamentalism, to frighten others. Whom do they mean to scare? Russian Muslims, who number more than 20 million? Or primarily Muslim countries in the near and far abroad, for whom Islam is the religion of their fathers and forefathers? Yes, terrorist and criminal organisations in various countries of the world do make use of the banner of Islamic fundamentalism, but even here the husk must be separated from the grain, and Russia's allies (even potential ones) from its opponents. For example Saudi Arabia, the classical country of Islamic fundamentalism, is known for its stability and also maintains good relations with the United States, which paradoxically is regarded as the world's main fighter against Islamic fundamentalism. Ironically, Islamic Iran lends help to Christian Armenia.

S. A. Bagdasarov, who knows this region very well, states that there might be only one course of action: to nip in the bud all attempts to bring about the disintegration of the Russian Federation under the Islamic banner or any other; but Russia need not fight against religion. The plans to drag Russia into bloody and endless conflicts between nations and confessions will trouble the West to eliminate Russia from the international political arena for a long time or for forever. For some Western ideologists this is strategic task number one (after the Soviet Union's dissolution) to direct a powerful Islamic wave against Russia.

Russia must keep the situation in Tajikistan under its control and should not give the United States and other powers the opportunity to interfere in its affairs. Russia must take the initiative and bring about national reconciliation in Tajikistan, followed by the formation of a coalition government with broad representation of regional interests and ethnic communities. Both historical and current realities must be taken into account in this process. Other countries, considering the balance of interests in a multipolar world, are best advised to stop interfering in this area.

In the West and even in Russia itself there are those who strive for the disintegration of Russia. They are the same people who are standing in the way of Russia's close integration with the CIS countries. The expansion of NATO to the east would play a negative part in this respect. As mentioned in the Russian press, this policy of opposing Russia to Eurasia's Islamic mass contains the hidden temptation to bring into conflict the waves of instability in the Muslim and post-socialist space, so that they can neutralise each other. But some political figures and strategists fail to realise that the disintegration of the Russian Federation would entail numerous conflicts on the Eurasian continent. Considering that these would take place on territory where there are vast stores of nuclear weapons and atomic power stations, it is evident that such events would present a real danger to the entire world. That is why Russia must be ready to confront the entire world by political, economic and other means.

On issues of defence, it would be economically beneficial and strategically expedient for the CIS in general and all the republics within it to have a joint defence system and a united military force, integrated at least to the same degree as the NATO countries. While military union would consolidate the republics, its absence could lead to disintegration and the sharpening of differences. Russia must make every effort (even at the cost of making concessions on certain other issues) to incorporate a defence network into the structure of the Commonwealth in concordance with other sovereign states.

In the case of coordinated defence, Russia would be supported by the defence structures of other republics, while in the case of national defence in individual territories, some of the neighbouring republics might find themselves in positions of military confrontation, and perhaps in alliance with states that were not part of the former Soviet Union. The economic situation in these republics prevents them from having adequate military forces and a reliable defence system. That is why they are particularly interested in military alliance with Russia and are arranging a mutual defence system within the CIS. For Russia and other CIS states, settlement of the situation in Tajikistan is of primary importance.

In order to strengthen cooperation among the CIS countries, Russia and the other republics of the CIS should refrain from joining NATO or any other military – political union or bloc. Economic associations with other states could be established, but military union should be restricted to the CIS. Otherwise the CIS will disintegrate and Russia could be opposed not only by individual republics that have seceded from the CIS, but also by military blocs, especially in the south.

Russia needs to adapt a very careful approach to the revival of the Cossack movement, which in the past clashed with Muslims. Before 1917 in Kazakhstan and on the northern frontiers of Central Asia there existed Astrakhan, Ural, Semirechensk and Orenburg Cossack troops. In today's circumstances, while encouraging in all possible ways the cultural revival of the Cossacks, it is desirable not to permit the formation of Cossack armed forces. As long as the CIS exists and its frontiers are open, these formations will not be needed as they would only worsen Russia's relations with Kazakhstan and the Central Asian republics.

Finally, it is imperative that Russia, when making vital decisions on questions of domestic and foreign policy, should take the Islamic factor into serious consideration.

Conclusions

First, as in all periods in its historical existence, Russia embraces several civilisations, where Islam takes its rightful place. That is why the Islamic factor should not be used as a means of intimidation. It is imperative for the government to recognise the need for genuine methods of cooperation and collaboration with Muslims within Russia and Muslim countries abroad. In its own interests, Russia should be able to compete with other countries for influence in the Islamic states.

Second, Islam is one of the leading religions of the world, and as with other religions the majority of believers adhere to the ideals of peace and collaboration between peoples and confessions. There is a moderate wing of Islam that opts for concord between religion and secular aspects of society. As with other religions there are also extremist wings, and in the interests of political struggle the latter are often used by certain powers to engage in terrorist and other unacceptable acts. But this must not cast a shadow on the whole of the Muslim world. Peace and tolerance are the essence of Islam.

Third, attempts by political forces to use Islam in the struggle against Russia and other countries have been fraught with danger. It was easy, for instance, to provide the Afghan Mujahiddin with arms, but disarming them and bringing them back to a peaceful life is a different matter altogether. Bosnia and Chechnya also serve as examples in this respect. Instead the leading countries of the world should be seeking mutually acceptable ways of cooperating with the Islamic world. Taking into account the fact that many Muslim countries were colonial possessions for a long time and have weak economies, the United Nations and other international organisations should consider the possibility of rendering them substantial economic assistance.

Finally, if Russia is to achieve good cooperative relations with Muslim countries it is very important for it to show respect for the needs and culture of its own Muslim inhabitants.

References

1. Vestnik ITAR-TASS, 17 April 1992, no. 75.
2. *'USA: Economics, Politics, Ideology'*, no. 11 (1992), p. 6.
3. *'Mezhdunarodnaya zhizn'*, no. 9 (1993), p. 52.

8
Political Perspectives of Islam in Bashkortostan

Aislu Yunosova

There are many debates in Russia about Islamic political activity and its potential threat to the Russian Federation. The politicisation of Islam is the main cause of agitated discussions on the subject. The Islamic revolutions in Libya and Iran, and unrest in Jordan, Tunis and Algeria resulted in Islamic parties engaging in political activities in the Muslim world. Their political activism gave rise to a surge of international terrorism in the 1970s and Islam later became a catalyst of the struggle between ethnic groups in Yugoslavia.

Political Islam and terrorism are joined together in the public mind as Islamic fundamentalism. Since the 1980s the word 'fundamentalism' has become synonymous with 'Islamic' and associated with social movements that are presented as anti-Western, anti-Russian, anticommunist and so on. Some of these do use fundamentalist slogans, but others have moderate views and function legally, including Birlik in Uzbekistan, the Party of Islamic Revival in Tajikistan and Johar Dudayev's supporters in Chechnya. Their leaders appeal to Islam in order to gain moral support.

The views held on political Islam are noticeably incoherent. Unfortunately journalists, who are obliged to respond to events immediately, try to bring Islamic fundamentalism into every event in the Muslim world. In their presentations, Islam becomes 'Islamism', 'extremism' or 'terrorism', and Muslims become 'Muslim fanatics'. Consequently the supposed threat of Islamic fundamentalism has grown into a worldwide threat.[1]

Historians, especially Islamic researchers, take a more professional approach.[2] Firstly, they suggest that Islamic radicalism is a reaction to social problems. A classical example is the emergence of the anti-Western revolution in Iran. Second, the term 'fundamentalism' is not used in the Muslim world, although *saf Islam* (clear and pure Islam) is sometimes used in a positive religious context. Third, in journalistic speculations Islam's threat to Russia has military implications, providing justification for the wars in Afghanistan, Chechnya and Tajikistan. Their slogan is 'Only Russia's army can restore order in the Muslim regions'. Finally, historians assert that radicals, extremists and terrorists exist everywhere, and there is no need to underline their national and religious affiliations.

We think that the thesis on Islam's potential threat to Russia and its political implications in the Muslim regions, especially Bashkortostan, demands special objective analysis. One should remember that Russia's Muslims live in a non-Muslim world dominated by Christians. Muslims (Tatars, Bashkorts and north Caucasian peoples) constitute less than 10 per cent of the population of the Russian Federation. They live in the Volga–Ural region, Siberia, Moscow, St Petersburg and the northern Caucasus. The rhetorical question could be asked: is it possible for Muslims, dispersed as they are all over the country and living amidst the mainly Christian population, to achieve political objective such as Islamic fundamentalism?

Moreover fundamentalism implies the restoration of a religion's foundation stone. In the Muslim world it means restoration of the Muslim *ummas* (state rules), which is possible in those countries where the caliphate once existed and the *umma* state flourished. Caliphate lands were ruled by (1) the economic principles of Muslim *umma* (joint possession of lands, water, pastures; *sadaka* and *zakkat*); (2) Muslim laws (family law and criminal law) and *sharia* Courts; (3) a caliphal political system, with the caliph – as the prophet's successor – at the head; and (4) *jihad*. Were these principles transferred to Russia along with the Islamic religion? To answer this question we need to examine the history of Islam in Bashkortostan.

The historical development of Islam in Bashkortostan

The earliest evidence of an Islamic presence in Bashkortostan dates from the ninth and tenth centuries. Caliphate coins found in the Levashov burial mound date from 712 to 892 AD. Archaeologist P. Mihaylov, who found the coins, writes: 'Judging from the kufic inscriptions they were put in the burial mound long after they were minted, and they spread to the South Ural steppes by the 'trade way – God's way'.[3] Levashov based his findings not only on the Muslim coins, but also on the position of the skeletons, which were lying face up, arms along the body and head towards the west. Consequently we are confident about the early spread of caliphate trade right up to the Urals.

In the tenth century Islam appeared in the region through trade and missionary activities. The great embassy from Baghdad, with Ibn-Fadlan at its head, arrived in 922 AD. That year is also thought to be the one in which Islam was adopted by the Bulgars, who had established a large state of their own along the river Volga in the ninth century. According to Ibn-Fadlan the Bashkort tribes were pagans – some worshipped birds and animals, others worshipped up to 12 gods, who personified nature, life and death. As Ibn-Fadlan wrote, Bashkorts also worshipped the phallus.[4] At the same time the Bashkorts sought to expand their religious horizon, looking for novelty in a world outlook. An early Bashkort to convert to Islam was a member of Ibn-Fadlan's embassy, and Ibn-Fadlan also wrote of Muslim burials among the Bashkorts,[5] we can say that Islam was adopted by some Bashkorts even before 922.

The Islamisation of Bashkort lands was rapid and closely connected with their becoming part of the *Zolotaya Orda* (the Golden Horde), which lasted from 1256 to 1502. Khan Uzbek (1312–42) declared Islam the official religion of the Golden Horde. He also sent many Muslim missionaries to Bashkortostan. There are about 20 missionary burial sites along the rivers Belaya, Urshak, Dim, Chermasan and Ik.[6] Among these is Hussein-bek's mausoleum (1339), not far from Ufa. During the thirteenth and fourteenth centuries there was a decline in pagan culture and an increase in the number of bodies being buried according to Muslim rules.[7] Islam's spread in Bashkortostan took place in several stages and was completed in the fourteenth and fifteenth centuries.[8] Since that time Islam has been an important religious system in Bashkortostan.

Some features of the Islamic expansion in Bashkiria are specifically related to politics, economics and ideology. First, Islam appeared in the Volga–Ural region because of missionary activities and economic connections with the Muslim world, not as a result of conquest. The Turkic peoples of the Volga–Ural region were not forced by Muslim countries to convert to Islam. Islam became a mode of life that included Muslim beliefs, ethics, family law, culture and education, but not a political system. It was adopted by Tatars, Bashkorts and other Turkic peoples as a main ideological system, reflecting the tendency for social stratification. Islam never dominated the Turkic life as a political system in the Volga–Ural Basin. While the Tatar khans in the Bulgar state the Golden Horde, Nogay Horde were Muslims, not one of them declared himself a caliph's successor. So the state and Islam remained separate and were never united into a whole in the Volga–Ural region. When the latter was absorbed into the Russian state, where the Russian Orthodox Church dominated, Islam in Russia became a religion of national minorities.

Second, economic relations in the Bulgar state and the Golden Horde remained in the traditional form of *yasak* (tribute), which also defined economic relations between Russia and the Tatars and Bashkorts until the sixteenth century and beyond. The main economic principles of Islamic state, including *sadaka* (irrevocable charitable gift) and *zakat* (alms-tax), virtually amalgamated here as *sadaka*, meaning voluntary donations. These donations were distributed among *madaras* (religious schools) and mosques to pay for their maintenance. As they were offered during religious holiday, such donations usually signified personal expiation as well. But neither *sadaka* nor *zakat* ever formed the economic foundations of the Tatar and Bashkort societies.

Waqf is another very important feature of the Islamic state, but it reached perfect development in the Bashkort lands and Russia. Some historians have confused the presence of Muslim mullahs as *waqf*, but this is not correct. *Waqf* in the Muslim world means a property of religious endowment, including mosques, *madaras* and *muftiats* (religious organisations). They are part of the state and do not pay taxes. In Central Asia before 1917 mosques possessed plots of land, irrigation systems and shops – all of which brought in some profit. There were many personal *aqaf* to provide for the descendants of sheikhs and famous clergy. Here, mosques were large landowners and possessed about 20 per cent (Bukhara) to 30 per cent (Khiva) of all arable lands.[9]

Nothing of this kind of endowment was visible in inner Russia and the Bashkort lands. The state imposed a tax upon mosques in 1711 – about five rubles for each mullah and about one altin for every person entering the mosque.[10] It was imposed as a punishment for the popular Bashkort uprising of 1705–11. Another uprising in 1734–40 led to increased government pressure on Muslims and Islam in the Volga–Ural basin and Bashkort and Tatar mullahs were stripped of their right to own land.[11]

In the nineteenth century some shops and plots of land became the property of Russian mosques, but they were not large. At the end of the nineteenth century prosperous merchants invested money in the construction of new mosques and *madaras* and endowed shops and land to them. Merchant Mazhitov endowed five shops to Sterlitamak *madaras*, and Mufti Tevkelev's widow endowed to the Orenburg Muslim Council some land with buildings.[12] In 1889 the Orenburg Muslim Council possessed about 23 *aqaf*,[13] which were not enough. There were about 200 *aqafs* at the beginning of the twentieth century, almost all of them for *madaras's* buildings. Even in 1913 *aqaf* were on the decline.[14] Moreover the Russian state could confiscate *aqaf*. For example a Bashkort caravan-serai in Orenburg was confiscated in the middle of the nineteenth century.[15]

Clearly the political and economic functions of Islam were curtailed in Tatar and Bashkort society. They were further curtailed after the Volga–Ural region was taken over by the Russian state. After 1552 the majority of Muslims from Kazan migrated to the South Urals and hid themselves in Bashkort lands to avoid forceful Christening. This development strengthened the position of Islam in the area. The Bashkorts' willingness to join Russia in 1557 guaranteed the preservation of Islam and Islamic traditions for the Muslims of the Bashkort lands. From the seventeenth century, Islam became a minority religion and Muslims were persecuted throughout the Volga–Ural region because Kazan was not only the regional centre of Islam but also the stronghold of resistance to Russia. In 1788 the Orenburg Muslim Council was established in Ufa and Islam became a 'permitted' but 'controlled' religion. The Orenburg Muslim Council was an official bureaucratic body, and followed the orders of the tsarist government. Muftis from the Muslim Council took part in the Russian conquest of the Kazakhs. By the end of the eighteenth century Islam had strengthened in the Bashkort lands and other Muslim regions. More than a thousand mosques were built in the Orenburg *guberniya* (province) and there were about four or five mosques in each village.

Third, a distinctive feature of Russian Islam is that during its long history many elements of paganism have survived and remain part of the Muslim culture. Many scholars have written about the subject, especially with regard to shamanistic practices among Bashkorts, Kazakhs, Turkmen and Abkhases. Islam does not exclude pre-Islamic religions and traditions: magicians, sorceresses, sorcerers and shamans usually play a part in Bashkort life.[16] Very often mullahs perform the duties of shamans: 'They treat the sick by whispering, reading the Qur'an, blowing and spitting on their face... . Sometimes, in a serious case, an animal is sacrificed. The Mullah gets the skin, and a person who is present eats the meat'.[17] Paganism is at the root of most of such offerings. Even in the middle of the nineteenth century some mullahs did not believe in God and instead worshipped the crane, an ancient tribal symbol.[18]

Gabdulkadir Inan[19] and contemporary ethnographers have also observed remnants of shamanism among the Bashkorts, most noticeably the presence of magical lexicons in the contemporary Bashkort language. The widespread consumption of egg dishes (*chak-chak*, *baursak*) testify to the ancient bird cult. Yanbukhtina underlines the fusion of Muslim and pagan decorative elements in modern Bashkort dwellings, such as *shamails* (prayer carpets brought from Mecca) and talismans made from wood-grouse tails to guard the home.[20] Pilgrimages to 'holy places' were part of the life of Bashkort pagans in the distant past. The worship of idols passed into modern Muslim practices as *ziyara*. All of these elements testify to remains of the tribal system among the Turkic and Caucasian nations.[21]

The moral substance of Islam in the Bashkort lands was provided by Ishanism (Sufism), which emerged as a result of the imposition of Islam over tribal cults. Ishans exercised great authority over the Bashkorts and their influence passed from generation to generation. There were two highly influential dynasties in the Bashkort lands – the Rasuly and the Kurbangaly – and both played an important role in cultural and political life. At the beginning of the twentieth century the adherents and opponents of the Rasuly and Kurbangaly split into their political factions. Supporters of the Rasuly became adherents of Zaki Validy, while Kurbangaly followers supported Kolchak. These examples indicate that ideologically Islam has not been the dominant system in the Bashkort lands.

During the nineteenth century Islam played no political role and the lives of all the Muslim peoples of Russia were regulated by the tsarist government's statutes for aliens – subject, non-Slavic peoples such as the Bashkorts, Kazakhs and Caucasians. However at the beginning of the twentieth century Islam acquired a political content. The tzar's edict of April 1905 about religious liberty and proclamation of October 1905 stirred the Muslim masses into action. In 1917–20 three all-Russia Muslim congresses were held and important decisions were made with regard to the election of muftis, the structure of the Muslim Council, educational reforms, participation in the democratic movement and election to the *Uchreditelnoye Sobranie* (local Councils). National concerns dominated the Russian Muslim opposition movements. Islamic and Muslim traditions comingled in almost all the national movements, whose leaders included Zaki Validy, Mirsaid Sultan-Galiev, Mullanur Vahitov, Ahmed Tcalikov, Bukeikhanov and others. However Islam could not transform the national movements into an Islamic political movement and pursue political ends such as the establishment of an Islamic state. In 1917–20 the democratic movement of Russian Muslims included Tatars, Bashkorts and Turkmen: (we are unable to describe it as a 'Muslim movement' in Russia, but only as a Muslim minority's movement.)

The October Revolution overturned the Muslims' lives. In a Bolshevik decree of January 1918 all religions and clergy were declared illegal and all religious establishments were deprived of their juridical status. Before the October Revolution there were about 13 000 mosques in Russia, including 2500 in Bashkortostan. During the 1920s and 1930s thousands of mosques were destroyed all over the Soviet Union. Only 80 mosques remained in Russia, just 12 in Bashkortostan. Thousands of mullahs were persecuted, including Zia Kamaly, Kashaf Tadjimany, Mutigulla Gatay, Mutagar Kamaly and Gabdulla Shamsutdin, and the Muslim Councils were disbanded. In comparison with the Christians, Muslims suffered far more from the state's aggressive atheism. A large number of books in Arabic script were destroyed, halting the development of the Muslim culture and severing its links with the past.

The Second World War compelled the state to reduce its pressure on religion to a certain extent. Some historians explain the Soviet state's more relaxed policy towards religion during that period by the clergy's loyalty during the war. For example Mufti Rasulev offered the Red Army 40 000 rubles, as acknowledged by Stalin in *Izvestiya*.[22] But the real reason for the change was the government's fear of rebellion.

Despite state repression the Islamic and Muslim traditions were kept alive in the consciousness of the Muslim minorities, and today we can see the restoration of Islamic positions in society, the building of new mosques, the publication of Muslim religious and historical literature, and the celebration of Muslim holy days and festivals. There are now about 500 mosques in Bashkortostan, and 50 new Muslim schools have been established in Ufa, Oktyabrsk, Kazan, Nabereszhhnie Chelni, Moscow, Omsk, Tyumen and Novosibirsk.

However, politically Islam cannot be restored – there is nothing to restore! Islam has no political strength in Russia today and nationalism and national separatism in the Muslim regions have no Islamic content. Not one of the national parties or unions includes Islam in its programme; such is indeed the case with 'Urals' in Bashkortostan, 'Ittihad' in Tatarstan and 'Birlik' in Central Asia. Even in the Chechen *jihad*, led by Dudayev and his followers, Islam played no role. Nor has an Islamic voice been heard to condemn the Russian state's actions in Chechnya.

The fact is that the Russian Muslims are too fragmented. The Central Muslim Council of Russia fell apart in August 1992 when the Bashkortostan and Tatarstan Muslim councils appeared. Since 1992 about ten new Muslim councils have appeared in Russia and every region has its own council. There are two in Moscow and four in Bashkortostan. At least two claim to be central councils for all Russia. One is headed by Nafigulla Ashirov and professes to be the coordination centre for all Muslim councils in Moscow. The second, which is located in Ufa and led by Supreme Mufti Talgat Tadjuddin, claims to be the central Muslim council for the European part of Russia and the CIS countries.

The same fragmentation can be seen in Bashkortostan. The struggle between the Bashkort and Tatar clergy began in 1917 and soon acquired a nationalistic character, reaching full strength by November 1995. Bashkortostan governmental bodies participate in the Bashkort Muslim Council. An attempt was made to interfere with the activities of the Central Muslim Council when state representatives tried to hospitalise Mufti Talgat Tadjuddin for mental problems. He was castigated for allegedly using narcotics and disregarding Muslim religious and social rules. All this tended to divide the Bashkortostan Muslims into two camps according to their ethnic identity.

There are three Muslim councils in Bashkortostan, located in Ufa, Salavat and Tatishli. The one in Ufa is supported by the Bashkortostan government and its leader, Hurmuhammet Nigmatullin, is a former imam of the First Ufa Mosque. At present he has authority over about 250 mosques in southern Bashkortostan. The council in Salavat is led by Talgat Tadjuddin. Both councils claim to have authority over the same mosques and all three have declared themselves to be the main council for Bashkortostan. The council in Tatishli was established by Talgat Tadjuddin as the centre for the mosques of the southern Urals. At present this council has no real influence.

These developments are the consequence of separatism in the former Soviet Union and the struggle for power among the Muslim clergy. Muslim clergy dissidence, the Muslim Council's fragmentation and the formation of the national Muslim councils reflect the struggle for power in Muslim society. Rivalry between the Muslim clergy does little to strengthen Islam; rather it reflects Islam's weakness in Russia – although the Russian Muslims have been freed from state restrictions they do not struggle for Islam, nor have they for the last fifty years.

Economic weakness is noticeable too. Muslims, like all the other people of Russia, are in a difficult economic situation and have few resources, which is why many mosques are only partly completed. Besides, as a result of the Bolsheviks' brutal antireligious policies today's Muslims have lost sight of their Islamic traditions and history and often cannot read the Qur'an. With regard to politics, the orientation of the Islamic leaders is another problem. Some of them look to Turkey as the model of Islamic development, others to Saudi Arabia. Both countries have flooded Bashkortostan with preachers and teachers, some of whom are mere adventurers.

Another problem is related to the generally accepted ideology as a means of control over Muslim voters. The presidential election of June 1996 revealed that Muslims are under communist influence. In the first round the communists won a majority of the Muslim votes in Bashkortostan and Chechnya and about half in Tatarstan. In the second round, great efforts were made to reduce this influence.

Is the communist influence a paradox? No, not really. Bashkortostan and some other Muslim regions have preserved the *kolkhos* (cooperatives) system, with a few insignificant and token changes. Who helps to build mosques today? Clearly the *kolkhos* administration. Who provides money for pilgrimages and Muslim schools? Indeed the *kolkhos* administration. The chiefs of the kolkhos movement (AKH) visit mosques, invite Muslim clergy to festivals, go on pilgrimage to Mecca. Bashkortostan's President Rakhimov also visited Mecca as a pilgrim. In the common consciousness, religion and power have united. This is the real picture, not only of Bashkortostan and Tatarstan, but also of Russia as a whole.

The weakness of Islam in Russia fills us with apprehension for at least three reasons. First, Islam in Russia is too personified: public opinion on Islam is determined by the Muslim clergy's behaviour, and not by real knowledge of Islamic principles. Hence Saratov's Mullah Mukaddas Bibarsov is said to be a 'fundamentalist' only because of his great Islamic influence on politics today. There has been much talk about Talgat Tadjuddin's private life and his weaknesses have been used as an excuse to decentralise the Muslim Council in Ufa.

Second, Islam has been used for the purpose of political and national struggle. This was evident during the parliamentary elections of December 1995. Two Muslim political movements – Nur and the Russian Muslims Union (RMU) – surfaced just before the elections. The leaders of both movements had connections with the Liberal-Democratic Party of Zhirinovsky. It is not clear why Muslim interests became so much stronger on the eve of the elections that they forced Ahmet Halikov and Halit Yahin to set up their own political parties.

On 10 August 1995 the first meeting of the RMU took place in Sibay (Bashkortostan), and although there was a wide geographical representation attendance was poor. The main item on the agenda was preparation for elections. Ahmet Halikov was sure of success, but in the end the RMU did not even participate in the elections. Nur did take part but received only 1.2 per cent of the votes (35 317) in Bashkortostan and about 0.1 per cent in Russia.[23] It was noticeable that the political programme of the religious unions were not even commented upon in the press. There was only one area of interest: the struggle between communists and democrats.

Finally, the threat of Islam is used to justify foreign intervention in countries of the Muslim world – Afghanistan, Tajikistan, Turkey, Bosnia, Iraq and so on. Such intervention is usually followed by military action.

Notes and references

1. V. Titorenko, 'Islam i interesi Rossii', *Mezhdunarodnie otnoshenia*, no. 1 (1995); Yu Tissovskiy, 'Islamskiy fundamentalism', *Modus vivendi International*, no. 11 (1993); V. Danilov, 'Turcia i postsovetskaya Centralnaya Asia' *Asia i Africa segodnya*, no. 2 (1994).
2. A. Kudryavteev, 'Islam i gosudaratvo v Chechenskoy respublike', *Vostok*, no. 3 (1994); V. Livshic, 'Politicheskaya situacia v Tadjikistane', *Rossia i musulmsnskiy mir*, nos 10, 11 (1993); A. Malashenko, 'Musulmanskoye duhovenstvo i politika', *Nezavisimaya gazeta*, 24 October 1992; D. Mikulskiy, 'Musulmanskiy fundamentalism v SNG – pravomerna li postanovka voprosa?', *Rossia i musulmanskiy mir*, no. 12 (1993); M. Olimov, 'Ob etnopoliticheskoy i konfessionalnoy situateii v Tadjikistane i veroyatnosty mezhetnicheskih konfliktov', *Vostok*, no. 2 (1994); A. Sultangalieva, '*Islam v Kazahstanee*', *Vostok*, no. 3 (1994), A. Yunusova *Islam v Bashkirii, 1917–1994* (Ufa, 1994).
3. CGIA RB. F. 4423. O. 1. D. 4. L. 28–31.
4. S. I. Rudenko, 'Bashkiri. Opit etnologicheskoy monographii', in *Bit Bashkir* (Ufa, 1925), p. 299.
5. *Hrestomatii po istorii Bashkortostana* (Ufa, 1996), pp. 67–8.
6. R. G. Kuzeev, *Istoriceskaya etnographiya bashkirskogo narioda* (Moscow, 1978), p. 59.
7. N. Mazhitov and A. Sultanova, *Istoria Bashkortostana s drevneishih vremen do XVI veka* (Ufa, 1994), pp. 262–6.
8. N. V. Bikbulatov, *Bashkiri. Etnographicheskiy ocherk* (Ufa, 1995); R. G. V. Kuzeev, *Istoriceskaya etnographiya bashkirskogo narioda* (Moscow, 1978); N. Mazhitov and A. Sultanova, *Istoria Bashkortostana s drevneishih vremen do XVI veka* (Ufa, 1994); G. B. Faizov, *Gosudarstvennoislamskiye otnosheniya v Povolzhye i Priuralye* (Ufa, 1995).
9. T. Saidbayev, *Islam i obschestvo* (Moscow, 1983), p. 81.
10. A. Asfandiyarov, 'Religioznaya politika tzarizma v Bashkirii v period feodalizma', *Bashkirskij kraj*, vol. 1 (Ufa, 1991), p. 4.

11. A. Asfandiyarov, 'Religioznaya politika tzarizma v Bashkirii v period feodalizma', *Bashkirskij kraj*, vol. 1 (Ufa, 1991), p. 4; N. Kulbahtin and Yu Sergeev, 'Religioznaya politika tzarizma v Bashkirii v XVIII v', *Socialno-economicheskoye razvitie i klassovaya borba na Yuzhnom Urale i v Srednem Povolzhje* (Ufa, 1988), pp. 37–8.
12. A. Yunusova, *Islam v Bashkirii* (Ufa: 1917–1994), p. 47.
13. L. Klimovich, *Islam v tzarskoy Rossii* (Moscow, 1936), pp. 97–109.
14. 'Shkolni vopros v russkom musulmanstve', *Mir Islama*, vol. 7, no. 2 (1913), pp. 459–60.
15. *Caravanserei* (Ufa, 1995), pp. 11–12.
16. *Hrestomatii po istorii Bashkortostana* (Ufa, 1996), p. 160.
17. Rudenko, 'Bashkiri', op. cit., p. 314.
18. Central Historical Archiv of Bashkortostan, F. 295. O. 2. D. 27.
19. Abdülkadir Inan, 'Baskurt Türklerinde Samanizm kalintilari', *Türk Folklor Arastirmalari*, no. 9 (1965), pp. 1–191.
20. A. Yanbuhtina, *Narodnie traditeii v ubranstve bashkirskogo doma* (Ufa, 1993), pp. 53, 81.
21. Rudenko S. Bashkiri, *Opit etnologicheskoy monografii* (Leningrad, 1925), ch. 2; G. Georgy, *Opisanie vseh obitayuschih v Rossiyskom gosudarstve narodov* (SPb, 1799); Inan, 'Baskurt Türklerinde Samanizm kalintilari', op. cit.; T. Saidbajev, *Islam i obschestvo* (Moscow, 1983); N. Basilov, *Kult sviatih v Islame* (Moscow, 1970); B. Karmisheva, *Ocherki etnicheskoy istorii yuzhnih raionov Tadzhikistana i Uzbekistana* (Moscow, 1976).
22. *Izvestiya*, 3 March 1943.
23. *Bashkortostan*, 1 March 1996.

9

Tatarstan's Quest for Autonomy within the Russian Federation

Hafeez Malik

In February 1994 Tatarstan and Russia signed a treaty defining their political and economic relations within the Russian Federation. This came as a big surprise, as well as a disappointment, to the Tatar national movement, which expected the treaty to bring about a well-defined independence. However President Boris Yeltsin saw it as a major achievement as he could use the treaty as a model to settle Russia's relationships with the other twenty autonomous republics and some of the *oblasts* that were aspiring to become autonomous republics. In this chapter an attempt is made to analyse the nature and scope of this treaty in the light of current dynamics and the historical perspectives which Tatars and Russians have nurtured since the middle of the sixteenth century.

Duality of power and Yeltsin's success

When in December 1991 the Soviet Union unexpectedly collapsed, there was widespread fear in Russia that the multi-ethnic Russian Federation would not be able to preserve its territorial integrity and that Russia would use force to keep the Muslim-Turkic regions within the Russian Federation. Some observers, both within Russia and abroad, expected the emergence of at least two independent states: Tatarstan in the Volga–Ural Basin and Chechnya in the Caucusas. These regions were focal points of discontent and calls for political sovereignty. The prospect of the Russian Federation breaking up was heightened by the duality of power that prevailed in Moscow between the Russian Supreme Soviet, which was still dominated by the communist old guard, and President Yeltsin. The struggle between the two reached its climax in September 1993 when Yeltsin dissolved the

Supreme Soviet and called for new legislative elections to be held in December 1993 and presidential elections in June 1994.

The Russian Constitutional Court ruled on 22 September 1993 that Yeltsin had violated the constitution and could be impeached, while the defiant vice president, Aleksandr V. Rutskoi, denounced the move as a *coup d'état* and assumed full state powers. The parliament's chairman, Russlan I. Khasbulatov, a Chechen Muslim, called on the armed forces to disobey Yeltsin. The Congress of the Peoples Deputies voted to call simultaneous parliamentary and presidential elections before March 1994, but Yeltsin rejected the call and ordered the Interior and Defence Ministries to disarm the guards at the White House (parliament) and evict the legislators. Russian troops duly sealed off the White House in order to 'maintain law and order' in the vicinity, and then assaulted the building with tanks, forcing out the legislators. Yeltsin was the undisputed victor of this showdown and he promptly disbanded the communist and ultranationalist parties. Physically exhausted and bedraggled, Khasbulatov sat in a chair in the White House and muttered: 'I never thought he [Yeltsin] would do this. Why isn't anyone coming to help us'.[1]

Like the communists who led the abortive coup in August 1991 against Gorbachev, Rutskoi and Khasbulatov were convinced that the silent majority and the armed forces were on their side and longed for the return of the Communist Party's centralised and authoritarian rule. They were wrong. Communism and its stalwarts had lost the sympathy and support of the common people in Russia and other republics.

Whether or not Yeltsin's action against the parliament was legal is now a moot point. However 'the Yeltsin coup' had a profound psychological impact on the Russian citizens and the leaders of the 88 regions that make up the Russian Federation. In particular, Yeltsin had conveyed the message to the 21 autonomous republics, including Tatarstan, that he would not hesitate to use force against his personal opponents and secessionist leaders in the regions. Consequently Tatarstan's negotiations for independence and sovereignty must be analysed against the backdrop of the coup of August 1991 against Gorbachev and that of October 1993 by Yeltsin against the Russian parliament. Fear of the Russian Bear once again prevailed in Tatarstan, weakening the national resolve for independence.

During 1990–91, when Yeltsin was engaged in his struggle for power against Gorbachev, he visited Tatarstan and encouraged the Tatar leaders with a statement that subsequently returned to haunt him: 'Take as much sovereignty as you can swallow'.[2] Consequently on

13 March 1992 Tatarstan, along with Chechnya, refused to sign the treaty offered by Yeltsin that would grant some autonomy to the ethnic autonomous republics in matters of finance, infrastructure, the environment, social protection, foreign relations, natural resources and state of emergency requirements, and in a convoluted formula recognised the 'state sovereignty of the republics within the Russian Federation'.

In July 1993 the constitutional conference set up by Yeltsin in defiance of the parliament extended to the autonomous republics the opportunity to adopt their own constitutions, national anthems and flags. In response to this liberal policy Yakaterinburg (Yeltsin's former fiefdom as a Communist Party secretary) declared itself the Republic of the Urals, Vladivostok threatened to proclaim itself a maritime republic, and Krasnoyarsk planned with Irkutsk to create an east Siberian republic. These *oblasts'* proclamations were not necessarily viewed as leading to the break-up of Russia in the way that the Soviet Union had been split up. Nevertheless the Russian right wing exploited these developments to attack Yeltsin as weak and indulgent, encouraging the centrifugal forces unleashed by the ethnic republics. The right wing's criticism took on an added sting when it was known that Tatarstan, Bashkortostan and Yakutia had stopped paying federal taxes.

In the second week of July 1993 the Russian constitutional conference adopted a new constitution for the federation by 433 votes to 62, with 63 abstentions. Only eight of the 21 ethnic republics and about two-thirds of the *oblast* leaders initialled the draft. These interrelated developments generated the constitutional crisis that culminated in the attack on the Russian parliament, which had refused to accept the legality, as well as the legitimacy, of the constitutional conference organised by Yeltsin in order to bypass the parliament.

The Tatars' historical encounters with Russia: conflict of national characteristics

From 1991 to February 1994 Tatarstan's negotiations with Russia dragged on inconclusively. The negotiations between the two sides reflected not only the psychology of each in political terms, but also the Tatars' historical encounters with Russia and their never-ending desire for national freedom. Islam plays a defining role in their psychological make-up and aspirations. Without Islam, the Tatars assert, they would have been assimilated into the Russian culture and swallowed up by Russian Orthodox Christianity, retaining no trace of their own Bulgar–Tatar identity.

The Bulgars, the ancestors of the Tatars, were Turkic people who settled in the middle Volga and lower Kama regions during the first half of the eighth century. Islam first appeared among them in the ninth century, but in 922 a determined effort to spread Islam among the Bulgars was made by an Abbasid caliph, Jafar Al-Muktadir, who sent Ahmed Ibn-Fadhlan, a missionary, to the Bulgar state. By the end of the tenth century practically all the Bulgar population had been converted to Islam.

At that time Russia was confined to Kiev and the lands of Moscovy. In the eleventh to twelfth centuries the Bulgar state expanded and its borders reached the River Zai and touched Samara in the south. From the tenth to the thirteenth centuries the Bulgar state and the Russian principalities conducted trade relations, but also frequently clashed with each other. In 1223 the fear of the Mongol invasion temporarily ended the hostilities. During these centuries the Bulgar state achieved a high level of culture and civilisation. (Ruins of their magnificent mosques and palaces still exist in the port city of Bulgar, not very far from Kazan, which the author visited in the summer of 1993.) Khorazmian Turkic – in Arabic script – was widely used as the literary language, as it was in Crimea.

The long-feared Mongol invasion became a reality in 1236 when Genghis Khan's (d. 1227) grandson, Batu (d. 1255), invaded and conquered the Bulgar state. Batu's army went on to conquer Russia in the winter of 1240. Because Bulgars had been drafted into this army as Tatars (the conquered people) the Mongolian invasion of Russia came to be known as the Tatar conquest.

The Mongols (or in Russian historiography, the Tatars) ruled over Russia for 250 years. Commenting on their rule, D. Mackenzie Wallace (writing in the 1870s) stated that 'The Khans never dreamed of attempting to Tatarise their Russian subjects. They demanded simply an oath of allegiance from the Princes, and a certain sum of tribute from the people. The vanquished were allowed to retain their land, their religion, their language, their courts of justice, and all their other institutions'. It is a strange quirk of history that Batu's descendant, Berke Khan (ruled 1256–1266) adopted Islam, the religion of the Tatars, instead of Christianity, the religion of the Russians. This conversion of the Mongols to Islam led to the blending of the Mongol and Tatar cultures and eventually the Mongols became totally assimilated. Consequently Mongol history became the Tatar patrimony.

The Kazan khanate, the successor to the Bulgar state and the Golden Horde, was located in the mid Ural Basin, around the confluence of the Volga and Kama Rivers. This territory corresponded approximately to the Tatar autonomous Soviet socialist republic, established in 1920 by Lenin. The present republic of Tatarstan covers 67 800 square kilometers and is bordered by the republics of Mariy-el, Udmurtia, Chuvashia and Bashkortostan. The latter is Turkic-Muslim and Bashkorts speak the Tatar language with regional variations. The population of 3.68 million comprises 48.5 per cent Tatars, 43.3 per cent Russians, 3.7 per cent Chuvashes and 4.5 per cent other nationalities.

The protracted conflict between the Tatars and the Russians reached its climax in 1552 when Ivan the Terrible conquered the Tatar state and firmly established Russian rule. For the first time the Russian state came to include a non-Slavic, non-Christian population that was essentially Central Asian in its cultural make-up. Before the conquest of the Kazan khanate the Russian tsardom had covered 47 000 square miles, but after the conquest it grew to 125 000 square miles. Ivan the Terrible and his successors ruled the Tatars with repressive policies that included anti-Islamic campaigns and the forcible conversion of Muslim Tatars to Christianity; cultural assimilation; confiscating fertile Tatar lands in river valleys and allotting them to Russians; and dispersing the Tatars to Central Asia.

In his book *Russia* (1877) Mackenzie Wallace shed light on the anti-Islamic campaigns and the mass conversion of the Tatars (the present author was informed in the summer of 1994 that there were still approximately 100 000 baptised Tatars in Tatarstan). Converts were called upon to hold firmly and unwaveringly to the Christian faith and its dogmas. According to Wallace, the government ordered its officials to 'pacify, imprison, put in irons, and thereby unteach and frighten from the Tatar faith those who, though baptised, don't obey the admonitions of the metropolitan [the highest religious authority of the Russian Orthodox Church]'. Any person convicted of converting a Christian to Islam was stripped of all civil rights and sentenced to imprisonment with hard labour for a term of 8–10 years. It was estimated that by 1725 some 40 000 Tatars had been baptised. In 1740 the Russian government ordered that all newly built mosques be destroyed and the construction of new ones was prohibited.

Forced conversion led some Tatars to drown themselves in the Volga. Even today, with tears in their eyes Tatars relate to their children the tragedy of these doomed people, who became *shahid* (martyrs) in their eyes. The confiscation of fertile lands forced others to flee to Siberia

Table 9.1   Location of Tatars in the Soviet Union Republics 1926–89

Republic	1926	1937	Population 1959	1970	1979	1989
Russia	3 214 043	3 610 718	4 074 669	4 757 913	5 016 087	5 543 371
Ukraine	22 281	24 242	61 527	76 212	90 542	133 596
Belorussia	3777	3475	8654	10 031	10 911	12 552
Uzbekistan	28 297	27 960	44 810	573 733	648 764	656 601
Kazakstan	79 758	92 096	191 925	287 712	313 460	311 151
Georgia	599	–	5441	5856	5165	4714
Azerbaijan	9948	–	29 552	31 787	31 350	28 564
Lithuania	–	–	3023	3460	4006	5188
Moldavia	–	–	1047	1850	2637	3477
Latvia	–	–	1836	2688	3772	4888
Kirghizstan	4902	17 483	56 266	69 373	72 018	72 992
Tajikistan	982	16 604	56 893	70 803	79 529	79 442
Armenia	27	–	577	581	753	506
Turkistan	4790	–	29 946	36 457	40 321	39 277
Estonia	–	–	1535	2205	3195	4070

Source: R. M. Muhammetshin (ed.), *Tatars and Tatarstan* (in Russian) (Kazan: Tatar Book Publishing Co., 1993), p. 25.

and Central Asia, where Tatar communities still exist today. Moreover, Tatars were forbidden to live in Kazan and its environs. The distribution of the Tatar diaspora in the twentieth century is presented in Table 9.1.

After more than 200 years, the Russian State persecution of the Tatars was modified under Catherine the great: a law of 1776 revoked the rules restricting the trading activities of Tatar merchants, and in 1784 Catherine reestablished the rights of the Tatar gentry, who had demonstrated their loyalty to her by opposing the rebellion led by Pugachev. (Bashkorts, on the other hand, under their national leader Salavat Juliev, supported Pugachev's campaigns. An impressive statue of Salavat Juliev stands on a massive height in Ufa, not far from the Bashkort Supreme Soviet.) This act of 1776 organised the Muslim ecclesiastical structure and laid the foundation for Islamic education, making possible the subsequent development of Tatar national life.

In 1917, on the eve of the Bolshevik revolution, the bases of the Tatar culture were Islam, free trade (which had spread to Central Asia) and strong nationalism. These could not coexist with the so-called internationalist, egalitarian, atheistic and consequently anti-Islamic principles of the new Russian rulers, who were determined to Russify the Tatars in the name of secularism.

To cope with Bolshevism some Tatar leaders, particularly Mir Said Sultan Galiev, developed the ideology of national communism, implying that there existed proletarian nations that were exploited by others – a clear reference to the Tatars' repression by the Russians. Ideologically, non-proletarian nations could bypass the capitalist stage of development and leap directly from feudalism or precapitalism to socialism. In his very shrewd interpretation of Marxism–Leninism, Galiev stated that 'All Muslim colonised peoples are proletarian peoples and as almost all classes in Muslim society have been repressed by the colonialists, all classes have the right to be called proletarians ... therefore it is legitimate to say that the national liberation movement in Muslim countries has the character of a socialist revolution'.

Galiev and other national communist leaders were highly instrumental in promoting the concept of the Idel-Ural Republic, which was conceded in principle on 23 March 1918 when *Pravda* printed the NARKOMNAT (Peoples' Commissariat of Nationalities) decree proclaiming the 'territory of southern Ural and middle Volga the Tatar Bashkir Soviet Republic of the Russian Soviet Federation'. The decree carried the signatures of Joseph Stalin, Mullah Noor Vahitov, Sh. Manatov and G. Ibragimov. The decree was not approved by the Bolshevik Party organisation, but it attracted a great deal of support from the Tatars and even some Bashkorts. In May 1918, the Chuvash and Mordivinian people also expressed their support, and requested that their territories be included in the proposed Idel-Ural republic. Only some diehard communists in Kazan and Ufa and the Ural Soviets opposed the idea on the ground that it would encourage nationalism.

Sultan Galiev formally submitted the Idel-Ural Republic proposal to the second All-Russian Congress of the Organisations of the Peoples of the East, which met in Moscow between 22 November and 3 December 1919. However on 13 December 1919 the Central Committee of the Russian Communist Party's Politburo, which at the time was completely dominated by Lenin, decided against the idea. Instead Lenin split the Bashkorts from the Tatars and on 23 March 1919 created the Bashkir Autonomous Soviet Socialist Republic (ASSR). On 27 May the following year the Soviet government issued a decree establishing the Tatar ASSR. Only 1 459 000 of the 4 200 000 Tatars living in the middle Volga area were included in the republic. On 14 June 1922 the Soviet government also excluded the districts of Beleveev, Birsk and Ufa (where Tatars represented the majority of the population) from the Tatar republic and incorporated them into Bashkortostan, thus making

Table 9.2 Population of the Ufimskaya (Ufa) *guberniya*, 1987

Ethnic group	Number	Percentage of total
Russia (including Ukrainian and Belorussian)	839 635	38.20
Bashkort	899 910	40.90
Tatar	184 817	8.40
Mesheryak	20 957	0.95
Teptyar	39 955	1.80

Source: Census of Ufimskaya (Ufa) *guberniya*, 1897.

the Tatars the second largest ethnic group in Bashkortostan after the Russians.

Tatar nationalists continue to maintain that the Soviet government promised to hold a referendum in these districts in order to determine the wishes of the population, but the Bashkorts vehemently deny it. In fact the Bashkorts assert that in the 1920s Bashkorts were in the majority in these three districts, rather than the Tatars; and that subsequent mass repression of the Bashkorts by the Bolsheviks depopulated these regions, eventually turning the Bashkorts into a minority.

In the summer of 1994, when I raised this territorial issue with Bashkort nationalist leaders, they gave me a copy of a memorandum of 5 May 1990 from the Presidium of the Supreme Soviet of Baskorian ASSR to Murtaza G. Rahimov (later president of Bashkortostan) indicating the demographic predominance of Bashkorts in the 1920s (Table 9.2).

Thus Lenin's socialist government drove a wedge between the Bashkorts and Tatars, two Muslim-Turkic peoples sharing a common language and culture but with different ethnic backgrounds. Despite the Bashkorts' claim, which is backed up by reliable statistical data, the fact remains that today Bashkorts are only the third largest group in Bashkortostan, after the Russians and Tatars. This demographic anomaly is a source of friction between Tatarstan and Bashkortostan, and the Bashkort leaders suspect that the Tatars in their republic would like to rejoin their own republic, reducing Bashkortostan to a much smaller size. This potentially irredentist issue has prompted a tacit alliance between Bashkorts and Russians, directed against the Tatars within the body-politic of Bashkortostan.

Since 1552 Tatars and Russians have developed stereotypes of each other. In the Russians' perception Tatars are 'cruel', 'uncivilised', 'aggressors' and 'an eternal enemy' who made them carry the Tatar yoke for 250 years. These negative images have been passed down through the generations. Tatars, for their part, look upon the Russians as 'lawless rulers' and 'oppressors of other nationalities', who are determined to Russify them in order to wipe them out. (Lenin, in a fit of liberality, once called the Russian state 'a jailhouse of nationalities'.) The concept of the Tatar yoke provides eternal justification for Russia's domination of the Tatars. It is overlooked, however, that Mongol aggression disappeared from the Russian lands, and that the Russian people did not have to endure the process of Tatarisation. Russian domination of the Tatars, on the other hand, has acquired a seemingly endless character. Russia looks upon the Tatar lands as its own and the Tatar population as an ethnic minority.

The memory of the Tatar yoke was also present in Lenin's mind when he refused to accord the status of union republic either to Tatarstan or to Bashkortostan. When in December 1919 the Idel-Ural proposal was submitted to him, it included not only the territory of Tatarstan but also of Bashkortostan and three *oblasts*: Orenburg, Magnitogorsk and Chelyabinsk. Lenin instead established two autonomous republics – Tatarstan and Bashkortostan – and then interposed between Kazakhstan and Bashkortostan the three *oblasts* of Orenburg, Magnitoyorsk and Chelyabinsk, thus surrounding the conceptual state of Idel-Ural by Russian territory. This also denied the two autonomous states the constitutional right to secede from the Soviet Union as they were now surrounded by Russian territory. The right to secede was, however, conceded to the 15 union republics.

Without a grasp of the past and present dynamics of Russian–Tatar relations their current negotiations cannot be appreciated. In the process of negotiating a new set of relations in the post-Soviet period, both sides have made constant references to the past as well as to contemporary imperatives.

Russian–Tatar negotiations for sovereignty

Between 1990 and 1994 four rounds of negotiations were held in Moscow between the two parties. The Tatar government's strategy was by no means to collide head-on with Russia but to maintain social peace in the republic, despite the fact that Tatar nationalist leaders and parties were not reluctant to take up arms against Russia in order to obtain national self-determination. President Mintimer Shaymiyev's government and the opposition parties reached a tacit understanding to pursue the following objectives: (1) a confederal arrangement with Russia while retaining complete independence; (2) membership in the United Nations; (3) international recognition of Tatarstan's sovereignty, with a guarantee of economic independence; and (4) full control over Tatarstan's natural resources, particularly oil.

Under Mintimer Shaymiyev's leadership the Tatarstan Supreme Soviet took its first bold step: on 30 August 1990 it declared state sovereignty and that the economic resources of the republic would henceforth become its 'exclusive property'. This declaration should not be read as a declaration of secession – the Supreme Soviet only 'reformed' Tatarstan's status to that of union republic, equal to that of the fifteen other republics. It also made Russian and Tatar joint state languages. In 1991 the positions of president and vice president were introduced, and on 21 June Mintimer Shaymiyev was elected the first president and Vasily Likhachev vice president.

First round of negotiations

The Tatar leaders' negotiations with Russia on union republic status began on 12 August 1991. Well-known members of the Tatar delegation were Rafael Khakimov, then principle advisor to the president of Tatarstan, and Indus Rizzakovich Tagirov, a leading Tatar scholar and dean of the history faculty at Kazan University. President Yeltsin's principle negotiator was his state secretary, Gennady Burbolis. The Tatar delegation relied heavily on the past Soviet commitments; however under the changed circumstances these had ceased to imply any moral obligation on the part of Russia. The Tatar delegation nevertheless invoked resolutions passed by the third Russian Congress of the Soviets in January 1918 that (1) the Russian Federation would be based upon the principle of freedom and equality among the Soviet republics; (2) the republics were to join the federation voluntarily; and (3) the republics could decide for themselves whether or not to join. While Burbolis confirmed the accuracy of this historical invocation, he treated it as mere ideological rhetoric. Furthermore the 19 August coup against Gorbachev occurred during the negotiations and radically changed the political dynamics.

During the negotiations Burbolis proposed that a referendum be held in Tatarstan to determine the preference of the population. Perhaps he was counting on the loyalty of the resident Russians to vote negatively on the question of sovereignty for Tatarstan. The Tatar leadership accepted the challenge and organised a referendum for 21 March, 1992 on the question: 'Do you agree that the Republic of Tatarstan is a sovereign state, subject to international law, and forming its relations with the Russian Federation, other republics and states on the basis of legal agreements?' The question, however, went beyond the scope of a declaration of state sovereignty when the last clause was changed to 'on

Table 9.3   Results of the referendum on Tatarstan sovereignty, 21 March 1962

Total number of eligible voters	2 600 297
Number of citizens who received ballots	2 134 271
Number of participants	2 132 357
Number of citizens who answered yes	1 309 056
Number of citizens who answered no	794 444
Number of invalid ballots	28 851

Source: *White Book of Tatarstan* (Kazan: President's Office, 1993), p. 14 (personal copy).

the basis of equal agreement'. Stunningly, the result of the referendum was 61 per cent in favour of independence in a 79 per cent turnout. The breakdown is shown:- in Table 9.3.

On the eve of the referendum Yeltsin had said in a televised address that the referendum was aimed at secession and could lead to ethnic violence. President Shaymiyev adopted a moderate and conciliatory stance and denied any plan to secede immediately. For its part the Tatar delegation now had a clear understanding that Russia was not prepared to accept Tatar sovereignty and independence. Burbolis suggested that relations between Tatarstan and Russia would be asymmetrical and based on some elements of confederation. When the Tatars pressed Burbolis to include the concept of Tatar sovereignty in a new treaty between the two republics, Burbolis shot back: 'Then the sovereign rights of Russia must also be included in the treaty'.

In order to assert Russia's sovereign rights, Burbolis suggested that the terms of the Federal Treaty of 13 March 1992, which other autonomous republics had signed, should be integrated into any future treaty with Tatarstan. The Federal treaty divided political power into three categories: (1) powers of the Russian Federation; (2) areas of joint jurisdiction; and (3) full powers of the republics. Article I of the treaty listed 20 items of Russian state power, including, significantly: (1) the federal constitution and its observance; (2) the protection of human, civil and minority rights; (3) the formation of federal state bodies; (4) the protection and management of state property; (5) the establishment of federal policies and programmes for economic, social, cultural and national development throughout the federation; (6) the establishment of a unified market, plus control over finance, currency, credit and customs regulations, the issuing of money, pricing policy, and federal economic services, including federal banks; (7) the federal budget, federal taxes and fees, and federal funds for regional development; (8) federal power engineering systems, nuclear power engineering and fissionable materials, transportation, railroads, information and communications, and activities in outer space; (9) foreign policy, international relations and issues of war and peace; (10) foreign economic relations; (11) defence and security, including defence production and determination of the procedures for the sale and purchase of weapons; (12) the protection of state borders, territorial waters and the continental shelf of the Russian Federation; (13) the judicial system and its related structures. These thirteen categories of power were so comprehensive that no autonomous republic could possibly escape Moscow's domination.

Article II listed 11 items that would be subject to joint jurisdiction and Article III listed three items over which the republics would enjoy

Table 9.4   Autonomy of state

Joint jurisdiction	Full state power by the republics
1. Ensuring that the constitutions of the republics correspond to the Russian laws and constitution	1. Independent participation in international and foreign economic relations, if not at variance with the constitutional laws of Russia and the treaty. Coordination to be exercised by Russia
2. Law and order, public safety	2. Russian law and republic legislation to regulate use of land, subsidy resources, water and other natural resources
3. Use of natural resources, ecological safe guards	3. A republic's preliminary consent is needed to proclaim a state of emergency in that republic
4. Education, science, culture, sports	4. A republic and the Russian Federation can transfer the exercise of power to each other (Articles IV and V)
5. Social security, family protection, public health	
6. Natural disasters and epidemics	
7. Taxation in the republics	
8. Laws on labour, family, land, housing	
9. The notary office system	
10. Protection of small ethnic communities	
11. Local government	
12. Federal principles of legislation to be followed by the republics	

Source: 'The Text of Russia's Federal Treaty', *Rossiiskaya Gazeta*, 18 March 1992; CDSP, vol. xliv, no. 13 (1992).

full state power. Table 9.4 highlights the extent to which the autonomous states retained their cherished autonomy.

By 13 March 1992 only 18 autonomous republics had signed the treaty. Bashkortostan signed it with a four-point economic supplement; Tatarstan and Chechnya refused to sign. Designed to reestablish Russian control over the destiny of the autonomous republics, the Federal treaty was seen in its true colours by the Tatar negotiators, who rejected it outright. Clearly Article I of the treaty gave sweeping powers to Moscow over the autonomous republics, Article II further reduced the scope of the republic's authority, and Article III lowered the republics to the status of minor municipal corporations. The Russian delegation, however, wanted the negotiations to continue and a second round was organised.

Second round of negotiations

The second phase began in March 1992 and ended in January 1993. By 15 September 1992 a tentative understanding had been reached that a bilateral treaty would be signed. At that point Yeltsin cancelled his scheduled visit to Japan, which had been organized by Burbolis. Right-wing nationalists had mounted a vitriolic campaign against Burbolis, who was accused of being 'soft' on the republics. Sergei Borisovich Stankevich, a member of the Russian negotiating team, was uncompromisingly against the Tatars' aim of independence and sovereignty, and conducted a vigorous campaign against Burbolis in the Russian Supreme Soviet. Consequently Burbolis was removed and Sergei Mikhailovich Shakhrai, who later became Russia's vice premier, took over the principal role in the negotiations.

The two sides signed a treaty on economic cooperation on 22 January 1992. Russia conceded that Tatarstan could 'control the exploitation, output and sale of national resources without outside interference', starting with the sale of oil and oil and gas products. Russia would receive its share of oil through 'mutually beneficial annual agreements'.

By 15 August 1992 Tatarstan's draft of the treaty had been submitted to the Russian negotiators. A substantial area of disagreement between the two parties remained. The draft clearly declared the Republic of Tatarstan a sovereign state with full state authority. Tatarstan also claimed the right to have an independent foreign policy and conduct its own foreign economic relations, to establish a military service and to authorise the distribution of Russian Federation military units within Tatarstan. This was a substantial step forward because the draft was signed by I. F. Boltenkova, head of the Russian experts, and F. G. Khamidullin, head of the Tatar experts, and hope was raised that

Tatarstan's sovereign status might be accepted by Russia since the political leaders of both sides had signed the draft.

The meetings were then adjourned until February 1993. The Tatar delegation, however, refused to participate in the proceedings of the constitutional conference.

Third round of negotiations

By this time it was widely perceived within Russia and abroad that Tatarstan was determined to secede from the Russian Federation. Yeltsin and his advisors feared that the other autonomous republics might follow suit, causing the break-up of the Russian Federation. In order to forestall this eventuality Shakhrai went to Kazan in June 1993 and persuaded President Shaimayev to participate in the constitutional conference. This bargaining position was very simple: 'If you refuse to participate, Moscow will refuse to continue the negotiations on the status of Tatarstan'.

The constitutional conference got underway in July 1993. There were five groups, one of which dealt with matters to do with the Federation. The Tatar delegation became active in this group. Among the participants were the leaders of various political parties, businessmen, representatives of local governments and representatives of the government of the Russian Federation. All issues, according to the rules, were to be settled by majority vote. At the conference the senior member of the Tatar delegation, Raphael Khakimov, encountered an unknown Tatar mullah who claimed to represent a Tatar political party in Moscow. Evidently the leaders of some conveniently created political parties were present in substantial numbers to vote according to the Russian authorities' wishes and checkmate the nationalist leaders of the autonomous republics.

Some of the negotiations were conducted at the highest level: Presidents Yeltsin and Shaymiyev personally presented their respective cases. Tatarstan reiterated its by now familiar position: Tatarstan was a sovereign state, subject to international law and 'associated' with the Russian Federation. Yeltsin proposed that the discussion on Tatarstan's status should be postponed and that issues amenable to negotiated settlement should be thrashed out first. Subsequently the two presidents could discuss the status question in order to find a mutually acceptable formula.

Consequently each side initiated proposals on areas of joint or exclusive authority. Russia wanted to have control over matters relating to outer space, standardisation, defence and military production, which was unacceptable to Tatarstan. In the category of 'mutual authority' Russia listed defence, the military – industrial complex, customs regulations, the banking system, payments to the Russian Federation, the apportioning of state property, defining joint property and scientific endeavours of all kinds. The Tatar delegation conceded in principle that military and defence-related installations in Tatarstan would remain under the jurisdiction of Russia, but was not sure how these matters could be handled under joint authority.

Russia reacted negatively to the Tatar position. In order to make the Tatars realise the extent to which their economy was dependent on Russia, Moscow withdrew its financing of the military – industrial complex in Tatarstan and state orders for various items were reduced by 40–90 per cent. As a result no meaningful industrial conversion could be implemented, so Tatarstan changed its position on the military–industrial complex and accepted joint control, with the following exceptions: where Russia financed the weapons it would have exclusive control; and in the civilian aspect of production Tatarstan would retain full control.

Despite the resolution of tangled issues no treaty between Russia and Tatarstan was signed – the latter continued to insist on complete independence in a confederal arrangement, with the right to representation in the United Nations in the way that Ukraine had had under the Soviet Union. Tatarstan also worked out a shrewd strategy with nine other autonomous republics for a coalitional approach to the constitutional issues of autonomy and sovereignty. The ten republics were agreed on their demand for sovereign status and that the Russian Federation Treaty should be structured on the basis of the new constitution. Tatarstan, however, added two demands of its own: that Tatarstan be excluded from Article 56 of the draft constitution, which enumerated the autonomous states; and that it would have special relations with Russia in accordance with Article 61 of the Tatar constitution.

Moscow's negotiator, Shakhrai, refused to discuss these conditions and handed over the task to the so-called Presidential Group of Negotiators, who subsequently discussed them, but negatively. Essentially the Tatars wanted the article on special relations to be inserted into the constitution first, and then to negotiate the scope of these relations. Yeltsin's team wanted the reverse – Tatarstan should join the federation first and then negotiate a treaty defining the relations. Consequently the Tatar delegation walked out of the conference.

However the delegates of the other nine republics remained, thus Yeltsin succeeded in isolating Tatarstan from its potential supporters.

In Kazan President Shaymayev's government declared that Tatar laws would have priority over Russian laws, and that old laws remained applicable but would be abrogated or amended in the light of changed circumstances. The Kazan government also let it be known that it would welcome other *oblasts* if they raised their status to that of autonomous republic. When the Saverdlovskaya *oblast* proclaimed itself an autonomous republic of the Urals, President Shaymayev's principal counselor, Raphael Khakimov, conveyed Tatarstan's congratulations and offered to exchange envoys. However Khakimov also believed that Shakhrai was deliberately encouraging *oblasts* to follow the example of Saverdlovskaya in order to accuse Tatarstan of leading a campaign to split up the Russian Federation.

Nonetheless an agreement was signed with Russia that enabled Tatarstan to establish strictly economic relations with Lithuania, Hungary, Turkey, Uzbekistan, Ukraine and Crimea. From its production of 600 000 barrels of oil a day, Tatarstan would supply oil to these countries. The economic agreement with Crimea went beyond oil supply to include vehicles produced at the KAMAZ installation, plus other industrial products. A Tatar delegation (consisting of the deputy prime minister, Filza Khamidullin, and Rafail Khakimov) visited Crimea in January 1993 and announced in Simferopol, the capital, that Tatarstan would provide assistance to the Tatar diaspora in Crimea, especially in matters of cultural development. This initiative might not have unduly disturbed Kiev, but alarm bells started to ring in Moscow and provoked headlines such as 'Kazan gains access to warm seas'. Tatar oil was to be transported to Crimea via a serpentine route: tankers would travel down the Volga and then through the Volga-Don Canal, coming out in the Sea of Azov and ending up in the warm water parts of the Black Sea. 'Tatarstan doesn't intend to stop there', *Nezavisimaya Gazeta* contentiously stated on 2 March 1993. Draft agreements with Kazakhstan, Estonia, Latvia and Turkmenia were prepared, but these bold and imaginative initiatives did not lessen Tatarstan's economic dependence on Russia, whose tight control over Tatarstan's affairs remained intact. Nevertheless the Yeltsin administration did not look upon these developments kindly, and perceived Tatarstan to be a very serious threat to the territorial integrity of the Russian Federation, and at best 'a dangerous example' for other autonomous republics.

Yeltsin's tank attack on the White House certainly brought about a psychological change in Tatarstan, facilitating a final settlement between the two sides and the signing of a treaty in February 1994.

Fourth round of negotiations

According to the treaty of 15 February 1994, Tatarstan would be governed by three legal documents: the constitution of the Russian Federation, the constitution of the Republic of Tatarstan and the treaty itself. The 1994 treaty closely followed the pattern of the Federal Treaty of 13 March 1992, but gave a wide margin of autonomy to Tatarstan. The sovereign status of Tatarstan was certainly not acknowledged, which was a source of great disappointment to the Tatar nationalists. Rather than being 'associated', as Tatarstan had wanted, it would be 'united' with the Russian Federation. Article II recognised the Tatarstan constitution and enumerated 15 areas over which Tatarstan would have exclusive authority, while Article III established 22 areas of joint authority.

Article II	*Article III*
Exclusive authority, Tatarstan	**Joint authority, Russia and Tatarstan**
1. Protection of human and civil rights	1. Civil rights and rights of national minorities
2. The republic's tax system	2. Protection of sovereignty and territorial integrity
3. Issues of jurisprudence and notary public	3. The national economy; production of armaments and military equipment; conversion of the defence industry (the share and participation of both parties to be determined by separate agreement)
4. Administrative, family and housing regulations; environmental protection and use of natural resources	4. Settlement of contradictory questions of citizenship
5. The granting of amnesty to individuals convicted in the Tatar courts	5. International and foreign economic relations

Continued

Article II	*Article III*
Exclusive authority, Tatarstan	**Joint authority, Russia and Tatarstan**
6. Possession, use and disposal of land, mineral wealth, water, timber and other resources, including state enterprises, organization, other movable and immovable property except units of federal property (state property to be defined by a separate agreement)	6. Pricing policy
7. Establishment of state governmental bodies, their organization and activities	7. Funds for regional development
8. Issues of republic citizenship	8. Monetary policy
9. Establishment of civil service for citizens who have the right to substitute their service in the armed forces	9. Management of Russian property in Tatarstan, which is transferred to common management (by separate agreement)
10. Maintenance of relations and conclusion treaties and agreements with republics, territories, regions, autonomous districts and the cities of Moscow and St Petersburg (which shall not contradict the three basic documents)	10. Coordinate work on geodesy, meteorology and calendar system
11. Participation in international affairs; establishment of relations and treaties with foreign states (which shall not contradict the three basic documents); participation in international organizations.	11. Funds for common programmes, e.g. national disaster relief
12. Establishment of a national bank (pursuant to a separate agreement)	12. Coordination of joint power system, highways, railways, pipe, air and tubing, communications and information
13. Independently conduct foreign economic activity (the delimitations to be settled by a separate agreement)	13. Management of duty-free movement of transportation, cargoes and production by air, sea, river, rail and pipeline

Continued

Article II	*Article III*
Exclusive authority, Tatarstan	**Joint authority, Russia and Tatarstan**
14. Conversion of enterprises (pursuant to a separate agreement	14. Environmental management; prevention of ecological disasters.
15. Establishment of state awards and honorary titles for the Republic of Tatarstan	15. Policy on social matters: employment patterns, migration and social welfare
	16. Health, family protection, education, science, culture, sport; tracing of national specialists for schools, institutions, culture, news media; native language literature, and research into history and national cultures
	17. Personnel for justice and law enforcement
	18. Settlement of litigation, arbitration and notary public questions
	19. Crime prevention; coordination of the activities of police agencies and security forces
	20. Establishment of common principles for the organization of state bodies and local government
	21. Legislation on labour, family law, housing, land, mineral resources surrounding environment
	22. Common use of land, mineral resources, water and other natural resources
	23. Execute other authority established by mutual agreement

Source: Treaty of 15 February 1994 between the Russian Federation and the Republic of Tatarstan (Kazan: President's Office).

In addition to 23 areas where Russia would exercise joint authority in Tatarstan, there were 17 areas over which it would have exclusive power. Some of these were couched in general terms as if they were applicable to the entire federation, but some applied specifically to Tatarstan (Article IV):

- Adoption and amendment of the Russian Federation's laws and constitution, control of their observance and implementation of the federal system.
- Protection of the rights of national minorities, civil rights and issues of citizenship.
- Establishment of federal legislative, executive and judicial power.
- Federal state property and its management.
- Federal policy and programmes for the economic, ecological, social, cultural and national development of the Russian Federation.
- Establishment of a common market, including finance, currency, credit, customs regulations, money supply, general pricing policy, federal economic agencies, including federal banks.
- The federal budget, taxes and duties; funds for regional development.
- The federal power (energy) system, nuclear energy, fissionable materials, federation transportation, communication and information systems and the space authority.
- Foreign policy and international relations; international agreements and questions of war and peace.
- Foreign economic relations *vis-à-vis* the Federation.
- Defence and security.
- State frontiers, territorial waters, air space, exclusive economic area of the Federation's continental shelf.
- The judicial system.
- Federal collision law (law of torts).
- The meteorological service.
- State awards and honorary titles.
- The federal state service.

Some of these powers were also listed in Article III (areas of joint authority), but their presence in Article IV means that Russia could take action in Tatarstan simply by invoking the latter article without the prior agreement of Tatarstan, even though Article VI states that both sides 'have no right to issue any legal acts on issues that do not relate to their area of responsibility'. Finally, each side agreed to provide plenipotentiary representation in the capital city of the other. Despite the latter agreement it should be kept in mind that the sovereigns rarely consult treaties and very seldom observe legal niceties, especially when dealing with subordinate entities in sensitive political circumstances.

So all in all, of the 55 areas of authority listed in the treaty, Russia acquired power over 40 including 17 exclusive and 23 joint ones, while Tatarstan retained jurisdiction over 15. If a strong nationalist government were to come to power in Tatarstan, the areas of joint authority would become a source of friction between Moscow and Kazan; if, however, a compliant regime existed in Tatarstan, then Russia's authority would certainly become overwhelming. In that eventuality the 15 areas of Tatarstan authority would pale into insignificance.

One month after the signing of the treaty in Moscow, elections were held in Tatarstan for two seats in the Federal Council of the Russian Federation. The overall turnout was 58.5 per cent, but in the district of Atnisky 99.7 per cent of voters went to the polls. The seats were won by President Mintimer Shaymayev (91.2 per cent) and the chairman of the Tatarstan Supreme Soviet, Farid Mukhametshin (71.1 per cent). In the five districts holding elections to the State Duma, two seats went to the communists, two to candidates supported by President Shaymayev's party (Unity and Progress) and one to a nominee of the local electoral bloc known as Equal Rights and Legality.

Russia's reaction to the treaty

In general the treaty was well received by the Russians. It had a calming impact on their taut nerves and dissipated the Yeltsin administration's fear that a centrifugal force would cause the disintegration of the Russian Federation. Sergei Filatov, Yeltsin's chief of staff, described the constitution of the Russian Federation, the federal treaty and the bilateral treaty of February 1994 as three major landmarks in the strengthening of the Russian Federation. He indicated that the treaty with Tatarstan could serve as an example in arriving at agreements with the autonomous republics of Kabardino-Balkaria, Bashkortostan and Kaliningrad; and also with the most recalcitrant state, Chechnya. Emil Pain, a member of the Presidential Council, described Tatarstan as leading the way in loyalty to Moscow.

Deputy Prime Minister, Sergei Shakhrai, who had taken an active part in the last round of negotiations between Russia and Tatarstan, had in fact developed with his state committee a distinct eleven point nationality policy of his own. Briefly, these eleven points included:

- Equal rights for all peoples of the Russian Federation.
- Recognition of those peoples' right to self-determination.
- Federalism.
- Territorial unity and integrity of the Russian Federation and its members.
- The depoliticisation of nationality policy.
- Reliance on elected bodies of power, whether the centre liked them or not.
- Political methods of settling conflicts.
- The indivisibility of economic policy.
- A nationality policy that would forestall crises.
- Consistency, even in minor matters.
- Mandatory consideration of the complexity of Russian society's religious make-up.

Shakhrai firmly believed that the *oblasts* and autonomous republics presented little threat to the territorial integrity of Russia, and that it instead stemmed from discord among the authorities in Moscow. Shakhrai, whose plan was not designed to concede sovereignty or complete autonomy to any unit of the Russian Federation, was naturally very pleased with the treaty and saw it as a good omen for the unity of the Federation.

To highlight the new status of Tatarstan within Russia and to develop joint mechanisms for implementing the provisions of the treaty, Yeltsin visited Kazan from 30 May to 1 June 1994. Yeltsin's route from the airport to the Kazan kremlin was carefully planned and the streets were hurriedly paved. Shabby buildings received a quick coat of paint. Yeltsin was escorted like a czar into the kremlin. The public response in Kazan to his visit was rather subdued, but to Yeltsin even indifference was a positive sign of the treaty's acceptance.

The negotiations between the two presidents involved the following issues:

- Economic problems.
- Repair of the KAMAZ plant, which had been damaged by fire.
- The modernisation and reconstruction of Kazan airport.
- The construction of a new automobile plant.
- The construction of a bridge over the River Kama.
- The launching of new shareholding enterprises.

For the last project it was agreed that Tatarstan would be given a tax holiday for one year and that the exercise would be a joint venture by both countries. The tax structure was subjected to a great deal of scrutiny because it was found to be discouraging foreign investment. It was also discovered that of the 30 per cent of taxes earmarked for the federal budget, Tatarstan was transferring only 5–6 per cent to the Treasury. The Russian government agreed to offer guarantees to foreigners who invested in Tatarstan's vehicle manufacturing industry, particularly with regard to the KAMAS joint stock company, to which the Export-Import Bank of Japan was willing to grant $400 million in credit.

The two presidents agreed to create a bilateral commission to monitor the implementation of the treaty between Russia and Tatarstan. Shakhrai would head the commission for Russia and Vice President Vasiley Likhachev would do the same for Tatarstan. The most reassuring elements for Yeltsin were that the treaty united Tatarstan with Russia, and that the mechanisms for the implementation of the treaty were being put in place.

While the treaty boosted the morale of the Russian public and most political parties reacted positively to it, critical comments came from the leader of the Communist Party of the Russian Federation, Gennady Zyuganov, who said that the treaty was unacceptable because it signified the 'creation of a confederation'. But even after a casual reading of the treaty no one could say that this was the case. For Zyuganov, the mere fact of Yeltsin negotiating with the president of the autonomous republic amounted to a loosening of Moscow's control, which in his eyes was unacceptable.

Tatar reaction to the treaty

The Tatar reaction to the treaty will be divided into three subsections: (1) President Shaymayev's defence of the treaty, (2) the moderate opposition's views and (3) the nationalists' criticism.

Akrinlap (gradualism): President Shaymayev's defence

Naturally, President Shaymayev was on the defensive. After compromising on the question of sovereignty and independence, Shaymayev suggested a policy of *akrinlap*. Indirectly he confirmed that independence and sovereignty would remain the Tatars' ultimate objectives, but that they could not be achieved in one fell swoop.

Basically, two realities had forced his hand: Tatarstan's economic dependence on Russia, and Russian political pressure. Speaking at a meeting of the Writers' Union in Kazan on 3 June 1994 (where the author was present) he dwelt at length on the economic stranglehold that Russia maintained over Tatarstan. He reminded his audience that Tatarstan's economic enterprises, manufacturing plants and agriculture were dependent on the Russian economy. During 1993, 500 oil wells had lain idle because of the absence of an agreement with Russia, which had used technical means to generate economic pressure – the Russian pipelines had 'failed' to function.

In order to develop economically and improve the living standards of Tatar citizens, Shaymayev's government needed large credits from Russian banks, especially for complex industrial projects, including vehicle manufacturing plants, repair shops at the KAMAZ centre, the modernisation of Kazan airport and a rather expensive bridge over the Kama River. Last, but not least, the kremlin in Kazan needed to be renovated and this would cost several hundred billion rubles. Where was this money supposed to come from? Being a part of Russia's economic space, Tatarstan could justifiably obtain help from Moscow.

Shaymayev ruled out any radical policy to deal with Russia. A radical approach, in his opinion, would result in civil war between Tatars and Russians, thus destroying social harmony in the republic and bringing untold misery to the population. Consequently the policy of *akrinlap* was the best one for Tatarstan. Shaymayev also believed that as a consequence of its treaty with Tatarstan, Russia was no longer a unitary state. However he conceded that the true significance of the treaty would have to be appraised when the need arose for close interpretation of its terms. Shrewdly, he stated that if Russia insisted on the need to bring the republic's constitution into conformity with the Federal constitution, then a ticklish problem would arise. Both parties had clearly recognised the existence of two constitutions; logically, therefore, Tatarstan would be within its right to ask for certain articles of the Russian constitution to conform with Tatarstan's constitution. Resolution of this issue would determine the degree of autonomy that Tatarstan had come to possess.

Shaymayev also highlighted the existence of positive changes in the daily life of the Tatar people. Tatars could now speak their language with pride. Tatar kindergartens, elementary schools, high schools and lyceums had been established in large numbers. Old mosques were reopening and new ones were being built. Muslim institutions of religious scholarship had appeared. Thirty-one Tatar newspapers and seven magazines were being published, as were 66 Russian–Tatar bilingual newspapers. The time allotted to programmes in the Tatar language on radio and TV had increased substantially. In other words the policy *akrinlap* had inaugurated a mini renaissance of Tatar culture.

Finally, in a grand gesture of patronage President Shaymayev donated six million rubles to the Writers' Union.

The moderate opposition's views

Moderate opposition to the treaty was voiced by President Shaymayev's political counsellor, Rafael Khakimov, who had participated in the negotiations with the Russians from 1991–94. A thoughtful and imaginative thinker, Khakimov was not opposed to a peaceful settlement of Tatarstan's relations with Russia, but he believed that a better treaty would have resulted if Shaymayev had been bold enough to stick to Tatarstan's objectives of independence and sovereignty. Khakimov also believed that since the treaty had not been submitted to the Tatar parliament for ratification, it lacked legitimacy.

Because of Khakimov's moderately critical stand a rift developed between him and the president. This rift was intensified during and after the negotiation process. Khakimov published five extensive articles in two well-known publications: *Vatanim Tatarstan* (30 March, 2–9 April 1994) and *Youth of Tatarstan* (numbers 13–16, 1994). These articles brought the rift into the public gaze. Stung by Khakimov's criticism, President Shaymayev eliminated the political section from his administration, forcing Khakimov to vacate his office in the Kazan kremlin.

Khakimov recognised the merits of the treaty, but believed that it did not go far enough with regard to autonomy. Khakimov's very exhaustive analysis of the treaty in the five articles mentioned above raised serious political questions. Now that Tatarstan was governed by three documents – the Russian constitution, the Tatar constitution and the treaty – what would happen if the treaty at some point contradicted the Russian and Tatar constitutions? As long as the treaty was not ratified, it would not be binding on Russia, which could arbitrarily insist upon the superiority of the treaty or of its own constitution. No neutral judicial mechanism existed for its interpretation.

Another important issue was Tatarstan representation in the legislature of the Russian Federation. Khakimov rightly pointed out that the participation of Tatarstan in the legislature was mentioned nowhere in the treaty. Consequently there was no legal basis for holding in Tatarstan elections for seats in the Federal Council of the Russian Federation. Elections were held in Tatarstan only because of political considerations and 'as a kind of compromise with the leadership in Moscow'. Khakimov also asserted that it was a reward to Yeltsin for signing the treaty, as well as a mutually convenient arrangement. In reality, Khakimov asserted, the whole exercise was a product of the fears 'that had influenced the adoption of such a decision – fear of social and economic problems, fear of chauvinism appearing in Russia, and political instability prevailing in that country'.

Finally, Khakimov presented US–Puerto Rico relations as a paradigm to be emulated by Tatarstan and Russia. According to Article 11 of the US–Puerto Rico Treaty, Puerto Rico has one representative in the US Senate and one in the House of Representatives, elected in accordance with the laws of the freely associated state of Puerto Rico. To Khakimov, the logic of US–Puerto Rico relations was clear: Puerto Rico had delegated a number of powers to the United States and adopted certain US laws; to supervise the adoption of laws according to the powers delegated to the United States, one representative for each house of Congress is elected from Puerto Rico, and these representatives are elected according to the laws of Puerto Rico and not those of the United States.

Accordingly Khakimov suggested that Tatar deputies to the Russian federal assembly should be appointed rather than elected, and that this provision did not contradict the constitution of the Russian Federation. Moreover the deputies' responsibilities should be strictly defined. In other words, Khakimov would have preferred Tatarstan to be associated with Russia in the same way that Puerto Rico was associated with the United States, since voluntary association, in his eyes, would not restrict the sovereignty of the republic. He believed that '*De jure* act of voluntary delegation of powers to Russia is much more preferable than what we have now – *de facto* performance of these functions by federal organs without any adequate procedure of their delegation.' The logic of Khakimov's argument is that what is voluntarily delegated can later be retracted by an analogous act, and that 'everything done *de facto* is done by the right of force and is given as a result of pressure'.

Tatar nationalists' criticism of the treaty

The Tatar nationalists' reaction was epitomised by Fauziye Bayromova (president of the Tatar Millia Majlis, president of the Ittifaq National party and a member of the Tatar parliament). She believed that the treaty contradicted the will of the people of Tatarstan because in a referendum they had voted for independence and national sovereignty. Consequently she believed that the struggle of the Tatar people would continue, but that it should be conducted by constitutional and legal means. A programme to mobilise international opinion in favour of

Tatars' rights would be launched and publications would be issued condemning the treaty. She added that perhaps another referendum should be held in the republic on acceptance or rejection of the treaty.

In obvious despair, Fauziye Baromova told this author that the treaty 'took everything from us, including our national aspirations'. She asserted that other autonomous republics within the Russian Federation had looked to Tatarstan to provide a model by which they could regain their national dignity and sovereignty. As a result of Tatarstan's treaty with Russia those republics were now discouraged and demoralised.

Some concluding observations

Tatarstan is surrounded on all sides by territory that Russia claims to possess by virtue of Ivan the Terrible's conquest in 1552. Tatarstan (along with Bashkortostan) occupy extremely valuable land in geopolitical terms. The Volga–Ural basin, which is the heartland of the two republics, artificially separates Central Asia from Europe, although this basin is actually part of the Central Asian land mass and was culturally Central Asian until 1552, when large-scale Russian penetration and settlement got under way. By virtue of its control over this area, Siberia and the far east of the Continent, Russia claims to be a Eurasian state. Consequently it plays a role in the politics of both Asia and Europe. It would be exceptionally difficult for Russia to grant total independence to Tatarstan, especially as nearly half the population of Tatarstan and Bashkortostan are Russian settlers.

It was within the framework of these geopolitical constraints that the leadership of Tatarstan negotiated the treaty with Russia. The treaty should be seen as a positive achievement because Russia had ruled over these areas autocratically since 1552, so the granting of autonomy within the Russian Federation was a significant milestone that should not be dismissed lightly. The Bolsheviks had also granted autonomy to Tatarstan, but very soon into their rule it was whittled away. What will happen under the new 'democratic dispensation' remains to be seen, although Khakimov's cautious approach was designed primarily to safeguard the republic against future dictatorial developments.

Despite the importance of the treaty, it should be pointed out that it lacks legitimacy and is on shaky ground legally. It was signed only by the presidents and prime ministers of Russia and Tatarstan. In order for it to acquire both legality and legitimacy it will have to be ratified by the Russian State Duma and the Tatar parliament. However if it were ratified by a referendum it might upset ethnic relations in Tatarstan.

If the treaty is to be ratified in the Tatar parliament, then naturally the legislature will first conduct hearings on the treaty, and as well as legal and technical points, political issues may be raised. Tatarstan citizens may want another round of negotiations between Russia and Tatarstan on certain issues. Renegotiated terms would add legitimacy to the treaty and elevate its status as a legal document in international law.

Finally, nationalists would insist that the treaty should not be seen as indefinitely binding, freezing Tatarstan's relations with Russia in the current dependent mould. They would demand periodic review of the treaty in order eventually to achieve the status of an independent and sovereign state with full power to establish diplomatic relations with states throughout the world. However, in recognition of Tatarstan's geographical constraints, they visualise their country as being neutral in power politics and as being 'associated' with Russia in respect of certain well-defined objectives of national security.

Appendix 9.1   Participants in the negotiations: 1991–94

Russia

Yeltsin, Boris Nikolaevich (president)
Chernomyrdin, Victor Stepanovitch, (prime minister)
Shakhrai, Sergei Mikhailovich (deputy prime minister)
Burbulis, Genady Eduardovich (secretary of state under the president of the Russian Federation)
Yarov, Yuri Fyodorovich (deputy chairman of the Supreme Soviet)
Tishkov, Valery Aleksandrovich (chairman of the State Committee of the Russian Federation for National Policy, minister of the Russian Federation)
Abdulatipov, Ramazan Gadzhimuradovich (chairman of the Soviet of Nationalities of the Supreme Soviet)
Gen, Nikolai Leonidovich (deputy chairman of the Committee of the Soviet of Nationalities for the National–State System and Interethnic Affairs of the Supreme Soviet)
Stankevich, Sergei Borisovich (adviser to the president)
Granberg, Aleksandr Grigorjevich (adviser to the president)
Turbin, Vitaly Borisovich (deputy minister of internal affairs)
Korolyov, Stanislav Andreevich (deputy minister of finance)
Mironov, Valery Ivanovich (deputy minister of defence)
Miroshin, Boris Vladimirovich (deputy head of the Legal–State Department under the president)
Yarov, Yuri Fyeodorovich (deputy prime minister)
Yusupov, Magomed Yusupovich (deputy minister for the economy)

Voronin, Yuri Mikhailovich (chairman of the Committee for Budget Plans, Taxes and Prices of the Supreme Soviet)
Lobov, Oleg Ivanovich (first deputy prime minister)
Fyodorov, Nikolai Vaciljevich (minister of finance)
The following were members of the group of experts: D. Dmitriyev, N. Bogajenko, O. Tiunov, G. Kalvan, Y. Melnik, Rashid Abdulovich Salikov, Igor Georgievich Kosikov, Lyubov Fyodorovna Boltenkova, Yevgeny Alekseevich Danilov, Aleksandr Ljvovich Mukaed.

Tatarstan

Shaimiyev, Mintimer S. (president)
Sabirov, M. G. (prime minister)
Mukhametshin, F. Kh. (deputy chairman of the Supreme Soviet)
Likhachev, Vasily Nikolaevich (vice president)
Valeeva, Zilya (first deputy chairman of the Supreme Soviet)
Khamidullin, Filzya Garifovich (deputy prime minister)
Kobelev, Gely Vasiljevich (chairman of a standing committee of the Supreme Soviet)
Kolesnik, Aleksey Alekseevich (chairman of a standing committee of the Supreme Soviet)
Khafisov, Rustem Shamiljevich (chairman of a standing committee of the Supreme Soviet)
Khakimov, Rafeal Sibgatovich (adviser to the president)
Arslanov, Shaukat Raufovich (minister for foreign economic relations)
Nagumanov, Dmitry Nagumanovich (minister of finance)
Salabaev, Albert Mikhailovich (justice minister)
Safiullin, Fandas Shakirovich (chairman of a standing committee of the Supreme Soviet)
Tagirov, Indus Rizyakovich (dean of the historical faculty at Kazan University)
Shamgunov, R.
Gazizullin, F. R. (deputy prime minister)
Nagumanov, D.
Safiullin, F.
Khamidullin, F.
Zheleznov, B. L. (member of the Committee for the Constitutional Control of the Republic of Tatarstan)

Notes and References

1. *New York Times*, 5 October 1994.
2. *Moscow News*, no. 22 (3–9 June, 1994).
3. Official Department, *Federal Treaty* (Treaty on Demarcation Objects of Justification and Powers Between the Federal Bodies of State Power of the Russian Federation and the Bodies of Power of the Republics Within the Russian Federation); *Russiikaya Gazetta*, 18 March 1992, p. 2 (*CDSP*, vol. XLIV, no. 13, 1992).

4. This conviction is articulated in scholarly Tatar literature. Moreover it has been stated in my presence on numerous occasions that it needs no documentation.

5. A. P. Kovalevskii (ed.), *Kniga Akhmeda Ibn-Fadlana i ego puteshestvie na volgu v 921–922g. Stat'i, perevody i Komentarii* (Kharkov, 1956), p. 131. There is an earlier edition of Ibn-Fadlan's work: I. Iu. Krachkovskii (ed.), *Puteshestvie Ibn-Fadlana na Volgu* (Moscow and Leningrad), 1939. Azade-Ayse Borlich, *The Volga Tatars: A Profile in National Resilience* (Stanford, CA: Hoover Institution Press, 1986), pp. 11, 198, fn 2.

6. A. Bodrogligeti, 'The Function of the Khorazmian Turkic Literary Language: The Problem of the Interference of Lexical Systems', *Tatarila* (Edendum Curavif Abdulla Tukain Kulttuurislura Y. Y.; Stulia ijn Honorem Yurai Daher, Anno, MEMLXX, Sexagenario), (Vammala, 1987), pp. 44–5.

7. D. Mackenzie Wallace, *Russia* (New York: Henry Holt, 1877), p. 347.

8. *Obrutchef: Voenno-Statistitcheski Sbornik* (St Petersburg, 1871); Mackenzie Wallace, *Russia*, op. cit.

9. Czar Ivan the Terrible was notorious for cruelty even towards his own family. For example he gave a thorough beating to his pregnant daughter-in-law because when he went into her room she was 'too scantily clad'. His son and heir protested, and in a fit of rage, his father struck him dead with a blow of his iron staff. Ivan the Terrible was unlikely to show more leniency towards the vanquished Tatars. V. O. Kliuchevsky, *A Course in Russian History: The Seventeenth Century*, trans. Natalie Duddington (New York: M. E. Sharpe., 1994), p. 13.

10. Mackenzie Wallace, *Russia*, op. cit., p. 159.

11. *Ulozhenie O Nakazaniakh*, pp. 184, 161.

12. Rorlich, *Azade-Ayse, The Volga Tatars: A Profile in National Resilience*, p. 41. *(Stanford, Ca.: Hoover Institution Press, 1986)*

13. A. Iskhaki, *Idel Ural* (Paris, 1933), p. 25.

14. Serge A. Zenkovsky, 'A Century of Tatar Revival', *American Slavic and East European Review*, no. 10 (1953), pp. 303–18.

15. A Arsharni and Kh. Gabidullin, *O Cherki Panislamizma i Pantuurkizma v Rossii* (Moscow, 1931), p. 78; Alexandre A. Bennigsen and S. Enders Wimbush, *Muslim National Communists in the Soviet Union* (Chicago, Ill.: University of Chicago Press, 1979), p. 42.

16. The decree was signed by M. Kalinin, chairman of the All-Russia Central Executive Committee, and is included in *Documents, Papers and Materials on the Formation of the Bashkortostan Autonomous Soviet Socialist Republic*, Central Archive of the BASSR (Ufa: Bashkirskoe Knizrol *Izdatelstva*, 1959), pp. 738–739 (in Russian).

10
Russia–Tatarstan: Economic Reform Problems

M. G. Galeyev

The search for a viable paradigm of development in the new Russia

The creation of a viable paradigm for the development of Russia in the new geopolitical environment is a problem for which there is no existing model. Internally a viable model would reduce the probability of significant social tensions; externally Russia would shift from a confrontational to an accomodative stance *vis-à-vis* the international community. The policy of confrontation exhausted the country's resources and led to its collapse in 1991. We would argue that the events of December, 1991 were not accidental or the result of human error, but were the natural outcome of the perniciousness of the previous system, which was based on the philosophy of opposition to the rest of the world. Any renewed attempt to act like a great power would have had even more disastrous consequences. The recent reforms of the post-Soviet environment show that a viable model of development has not yet been found. One of the reasons for this is that many of the initial premises were faulty and unable to provide the basis for renewal. For example, the premise of the (Moscow, 1996) address of the President of the Russian Federation to the Federal Assembly on the subject of national security, was that Russia was the natural successor to the Soviet Union. This was clearly an attempt to combine market reform with the prior great power pretentions which had overloaded the economy with military-industrial demands.

While the Soviet Union was one of the world's largest producers of a wide range of mineral resources, its living standards lagged far behind those of developed countries. This occurred because the economic structure was inefficient and the military consumed the lion's share of the economy. The military took precedence over all other institutions, including fundamental and applied science. Although there were obvious achievements in science and technology, the average citizen only benefitted marginally from them. Living standards did not improve in proportion to the resources invested and this undermined developmental incentives.

The ruptured economic ties between the countries of the former Soviet Union contributed to a drop in productivity and more recently gave impetus to a wave of support for reintegration. This public mood is especially strong in Russia and Belarus. According to some experts, only a 25–30 per cent of the drop in the Russian Federation's GDP was caused by reforms, while the rest was caused by the ruptured economic ties with the CIS countries, the Baltic states and the former COMECON countries. At the same time most of the CIS countries and especially the Baltic states wish to avoid reintegration by all means. This may be explained in terms of political and economic reasons.

For example, the integration that took place in the past was always under the strong control of the totalitarian state. Cooperative links forged by the center were often not economically sound. Moscow intentionally arranged the links so as to strengthen, often artificially, the existing interdependence. Thus Belarus, which is poor in minerals and other raw materials, became a major assembly line for Soviet metal consumption and machine building; and the Asian republics were turned into suppliers of raw materials, especially cotton, which were processed in the territory of Russia.

It is not surprising, therefore, that Belarus is striving to return to the safe industrial environment of the past. Other countries, both those with their own raw material base (such as the Asian republic of Kazakhstan) and those which lack such a base but enjoy the advantages of geographical position (the Baltic states) are attempting to find their own place by integrating themselves into the world community. The difficulties of this course are obvious, but preferable to a renewed loss of state independence and a return to the political status quo ante and the uncompetitive products manufactured within the former Soviet Union. In view of the above, it is not surprising that most of these states want to join NATO, although their motives are not aggressive. NATO membership would entail considerable additional cost. Here we should take into account the determination to influence Russia politically by turning the vector of support away from the military industrial complex, which is becoming increasingly ruinous for the Russian economy. Since many cooperative links were strongly intertwined with the military industrial complex, the severing of such links should not be considered a negative factor.

On the one hand the collapse of the Soviet Union severely hampered the country's productive capability, but on the other hand it precluded the possibility of returning to the ruinous structure of the previous economy. The danger of the present situation is that despite the significant drop in industrial production and the absence of any visible political lobbying in favour of the military industrial complex in Russia, the capacity to mobilise has been maintained, which means that a new spiral of militarisation might occur. There are, however, a number of factors that could hinder such a development.

First, there are problems related to the supply of raw materials: for the first time in many decades there has been no growth in the stocks of raw materials. The stability of the previous political system was based on a number of factors, one of which was the availability of a huge supply of cheaply produced raw materials, compared with average world prices. This enabled the Soviet Union to keep the COMECON countries within its sphere of influence and to bear incredibly high military expenses for a long period of time. The powerful military industrial complex became a key factor in the development of the whole economy and in the rise of the Soviet Union as a great power. For a long time the growth of the raw material stock exceeded the rate of its use due to the large-scale state financing of prospecting works. Now, however, the growth of the raw material stock lags behind even its falling rate of utilisation, not only because of the reduced financing of prospective works, but also because of the depletion of stocks. For instance oil production in Russia in 1991–95 dropped from 452 million tons to 298.4 million while stocks fell from 851.6 million tons to 182.8 million, which means that the stocks were being overconsumed. As the supply of cheap raw materials dwindled the ability to preserve the old political system weakened and that led to the collapse of the state. A large proportion of the huge supply of natural resources had been consumed by the military industrial complex and other energy-consuming sectors of the economy, which was developing in a closed, competition-free environment. The fact that these stocks no longer exist is sufficient reason to revise the paradigm of development. Despite the research conducted by economists from the 1970s to 1980s the Soviet leadership failed to recognise this need, and this also applies to the current Russian leadership.

Moreover it is impossible to manufacture enormous quantities of weapons and simultaneously conduct market reforms. The main buyer of these specific products can only be the state, which obtains the required funds from the budget, necessitating high taxes. However even the current rates of taxation are unacceptable and are impeding the stabilisation of the financial system. Furthermore the budget deficit is obviously speeding up inflation. The size of the deficit is comparable to the country's expenses, which shows the economic absurdity of the claim that the status of a great power can be preserved by increasing its military muscle.

The manufacture of large machinery and a number of other branches of the economy of Tatarstan are connected to the military industrial complex. Even light industries (clothing, furs, footwear) have been engaged in manufacturing products for the military. The profits they could earn from this (sometimes up to 50 per cent) encouraged such enterprises to work with outdated, non-flexible technologies and significantly hampered their quick adaptation to market conditions.

The problems of large enterprises are connected to the absence of profitable state orders and the drying up of a considerable amount of mobile capital, which became a formidable problem for producers wishing to undergo conversion. The alternatives here are obvious: either continue the ruinous course of sitting on two chairs and preserve the depressed state of industry, or conduct radical reforms, which would mean separation of military technologies from civil ones through targeted investment from various sources, thus making such technologies competitive and allowing growth.

In our opinion, there is no hope of supporting military production by means of increased exports. Certain bursts of activity in this respect are possible, but cannot be counted upon. Only conversion and total demilitarisation can stabilise the economy. Besides, this would create a more favorable climate for foreign investment from developed countries and aid the realisation of market reforms.

According to the treaty of 1994 on the demarcation of authority and agreements on property, Tatarstan can travel this road independently and irrespective of the unstable political situation of Russian leadership, which is hesitating between preserving a strong military economy and conducting market reforms. Long-term maintenance of this unstable situation may create a prolonged economic depression and is, in itself, fertile ground for political instability.

As a rule, enterprises which have attempted to combine military preponderance and market conversion have succumbed to economic depression. Weapons production should be transferred to a separate balance sheet and financed by the budget of the Russian Federation. Simultaneously some enterprises should be turned over to the state as soon as possible.

The Russian government maintains the current uncertain situation because it wishes to preserve the potential of the military industrial complex and place the maximum possible responsibility for this on the various regions. However this situation is inherently untenable since it contradicts the logic of reform. The economic situation can be improved by implementing full-scale market conversion and bringing the expenses of manufacturing marketable products to a competitive level. This can be accomplished only if finished products are actively exported on the free market. The prospects of making the economy wealthy through the export of raw materials are nil, since the stocks of cheap resources are already exhausted.

A market economy based on the balance between supply and demand cannot function efficiently in the framework of large scale state orders. Giant enterprises which are inefficient and have poor marketing practices must be dramatically modified if the economy is to grow. Unfortunately an important segment of the society still hopes to restore economic well-being without significantly altering existing large enterprises.

Disagreement and political uncertainty in the Russian leadership and differences in the levels of development of the various regions lead to the conclusion that simultaneous progress on all fronts in every region is impossible. Each region must consider all factors (including economic, geographic and political) and determine its priorities in promoting stabilisation and development. Tatarstan should utilise the political capital which it possesses in the form of the treaty and the agreements. The essence of the treaty is that some authority is held by the republic while other powers are transferred to the federal level. When considering the transferred powers, Tatarstan is a part of the Russian Federation, however in the case of the authority held by the republic, Tatarstan is a sovereign state.

Determination of the status is not a mere political formality, but a matter of great practical importance. There is no point in enacting legislation if the appropriate spheres of state and federal jurisdiction are not clearly demarcated and universally understood. The treaty recognises the right of the people of Tatarstan to own the land, mineral resources and property. It is necessary to develop operating procedures on these and other important issues.

Economic aspects of federal formation in Russia

Successful formation of federalism depends on adequate and simultaneous political and economic reforms and their implementation. There is little sense in speaking about federal structure if the constituent entities are not allowed to develop sufficiently. The existing budget of the Russian Federation does not support the federal structure because some 55 per cent of the taxes are allocated to the centre. Moreover this does not include the substantial revenues going into the federal budget (10-21 per cent) from foreign economic activity. These percentages are several times higher than those of the majority of countries, whose range typically is from 2–5 per cent. These figures bear witness not only to the protectionist foreign economic policy based on high customs fences, but to the redistribution of (natural resource) derived revenues from the regions to the center.

There are also additional factors which contribute significantly to the actual assets which are available to the federal centre. These include revenues derived from the issuance of state securities, which result in the outflow of financial resources from the regions and also serve as latent generators of inflation. Moreover, the illegal retention (of up to several months) by the centre of a significant portion of the liquidity generated by the regions results in an extra financial fund which can be manipulated by the federal centre. This inflicts economic losses on the regions, significantly impedes the democratisation of the society and causes internal tensions in the federation. The funds actually available to the federal centre constitutes 80–85 per cent of all federal financial resources. Therefore there is little point in speaking about federative relations. The situation closely resembles the one prevailing in the former totalitarian state which, although it was formally committed to regional development and prosperity, did not accomplish either.

Considering that well over half of the regions are chronically subsidised, it is problematic to speak about real federalism. If a federation is to be developed, each region must be encouraged to become fiscally self-sufficient and tackle its own social problems. If the dependency mentality is maintained it retards regional self sufficiency. Possible mechanisms to encourage regional development include the elimination of region to center financial flow and participation of the federal center in specific regional business projects. This latter approach has been employed in some federative states.

The evolution of political federalism plays an important part in demolishing the deeply rooted budgetary system of the unitary state. The (1994) treaty between Tatarstan and Russia provided a political solution to the economic centre–region problem; the region was accorded the opportunity of retaining the major portion of revenues which were generated in the republic. The basis for the development of the republic was laid by transferring the ownership of the land, mineral resources and property to the Tatar people and by budgetary agreements which make it possible to form a new federation in Russia. The huge size of Russia, differences in levels of development in the various regions, and diverse histories and political outlooks permit the formation of federalism in Russia solely on an asymmetrical basis characterised by differing degrees of regional independence. A contractual and constitutional form of emerging federation is a reality which has created a certain political balance inside Russia and any attempt to revise this balance threatens to disturb it.

The new status of Tatarstan: intensifying the reforms

In contrast to the prior system in which Tatarstan depended on Moscow for resources and was isolated from the outside world, the republic now intends to tackle its own problems by relying primarily upon its own resources and capabilities and by cooperating with other states on a mutually beneficial basis. Despite all the complications of this transitional period, this approach provides real possibilities for the republic to come out of non-existence and to occupy its own place in the world. Recognition of the right to own land, mineral resources and fixed and movable property created an important legal foundation for the republic's independence.

Any property is valuable only when it is efficiently used. Denationalisation and privatisation are essential elements of efficient market reform. Sufficient time has elapsed to suggest that the model chosen by Tatarstan will be successful. The principal elements of the model are as follows.

In the first stage, conditions are created whereby most of the property is owned by the republic. This is achieved by intentionally devaluing Russian vouchers, reevaluating basic funds to reflect their real market value and by creating individual privatisation deposits (IPD) which are attractive for the citizens. The second stage addresses the conditions which are necessary to attract investors. A number of legislative acts on this subject have already been promulgated and many others are pending.

Notwithstanding the importance of the privatisation process, the fundamental problem is the adaptation of the economy to market standards, i.e. the critical restructuring of the entire basis of the economy, which can be accomplished only with continuing investment. Since there is a wide range of industries in the republic and many are undergoing dramatic changes in technology and the structure of production, we will focus on principal industrial blocks.

The collapse of the centralised distribution system highlighted the necessity for the republic to achieve self-sufficiency in basic food stuff. Many countries regard this problem to be pivotal; for any country it is a main constituent of economic security. Two main indicators of the degree of foodstuff self-sufficiency are internationally recognised.

- Annual carryover stocks should not be lower than 60 days or 17 per cent of the total volume of consumption;
- Average per capita grain production should equal one Mt./year for food and fodder gains.

Since agriculture is an important sector of the economy and significant positive changes have been noted in this area, it has been comprehensively supported despite its low profitability. The problem of generating sufficient stocks of foodstuff has also been accorded marked attention in some highly developed countries (Japan, the Netherlands).

The production of wheat in Tatarstan has essentially begun in recent years with comprehensive government support. In 1996 an estimated 500 000 megatons of wheat were produced as compared with 178 000 in 1994 and 441 000 in 1995. Since these quantities fulfill the requirements of the republic, considerable hard currency, which had been earmarked for wheat imports was freed up for other uses. A programme to achieve similar self-sufficiency in sugar is also being implemented. In 1995 areas producing sugar beets doubled as compared with 1994, and these were cultivated with highly efficient industrial technology in active cooperation with leading French companies.

With the aim of increasing the efficiency of the entire process of sugar production from seeding to crop treatment to harvesting and processing, a programme to produce seeding machines and cultivators for sugar beets has been established in the republic. Sugar refineries are also being constructed. With the assistance of Pioneer, USA corn producing acreage also increased to 41 000 in 1995 from 11 300 in the preceding year. In the same years acreage planted with oil seed crops (rape, in particular) increased from 38 700 to 60 300. In light of these trends, there is good reason to believe that in the near future the republic will become self-sufficient in food, particularly in wheat, sugar and livestock, and will even be in a position to export a number of food products.

The process of connecting the civil sector of the economy (mainly the agro-industrial complex) with the extensive machine production of the military industrial complex, which for a long time was isolated from the interests of the republic, is now slowing quite rapidly. The defense complex is composed of fifteen large and extra-large enterprises. For decades it was barely connected with the economy of the republic. The fact that the military-industrial complex is now involved with agrarian as well as other market sectors should be regarded as an initial step towards basic structural changes which require firm measures to preclude a return to previous conditions.

Fundamental structural modification requires both technical and economic changes, of which the latter appear to be more difficult. Two years ago an attempt to manufacture components for KamAZ vehicles ended in failure because of the non-competitive prices offered by the military-industrial complex. This occurred because they attempted to underutilise the equipment so that, in case of need, it could simultaneously be used for military production with all costs being factored into the price of the civilian goods. Naturally this condemned the project to failure. Unfortunately a substantial segment of the society still feels that no significant changes need to be made in the production structure or economic norms.

Absurd ideas can be heard in favour of changing the political course and curtailing market reforms since the existing economy is inconsistent with the market. The fact is, however, that the existing economy has exhausted its resources and is unable to continue functioning. Therefore the reconstruction of the economic base of the economy is a necessity dictated by objective factors, not by the discretionary political views of a particular segment of the society. This explains the unsuccessful attempt made two years ago to organise a cooperative effort between the military-industrial complex and a large commercial enterprise.

Although the Russian government decreased the volume of state orders, they turned out to be insolvent even in regard to the products they did order. Russian government debts are numbered in trillions and there is no doubt that if this policy continues, their debts will remain outstanding year in and year out and become chronic. In fact, they already are! It is clear that this will be accompanied by the growth of manufacturing debt, unacceptably low profitability, loss of qualified personnel and further lowering of production quality.

In view of the ongoing political instability, the absence of an explicit military doctrine, and a programme of designing and manufacturing weapons, it is necessary to place civil production on a separate balance sheet and promote it in the marketplace with competitive prices. Under the circumstances, we have no alternative. Placing new production on a separate balance sheet will allow an increase in the rate of capital turnover. This in turn will be a prerequisite for the adaptation of the machine-building complex to the market economy with a moderate inflation rate. Russia needs to attract investments from capital markets and foreign banks to be satisfactorily integrated into the world economy. Accounting procedures, including qualified auditing and the maintenance of stable and active balances, must be brought in line with universally accepted standards. Upgrading and modernisation of the technical structure of production and the revision of economic and accounting procedures must occur in tandem. The earlier the directors of the enterprises realise the need for reforms the sooner the economy will overcome the crisis.

A number of procedural and economic steps designed to stimulate structural reorganisation were undertaken during the reform years. Several of these, including compilation of a list of business projects which would be tailored to the market, were favourably evaluated by international experts. However problems of quality and timing still remain.

After a project has been organised, investment must be obtained. Since the typical investor is cautious with his capital stringent requirements should be demanded of the project organisers. If they do not learn to make a qualitative study to accompany the proposed project, the problem of finding investors will remain unsolved. Unfortunately, in actual practice we find examples of this. Often the government grants temporary tax privileges provided the amount is used for purposes of reconstruction.

Another common problem concerns implementation. It often takes an unacceptably long time from the project's starting point to its conclusion. Meanwhile the market can change, the production methods can become obsolete and the amount invested may devaluate due to inflation. The accumulation of sufficient investment resources, which is one of the main problems, can be achieved in various ways: targeted credits, the establishment of (venture capital) financial-industrial groups and the use of funds obtained through privatisation.

The creation of a legal climate favourable for investments is also of key importance today. The passage of the Law on Foreign Investments in the Republic of Tatarstan was made possible because of independence in legislation. As compared with the analogous Russian law, the law of the Republic of Tatarstan provides foreign investors with many benefits. These include more rights, additional tax privileges and guarantees, the possibility of accelerated depreciation for enterprises with foreign shareholders, expedited registration for some enterprises, extension of the depositing period, and the possibility of partial loss coverage at the expense of the government budget. In order to create a favourable investment climate in the republic the Law on the Status of the Approved Investment Project with Foreign Investor Participation took effect in March, 1996. The envisages enhancement of the process of government approval for projects deemed to have a priority in economic importance. This permits a maximum tax privilege of up to 10 years, which is unprecedented in Russia.

Transferring the government's shares in a number of the republic's enterprises into the trust fund Tatinvest-Ross (USA) for five years is one way to attract investments aimed at technical reconstruction and increasing competitiveness. Currently shares of nine enterprises including Tatnefteproduct, Karpov Chemical Plant, Nizhnekamskshina, Polimiz, Alnas and Tatarstan Soete have been transferred and six more are in line. The proportion of shares transferred varies form 22 to 8 per cent. The shares were transferred without the right to sell; this will encourage new managers to look for private investments and to actively utilize their expertise. Potential investment in these enterprises could amount to US $200 to 300 million.

The political success of reform depends on economic stability and the perceptions of society regarding the effects of economic reform. Long-lasting recessions and depressions generate public weariness and apathy and the fear that Russia may come to another dead end if the reforms fail.

The treaty and agreements signed with Russia require that some parameters of Tatarstan's economic activity lie within the jurisdiction of Russian legislation. Any lag in Russian reforms concerning foreign economic activity has negative consequences. Since 1992, when reforms were initiated, legislation in this field has been unstable. Interference of the state in foreign economic activity has been unpredictable and unprecedented. Russian Federation revenues from foreign economic activity rose from a mere 6 per cent to 21 per cent in 1994, thereby lowering the competitiveness of many Russian goods. This type of Russian government influence in the economic sphere basically amounts to the restoration of some elements of state monopoly and is a step away from market reform. In most developed countries revenues from foreign economic activity vary from 1–3 per cent, whereas East European countries, which have recently embarked on the path of market reform, generated 5–8 per cent. Russia's obligations to the international community, undertaken to bring foreign economic legislation in line with internationally accepted standards by 1997–8, have not really been fulfilled.

Needless to say, this negatively affects the economy of Tatarstan. Economic agreements between Tatarstan and Russia envisage partial retention of the foreign economy revenues in the budget of the republic. Any delay in resolving this matter calls for political action by the government of the republic. The same logic applies to the question of free economic zones, which are also envisaged by the treaty. A legal framework and the establishment of free economic zones would stimulate business activity in the republic.

In summary, it is appropriate to note some positive changes in the structural adaptation to the market. First, the weight of foodstuff in the total volume of production has increased. This was accomplished because of the increased independence of the republic and the opportunity to control the funds earned in accordance with the interests of the citizens. In this economic sector, the responsibility accepted by the republic after the adoption of sovereignty had positive results. Some positive results were also achieved in industry restructuring and cooperative ties between the military-industrial complex and the civil sector of the economy became stronger. However, since there were delays and subjective obstacles are yet to be overcome, some problems still remain.

In the future there will be severe economic competition and struggle for customers and probably some will be adversely affected. But one thing is clear: the era of large-scale state orders has passed and there is now no alternative to market activity. This leads to the conclusion that economic well-being depends on the restructuring of production technology and a system of accounting adjusted to meet the standards of the international market. These contain stringent requirements regarding cost, quality, discipline and adherence to strict timetables.

Independence, achieved by the republic as the result of past political processes, speeds up development since the market favours those who are capable of thinking and acting on their own and are not afraid to assume responsibility and engage in permanent competition.

11

Tatar Renaissance in the Context of Eurasian Civilisation

M. H. Khasanov

The unique medieval phenomenon known as the Renaissance ranks particularly high in world history. The Renaissance brought cardinal changes to civilisation and showed the way to future development. It is no exaggeration to say that modern global culture in a broad sense sprang from the Renaissance, a very widespread phenomenon that exceeded the limits of separate national cultures. But at the same time we must not forget that the European Renaissance evolved from the revival of separate national cultures and gave birth to European nations, their languages and sovereign states.

In the context of the contemporary renaissance in Eurasia it is logical to ask: the revival of what and whom? Self-evidently, it is impossible to revive something that never existed. Even the European Renaissance, which by definition meant the revival of the classical heritage of Greece and Rome, was accompanied by the emergence of new nations and cultures that had no roots in the ancient world. Nevertheless it is possible to identify the main features of a renaissance and use them to judge whether the phenomenon has occurred or is occurring in other nations.

In this chapter an attempt is made to review the development of the Tatar nation, its culture and state organisation from this particular point of view. An analysis of Tatar renaissance is especially urgent today, not only from a historical point of view but also from the viewpoint of state-building and the spiritual rebirth of sovereign Tatarstan. The Tatar renaissance is unique but nevertheless includes some typical features of the European Renaissance. We shall examine the main components of the process from its recent beginnings in Tatarstan, but in so doing we shall try to keep away from historical economic structures, and persistent Marxist traditions will be set aside. From our point of view it is obvious that political dogma is unable to explain the complex processes involved in the development of human civilisation. In examining the Tatar renaissance a glance at the history of the nation is necessary. One has to answer the question: is there anything for the Tatars to revive? What stages of development have they passed through?

First and foremost, the Tatars are one of the few nations in the world to possess ancient traditions of social organisation. Volga Bulgaria, one of the most ancient states in Eastern Europe, was founded by the ancestors of the modern Tatars during the ninth and tenth centuries.

The most important event in determining the future fortunes of the nation was its official adoption of Islam in the tenth century, which enabled it to become part of the most progressive and dynamic civilisation of that time. After the fall of the Greek and Roman civilisations, Western Europe suffered a cultural decline and spiritual obscurantism. However the ninth to thirteenth centuries were considered to be the golden age of Muslim civilisation. While mysticism reigned in Europe and orthodox Christianity prevented the development of rational knowledge, the cultural heritage and social doctrine of Islam encouraged the development of science, medicine, literature and the arts. The Muslim world mastered the achievements of the Greco-Roman culture long before they were resurrected in Europe. In fact the philosophy of Aristotle, Plato, Socrates and other thinkers returned to Europe through the Arabs. The works of Muslim thinkers and scientists, including Ibn Sina and Ibn Rushd, were embraced in Europe during the Renaissance with Latinised names. Mathematical procedures such as algebra and algorithm were developed with Arab contributions.

The golden age of Muslim civilisation in many ways anticipated the Renaissance in Europe. Geographically, the Renaissance originated in southern Europe, particularly the Italian peninsula. Along with the internal circumstances that brought the Renaissance phenomenon to life, it was also influenced by the contacts that people living in Genoa, Venice and Florence had with the Muslim civilisation through their communications with the Mediterranean basin.

The development of the Tatar renaissance is impossible to understand outside the context of the Eurasian civilisation called the Golden Horde (1256–1502), known in medieval Europe as Tartaria, maps of which, as well as travellers' notes have been preserved. The Turkic people themselves called it Deshte Kypchak. The Golden Horde was the bearer of the peculiar civilisation of the Eurasian steppes. It successfully established a culture of settled people, particularly in Volga

Bulgaria. It gave the world organised postal and coach services and furthered the art of war, based on highly manoeuvrable light cavalry. When the Golden Horde came into existence Muslim civilisation had become mainly Turkic and Iranian.

After two centuries the Golden Horde broke up into several independent Tatar states: the Kazan, Crimean, Astrakhan and Siberian khanates. This coincided with the formation of the Moscow state, which was strengthened in the bosom of the Golden Horde. By this time the Renaissance in Europe was beginning to flourish. The weakening of Tatar state organisation took place against the background of the stagnation of Muslim civilisation on the one hand and the flourishing of European civilisation (after the medieval lethargy) on the other.

The Renaissance came to an end with the great geographical discoveries of the fifteenth and sixteenth centuries and the ideological development of mankind. Since that time the world has been viewed as a single whole by progressive-minded people. But the geographical discoveries gave rise to the darker side of the late Renaissance. Many colonial empires sprang up with the enslavement by leading European states of the people of 'less advanced' civilisations. By the time of the late Renaissance the Muslim world in particular had lost its former dynamism and fallen into stagnation. Its progressive position in science, culture, education and other fields was lost. Consequently many Muslim nations were unable to withstand the colonial expansion of the European states. One cannot understand the fate of the Tatar nation outside this context. Russia's colonial empire began with the seizing of the Kazan khanate in 1552, when the Tatars lost their independence. It coincides in time with the coming into existence of the world colonial system.

The beginning of the Tatar renaissance dates back to the middle of the nineteenth century, although the first positive movements in Tatar society began at the end of the eighteenth century, immediately after the liberal indulgences of Catherine the Great had been granted to the Muslims of the Russian empire. After the loss of their independence the Tatars had to bear the colonial yoke and during the next two centuries desperately struggle for individual and national survival. Their only support during this time was Islam and the sense of spiritual belonging to the Muslim civilisation and a culture that was alien to the conquerors. This strengthened the historical memories of the Tatars, who never forgot the greatness of their ancestors and their independent states. According to some scholars, in spite of their low status in the empire the Muslims never lost their dignity and had a sense of moral superiority over their oppressors.

At the beginning of the nineteenth century the first reformative signs appeared in the creative works of Tatar thinkers such as G. Utez-Imjani and G. Kursazvi. Like their predecessors in medieval Europe, they came to understand the fallaciousness of the scholastic education offered at that time in the Muslim environment and recognised the necessity of reforms in Tatar society. The Tatars were among the first in the Islamic world to start book printing, and Tatar accumulated capital, for trade with its specific requirements in the spheres of culture, education and professional training, came into existence.

These developments influenced the next generation of thinkers and public figures. Creative free thinking emerged in the religious reformative ideas of G. Kursavi, Sh. Mardjani and K. Nasiri. According to a well-known orientalist, A. Bennigsen, the Tatar religious reformers

> were one of the first Muslim thinkers, much earlier than Arabs, Turks, Persians and Indians who declared the right of any believer to look for answers to all political, social and religious questions in the *Qur'an* and *ahadith*. Their influence on the development of reformative movements not only in Russia, but also in the whole Muslim world, was exceptionally important. Due to their contributions which are not well known in the West and are being ignored by Muslim scholars, the road to reforms in other fields was paved: language, education and political organisation.[1]

It is generally believed that the liberation of Muslim religious and social thought from the chains of orthodox dogma began only at the end of the nineteenth century. For non-Russian Islam that might be so. Indeed Jamal-ud-Din Afghani initiated his reformative movement at exactly that time. It is also erroneously believed that he was the first to suggest the idea of *ijtihad* (innovative thinking) when interpreting the Qur'an and Hadithes. Until that time the principle of *taqlid* had reigned – that is, unreserved submission to the letter of orthodox dogma. But the principle of *ijtihad* had been expressed first by the Tatar thinker G. Kursavi at the beginning of the nineteenth century, almost one century before Afghanis. When Kursavi expressed his revolutionary ideas in Bukhara, conservative *ulamas* (Muslim theologians) condemned them as heresy and demanded that he be severely punished. Kursavi was obliged to escape from Bukhara and find santuary elsewhere. In Tatar society the principle of *ijtihad* was absorbed painlessly and contributed to the formation of the philosophy of *jadidism* (modernism).

Bennigsen insists that the preeminence of Tatar thinkers in the reformation of Islam was not accidental. Indeed Kursari brought the idea of *ijtihad* to the rest of the Muslim world. The fact is that Afghani studied in Bukhara, and it is likely that he became acquainted with Kursavi's ideas at that time (in any event this hypothesis deserves to be explored).

Now a few words about the Muslim renaissance, or *nahda* (elevation). The Muslim nations that were under the colonial control of the West during the nineteenth century were drawn into the world economy and this inevitably increased the influence of Western civilisation on their lives and culture. As in the European Renaissance, this was first reflected in literature and art, but then began the search for a new paradigm of Islam in the sphere of public thought. Among the founders of the Muslim renaissance were Jamal-ud-Din (Dzhemeletdin) Afghani (1839–97), Muhammad Abdo (1849–1905) from Egypt and the Indian Muslim thinker, Muhammad Iqbal (1873–1938). But the list would not be complete without Tatar thinkers and scholars, including G. Kursavi, Sh. Marjani, R. Fakhretdinov, M. Bigiev and G. Barudi. Indeed the Tatar Renaissance can be seen as part of the general process of Islamic renaissance. Summarising, it might be said that the combined achievements of the Western and Muslim civilisations are the characteristic features of the Islamic renaissance. The former power and advanced position of the Muslim civilisation in the spheres of science, culture and education are the natural points of orientation.

As indicated above, the second major contribution the Tatars made to the Eurasian culture was the development of *Jadidism*. Tatar religious reformers also managed to modernise the ideological and moral–ethical basis of Islamic dogma, but the *jadid* system of national education became their main priority. Modern schools (*madaras*) were the instrument of orienting people towards the new ideas. In *jadid* schools, as in the new schools of the European Renaissance, mathematics, history, geography and even gymnastics were taught. From this emerged the *jadid* movement, which very quickly exceeded the confines of pure enlightenment and developed into the national liberation movement of Muslim nations.

The abolition of serfdom by Alexander II was an important catalyst in the development of the Tatar renaissance. The post reform period in Russia, starting in 1861, was characterised by increased entrepreneurial activity and the rapid growth of the national economy. Tatars were in the front rank of this movement. The Tatar's capital for trade by its strength, caused jealousy among Russian capitalists, especially in Central Asia. Tatars also began successfully to master industrial production and Tatar owners of factories and gold mines appeared on the scene.

In the nineteenth century Kazan became the main centre of oriental studies in Russia, and one of the world centres of Muslim book printing. This fact is universally recognised and bears witness to the fact that the Tatar renaissance bore the main features of the Eurasian Renaissance. In turn the development of science and Muslim book printing in Russia stimulated a rapid rise in the educational level of the Tatar population. By the beginning of the twentieth century most were literate in their native language. Even in one of Lenin's scholarly works, which is based on official statistics, it is stated that Tatar literacy considerably exceeded that of the Russian population of the empire.

Naturally the growth of literacy and the successes in book printing brought to life a new order in Tatar society that was underlined by creative literary work. At the beginning of the twentieth century Tatar literature was elevated by the coming of bright masters of the pen who raised literature to a qualitatively higher level: G. Tukai, G. Ishaki, F. Amirhan, G. Ibragimov and G. Kamal. In principle, where literature successfully develops a literary language develops too. Clearly the Tatar renaissance repeated the main features of the European Renaissance – the literary languages of many European nations were formed during the Renaissance.

Music and theatre also blossomed. At the beginning of the twentieth century professional Tatar musicians began to appear and in 1906 the first professional theatre company was formed. Since that time theatre has been one of the most popular arts among Tatars. The medieval Renaissance in Italy and England was accompanied by the rapid development of theatrical art, but Tatar theatre, which appeared on the tide of national renaissance, can be considered a unique phenomenon. There was no Tatar cinematography but in many respects the theatre compensated for this, producing great Tatar playwrights, directors and actors.

Thus Tatars entered the twentieth century with their own national education system a growing and original body of literary works. A national intelligentsia was also formed at that time.

As important as the cultural and economic aspects of the Tatar renaissance was the introduction of a state structure based on ancient traditions. This deserves particular attention.

The reappearance of the Tatar state structure

The ups and downs of relations between ethnic groups, cultures and civilisations throughout history demonstrate that if national life is not organised into some kind of statehood a nation cannot have a solid future. The tragic fate of a number of national minorities serves as proof of this. We have recently witnessed the tragedy of the Chechen nation, whose self-determination was not recognised or accepted by some political and military figures in the Russian Federation.

At the beginning of the twentieth century the Tatar people came to the conclusion that a national state structure was necessary to the further development of the nation. Events in Europe influenced this realisation. At that time many new states were emerging in Europe and progressive Tatars watched the events with great interest. An unidentified secret service reported to the Kazan gendarme administration (the political police) that Tatar students were discussing Islamic reformation, perspectives of the Islamic world. The history of the Balkan wars and similar matters during their meetings (*majalas*). Greece, Bulgaria and Serbia became independent in the nineteenth century, Norway and Ireland at the beginning of the twentieth century, and these developments stimulated interest in the idea of a Tatar state organisation.

The Tatars were one of the first Turkic nations to articulate this idea, an idea that had remained with them throughout their colonial history. At the beginning of the twentieth century it became a reality thanks to the intellectual efforts of philosophers and public and political leaders such as Ysuf Akchura, Sadri Maksudi, Gaes Ishaki and Mirsaid Sultangaliev. In particular Sadri Maksudi and Mirsaid Sultangaliev were important theorists and instigators of the rebirth of Turkic nations.

On several occasions Sadri Maksudi acted as leader of the Muslim section of the Russian Duma. Persistent and naturally gifted, Maksudi received a European education and a law degree from the Sorbonne. His ideas on state organisation and law, federalism and self-determination are still important today. At a time when national rights and liberties were severely suppressed, Maksudi promoted the idea of cultural and territorial autonomy, of a federally organised Russian empire. He showed that elements of federalism were already present, citing the special rights and status enjoyed by Finland, Poland, Bukhara and the Khiva emirates, which were incorporated into Russia as distinct entities. His views on the problem of nation and nationalism also deserve attention. In a book entitled *Sociological Aspects of National Feelings*, he wrote that the aspiration of a nation to develop its culture and secure its independence and sense of nationhood did not contradict the interests of mankind as a whole. On the contrary, he argued that it was the only way to ensure the happiness and safety of all mankind. Accordingly he spoke out in the State Duma in defence of the rights and interests of the non-Russian peoples of the Russian empire.

In 1917 Maksudi headed the movement of Muslims of inner Russia for the resurrection of their state organisation. Milli Majlis (National Council of Tatars and Bashkirs), who worked in Ufa under Maksudi's leadership for several months, announced the intended formation of Idel–Ural, a self-governing state under the protection of Russia. Maksudi was unanimously elected as its future head of government. But the Bolsheviks severely clamped down on this attempt to revive the national state organisation of the Tatars. Nevertheless the Bolsheviks had to consider the expectations of the Tatars, who had retained their aspiration to revive their lost state through centuries of colonial oppression. On 27 May 1920 Lenin decreed the formation of the Tatar Autonomous Soviet Socialist Republic. It would not be right to downplay or ignore the significance of this decree – even though it only allowed for a restricted form of national state organisation – as it was the first step towards the formation of Tatarstan Republic.

Here it is important to briefly outline the facts of the national state order of the Soviet Union. The Bolsheviks made certain political capital with a slogan about the right of nations to self-determination. Many Turkic people at first believed this slogan, but then bitter disappointment grew because the Bolsheviks instead established a cruel class dictatorship aimed at creating a non-national society, according to their Utopian and dogmatic visions. In 1922 the so-called Agreement for the Creation of the USSR led to real inequality among peoples and their territories. Some of them became union republics, others autonomous republics, and the rest became 'nothing'. M. Sultangaliev was against Stalin's concept of Tatarstan autonomy, the hierarchical ranking of peoples and their state formations. Later Sultangaliev became a victim of the totalitarian regime and was executed. The democratic changes in the country after 1985 revealed all the past injustices. With the passage of time Maksudi's and Sultangaliev's correct political thinking has been confirmed.

Despite its declared federal organisation the Soviet Union was really a unitary and totalitarian state. Everything was done in response to directives from the centre and the strongly centralised planning system. The totalitarian regime cruelly ignored human rights. Nevertheless Tatarstan was outstanding amongst the other autonomous republics for certain historical reasons. The question of Tatarstan's status was raised by the republic throughout the Soviet period, particularly in 1924, 1936 and 1977, when new Soviet constitutions were adopted. As an economically developed republic with excellent scientific and cultural potential, Tatarstan strove throughout to achieve union republic status, a status which would allow it to secede from the Soviet Union.

Although the Bolshevik revolution brought a halt to the Tatar renaissance that had blossomed at the beginning of the twentieth century, it would be wrong to present the Soviet period of Tatar history in solely black terms. Of course the so-called dictatorship of the proletariat, the class approach to society, crushed the substance of national life and a significant proportion of national culture. There was also an attempt to deprive the people of their spiritual heritage – Islam. The best brains of the nation were obliged to emigrate, and those who stayed were subjected to repression. However there were also positive changes. First of all the Tatar national state organisation was revived after an absence of more than three centuries, albeit in a very limited form. Second, a state education system was created. Although this was limited to secondary education there were attempts to organise courses in the Tatar language at university level before the Second World War. Third, a scientific Tatar intelligentsia developed, guaranteeing the intellectual progress of the nation. Fourth, Tatars mastered the arts of symphonic music, opera and ballet during the Soviet period. Fifth, radio and television became available to the people. Although the hierarchical organisation of the Soviet republics strongly limited the possibility of autonomy, slow progress was made in this direction.

The totalitarian regime brought to a standstill the process of Tatar renaissance, but failed to eradicate it. A national Tatar movement began to develop at the end of 1980s and the beginning of the 1990s, but the turning point was the Declaration on the State Sovereignty of the Republic of Tatarstan on 30 August 1990. The declaration reflected a high degree of political maturity among the people of Tatarstan and their readiness to take on the burdens of state responsibility. A referendum on the status of Tatarstan in March 1992 and the adoption of a new constitution in November 1992 were notable landmarks in the construction of sovereign Tatarstan.

In 1996 the republic celebrated the sixth anniversary of the Declaration of Sovereignty. By that time markedly positive changes had taken place in national life and in the lives of the Tatar people. First of all, people had regained their dignity and pride in their state.

During the Soviet years nobody had bothered about the views of the people of union republics and the autonomous republics, but by 1996 many political and state leaders were listening to Tatarstan's points of view, and its voice had become more assured and significant in the Russian Federation. Around the world, people had started to talk about Tatarstan's model of national state reconstruction.

In the Declaration of Sovereignty Tatarstan announced its wish for equal partnership and voluntary relations with Russia, but this caused irritation in Moscow and was rejected. Of course the leaders of Tatarstan realised that compromise with Russia must come through federalism, through the creation of a true federation based on mutual agreement. In the referendum of 1992 the people of the republic supported this principle. Association with the Russian Federation was also laid down in the constitution of the republic, laying the basis for the formation of an asymmetrical federation, which found legal form in an agreement on the mutual delegation of rights between Tatarstan and the Russian Federation on 15 February 1994.

Basic human rights, protection of the interests of all ethnic groups and confessions, equality among languages and duel citizenship (Tatarstan–Russia) were all taken into account during the construction of the state system of Tatarstan, thus avoiding the many excesses that are so typical of the post-Soviet world.

At the end of 1993 a referendum was held throughout the Russian Federation on the acceptability of the new Federation constitution. Unfortunately the constitution had been written in a hurry immediately after the sad events of October 1993 in Moscow and did not include the ideas of Tatarstan and other republics. No wonder a large number of voters in the Russian Federation opposed it, and in Tatarstan only 13 per cent of voters took part. A later version of the constitution declared the existence of a democratic federation, but more and more members of the Federation are demanding specific rights and agreements.

Relations between Moscow and Kazan have always been strained. The negotiations (1991–94) between the official delegations lasted two and a half years. It required colossal patience, much intellectual effort and good will on both sides, but eventually a compromise was reached. Both sides agreed that renewed federation should be built on the principle of 'subsidiarity' (that is, control from the bottom up) in accordance with the will of the people. Tatarstan insisted on the mutual delegation of rights, and all agreements between Moscow and the regions should taken into account the division of rights. In this respect the agreement between Tatarstan and the Russian Federation is unique. Most importantly, the agreement removed the possibility of conflict and new opportunities developed for the statehood of Tatarstan.

Let us turn to the lessons of the Chechen tragedy. Started by certain authorities in Moscow, the war in Chechnya demonstrated how strong the idea of a Great State is in Russia and how deep are the roots of imperial thinking. Russia hoped to wage a quick and victorious war. This was a major step back from democracy and reminiscent of the days of the unitary, centralised state. Did they not understand in Moscow that their actions were deadly for Russia? It should not be forgotten that the peoples of historical territories want to regain their political rights. Some politicians in Moscow think of the struggle for national rights and statehood as capricious. Some of them still think that a new Russia can be built in total disregard of the interests of indigenous peoples and their republics. (This particular attitude, I believe, led to the tragic war in Chechnya, the consequences of which will poison the political atmosphere of the country for a long time to come.) The Chechen conflict shows how deadly it is to use force to solve a national question. Two years of war led to the death of tens of thousands of civilians and armed forces, and the destruction of hundreds of towns and villages.

Today we can say for sure that the agreement between Tatarstan and Russia will be fruitful not only for Tatarstan, but also for the entire Russian Federation. Nonetheless there are those in Moscow who still harp on about the necessity of bringing the Tatarstan constitution into line with the constitution of the Russian Federation. It is true that there are considerable differences between the two, but a sensible compromise was arrived at and many contradictions were removed. Both sides demonstrated patience and wisdom in the negotiation process, and by so doing they were able to satisfy several political forces. Experience shows that the most important questions of state formation cannot be approached unilaterally. It is evident that the constitution of the Russian Federation is still far from ideal and cannot be interpreted as the supreme authoritative document. For example the federal authorities have signed agreements with many members of the Russian Federation. Thus one can say that the Federation is being built on individual agreements. The constitution of the Russian Federation should accord with the Federation's agreements with the autonomous states.

It will be impossible to bring about stability in Russia without a well-planned national policy. Such a policy was approved by the president of the Russian Federation, but there is no mechanism for its realisation; that is why it cannot satisfy multinational Russia. At the moment the interests of indigenous peoples are not taken into account, neither in the constitution of the Russian Federation nor in the representational branches of power. National-state formations are unable to protect their rights by voting in the State Duma or the Federation Council. Even if they were able to vote for their interests they could not exceed 25 per cent of the votes. Thus they are deprived of any real possibility of solving their problems. People do not want and will not consent to this limitation of their rights, which is doing nothing to help bring about stability in Russia. All federal states need a well-thought-out national policy.

As experience has demonstrated, state organisation cannot be achieved instantaneously. The process is prolonged and demands laborious work, the nurturing of spiritual forces and mobilisation of the intellectual potential of the nation. That is why the Tatar renaissance is so important; it lies at the heart of the search for nationhood, which in turn requires a proper national state organisation.

It would also be fruitful to pay attention to progressive tendencies in the rest of the world. The experience of the European Union is interesting in this respect. There a confederate relationship has emerged between the members of the European Union whereby each state retains its sovereignty and is an independent subject of international law. For common concerns, special all-Union assemblies exist in the form of the European Council, the European Parliament and so on. Of course Russia, with its centuries-old tradition of unitarianism and resistance to change, especially among the ruling elite, perceives progressive innovations such as this in a negative light. But changes can take place even in a conservative country such as Russia, though painfully. Large ethnic and climatic variations, vast distances, and the impossibility of regulating life and all its minutiae from one common centre make it necessary to look seriously at Europe's progressive innovations. It is essential to introduce some elements of confederacy within the framework of the Russian Federation. Modern communications, international ties of the republic, make it the subject of international law. The time has come to legalise it officially. Tatar independence and sovereignty does not mean a complete break with Russia but rather the realisation of basic human rights and a free and equal relationship between nations as we stand on the threshold of the twenty-first century.

Reference

1. A. Bennigsen, *Muslims in the USSR* (Paris, 1983).

12
Tatarstan's Model of Cultural Revival

Engel E. R. Tagirov

The story of Tatarstan is one of a people who lost their nation-state for five centuries. This period was also characterised by losses of many other kinds, including the decline of the Tatar culture and its intellectual fund. By the end of the twentieth century the threat of total assimilation and the loss of the nation's main remaining feature, its language, were very real. The Tatars, as citizens of Russia and the former USSR, shared the general fate that befell all the people of the country. The Russian state did not condone the preservation of national cultures, and it was precisely self-preservation that led Tatarstan towards the goal of sovereignty. Therefore it is no accident that the basic component of Tatarstan's new model of development is the revival of its culture. Cultural–civilisational 'revolution' is a prerequisite for self-determination and real sovereignty of the people; it is an historical end in itself.

The Tatar revival has a legal and constitutional base: the Declaration of the State Sovereignty of the Republic of Tatarstan of 30 August 1990, which protects the republic from future dismantlement; and the Constitution of the Republic of Tatarstan of 6 November 1992, is in the form of a social contract and a treaty with Russia for national agreement. In the treaty, people of Tatarstan are defined as a multi-national association of citizens who have equal rights and duties regardless of their nationality and religion. The constitution gives the Tatar and Russian languages the status of state language, guarantees the development of all national cultures, and grants the right to dual citizenship. These constitutional rights have been laid down in special laws, including the State Language Law, the Citizenship Law and the Education Law. Among the many political and legal documents that facilitate Tatarstan's revival, the treaty between Tatarstan and Russia of

February 1994 is very important. This provides for the development of society's spiritual spheres and the blending of traditional national values with the achievements of Russian culture and it encourages Tatarstan to adhere to the well known cultural and civilisational values.

In the light of all this, can we now speak of a Tatar renaissance? Yes, we can! Many features of Tatar national culture are being revived, as evidenced by the opening of national elementary and high schools, lycées and national cultural centres, and the burgeoning of societies, song competitions, festivals and national holidays. At the moment this cultural reawakening is limited to the upper classes of society; so in order to complete the process, it is necessary to mobilize the full resources of society as a whole and all the latent potential of the people. Renaissance is only possible if the energy of the entire nation and the state is directed at the realization of the grand national goal.

In order to revive the spiritual personality of Tatarstan, to discover methods of political development, and to energise persons who are in doubt, Tatar leaders need to articulate one united ideal and value, or a national ideology. Ideology influences all peoples' development. In periods of national crisis, national ideology becomes national strength, and is easily understood, it becomes a short formula, a slogan or an appeal. The history of the last two centuries, which is known for intensive development of national states, provides several examples of institutionalised national ideas. For instance, in the United States, this took the form of the 'American dream'. Inspired by this dream, the first generation of businessmen arose. In Italy, the national idea was 'Risordgimento', the appeal to unite and rejuvenate the Italian nation. In Russia in the twentieth century, they tried to present the national ideal against the background of the union of the 'Orthodox faith, autocracy, and nationality'.

If the Tatars made a decision to form national-state idea as a pillar of hope, its nature must be understood. It is born from the interaction of two principal social sources – spontaneous (affective) and rational (cognitive). The former is a sort of 'irrational national idea', an emotional response to the primordial problem of collective identity: who are we, where are we going, what do we want, and what are our aims?

The rational principle is a basic element of state ideology, which has to measure the feelings and perceptions of average people and to connect their interests with state ideology. The national ideology should be able to respond to the following questions: What should be done by the state, taking into account society's needs and in which way should it be done? These two principals are always in the process of interaction; their interpenetration is the basis of the national-state idea.

The slogan, 'Tatarstan is for Tatars only' is inappropriate. Tatarstan is the preserve of the Tatar culture and spirit; it is the Motherland of the nation which was born within its confines. Consequently, the national idea will be built up according to the Tatars' ideal. If their ideal is noble it will benefit other nations. Tatars should play the role of a great nation, great in spirit and great in faith. Only a great nation can make its spirit and culture an advantage for other nations who reside in the same territory.

Historical evolution of the Tartar culture

The Tatar civilisation and culture is one of the oldest in the world. It developed deep roots when the Turkic khanate was established in the Volga. This later became known as Bulgaria. At the beginning of the tenth century the Arab geographer Ibn-Rusta was impressed by the Bulgars' high achievements in agriculture, crafts, culture, and science. Another Arab scholar, Al-Garnaty, noted their intellectual strength and declared that 'Boolgary is the state of scientists'. It is therefore not surprising that elements of Bulgarian culture entered the way of life of the nearest Russian neighbours, notably Kiev, Vladimir, Suzdal and Moscow, as well as Europe and the East. The father of Eastern sociology, Ibn-Khaldun, remarked on the fact that for the first time in world history the victors had adopted the language, culture and religion of the conquered people. Within the framework of the Golden Horde, the culture of Tatars also developed and influenced the neighbouring countries. For example, long before Copernicus in 1380 the Tatar poet Sabf-Sarai wrote in a poem that the Earth moves around the sun. The 'golden age' of the Tatar culture survived even in periods of tragedy and continued to influence others as noted by the Russian historian M. G. Khudaykov and linguist M. S. Trubetskoy, the American historian Richard Pipe and the Italian historian D. Boff. Thus Tatar culture, which was the product of different worlds, civilisations, cultures and religions, was a reference point for the development of other national cultures. Tatars were very tolerant of other religions, and a great number of churches and monastaries existed side by side with mosques. Neighbours and foreigners were surprised by the industriousness, initiative and quick-wittedness of the Tatars. Egyptian ambassadors noted the Tatars' efficiency in such diverse areas as diplomacy, education, military matters, farming, business, crafts and leather work. In the Middle Ages the Tatars built their towns according to European standards, and in some aspects they were ahead of the Europeans. For example, at a time when domestic waste in Paris was poured into the streets the Tatars had properly functioning sewage systems; and while there were public baths in France, they had existed in Bulgaria since the ninth century. Despite all this the Tatar culture remained untainted by national conservatism or arrogance.

The history of the Tatar nation is the history of the establishment, development and flourishing of the national spirit. One thing is indisputable about the Tatar culture that it is shaped by Islam, which is known to be a culture making source. Tatars look upon Islam as a complete logical and philosophical system. Islam's concept of monotheism is a source of unity, knowledge, and a way of life – Islam embodies for the Tatars the unity of three basic values: originality, national spirit, and the state. This is the key to understanding the revival of Tatar culture.

13
Revival of Nationalism in Bashkortostan

Hafeez Malik

Approximately the size of France, the autonomous republic of Bashkortostan is one of the largest republics in the Russian Federation and a neighbour of the autonomous republic of Tatarstan, a fellow Muslim and Turkic state. Before the middle of the sixteenth century the Bashkorts were a part of the Tatar Kazan khanate (1437–1552), and before that belonged to the Golden Horde (1255–1502). The latter state was established by Batu, the Grandson of Genghis Khan, who in 1228 conquered the Bulgar state, which had been established by the ancestors of the Tatars in the ninth century in the Volga–Ural Basin. Russia was then confined to Kiev. An Arab missionary, Ibn-I-Fadhlan, spread Islam among the Tatars and Islam became firmly established in the Bulgar state in the tenth century. Subsequently, through Tatar missionary efforts, it spread among the Bashkorts. When Batu conquered Russia in 1240, Bulgars who had been drafted into his Mongol army fought in the vanguard. Consequently for Russians the Mongol invasion came to be known as the Tatar yoke. The Mongol Tatars ruled over Russia for 250 years.[1]

Located in the middle of southern Urals at the crossroads of Europe and Asia, Bashkortostan's territory of 143 600 square kilometers contains about four million people. The titular nationals, the Muslim Bashkorts, whose historical ownership of Bashkortostan is acknowledged by Russia, rank third in number after Russians and Tatars (Table 13.1). Despite this the political apparatus is dominated by Bashkorts. Murtaza Rahimov, a Muslim Bashkort, was elected in December 1993 as the first president of the republic and a substantial member of his cabinet colleagues and senior officials are Bashkorts. Nevertheless the Bashkorts are conscious of their minority status and identify three important factors in their contemporary

Table 13.1   Demographic distribution in Bashkortostan, 1989

Ethnic group	Percentage of population	Number
Russian	39.3	1 548 291
Tatars (Muslim)	28.4	1 120 702
Bashkort (Muslim)	21.9	863 808
Chuvash (Christian)	3.0	118 509
Armenian (Christian)	0.1	2258
German (Christian)	0.3	11 023
Jewish (Jewish)	0.1	4911
Kazak (Muslim)	0.1	3564
Maris (Pagan)	2.7	105 768
Ukrainian (Christian)	1.9	74 990
Mordvinian (Christian)	0.8	31 923
Udmurt (Finno-Ugric)	0.6	23 696
Belorussian (Christian)	0.4	17 038
Latvian (Christian)	0.6	1956
Others	0.4	14 676
Total		3 943 113

Source: 1989 Soviet Census (Moscow, 1990).

national struggle: (1) their relations with Russia, which is the occupying power of their lands; (2) their interaction with Tatars, who are perceived as more articulate, sophisticated and dynamic, and 'dangerously' close to them culturally, linguistically and religiously; and (3) Bashkort nationalism, without which their national identity would be lost to the larger Tatar identity. These three factors are intertwined and Bashkort leaders are attempting to juggle them as adroitly as possible.

In 1557, after the conquest of the Tatar Kazan khanate (which included the Bashkort territory) by Ivan the Terrible in 1552 a delegation of Bashkorts arrived in Moscow and asked for their territory to be taken into Russian protection. Consequently the Russians have always asserted, and the Bashkorts have eagerly agreed, that the Bashkorts were not conquered but had voluntarily joined Russia.[2] In reality Russia never maintained a distinction between the territories acquired by treaty or conquered by force. The Russian political logic was that rebellion, after voluntary submission to Russia, amounted to treason. To the Bashkort leaders, however, rebellion against Russia was an inalienable right,[3] especially if the Russian state violated their national rights and usurped their lands.

During the next two hundred years Russia relentlessly colonised the territory by encouraging Russian peasants and small groups of Udmurts, Chuvashes and Maris to seize Bashkort land. Fertile land in north-western Bashkortostan was seized by members of the Russian gentry, the nobility and the Russian Orthodox Church. Moreover the region provided a substantial amount of revenue because of the tribute levied on the local population. In addition the Bashkort Urals became the centre of the Russian mining and smelting industry, which continued to grow very rapidly. By the end of the first quarter of the eighteenth century Bashkortostan had become a valuable colony, and Russia had no intention of relinquishing its control.

The never-ending Russian penetration of Bashkortostan provoked the Bashkorts to wage wars against Russia in 1662–64, 1675–83, 1705 and 1735–40, exploding the myth that after 'voluntarily joining' Russia the Bashkorts had lost the right to rebel. Nonetheless Bashkortostan remained a Russian colony, and in the process the Bashkorts lost their demographic majority in their own land.

With the incorporation of Bashkortostan and Tatarstan the Russian state became truly Eurasian; specifically, the conquest of Tatarstan extended Russia into Asia and the Caucasus, and the colonisation of Bashkortostan paved the way to Central Asia. By 1682 the Russian state covered 265 000 square miles (Table 13.2) – about 80 000 square miles in Europe and about 185 000 in Asia. The territorial acquisitions of 1533–1682 were truly dramatic, bearing in mind that in 1505 the tsardom of Moscow had consisted of only about 37 000 square miles.

The advent of Marxism–Leninism in Bashkortostan

Under Lenin, who described Russia as the jailhouse of nationalities, the nationality policy acquired a new dimension: reconciling the national

Table 13.2   Area of Russia, 1533–1682

Year	Square miles
1533	47 000
1584	125 000
1598	157 000
1676	257 000
1682	265 000

Source: D. Mackenzie Wallace, *Russia* (New York: Henry Holt, 1877), p. 506.

aspirations of large and small ethnic groups with Soviet imperatives. Eventually the age old policy of divide and rule was adopted within the Stalinist formula of 'national in form, socialist in content'. Under the monolithic rule of the Communist Party of the Soviet Union (CPSU), Stalinist policy meant political domination by Moscow, and the cultural and linguistic Russification of union and autonomous republics. In law the former had the 'right' to secede from the Soviet Union, the latter did not, so when the 15 union republics became independent in December 1991 the 21 autonomous republics, surrounded by so-called Russian territory, continued to be an 'inalienable' part of the Russian Federation.

What were the ideological principles that were supposed to govern the creation of the autonomous republics? In the Volga–Ural Basin the views of the Tatar and Bashkort leaders diverged. (Of course Moscow had a distinctly Stalinist policy of its own.) The Tatar Bolshevik leadership was dominated by Mulla Nur Vahitov and Mir-Said Sultan Galiev, who had articulated the theory of 'Muslim national communism' in the 1920s.[4] They envisaged a new state – Idel–Ural – that would be territorially broad and multiethnic, while the Bashkorts desired no more than an ethnic Bashkort state. However the demographic situation admirably suited the national aspirations of the Tatars (Table 13.3).

Obviously, under the generic title 'Turkic' the Tatar nationalist leaders included Muslim Bashkorts and other Turkic peoples who may or may not have been Muslim. It should also be kept in mind that the Russian census takers automatically included all baptised individuals in the category 'Great Russian' if they did not declare themselves as Mordivinian, Chuvash, Turkic or even Ukrainian. The Idel–Ural (Volga–Ural) state would include not only the present territories of Bashkortostan and Tatarstan, but also what are now the *oblasts* of Orenburg, Magnitogorsk

Table 13.3 Demographic Picture in the Volga–Ural Region

Ethnic group	Percentage of population	Number (million)
Turkic Tatar	51.0	7.848
Russian	28.0	4.290
Finno-Ugric Mongol	17.7	2.712
Germans	3.3	0.501
Total		15.351

Sources: 1926 Russian census and statistics preserved in the Volga–Ural region.

and Chelyabinsk, thus making the new state contiguous with what was then called Turkistan.[5] However Moscow interposed these three *oblasts* between Kazakhstan and Bashkortostan, and thus surrounded the conceptual state of Idel–Ural by Russian territory.

In 1918–19, when Bashkortostan was established, the Bashkort leaders were not enthusiastic about the planned Idel–Ural state. Zaki Velidi Togan,[6] who was then known as a Bolshevik leader in Bashkortostan, had previously established a military formation that had supported the anti-Bolshevik forces – the so-called White Russians, led by czarist General Kolchak – but had shifted his support to the Bolsheviks when the White Russians appeared to renege on their promise of self-determination for the Bashkorts. Under Stalin, Togan was denounced as an anti-Soviet nationalist and he took asylum in the Republic of Turkey, where he eventually died. Recently he has been resurrected as a Bashkort national hero and is idolised by the Bashkort government.

The Bashkorts' national aspirations fitted neatly into Stalin's four criteria for nationality – territory, language, psychological make-up and economy. Thus the Bashkort Autonomous Soviet Socialist Republic was established on 23 March 1919.[7] But in allowing Bashkort national autonomy, Moscow created an irredentist issue between the kindred states of Tatarstan and Bashkortostan. This was also related to the Soviet government's decision of 14 June 1922 to exclude the districts of Beleveev, Birsk and Ufa (where Tatars represented the majority of the population) from the Tatar Republic and to make them part of Bashkortostan. This made the Tatars the second largest ethnic majority after the Russians in Bashkortostan and is the Tatars' explanation of their numerical superiority in the republic.

Tatar nationalists assert that the Soviet government had promised referendums in these districts in order to determine whether the people would prefer to remain with Bashkortostan or join the Republic of Tatarstan, but that the promised referendum had been cancelled in 1922.[8] However the Bashkorts vehemently deny this and maintain that no such commitment had been made by the Soviet government.[9] To support their assertion they refer to the volume entitled *Documents, Papers and Materials on the Formation of Bashkortostan Autonomous Soviet Socialist Republic*, published in Russian in 1959, which is supposed to contain all relevant documents on territorial issues but contains nothing on the supposed referendum. In addition the Bashkorts claim that in the 1920s the Bashkorts had outnumbered the Tatars in these three districts, but that the subsequent mass repression of the

Bashkorts by the Bolsheviks had depopulated these regions and eventually turned the Bashkorts into a minority.

When I raised this territorial issue with Bashkort nationalist leaders in the summer of 1994, they gave me a copy of a memorandum of 5 May 1990 from the Presidium of the Supreme Soviet of the Bashkortostan ASSR to Murtaza G. Rahimov (later the president of Bashkortostan). This memorandum showed the demographic predominance of Bashkorts in the 1920s (see Table 9.2).

Writing in the 1950s, Serge Zenkovsky offered another thesis that highlights the Bashkorts' steady demographic decline from 1789, climaxing with the great famine of 1921 in the Volga–Ural Basin. According to Zenkovsy, Tatars started to migrate to the Bashkort lands during the sixteenth and seventeenth centuries, after the Russian conquest of the Kazan khanate in 1552. In 1789 the Russian government established a 'special privileged Bashkir ' *Voisko*', an autonomous military organisation. At that point many Tatars registered as Bashkorts and began to identify themselves as Bashkorts, but when the *Voisko* was dissolved and the Bashkorts' privileges were removed the Tatars once again began to call themselves Tatars. Naturally this distorted the official population statistics, but according to Zenkovsky 'There were only 95 000 Bashkorts in 1767, 1 493 000 in 1897, 741 000 in 1926, and of the latter only 393 000 spoke Bashkort, while the remainder used Tatar.'[10]

The famine of 1921 spread throughout Russia but it took a particularly heavy toll on the Bashkort population. 'In Bashkort territory alone, the population diminished by 25.1 per cent during the period 1917–1922. While Russian and Tatar agricultural areas in the Urals lost from one fifth to one sixth of their population, among the semi-nomadic Bashkorts nearly one third of the people starved to death.'[11] Between 1920 and 1926 the Bashkort population fell from 36.4 per cent to 23 per cent of the total population. According to another estimate, mortality among the Russian population of the Bashkort ASSR was 16.2 per cent, among the Tatars it was 19.2 per cent and among the nomadic Bashkorts it was as high as 29.1 per cent.[12]

This demographic anomaly is a source of friction between Tatarstan and Bashkortostan. The Bashkort leaders suspect that the Tatars in Bashkortostan want to rejoin their own republic, reducing Bashkortostan to a much smaller size. This irredentist issue has led to a tacit alliance between Bashkorts and Russians, which Tatars perceive as directed against them within the body-politic of Bashkortostan.

Without a grasp of the current and historical dynamics of Tatar–Bashkort relations the significance of the Bashkorts' national *Kurultai* (which was held on 1–2 May 1995 and will be discussed below) cannot be fully appreciated.

National reconstruction in Bashkortostan

The national reconstruction of Bashkortostan acquired political significance after the founding of the autonomous republic in 1919. The Bashkort leaders in the local CPSU dared not tackle this issue for fear of being branded as nationalists, and consequently as anti-Soviet. The opportunity eventually came their way during the declining years of the Soviet Union (1985–91). Bashkortostan proclaimed its sovereign status on 11 October 1990 and revealed its determination to achieve real rather than quasi autonomy. In December 1993 the first president in the republic's history, Murtaza Rahimov, was elected with 64 per cent of the votes.[13] and a new constitution was adopted. In the Bashkort parliament the ethnic mix among the 280 deputies was 35 per cent Russian, 27 per cent Bashkort and 27 per cent Tatar, while the national demographic figures were 39 per cent Russian, 28.4 per cent Tatar and 21.9 per cent Bashkort. The electoral success of the Bashkorts increased their clout in the state apparatus of the republic.

In respect of Russia, President Rahimov, and the Bashkort leadership in general, stated unequivocally that 'Bashkortostan is forever with Russia'.[14] Simultaneously, however, they demanded economic sovereignty. Not mentioned was the concept of political sovereignty, which of course remains the Tatars' ultimate national objective. The issue was crystallised in the all-Russia referendum of April 1993, when the Bashkort leadership inserted a fifth item into the referendum, emphasising Bashkortostan's economic sovereignty. Tatar and Russian public centres objected to the inclusion of the fifth item and urged the Tatar and Russian citizens to boycott the referendum. Nevertheless 74.9 per cent of voters endorsed economic sovereignty for Bashkortostan; 40.2 per cent voted for Yeltsin, and 36.5 per cent endorsed his economic policies.[15] Obviously the Russian and Tatar citizens exercised their own discretion and disregarded their leaders' advice.

Subsequently the Bashkort leadership reached a consensus on the republic's future relations with the Russian Federation, the central elements of which were that Bashkortostan would remain an integral part of the Russian Federation but with economic autonomy (or sovereignty as they described it), and that Russia would have exclusive power over matters of defence, communications, foreign policy and defence-related industries. The Bashkort leadership also demanded the right to establish economic relations with foreign countries, pointing out that such relations had already been established with Austria, Germany, Hungary and Turkey. Their emphasis on economic autonomy made a great deal of sense, especially in the light of Bashkortostan's past experience with the Soviet Union, with Moscow exercising direct control over 97 per cent of the republic's industries and only 3 per cent of small industries being managed by Ufa. Even the smallest issues had had to have the Soviet government's approval, and Moscow reserved the exclusive right to make all important and minor appointments.

Consequently when Bashkortostan signed the Federal Treaty with Russia on 31 March 1992 it included a five-point economic addendum that allowed the republic to legislate on matters relating to 'land, natural resources, properties of its multinational people, issues of ownership, usage and disposal of their properties, and define general principles of taxation for the Republic's budget'. Incidentally this treaty was also signed by 18 other autonomous republics, while Tatarstan, Ingushtia (which had recently split off from the Chechen–Ingush Republic but had not developed a state apparatus) and Chechnya refused to adhere to the treaty.

Finally, on 3 August 1994 President Rahimov signed a treaty with President Boris Yeltsin defining each country's areas of jurisdiction and the mutual delegation of powers between Moscow and Ufa. Rahimov stated that the treaty signified 'official consolidation of the results of the referendum of April 25, 1993', indicating Bashkortostan's determination 'to have the status of a sovereign state within the Russian Federation'. He added that 'in some respects we have more powers than Tatarstan'.[16] This may be an overstatement, but the fact remains that the August 1994 treaty implied Russian acknowledgement of the Bashkorts' ownership of their ancestral lands, This provided an enormous boost to the morale of the Bashkorts in general and President Rahimov in particular.

Consequently the stage was set in 1995 for nation-building activities. After a lapse of nearly 200 years, an international Bashkort *kurultai* (national assembly) was called for 1–2 June 1995 to review the state of the Bashkort nation, its current problems and future prospects. This was to be a major watershed in the revival of Bashkort nationalism. (D. K. Uzbekov, the executive director of the organising committee, sent the author an invitation to attend the *Kurultai* as an observer. The analysis of the *Kurultai* proceedings is largely based upon personal observations.)

Table 13.4   Number of delegates attending the Bashkort *Kurultai*, 1–2 June 1995

Foreign countries			
Germany	2	Turkey	6 (+ 11 non-Bashkorts)
Japan	1	USA	7
Finland	1	Switzerland	4
Italy	2	France	1
Poland	1	Peru	1
Hungary	6	Hong Kong	1
China	1	Total:	45
Former republics of the Soviet Union			
Ukraine	2	Tajikistan	2
Uzbekistan	7	Moldovia	1
Kazakhstan	8	Latvia	1
Azerbaijan	1	Turkmenistan	2
Khirghistan	1		
Belarus	1	Total:	26
Russian *oblasts*			
Chelyabinsk	50	Orenburg	17
Prem	17	Tyumen	15
Kurgan	12	Sverdlousk	15
Moscow	20	Samara	2
Kernerovo	1	Sarafov	1
Novosibirsk	2	Krasnoyarsk	1
Magadon	1	Uliyanovsk	1
Omsk	2	Tomsk	1
Myermansk	1	Kamchatka	1
Leningrad	1	Kirov	2
St. Petersburg	3	Total:	166
Autonomous republics within the Russian Federation			
Tatarstan	6	Dagestan	1
Komi	1	Mari El	1
Mordovia	1	Udmurtia	1
Chuvashia	1	Yakutia	1
The Kabardino – Balkan Autonomous Republic	1		
		Total	14

The Bashkort delegates can be divided into four categories: those from (1) foreign countries, (2) former republics of the Soviet Union, (3) various *oblasts* within Russia and (4) the autonomous republics within the Russian Federation (Table 13.4).

Altogether 251 Bashkort delegates attended the *Kurultai*, representing 56 different communities. The *Kurultai* had evidently been blessed by Moscow as it was represented by Vladimir Shumeiko (chairman of the Federation Council), Yuri Yaro (deputy chairman of the Russian government) and Alexander Kazakov (head of the department of Administration for the Russian President). Nine autonomous republics sent either high-ranking officials or ministers. Tatarstan sent the largest contingent – six delegates headed by the prime minister, Farid Mukhamedshin. The tiny Ingushtia Republic, which had split off from Chechnya with Moscow's blessing, was represented by its president, Ruslan Aushev. Particularly significant was the participation of the Russian commander of the Volga military district, Colonel General Anatoli Sergheyev, whose presence symbolised Moscow's lordship over these possessions.[17]

On 1 May the inaugural session got underway and delegates started to pour into the auditorium from the main entrance of the Social and Political Centre in Ufa. On the spacious forecourt of the building, singing and dancing to Bashkort folk music, men and women in their fifties and sixties welcomed contingent after contingent of official delegates. The external ambience was more that of a folk festival than a serious national conference.

Inside the auditorium the session started with President Murtaza Rahimov's thoughtful keynote address, which laid out the framework for serious deliberations on national problems. Rahimov highlighted several themes, including Bashkortostan's relations with Russia; the problem of the Bashkorts' spiritual revival and fear of assimilation; and the role of economy in national rejuvenation. The other topics fell within these themes.

Relations with Russia

Skilfully and in soothing words, Rahimov repeatedly professed loyalty to Russia while at the same time indicting the 'perfidious' policies that Russia had pursued towards the Bashkorts since 1557. Expressing his 'special pleasure' in welcoming the Russians, he looked them in the eye and said: 'khush kildeghez, tughandar' (welcome our dear friends). He assured the gathering that the Bashkort nation was alive and prospering'. It had not disappeared, nor had it 'yielded under the burden of hardest trials'. Bashkorts had not been 'lost on the dusty and blood-soaked roads of history'. Stretching from the Ural mountains to the Caspian Sea, Bashkortostan was the land of the Bashkorts. Other peoples, Rahimov implied, including the Tatars, Udmurts, Russians,

Chuvashes, Maris and other fellow citizens had merely settled on Bashkort ancestral land.

On a more conciliatory note, Rahimov pointed to the presence of delegates from Ukraine, Kazakhstan, Latvia and Russian cities, and then generously stated that their presence was an 'invitation to a reunification of the former Soviet Union nations, whose disunion had not been of their own free will'.[18] This statement was music to the Moscow emmissaries' ears.

Rahimov then asked, who are the Bashkorts, and what has been their fate since they were incorporated in Russia? Emerging on the world scene in the middle of the first millenium, Bashkorts had settled in the southern Urals. To prove this claim, Rahimov cited Ahmad Iban Fadhlan, who had noted the presence of Bashkorts in the first half of the tenth century. In 921 Caliph Al-Maktadir had sent Ibn Fadhlan, an Islamic missionary, to the Bulgar state, which the Tatars had established in the Volga–Ural Basin.[19] Both Tatars and Bashkorts had converted to Islam. For many centuries, Rahimov pointed out, the Bashkorts had been 'surrounded by or incorporated into mighty neighbours'. Clearly this referred to the Bashkorts being part of the Bulgar state from the tenth to the twelfth century, and then becoming part of the Golden Horde (Orduyu Mauzzam) from 1256–1502 and the Kazan khanate from 1437–1552.

Finally, the Bashkorts had been incorporated into Russia in 1557 under Ivan the Terrible. Rahimov applauded the Bashkort tribal chieftains' request for Russian protection and described it as 'a wise political decision'. In his perception, this new relationship – based on the 'voluntary joining' of the Bashkorts with Russia – had been in the nature of a social and political covenant, sealed by 'a *gramota* or a deed executed between Czar Ivan and the Bashkort tribes'. This covenant had bound the Russian government to allow the Bashkorts to remain on their land and profess their religion (Islam) protected from external enemies and 'living according to their own laws and customs'. In return the Bashkorts had undertaken 'to pay taxes and serve in the army'.[20]

Bashkortostan's integration into the Russian state, according to Rahimov, had been in the long-term interests of both countries. However, when the Russian state had grown stronger the czars, while officially upholding the unification terms had started surreptitiously to violate them. Starting in the eighteenth century, Moscow had established a feudal colonial relationship with Bashkortostan. Consequently, according to Rahimov, Bashkortostan's 'faithful sons' – Seit, Aldar,

Kusyum, Kilmyak, Karasakal, Batyrsha, Kiza and Salvat Yulayet – had led liberation movements against Russia. Despite these justifiable rebellions, Rahimov asserted, when external enemies had invaded Russia, Bashkorts had eagerly joined the Russian army 'to help protect the fatherland', and this should never be forgotten.

Another opportunity to transform social and political relations between the Bashkorts and the Russians had come about in 1917–19 when the Bolsheviks triumphed in Russia. Ahmed Zaki Validi Togan had led the way when the Soviet government signed an agreement in March 1919 to establish 'the autonomy of Bashkiria'. This act had been the second most significant historical accomplishment after the Bashkorts' voluntarily union with Russia in 1557. However Lenin's promise immediately after the revolution that Muslims would be free to live according to their laws and customs had soon been forgotten, and the declared doctrine on peoples' right to self-determination had been jettisoned. This had been the second betrayal, according to Rahimov, which he illustrated by two incidents.

First, in 1922 the Boslshevik Party had debated the question of the future state structure. A proposal to bring the status of the autonomous states into line with that of the union republic had been supported by Mir Said Sultan Galiev, a prominent Tatar leader born in Bashkortostan. The proposal had also been strongly endorsed by the Bashkort leaders, including A. Adigamov, A. Bikbavov and C. Murzabulatov, who were subsequently executed by Stalin during the infamous purges. However the proposal had been rejected.

Second, in 1936, when the draft of a new constitution for the Soviet Union had been discussed, a proposal had been made to elevate the autonomous states of Tatarstan and Bashkortostan to union republic status. Stalin had personally rejected the proposal in his speech at the Eighth Congress of the Soviets on 25 November 1936, saying that they could not be transformed into union republics because they were surrounded on all sides by union republics and Soviet regions; consequently, they could not secede from the Soviet Union.

Despite the loss of autonomy and the failure to achieve union republican status, Rahimov conceded that during the Soviet period Bashkortostan had made considerable economic and cultural progress: the state had been industrialised; agriculture had been mechanised; oil had been discovered and extracted; engineering, chemical and petrochemical industries had been developed; urbanisation had been accelerated; illiteracy had been eradicated; a national educational system had been established; and intellectuals and scientists had been nurtured. On the debit side, the command economy had remained quagmired in the administrative jungle.

During Gorbachev's *perestroika* years (1985–91), Rahimov pointed out, the Bashkort leaders had supported the democratisation and renovation of the Soviet Union. Sadly, he added; 'It is not our fault that the Union Treaty was never signed, and the Soviet Union was dissolved in December 1991'.[21]

The third phase of the relationship with Russia had gotten underway in the post-Soviet period when a definitive treaty had been signed on 3 August 1994 and economic autonomy ('sovereignty') had been achieved, independent legislative and judicial systems established and a procurator's office created. This accomplishment, according to Rahimov, had led the way to the construction of 'a real federal state' in Russia. In a short period of time Bashkortostan had 'adopted 13 republican codes and more than 160 laws', dealing with 'issues of statehood construction, social–economic and cultural–spiritual development'. However, he warned, 'there are people in Russia's upper echelons of power who would like to degrade the significance of the Federation Treaty, and to neglect the obligations fixed by the Treaty'.[22]

Rahimov softened this criticism of the Russian leaders by reiterating that 'for four centuries Bashkortostan has been loyal to its historic choice [of voluntarily joining Russia in 1557]. There has never been and never will be a single political movement which questions Bashkortostan's status within the Russian Federation.'[23]

The fear of assimilation

More than the fear of the Russian bear, Rahimov was 'alarmed' by the Bashkorts' assimilation into other cultures – they were losing their 'national features and peculiarities'. Moreover, increasingly fewer Bashkorts were able to speak their mother tongue[24] and many had lost sight of their national culture, history, customs and traditions. He also lamented the fact that a number of Bashkorts were losing their national and historical self-awareness. In Rahimov's eyes this was unacceptable since Bashkortostan was their 'historical native land, and the only place on earth where the Bashkort nation can consolidate [itself]'. However, he asserted, other peoples bare a special responsibility for the Bashkorts' national development: it was in their national interest 'to create favourable conditions for Bashkort self-development and to remove age-long obstacles on the road to spiritual self development'.[25] This proposition was directed primarily at the Russians and to a lesser extent at the Tatars, but Rahimov did not elaborate on the nature of their responsibilities.

Within the multiethnic state, Rahimov proposed several measures for the special development of the Bashkort people, and that these measures be passed into law by the state legislature. First, the Bashkorts and their language and culture belong to world history, and the State of Bashkortostan should guarantee the preservation of the Bashkort people, culture and language. Second, the legislation should 'take into account the interests of the whole of the Bashkort nation, irrespective of their residence and citizenship', and these interests should be coordinated with 'those of the entire multinational population of the republic'.

Third, Bashkorts should receive special training for state positions and they should be sent to leading Russian and foreign educational centres for the purpose. To achieve these objectives, Rahimov pointed out, a Commission on Personnel had been established and functioned under the guidance of the Presidential Council.

Fourth, the Bashkorts' standard of living should be improved by means of employment, and their migration to other areas should be discouraged as there had been a steady decline in the number of Bashkorts living in the republic. Bashkorts returning to the republic from former Soviet republics should be allotted housing and jobs. To these ends he proposed that economic agreements be negotiated with Kazakhstan, Uzbekistan, Kirghyzstan, Moldova and the Baltic states. Finally, further measures should be taken 'to elaborate the basics of interethnic and interstate relations'.[26]

Closely related to the issue of cultural development was Rahimov's emphasis on 'the legal guarantee of preserving and developing the [Bashkort] mother tongue'. However the issues of language and assimilation were intertwined and would have to be disentangled for the purpose of analysis and to discover what was implicit in their formulation.

The assimilation process operates at two levels in Bashkortostan. First, Bashkorts have extensively assimilated with their kindred coreligionists (Sunni Muslim), the Tatars. In western Bashkortostan in particular, up to 55 per cent of all marriages are between Bashkorts and Tatars. Second, the republic as a whole, intermarriage between Bashkorts and Russians is about 8–10 per cent (as a part of the policy of Russification the CPSU encouraged intermarriage between the Russian and non-Russian peoples of the Soviet Union).

The Bashkort national leadership frowns upon such assimilation, and especially intermarriage between the Bashkorts and the Tatars. Why? Perhaps the explanation lies in the language issue. Is the

Bashkort language distinctly separate from Tatarski? According to the rules of linguistics the differences between them are minimal. There is no difference between grammar, script (which was Arabic before Cyrillic was adopted, literary forms and vocabulary. Whatever lexical or phonetic differences there might be are only regional variations, especially among Bashkorts who have traditionally lived in isolation in the southern Urals.[27] It is by no means a simplification to say that when Tatars speak the language it is Tatarski, when Bashkorts speak it, it becomes Bashkort. It is, however, true that Tatars and Bashkorts are different in their ethnic origins.

What is more dangerous to Bashkort survival: assimilation with the Russians or with the Tatars? Bashkort political and cultural leaders were stunned into silence when I demanded an answer to this question, but they eventually replied: 'assimilation with the Tatars of course'. The exception was the mufti of Bashkortostan, who gave a delightfully evasive Islamic answer: 'Muslims should marry only Muslims'.[28]

Ironically, in Bashkortostan it is the assimilation of one Islamic community into another that is the crux of the problem. Consequently a tacit alliance has developed between the Bashkorts and the politically and demographically dominant Russians that is likely to sour relations between the Bashkorts and Tatars. Against this, it should be pointed out that the Tatar National Centre in Ufa has also adopted a counter-productive policy on the language issue, especially in demanding equal status between Tatar and the Russian and Bashkort languages. I asked Tatar leaders why, if there was virtually no difference between the Bashkort and Tatar languages, they were demanding protection of the Tatar language.[29] No convincing explanation was given, but I gained the impression that the issue really revolved around the interethnic struggle for power and the Bashkort leadership's determination to utilise the state's resources to establish their separate identity and preserve for themselves a dominant position, with Russian support.

The role of the economy

In his keynote address Rahimov tackled the issue of the Bashkortostan economy. The republic, he pointed out, ranked 'among the six most developed republics of the former Soviet Union'. However the economy remained unstable, and the reform programme, which had laid the foundations for 'a socially-oriented market economy', had not in any significant way improved the standard of living. In order to improve the economy and modernise industry, a substantial injection of capital was needed, but was not available.

However Rahimov presented an impressive picture of production, research and development in the republic:

- Bashkortostan was rich in oil, natural gas, ferrous, non-ferrous and precious metals, timber, coal, building materials, water resources and raw materials for the chemical industry.
- It annually produced about 20 million tons of oil, 1.1 million tons of coal, 25 billion kilowatt hours of power, more than 200 000 tons of steel, 250 000 tons of mineral fertilisers and 116 000 tons of polythene.
- It ranked among the top producers in terms of gross agricultural output.
- The standard of equipment, machinery and technology had not been degraded.
- In the engineering field 182 competitive new items had been developed during 1990–95 because Bashkortostan was one of the leading centres of fundamental and applied research.
- Operating in the republic were an Academy of Science, a research centre in Ufa, 24 research and development institutes, 13 academic institutes and 'dozens of design businesses'.[30]

Consequently, Rahimov asserted, the industrial slump of 1994 had not been as severe in Bashkortostan as in the Russian Federation as a whole. He invited foreign businessmen to invest in Bashkortostan, and promised to provide all the necessary conditions for success and the profitable application of their funds. He also spoke of harmonising the republic's economic development with the spiritual development of its citizens.

After this extensive survey of Bashkortostan's political and economic landscape the delegates were split up into ten panels, each dedicated to discussing one of Bashkortostan's national concerns: (1) lessons of history: demographic problems; (2) the state system; (3) the Bashkort diaspora; (4) the Bashkort language; (5) the environment, health and preservation of the gene pool; (6) economic relations; (7) Bashkort social and political movements; (8) Bashkort ethnos: rebirth and perspectives; (9) women and the family; and (10) Bashkort youth. Altogether 65 papers were presented at these panels.

At the invitation of his host, Professor Rail Gumerovich Kuzeev, the present author attended the first panel (the lessons of history). A well-known scholar in Bashkortostan, Professor Kuzeev belongs to the Kothaj clan, which has settled in the north-east of Ufa. In addition to being director of Bashkortostan's Museum of Archaeology and Ethnography, he is a member of the Russian Academy of Sciences and an academician at the Bashkortostan Academy of Sciences.

The panel also included Irek Gaisievich Akmanov (professor of Bashkort history at Bashkort State University), Niz Abdul Haq Mazhitov (a member of the Bashkortostan Academy of Sciences), R. Z. Yanguzin (professor of history) and Rosa Gafarovna Burkanova (candidate for a doctorate in history and senior lecturer at the Bashkort State University). Five others were invited to participate in the discussions: Jyhat Sultanov (a freelance writer), Saima Gazatullina (an educator), R. Utagulov (a Bashkort activist from Sibai in eastern Bashkortostan), A. Yainullin (also a Bashkort activist) and Yanturin Diaz (a historian at the Bashkortostan State University). Dr Isenbike Togan (daughter of the Bashkortostan national leader, Zaki Velidi Togan, and a professor at Istanbul University in Turkey) sat silently through some of the discussions and then left without a word of explanation.

In their passionate presentations, which were full of the fervour of revived Bashkort nationalism, the four official speakers followed in the footsteps of President Rahimov and spoke on the Bashkorts' demographic decline; the threat of assimilation; Russia's perfidious behaviour towards those Bashkorts who had 'voluntarily joined' Russia in 1557; Bashkort rebellions, especially the one associated with Pugachev in 1773–75 and supported by the charismatic poet-warrior Salavat Yuliev, now Bashkortostan's national hero (a gigantic statue of him dominates the environs of the Bashkort Supreme Soviet in Ufa); Russia's confiscation of Bashkort lands after each rebellion and the expulsion of Bashkorts to other lands; and Russia's forceful, relentless but unsuccessful attempts to convert Bashkorts to Christianity.

Yanguzin proposed an interesting demographic theory to explain the decline of the Bashkort population. Referring to the presence of Teptiars in the nineteenth century, he asserted that they were not Tatars. Teptiar, a sociological term, was a corruption of *dafter*, (register) an Arabic word, and certain people who were registered in official registers came to be known as Teptiars. Subsequently they were erroneously listed as Tatars. He bemoaned the fact that Bashkorts living in the Menzilaski area (which had been transferred to Tatarstan when that republic was created in 1920) had been assimilated into the Tatar nation. Moreover a large number of Bashkorts living in the Chelyabinsk *oblast* had been educated in Russian, and not in the Bashkort language. In the 1979 Soviet census more than 37 per cent of Bashkorts had registered Tatar as their mother tongue. In northern and

western Bashkortostan, which includes Ufa, 200 000 Bashkorts erroneously thought, asserted Yanguzin, that their mother tongue was
Tatar. He concluded that Bashkortostan's basic national problem was
assimilation into the Tatar nation.

Plowing back through ancient history, Utagulov claimed
Chelyabinsk back for the Bashkort motherland: 'It is our land, which is
the cradle of Arkiam civilisation.'[31] The Arkiam civilisation, according
to the Russian archaeologists who discovered it in 1987, was an impressive Bronze Age culture and contemporary to the civilisations that built
the pyramids in Egypt and the Cretan–Mycenaean palaces. The sites of
the Arkiam civilisation stretch along the eastern slopes of the Urals for
almost 400 kilometers from north to south in the Chelyabinsk *oblast.*
'The geography described in the earliest parts of the *Rigveda* and *Avesta*
coincides with the historical geography of the southern Urals in the
18th–16th centuries B.C.'[32] Consequently Russian scholars hypothesise
that the land occupied by the Arkiam civilisation was the original
home of the Indo-Iranians (or Aryans)[33] who migrated to India, Iran
and Europe.[34]

Historically, most if not all the lands now incorporated into
Bashkortostan's neighbouring *oblasts* of Orenburg and Chelyabinsk
belonged to Bashkortostan. Consequently there is a muted but simmer-
ing irredentist claim by the Bashkorts against Russia. Utagulov also
proposed that a territorial claim be made on a historical Karawan
Saray, which was supposedly built in Orenburg by the Bashkorts' forefathers in ancient times. 'The government of Bashkortostan must proclaim it an extraterritorial property of ours, and maintain it at our own
expense.' Utagulov forcefully urged the delegates to adopt his views as
an official *Kurultai* proposal.

Yanturin Diaz enthusiastically joined in the discussion on
Chelyabinsk, highlighting the little known fact that a nuclear accident
had occurred there in 1957 but had been hushed up by the Soviet
Union. Diaz maintained that the Chelyabinsk accident had been far
more serious in terms of radioactive fallout than the world famous
Chernobyl accident. He suggested that the United Nations should
recognise it as a disaster area, and that the Russian government should
compensate the Bashkorts, the main victims of the fallout.

It might be added that in March 1993 more than 160 000 Bashkorts
living in the districts of Argaishkii, Kunashakskii and Sunsnowskii
gathered in a *Kurultai* in Chelyabinsk, where they articulated two
major grievances against Moscow. First, in 1957 the Bashkort population had suffered the medical and genetic consequences of nuclear

explosion in Miaak. Repeated explosions had caused radioactive pollution of the area, eventually forcing the transfer of the Bashkort population to non-Bashkort areas. The people who had been poisoned by radiation had received no compensation (A copy of a very detailed memorandum articulating these grievances was handed to the present author in April 1993 in Ufa with the request that it be passed on to Mr Boutros Boutros-Ghali, secretary general of the United Nations.) Second, in 1934 Bashkort land, unlawfully and against the will of the Bashkort people, had been transferred to Chelyabinsk *oblast*, where the Bashkort language had been suppressed in schools and colleges and all publications in the Bashkort language had been banned, lowering the percentage of those speaking the language from 95 per cent in 1959 to 84 per cent in 1989.[35]

Diaz went on to criticise fellow Bashkorts who were not making a serious effort to contain the Tatars' activities. Certainly the Russian government was indifferent about Tatars flooding western Bashkortostan with Tatar publications and 'converting Bashkorts into Tatars'. Some Bashkorts were 'culturally subversive', Diaz asserted, and must be 'declared enemies of the nation' because they had adopted an 'alien' language and Tatar culture. Even President Rahimov had delivered his speech in Russian; how appropriate was that? In reexamining Bashkort relations with Russia, Diaz debunked the officially preferred theory that the Bashkorts had 'voluntarily joined' Russia in 1557. Rather it had been *vaulap alyn*, a Russian conquest of Bashkortostan. Not even Zaki Validi Togan had been in favour of union with Russia in the 1920s. With considerable justification Diaz maintained that even Russia had not subscribed to the theory of voluntary union before the Second World War.

The 'unkindest cut of all' was that Matrosov, a Second World War hero whose statue stands resplendently in a park in Ufa, had been misappropriated by Moscow as a Russian. Born in 1923 in the Uchaly district, the orphaned Shakiryan Mukhamet (Muhammad), a Bashkort Muslim, had been drafted into the Soviet Army with the Russified name of Matrosov. During a battle he had covered with his own body a German machine gun situated in an earth dugout, thus opening the way for the 1943 Russian offensive in central Russia. Diaz pointed out that Matrosov had not hidden his origin from his friends, but since he did not have a typical Bashkort appearance, he could easily pass for a Russian.

In conclusion, Diaz proposed a solution to the Bashkorts' demographic dilemma. Bashkorts must raise large families, larger than the

Tatars and Russians. The Uzbeks had emerged triumphant because they had bred many children. 'Let us emulate them, and have many, many children.' However not every one agreed with him!

Speaking after Diaz on a deep-seated Bashkort fear, Yainullin denounced the possibility of any union between Tatarstan and Bashkortostan, and urged the *Kurultai* to recommend the adoption of the Bashkort language as the official national language of Bashkortostan.

The last session of the *Kuraltai* was devoted to the adoption of eight resolutions. Seven were more or less operational; the eighth was in the nature of seven addresses to draw the attention of (1) the Bashkort nation at large, (2) the peoples of the Republic of Bashkortostan, (3) the State Assembly of Bashkortostan, (4) the president of the Russian Federation, (5) the Federal Assembly of the Russian Federation, (6) the administration of the Russian Federation and (7) the United Nations.

The preamble of the first resolution emphasised that the 'Bashkort people have inhabited the southern Urals for more than 1000 years, struggled for freedom and independence, and managed to preserve their language, mode of life and culture.' The *Kuraltai* decided to establish an executive committee and declare the city of Ufa as the *Kuraltai's* permanent venue. The executive committee was assigned the following responsibilities:

- Implementing the *Kuraltai's* decisions.
- Helping with the realisation of the state programme on the revival and development of the Bashkort nation.
- Undertaking an intermediary role in settling regional conflicts on a democratic basis and meeting the spiritual demands of Bashkorts living outside Bashkortostan.
- Establishing a fund for the Bashkort nation.
- Encouraging the state assembly of Bashkortostan to adopt laws on the revival and development of the Bashkort nation and the languages of the nations of the Republic of Bashkortostan.
- Monitoring the progress of programmes by the Bashkortostan Cabinet of Ministers on the restructuring of the economy, combatting unemployment (including that of the native population), the development of higher education and secondary vocational training, improving the ecological and demographic situation, improving health standards and increasing the birth rate, improving communications and interaction, the introduction of satellite television, and reviving the Bashkort language, culture and traditions.[36]

The resolution addressed to the Bashkort nation was noteworthy because it involved Islam in bringing about social reforms among the Bashkorts. Alcoholism was condemned as it violated Islamic canons. The republic was urged to introduce anti-alcohol instruction in all Bashkort schools and institutions, and 'to stigmatise all those [who] trade in alcohol in pursuit of quick personal enrichment at the expense of peoples' health'. Bashkorts should strive for a higher standard of education and morality, be fluent in their mother tongue and skilful in making public speeches in other languages, and sufficiently knowledgeable about Russian and Bashkortostan history, philosophy, religion and morality. (It should be pointed out that during the panel discussions, especially the one attended by the present author), some participants took exception to the suggestion that Bashkorts were addicted to alcohol. One critic even called it a slanderous statement, 'maligning the good Bashkort name'.

The issue of intermarriage, leading to Bashkorts being assimilated into other cultures, was also raised in this address. It was categorically stated that 'We are not opposed to intermarriage', yet the tenor of the discussions weighed heavily against Bashkorts marrying non-Bashkorts without being 'concerned for the fate of ethnic groups they represent'. The resolution also bemoaned the fact that in some Bashkort villages there were too few girls of marriageable age: 'the number of unmarried [Bashkort] men is exceedingly high'. This national problem was crying out for solution.[37]

Pointing to the tragedy of Chechnya, another resolution urged the peoples of Bashkortostan to cultivate harmony and interethnic trust and friendship. All problems and conflicts should be resolved peacefully and in a civilised manner. This was in fact a message to the Russian leadership. Simultaneously, however, in the address to the State Assembly of the republic, the *Kurultai* lamented the fact that for centuries other peoples from the central regions of Russia had been settling in 'time-honoured Bashkort lands', facilitating the assimilation of Bashkorts while 'the forced migration of Bashkorts to other regions of Russia and the former Soviet Union took place'. Consequently the Bashkorts had become only the third largest group in the republic. This fact, it was asserted, had become a political 'trump in the hands of those [who were opposed] to preserving the integrity of Bashkortostan and interethnic stability within it'.

In the light of these factors the *Kurultai* called on the Bashkortostan legislature to adopt laws on the revival and development of the

Bashkort people; ensure that the Bashkort people would undergo 'worthy political, social, economic, cultural and spiritual development'; protect and develop the Bashkort language 'on equal terms with the languages of the other people living in the Republic'; and protect the people against unemployment, inflation and material and spiritual destitution.[38]

In another resolution the *Kurultai* called on the regional administrative heads of the Russian Federation, especially those in regions where Bashkorts lived in significant numbers, for example Chelyabinsk and Orenburg, to help their Bashkort minorities to learn their native language, preserve their traditional customs and give up their addiction to alcoholic beverages. Moreover radio and TV schedules should include programmes in the Bashkort language. Likewise, newspapers, theatres, concerts and education should be arranged through the medium of the Bashkort language. Special credit was given to the Chelyabinsk State University and the Orenburg State Teachers Training Institute, which trains language specialists for Bashkort schools.[39]

In resolution addressed to the Federal Assembly of the Russian Federation the *Kuraltai* reiterated historical Bashkort grievances against Russia and articulated its fears about Russia's future intentions. The treaty of 3 August 1994 between Russia and Bashkortostan had regularised their relations, demonstrating 'a civilised path of development of truly federal relations between the Russian Federation and its subjects', but the relationship was now being threatened by 'Russian Supreme bodies which favour the replacement of the federation of national and state formations by cultural and national autonomy'. In other words Moscow was now threatening to abrogate the treaty unilaterally in order to convert the ethnic autonomous republics into *oblasts*. Against this political background the *Kurultai* delivered a blunt warning to Russia: if Moscow were to pass a law to set aside the treaty it would 'result sooner or later in ethnic conflicts in Russia, and eventually in Russia's disintegration'.[40]

A similar resolution was addressed to President Boris Yeltsin, reminding him of the dangers lurking in the structure of the Russian Federation, and the threat that would be posed to its integrity if attempts were made to abrogate the treaty of 1994. The *Kurultai* again pointed to Bashkortostan's loyalty to Russia since 1557, and attempted to reconcile the multiethnic character of the Russian Federation with ethnic formations. 'Remember, Boris Nikolayevich Yeltsin, the might of the Russian State depends upon the prosperity of each separate nation, each ethnic community, each region'.

Finally, not fully recognising the United Nations' impotence, and its inability to solve political problems and preserve the independence and integrity of small nations, the *Kurultai* addressed a resolution for its consideration. The crux of the resolution was the necessity 'to proclaim national sovereignty as one of the main principles of solving ethnic issues'. Finally, the resolution urged all the nations of the world to unite 'to solve both global and ethnic issues'.[41]

The *Kurultai* was officially adjourned when the ten panels had ended their discussions. That evening was filled with festivities, including concerts, folk dances, banquets and fireworks.

Despite the joyous mood of revived nationalism the Bashkort elites remain preoccupied with the destiny of their nation. Demographically, the Bashkorts' 'voluntary' union with Russia has taken a heavy toll on their numbers and no amount of extra breeding is likely to reverse the balance in their favour. They are likely to remain a minority in their own republic. This gnawing fear continually haunts them.

Islamic reassertion and Bashkort nationalism

Consequently the assimilation of Bashkorts with Tatars is decried by the leaders, and Bashkort–Tatar intermarriages are presented as a threat to Bashkort national survival. This political–cultural 'defensive attack' makes no waves at the grass roots level because social harmony and mutual admiration exist between the two Islamic-Turkic communities. While the Bashkort political leadership emphasises their different ethnic origins, Islam and their common language and culture magnetically draw the two peoples together, leading to a substantial number of intermarriages between Bashkorts and Tatars. This mutual attraction is not likely to diminish unless Bashkort nationalism degenerates into a virulent form of chauvinism and tears apart the social fabric of Bashkortostan.

Much to the evident discomfort of Bashkort political leaders, Islamic leaders in the mufti's office in Ufa emphasise Islamic solidarity and tacitly condone intermarriage among Muslims of diverse ethnic backgrounds, especially if they, like the Bashkorts and Tatars, happen to be Sunni Muslims. This Islamic social policy is likely to spread widely with the Islamic resurgence that is now underway in Bashkortostan.

When describing the resurgence of Islam in Bashkortostan, the mufti of Ufa informed the present author that in order to provide *imams* for the mosques, three new *madaras* were established by 1994 in the towns of Oktyabrsky, Ayidel and Belorezk. Plans are also on the drawing board to build two more in the towns of Sibaiy and Sterlitamak. In the three functioning *madaras*, 150 students are enrolled for a two-year Islamic studies course. For further studies, some religious students have been sent to *madaras* in Tatarstan; two advanced scholars are studying in Saudi Arabia, and two in Sudan. These trained scholar-*imams* will staff the mosques that are now being built in Bashkortostan' to compensate partially for the 1500 mosques destroyed by the Soviet Union.[42]

Despite the revival of Bashkort nationalism the *imams* are unlikely to discourage Bashkort–Tatar intermarriage and may thus encourage the nationalists to step up their campaign against assimilation. However this is an uncertain prediction; after all, Islam has been exploited by the powers that be for all kinds of purposes.

The demographic pendulum would swing more in the Bashkorts' favour if they accepted the transfer of Tatar-dominated regions to Tatarstan. However they would still only be the second largest group. Furthermore this suggestion would be seen as heresy as it would reduce the size of their republic and result in a substantial reduction of their industrial and agricultural resources. Instead the Bashkorts have entered into a tacit alliance with the Russians to ensure a dominant political role for themselves. 'The land belongs to us; other nationalities are only settlers' is the cornerstone of their policy, which is aimed at their achieving positions of power in the republic's political system and apparatus, a dominant role in policy making and a revival of Bashkort nationalism in order to stop their assimilation with Russians and Tatars. In their perception this is the best course to take, but it is fraught with political dangers.

The Bashkorts' loyalty to Russia since 1557 has never been fully rewarded. Russia has repeatedly ignored even minimal Bashkort national cultural and political aspirations. The communists delivered heavy blows to their sacred convictions, as enshrined in their Islamic heritage, and the previous tsarist regimes tried relentlessly to convert them to Christianity. The ink was barely dry on the treaty of August 1994 when strident calls were made in Moscow for the abrogation of the treaty. With this dismal record, covering more than four centuries, how can the Bashkorts depend upon Russian magnanimity in safeguarding their national aspirations? The answer to this rhetorical question lies in the hope Bashkorts are placing on the democratisation process in Russia, where the representatives in the Duma supposedly reflect the conscience of the Russian nation.

While the reopening of the Duma was a welcome sign of the demise of communist totalitarianism, it is by no means a respected institution or firmly established in Russian political culture. The first Duma in the history of Russia was elected in April 1906, but it existed for only 72 days. The second, which started in 1707, lasted a bit longer – 103 days. The third functioned from 1907 to 1912. The fourth ended two months short of its five-year term. After the February revolution of 1917 the Duma deputies had to dismiss themselves in favour of a temporary Duma Committee, which included some well-known Russian politicians of the tsarist period, such as Kerensky (who later became prime minister), Rodzianko, Gutchkov, Milyukov and Nakrasov. In October 1917 the 'new revolution' began, and on 14 December Vladimir Lenin, chairman of the Council of People's Deputies, signed a decree to dissolve the Duma.[43]

For 72 years Russia functioned as a communist totalitarian system. Under Gorbachev's leadership (1985–91), in March 1989 the first competitive elections were held for the Supreme Soviet and many Communist party candidates were defeated. In June 1991 Boris Yeltsin was elected to the newly created Russian presidency. On 30 December 1991 the Supreme Soviet was forced to dissolve itself as two days previously the Soviet political leaders, headed by Yeltsin, had dissolved the Soviet Union. A new chapter opened in the struggle between President Yeltsin and the Russian Congress of People's Deputies, which had been elected in March 1990. This conflict ended tragically in October 1993, when on Yeltsin's orders Russian tanks opened fire on the White House, home of the Russian Duma. In January 1994, in line with the new Russian constitution, an emasculated Duma was inaugurated in a building near the Kremlin.[44]

Will the new Russian Duma be more fortunate than its predecessors? Only time will tell, but this author has serious doubts about the survival of Russian democracy. Is it wise for the Bashkorts to pin so many of their hopes on such a fragile democracy, which is likely to continue to experience serious political convulsions in the foreseeable future? Russian nationalist leaders, including Yeltsin's closest advisers, resent Russia's treaty relations with the autonomous republics, which they perceive as simply vassal states. Their resentment is focused primarily on Tatarstan, which was the first republic to insist successfully upon a negotiated settlement of its relations with Moscow, and Bashkortostan, which essentially exploited the Tatar-created precedent.

The Bashkort leaders' policy of maintaining good relations with Tatarstan is an astute one because Moscow is sensitive to the combined strength of the two republics in the Volga–Ural Basin. Arising from the fear of assimilation, the artificially created tensions between Bashkorts and Tatars within Bashkortostan could get out of control and eventually embitter Bashkortostan–Tatarstan relations and inflict incalculable damage on both, as well as shatter the social harmony within Bashkortostan. The Bashkort leaders' present game of *ménage à trois* is not without substantial risks, and they should be more sensitive to its danger than they have been so far.

Notes and references

1. Bernard Pares, a well-known British historian of Russia, has described Mongols as Tatars and *vice versa*. See his *History of Russia* (New York: Alfred A. Knopf, 1960), pp. 54–5. This myth is deeply embedded in Russian historiography and repeated *ad nauseum* in Russia as the Tatar yoke.
2. 'In 1557 Bashkiria joined Russia voluntarily'; so states a document published by the Chamber of Industry of the Republic of Bashkortostan (Ufa, 1994), p. 14.
3. Alton S. Donnelly, *The Russian Conquest of Bashkiria, 1552–1940* (New Haven, CT: Yale University Press, 1968), p. 19.
4. Alexandre A. Bennigsen and S. Enders Wimbush, *Muslim National Communism in the Soviet Union: A Revolutionary Struggle for the Colonial World* (Chicago, Ill.: University of Chicago Press, 1974), pp. 37–60.
5. Alexandre Bennigsen, 'Marxism or Pan-Islamism: Russian Bolsheviks and Tatar National Communists at the Beginning of the Civil War, July 1918', *Central Asia Survey*, vol. 6, no. 2 (1987), p. 56.
6. Ahmed Zeki Validov (Zeki Velidi Togan) (1890–1969) was a Bashkort political leader and historian, born in the southern Urals (village of Kuzen), son of an *imam*, studied in the *medrasseh* of Kasymiyeh (Kazan) and graduated from the University of Kazan. In 1909 he was a professor of history at the University of Kazan. In May 1917 he took an active part in the First All-Russia Muslim Congress as the leader of the Bashkort national movement. He was at certain times president of the Bashkort *Shura*, and of the Bashkort government (1918), and head of the Bashkort army during the civil war. Disgusted with Kolchak's antiminority policy, he joined the Bolsheviks. From 1919–20 he was the war commissar of the Soviet Socialist Republic of Bashkiria. In 1919 he represented the RCP at the First Congress of the Komintern, but in June 1920 he was the first of the Muslim leaders to understand that no cooperation was possible with the Bolsheviks. Together with some of his Bashkort comrades he fled to Turkestan and joined the Bashmachis. In 1922 he left Turkestan for Afghanistan and then Turkey. He was a brilliant scholar and became director of historical studies at the University of Istanbul in the Republic of Turkey. Bennigsen and Winbush, *Muslim National Communism*, op. cit, pp. 210–11.
7. The decree was signed by M. Kalinin, chairman of the All-Russian Central Executive Committee, and is included in *Documents, Papers and Materials on the Formation of Bashkorian Autonomous Soviet Socialist Republic*, Central Archive of BASSR (in Russian) (Ufa: Bashkirskoe Knizrol Izdatelstva, 1959), pp. 738–9.
8. Raphael S. Khakimov, 'Political Life of Tatarstan', *Tatars and Tatarstan* (in Russian) (Kazan: Tatar Book Publishing Co., 1993), pp. 94–7.

9. Author's interviews and discussion with the director (Dr Zinnur G. Uracsin) and his colleagues, Rimat Yussupov (head of the Anthropological Section), Khamza Usmanov (head of Bashkort History) and Salawat Kasimov (Department of Muslim Bashkort History) at the Institute of History, Language and Literature of Bashkortostan, Ufa, June 1993.

10. Serge Zenkovsky, *Pan-Turkism and Islam in Russia* (Cambridge, Mass.: Harvard University Press), p. 207.

11. Ibid.

12. Rahimov's rival in the presidential election was Rafis Faizovich Kadyrov, who is described in his internal passport as a Bashkort, but 'he does not know the Bashkort language', implying that in reality he is a Tatar. Author's interview with officials of the Bashkort National Centre, Ufa, 8 June 1994.

13. *Bashkortostan* (Ufa, 31 March 1995), p. 2.

14. Sh. Tipeev, *Bashkorstan Tarihi* (Ufa, 1930), p. 94.

15. Information provided to the author by the president's office in Ufa on 26 April 1993.

16. Radik Batyrshin, 'Russian Federation: Yeltsin and Rahimov Reach an Agreement', *Nezavisimaya Gazata, The Current Digest of the Post Soviet Press* (CDPSP), vol. XLVI, no. 31 (31 August 1994), p. 14. For Tatarstan's treaty negotiations and an analysis of the final treaty see Hafeez Malik, 'Tatarstan's Treaty with Russia: Autonomy or Independence', *Journal of South Asian and Middle Eastern Studies*, vol. XVIII, no. 2 (Winter 1994), pp. 1–36.

17. Author's personal notes, taken in the auditorium.

18. Text of President Rahimov's typed speech, p. 2 (personal copy).

19. Azade-Ayse Rorlich, *The Volga Tatars: A Profile in National Resilience* (Stanford, CA: Hoover Institution Press, 1986), pp. 10–11.

20. Ibid., p. 4.

21. Ibid., p. 12.

22. Ibid., p. 13.

23. Ibid., p. 16.

24. Ironically, Rahimov delivered his speech in Russian rather than in his mother tongue.

25. Rorlich, *The Volga Tatars*, op. cit., p. 22.

26. Ibid., pp. 23–25.

27. Bashkort leaders and scholars repeatedly spoke to me of the identical nature of Bashkort and Tatarski, but they emphasised phonetic differences in the Bashkort tongue. See also Hafeez Malik, 'Bashkortostan's Dilemmas of National Self Determination', *The Muslim* (Islamabad), 14 July 1993.

28. Interview in Ufa, Bashkortostan, June 1994.

29. Ibid.

30. Text of Rahimov's speech, pp. 19–21.

31. Author's notes, taken on 2 June 1995.

32. *Rigveda* is the oldest of the four *vedas*, which were probably composed by Indo-Aryans between 1500 and 1000 BC. Percival Spear, *India: A Modern History* (Ann Arbor: The University of Michigan Press, 1965), pp. 32–33

33. Chelyabinsk State University (bulletin), 'Arkaim: A Monument of Proto-urban Civilization' (Chelyabinsk, 1995?).

34. 'They [the Aryans] shared a common language group which is known as the Aryan group of languages, and to which most of the languages of modern Europe belong'. Percival Spear, *India: A Modern History* (Ann Arbor: University of Michigan Press, 1961), p. 32.
35. For the full text of this memorandum see Hafeez Malik, 'Tatarstan: A Kremlin of Islam in the Russian Federation', *Journal of South Asian and Middle Eastern Studies*, vol. xvii, no. 1, Appendix A., pp. 25–7.
36. Personal copy of the resolutions.
37. Personal copy of the two-page address.
38. Personal copy of the one-page address.
39. Personal copy of the one page-address to President Boris Yeltsin.
40. Personal copy of the one-page address to the Federal Assembly.
41. Personal copy of the one-page resolution addressed to the United Nations.
42. Interview with the mufti of Bashkortostan, Ufa, June 1994.
43. Vasily Ustyuzhanim, 'The History of Russian Parliamentarianism', *Passport to the New World* (Moscow: March–April 1994), pp. 82–3.
44. Archie Brown *et al.* (eds), *The Cambridge Encyclopedia of Russia and the former Soviet Union* (New York: Cambridge University Press, 1994), pp. 361–3.

14

The Role of Bashkortostan National Sovereignty in the Russian Multinational State

D. Zh. Valeyev

The social and political crisis in the territory of the former Soviet Union – caused by an unviable economy, the absence of scientific orientation in politics, lawlessness and low morals – entails the crisis of man, the crisis of ethnic and national orientation. As no cultures are devoid of national content (even global culture has its ethnic roots), the moral lapse in modern spiritual life is to a great extent due to the disintegration of ethno-national organisations over the millenia. Many ethnic groups are on the brink of extinction for want of adequate social institutions and politico-legal mechanisms for self-organisation and self-defence.

The current global ethnopolitical situation prompts the question: what is the optimum way for ethnic groups to coexist within a multinational state? Federation or confederation at its highest manifestation proved to be the best form of statehood in terms of the aspiration of ethnic groups for self-determination.

The federal state, in the true sense of the word, offers the best legislative protection to its citizens. At the basis of federal relations in multiethnic states lies a certain universal idea or absolute value – national sovereignty.[1] As the Lithuanian scientist Antanas Burachas rightly states, 'National sovereignty in modern conditions comes to the fore and plays a vital role as a means of restoring human values in world politics in the information age.'[2]

The ontological basis for a nation's right to sovereignty are the values and integrity of the ethnic group itself and its culture, which means that each ethnic group, by the fact of its existence, has the same right to a worthy life as large, dominant ethnic groups, which frequently treat smaller ones as inferior and impose on them their will, their way of life and social institutions. There are examples from the former Soviet Union and Russia to testify to this.

For example in January 1934, following a resolution by the All-Union Central Executive Committee (ACEC), two administrative districts in The Bashkirian Autonomous Republic (Argayashskiy and Kunashakskiy) were transferred to the newly created Chelyabinsk *oblast* (region) without the agreement of the people inhabiting these districts or the republic's administration. The ACEC resolution had specified that the two districts would be transformed into the autonomous Argayashskiy Bashkort national district,[3] but this proved to be fraudulent as ten months later the ACEC rescinded its promise.[4] This was a violation of both human rights and national sovereignty. Many years later (1993) the inhabitants of the two districts renewed their call for autonomy[5] but the Russian-dominated Chelyabinsk legislature paid no heed. This would not have been the case if the Bashkort populace, which numbered about 170 000 had had at least one deputy to represent its interests in the Chelyabinsk regional Duma (its highest legislative body), but in the event the problem could and *krais* are named by the same term – it is stressed in the preamble that 'it stems from universally accepted principles of equality and self-determination of nations'.[11]

In all probability the above statements would not have been issued by the secretary for national affairs if it had not been for contradictions in the text of the constitution according to Article 66, part I: 'The status of the republic is determined by the Constitution of the Russian Federation and by the Constitution of the republic.'[12] The problem is not only that in the text of the constitution the phrase 'by the Constitution of the Russian Federation' goes before the phrase 'by the constitution of the republic' (the status of a sovereign republic must be determined by its own constitution!) but also that according to Article 125(b) it is up to the Supreme Constitutional Court of the Russian Federation to decide whether or not a republic's constitution corresponds to the constitution of the Russian Federation, which diminishes the republic's sovereignty and makes it dependent on the centre.

Nonetheless there has been progress in the constitutional development of the Russian Federation. Possession of this status should entitle ethnic groups to UN membership. Currently, however, the UN embraces states but not nations, contrary to what its name implies. All the ethnic communities of the world should have representatives in the UN. By analogy all the ethnic groups of Russia should be represented in both chambers of the parliament of Russian Federation – the Federation Council and the State Duma – but neither of these bodies adheres to the principle of equal national representation. A balance could be reached by imposing a quota system. At the moment the 600 000 Bashkorts residing outside Bashkortostan are not represented in the Russian parliament.

The above considerations are not just idle fantasies but are born out of dismal reality. The crisis of federalism, characteristic of many multinational states (the disintegration of the Soviet Union and Yugoslavia), speaks against the established models of federalism and for the necessity to find new forms, which should not only be based on the territorial principle but also take into account the specific national features of the regions in question. Modern Russia, for instance, should be a federation based only on the territorial principle. In this connection it should be noted that there is a view among Russian politicians that Russia should be a purely territorial federation, laying aside the principles of national statehood for republics and the national-territorial character of relations with autonomous regions. The current Russian Federation combines various forms of federalism: *oblasts* (regions), *krais* (provinces), sovereign republics and autonomous *okrugs* (areas). In addition certain sovereign republics (for instance Tatarstan) have the status of associated states. This should be fixed in the constitution of the Russian Federation.

The most democratic and just form of federation – taking heed of national interests and regional particularities – is confederation. Confederal arrangement is for Russia as a whole and to all its subjects, whose subdivision is based on both territorial and national principles. It would benefit those units which are based on a territorial principle since they will gain economic independence, and those based on the national principle will gain their autonomy, politically, spiritually and in the sphere of legislature.

The problem of national sovereignty in sovereign republics is closely related to state sovereignty. This interrelationship is not simple and requires thorough analysis. Although not identical, the concepts of national sovereignty and state sovereignty are interdependent as all the sovereign republics within the Russian Federation came into being as national republics. The state sovereignty of today's national republics within Russia stems from the process of national self-determination among those ethnic communities that gave their names to the republics. This means that national sovereignty at the republic level is the historical basis of the state sovereignty of the republics. In other words the state sovereignty of the republics is a manifestation of national sovereignty. The above view found expression in the constitution of the Republic of Bashkortostan (Article 69), to wit: 'The Republic of Bashkortostan is formed as manifestation of the right of the Bashkort nation to self-determination and it stands for the interests of its multinational people.'[7] Here there is a distinct correlation between the national sovereignty of the Bashkort people and the state sovereignty of the Republic of Bashkortostan. This constitutional article confirmed the status of Bashkortostan as a national republic, testifying to the national–federal character of the national sovereignty of Bashkort people. This article also underlines the status of Bashkorts as the ethnic group that has given its name to the republic, the indigenous people of Bashkortostan.

Taking all the above into account, we offer the following definition of national sovereignty. National sovereignty is the freedom of the ethnic community to dispose of its own fate, its territory and its riches, and to choose its own way of living, and managing its property as well as its socio-political order.[8]

In the light of these reflections it is proposed that an article setting out the right of all ethnic communities to national sovereignty and the method of its realisation be included in international legislation and in the legislation of modern multinational states. Modern legislation does not operate within the concept of national sovereignty, which can vary in form from an independent state, to a sovereign republic within a multinational state to a self-governed territory under the aegis of the UNO. By right the form adopted should be determined by a referendum of the entire ethnic community, and the economic structure, political institutions and spiritual values of the nation should not be imposed from outside.

It follows that federal relations in multinational Russia should be based on the ethno-national sovereignty of the peoples inhabiting the country, as national sovereignty is the best means of safeguarding national interests. Sooner or later the world community will have to give serious attention to the problem of national sovereignty as to ignore it will result in further ethnic conflicts.

In this connection the following considerations of the former secretary for national affairs, Sergei Shakhrai, seem highly disputable. In his article 'On the Conception of State Regional Policy', he writes: 'Since the early 1990s, more spontaneously than consciously, the structure of our federation has gradually changed to a territorial model. The republics, *krais* and *oblasts* of the Russian Federation have become essentially territorial subjects, but not ethnic communities.[9] Thus instead of federalism based on national ethnic principles, and ignoring the fact that there exist sovereign republics and national territorial regions, Shakhrai presents a homogeneous, unitarian structure of Russia.

With regard to national ethnic problems, Shakhrai suggests the principle of national cultural autonomy: 'The role and significance of local self-government ... is determined by the fact that combining local self-government with ... national cultural autonomy makes it possible to work out practical ways of addressing national problems which are very hard to solve in Russia.'[10] Regretfully the solution offered by Shakhrai is dictated by the idea of bolstering stern autocratic centralism and does not address the question of national-federal or national-territorial make-up, which is preferable for ethno-national communities which would determine their status, based on the most essential principles of – a people's right to national self-determination.

Moreover Shakhrai's analysis is not in line with new developments in the spheres of politics and law enforcement in Russia. The fact is that Article 5.2 of constitution of the Russian Federation adopted on 12 December 1993, recognises the sovereign-republics as states. Although in the new constitution all the republics, *oblasts* have been solved painlessly if the Chelyabinsk regional administration had shown more good will and humanity.

In 1957 the people of the two districts fell victim to radioactive poisoning after a leakage of radioactive substances from the 'Mayak' radiochemical works. They received neither financial nor moral compensation for the damage inflicted on them. It would be appropriate for these people to unite and take their case to the international court. The Chernobyl catastrophe was on a smaller scale but received much greater attention in the rest of the world.[6] Whatever reason for the unequal and discriminatory treatment of the victims of this tragedy, it is obvious that if they had had national and territorial status as autonomous districts it would have been easier for them to stand up for their rights.

Returning to the question of national sovereignty, In Article 1 of the treaty signed on 3 August, 1994 between the Russian Federation and the Republic of Bashkortostan, it is clearly written that 'the Republic of Bashkortostan is a sovereign state within the Russian Federation'. By recognising Bashkortostan as a sovereign state, the bilateral treaty also recognised the national sovereignty of the Bashkort people. (This tact is also emphasised in the preamble of the Constitution of the Russian Federation.) One detail is significant about this treaty: the text is in two languages – Bashkort and Russian. Although nothing is said about the status of the Bashkort language in the Constitution, its very use in the treaty, along with the provision in the Bashkortostan' Constitution that the president of Bashkortostan must be able to speak both Russian and Bashkort, provide ample legal ground for imparting to the Bashkort language the status of state language. Furthermore, while Article 68 of the constitution of the Russian Federation states that the state language throughout the Russian Federation (including Bashkortostan) is Russian, it also says that republics have the right to establish their own state languages.[13] This clearly implies that there can be two state languages in a republic – the language of the nation that gave its name to the republic, and the Russian language as the language of international communication, and the official language of the federation as a whole.

Language policy in the sovereign republics of Ingushetiya, Komi, Yakutiya-Sakha, Tatarstan, Chuvashiya and elsewhere, follows the same logic. In these republics the state languages are Russian and the languages of the indigenous peoples that gave their names to the republics. This gives a legal precedent for Bashkortostan to declare Russian and Bashkort as its state languages. Bashkortostan's lagging behind other sovereign republics in this respect, regardless of the linguistic inadequacy of the Bashkort population (only 74.2 per cent of Bashkort residents speak Bashkort as their mother tongue, while other ethnic groups in the republic – Russians, Tatars, Chuvashes, Maris, and so on – have a much higher percentage) is not only an anachronism but, to put it mildly, looks like laziness or, worse, sheer indifference to the fate of a people whose history and culture go back millenia.

When discussing the national sovereignty of the Bashkort people, one should not overlook the national interests of the non-Bashkort population, especially as the two numerically strongest groups – Russians and Tatars – outnumber the Bashkorts. Of course, there is no denying the fact that every ethnic community has its legitimate claims.

The difficulty of tackling the problem of the national sovereignty of the indigenous peoples of the republic – the Bashkorts and other national groups, lies in the definition of 'indigenous peoples'. We suggest that national sovereignty within a multinational state may be present at various levels and have a different status for different ethnic groups. The status of national sovereignty of the indigenous people which is determined by historic facts (the formation of the ethnopolitical entity with its material and spiritual culture), is characterised as national-federal sovereignty. National-federal sovereignty means that the indigenous population of the republic can enjoy the right to statehood. The indigenous nationality should also have the right to name the republic after its own name; declare its language as the state language; and reflect special features of its culture in its national emblem, flag and anthem. All these rights should be legalised.

Non-indigenous ethnic groups have no right to national statehood in the territory of Bashkortostan. Acknowledging the right of every ethnic group in the republic to national-federal sovereignty, we would come to absurdity, as dozens of ethnic groups are citizens of the republic. However, these ethnic groups enjoy curtailed national sovereignty: they educate their children at schools in their native language; publish newspapers and magazines, and broadcast radio and television programmes in their native language, do their office work and conduct business correspondence in their native languages in the localities of their compact settlement.

While the doctrine of national sovereignty is an essential mechanism for the realisation of national-ethnic interests, it has not been given adequate attention both theoretically and practically in solving the problems of national relations in the Russian Federation. In dealing with the Republic of Bashkortostan, the concept of national sovereignty has been highlighted in three works: the article 'Thorny Way of Bashkirian Sovereignty'[14] and 'National Sovereignty and Self-Determination of Peoples',[15] an article written jointly by F. S. Faizullin, D. Zh. Valeyev and F. B. Sadykov,[16] and a book on national sovereignty.[17]

Suffice it to quote the main points made by Faizullin *et al.*, who primarily stress the methodological significance of national sovereignty: 'The category of national sovereignty is characterised by rich and complex content; it has the genetical and practical regulatory functions simultaneously. The application of the one aspect of this category makes it possible to investigate ethnic communities (tribe, populace, nation) as a single organism, while the other concept of national sovereignty enables the researcher to consider concrete problems of ethnic development specifically applied to the interests of every given nation.' The latter possibility is especially important for those Bashkorts who for a variety of reasons reside out of the Republic of Bashkortostan. Guided by the concept of national sovereignty it is possible to pose the question of reestablishment of Argayashskiy Bashkirian okrug (district), illegally abolished by Stalinist regime in November, 1934. Nowadays, after the adoption of the Law 'On Rehabilitation of Repressed Peoples' this possibility comes closer to its realisation, as Articles, 2, 3, and 6 of the law unambiguously and clearly testify to it.'[18]

In promoting the national-federal sovereignty of the nation, especially when it joins a federation it should be noted that a republic acquires the status of an associate member of the federation, having equal rights with other members. The Republics of Bashkortostan and Tatarstan could have become associated members within the Russian Federation, which is likely to become a confederation in the future. This is an adequate solution to the problem of a sovereign republic's membership within a federative or confederative state; this solution is devoid of logical contradictions. The attempts to hold fast to the pattern of national relations of old times, which denied the right of peoples to national sovereignty, and national self-determination are fraught with contradictions and interethnic conflicts.

The views on national sovereignty expressed by the former executive secretary of the Constitutional Committee of the Russian Federation, Oleg Rumyantsev, and his adherents are nothing but clinging to old stereotypes. They insist on pursuing hard line policy in regard to sovereign Tatarstan, claiming not only to bring the constitution of Tatarstan to conform with that of Russia in a short period of two months, but also insist on full identity of the constitution of Tatarstan and Russia. Otherwise, Rumyantsev proposed to declare economic blockade on Tatarstan, stop financing conversion projects, and the enterprises of military–industrial complex.[19]

In our opinion, in the present delicate situation of Russia the most appropriate policy should be the creation of unity among sovereign states, who should be associated in a single federation on contractual basis. This policy would be against turning the republics into something similar to the status of oblasts and krais of Russia; secondly, it would prevent Russia from turning itself into a new empire. The apprehension about Russia becoming another empire is not without reason; it is heightened by the fact that a war is going on against the Chechen Republic, which attempted to establish an independent state. One can hear not always well considered declarations of some politicians about the necessity of turning sovereign republics into provinces.

Bashkortostan, an associated member within the Russian Federation, is surrounded by Russian territory, which makes separation of Bashkortostan from Russia an inconceivable enterprise. It also means that the Republic of Bashkortostan as an associate state must be an equal member along with Russia and other republics in the structure of the Russian Federation as one of cofounders of this union.

If these sound propositions are not taken into account there would develop 'centrifugal' aspirations leading to national independence of Bashkortostan. Then the movement would be labelled as national-separatism by adherents of unitarianism, and the proponents of national revival of Bashkorts would rightfully call their initiative as a movement towards self-preservation of ethnic communities. Each party would be right in its own way, as it will stand for its own interests. Undoubtedly, the truth would be on that side whose actions will be in harmony with universal humanistic values. A reasonable question may be asked: which nation will benefit if the Bashkort people with their unique culture disappear?

Disappearance of Bashkorts would be beneficial for the nation which strives to expand its living space and increase its population through the assimilation of others. Mankind will never gain anything but only lose much from the disappearance of a small nation, which has its unique history, culture and language. No one but larger domineering nations should be blamed for the disappearance of national minorities. An 'ethnocide' of smaller ethnic groups is no less dangerous than an ecological catastrophe or nuclear war. The death of an ethnic community is a tragedy of the whole civilisation and it will be naivete to think that this process can be bypassed. This tragedy will hound larger nations. The moral crisis which confronted the peoples of the former Soviet Union was the consequence of the fact that the national question remained unsettled.

In conclusion, we will outline the measures which are designed to defend national minorities from the processes of assimilation by larger ethnic groups. The preamble to Convention number 169 'About Indigenous Peoples and Peoples Leading Tribal Way of Life in Independent Countries' adopted by the General Conference of ILO (International Labour Organisation) at the 76th session on 7 June, 1989, stated that changes taking place in the lives of indigenous peoples and peoples leading tribal way of life create 'the necessity to adopt new international norms concerning this question with the purpose of eliminating the tendency to assimilation.' In Article number 7 of the same convention, number 169 is written, 'Nations have their own rights to make decisions concerning the choice of their own priorities for the processes of their development to the extent which is adequate for their mode of life, their beliefs, social institutions, spiritual well-being, the lands they occupy and cultivate in some way or other, and the right to execute control within possible limits over their own economic, social and cultural development. Moreover, they participate in the preparations, implementation and evaluation of plans and programs of national and regional development which may directly touch their interests.' This article may refer to all ethnic groups, including those sovereign republics where they do not constitute the majority of the population. In Bashkortostan where indigenous population constitutes only 21.9 per cent laws about indigenous peoples which would declare among other measures that the Bashkort language, along with the Russian language, be the state language on the territory of Bashkortostan. Moreover, in the law on indigenous peoples the priority rights of Bashkirs migrating from other regions of Russia could be fixed. The proposed measures would not entirely stop the processes of assimilation, but they will play a positive role in combination with other measures.

Our next suggestion refers to the question of official recognition of ethnic communities as subjects of international law, and as the members of the United Nations. The United Nations has not yet become the institution, which defends the interests of ethnic minorities from assimilative influence of larger ethnic communities. The United Nations must be the organization which protects nations and peoples from every form of ethno-national discrimination in the modern world.

Notes and references

1. The term 'national sovereignty' implies here ethno-national sovereignty, that is, the sovereignty of a given ethnic group (nation) as a political unity. In earlier and current publications by Russian scholars the term 'national' is identical to 'ethnic'.
2. A. Burachas 'Suverenitet', *Opyt slovarya novogo myshleniya* (Moscow, 1989), p. 521.
3. *Izvestiya*, 17 January 1934.
4. Ibid.
5. In March 1993 the First Congress of Bashkorts residing in the Chelyabinsk region appealed to the UN secretary general for help. The appeal was published in the *Journal of South Asian and Middle Eastern Studies*, issued in the United States in 1993, for which we are indebted to the chief editor of the journal, Professor Hafeez Malik.
6. When the radioactive leakage at the 'Mayak' works near Kyshtym (the southern Urals) took place in 1957 there was a fallout of 70–80 tons of radioactive substances. Eighteen thousand inhabitants of the Argayashskiy, Kunashakskiy and Kaslinskiy districts were evacuated from the contaminated area. According to experts, no other area in the world has been contaminated to the same degree or been as dangerously explosive. M. Feshbach and A. Friendly Jr. Ecotsid. V SSSR. Zdorovye i priroda na osadnom polozhenii. M.: NPO 'Biotekhnologiya' i izdatel' sko-informatsionnoye agentstvo 'Golos', 1992. – pp. 141–2.

7. Constitution of the Republic of Bashkortostan (Ufa, 1994), p. 25.
8. For details: see D. Zh. Valeyev, *Natsionalny suvernitet i natsionalnoye vozrozhdeniye* (Ufa: Kitap, 1994), p. 17.
9. S. Shakhrai, '0 Kontseptsii gosudarstvennoi regional'noi politiki', *Nezavisimaya gazeta*, 12 May 1994.
10. *Ibid.*
11. *Izvestiya*, 28 December 1993.
12. *Ibid.*
13. *Ibid.*
14. D. Zh. Valeyev, 'Ternistiy put' bashkirskogo suvereniteta', *Agidel*, vol. 12 (Ufa, 1992), pp. 132–41 (in Bashkort).
15. D. Zh. Valeyev, 'National'niy suverenitet i samoopredeleniye narodov', *Yadkar. Vestnik gumanitarnykh nauk*, no. 1 (Ufa, 1995), pp. 37–46.
16. F. S. Faizullin, D. Zh. Valeyev and F. B. Sadykov, 'National'niye otnosheniya v sovremennom Bashkortostanye', *Izvestiya Baskortostana*, 25, 29, 31 December 1992.
17. D. Zh. Valeyev, Natsional'niy suverenitet i natsional'noye vozrozhdeniye, op. cit., p. 160.
18. Faizullin *et al.*, 'Natsional'niye', op. cit.
19. L. Shakirova, 'V nadezhde na liberalov', *Moskovskiye novosti*, 13 December 1992.

15
The Turkic Peoples of Russia: Historical Ethnopolitical Perspectives and a Case Study of Bashkortostan

Rail G. Kuzeyev

An historical investigation leads us to believe that the process of restructuring ethnic relations is continuous. Further, it leads us to assume that developments in the territory of modern-day Russia – which is currently characterised by fragmentation, the restructuring of interethnic, international and interstate relations, and even conflicts and local wars – will result in the establishment of a new type of cooperation between peoples. The factors that will promote progress in this direction are not only the will and aspirations of democratically minded people, who are tired of chaos and uncertainty, but also a growing acceptance in all strata of society of the need for cooperation and economic and cultural integration. The basis of such an optimistic assumption is the prolonged period of interethnic peace on the territory of the former Soviet Union and long-term cooperation between the different peoples living in the Eurasian region. This cooperation may be subject to stress, even partial destruction, but it must not be lost altogether and allowed to sink into oblivion.

In the light of these considerations, this chapter presents the logic of the historical development of national movements in the Volga–Ural Basin, but some observations may be relevant to Russia as a whole.

Historical overview

National processes and civil movements for sovereignty and federalism have a long history. The national movements of Turkic peoples in Russia, which reached their height at the end of the nineteenth and the beginning of the twentieth century, can be divided into four stages.

First, the national democratic stage lasted approximately from the end of the nineteenth century to the revolution of 1905. The main motive for this struggle was the Turkic peoples' desire for education and social reforms, the revival of national cultures and languages, and equality and parity between Turkic Muslims and Slavic Christians in Russia's political development. Ismail-bey Gaspraly (Gasprinskiy), a leading figure in this movement, wrote: 'possibly in the nearest future, Russia will turn into one of the significant Muslim countries, which, I think, will in no way diminish its significance as a great Christian power'.[1]

Second, the social democratic stage (1905–1919/20) was characterised by increasing calls for national self-determination. The interpretation of the concept of 'self-determination' was, however, quite broad and included independence for national Turkic states, national territorial–state federalism in Russia, and national cultural autonomy for its parts. Consequently, in a resolution of the First All-Russia Muslim Congress in May 1917 it was noted that 'the most appropriate to [the] interests of the Muslim peoples ... is a democratic republic on national-territorial federative principles'.[2] The National Congress of Muslim Peoples, which met in November 1917, adopted a resolution on 'the creation of a special Turko-Tatar Idel-Ural autonomous state with extensive rights as a step toward independence in case of the impossibility of co-existing with Russia'.[3] Finally, the Alash Orda party declared that Russia must become 'a democratic federative republic'.[4] Despite the multitude of trends and views, the idea of democratic federalism prevailed in the national movements of 1917–18.

The idea of cultural autonomy was also gaining ground and took two forms: national cultural (nationally personalised) autonomy, and cultural national autonomy. The first type implied the formation of self-governed national communities under state protection; the second, culturally autonomous national communities free from state interference. It is noteworthy that the idea of national cultural autonomy gained recognition among the Muslim communities and was reflected in Islamic political trends. However the idea of cultural autonomy could not develop into a clear conception and failed to gain ground. This problem and the practical task of organising communities on national cultural principles in Russia require further research.

Third, the Bolshevik stage (1919–20) opened under the revolutionary slogans of 'Land to peasants', 'Self-determination to nations and peoples', and 'Decree for peace'. Consequently national liberation movements were channelled into the revolutionary class struggle. The movement underwent a process of differentiation and the leftist radical wing was singled out. Its most outstanding representative was Mir Said Sultan-Galiyev, who stood for the 'worker–peasant' Tatar republic and advocated the idea of the 'red banner of Bolshevik class struggle' being carried through all Oriental countries.[5] A major event of this period was the founding of the Soviet Union in 1922, which united (directly or through the Russian Federation) more than 50 autonomous republics, national regions and districts, which were organised until the 1940s according to the principle of 'national sub-division'. However their frontiers were determined by subjective political considerations rather than ethnicity, the negative consequences of which have strongly affected interethnic relations to this day. The ideas of national cultural and cultural national autonomy were condemned as bourgeois, hence there was no possibility of experimenting in this sphere.

Finally, the fourth stage started in the second half of the 1980s. To a great extent it was a revival of the second, social democratic stage under the changed conditions of the last decades of the twentieth century.

The defeat of national liberation movements

The third stage (the Bolshevisation of the national liberation movement) halted the disintegration of the Russian Empire, a process that had also affected the Ottoman and Austro-Hungarian Empires in the first decades of the twentieth century. Poland, Finland and the Baltic states had already seceded from Russia, the Caucasian and Central Asian peoples were on the way to secession, and a similar process had started in the Middle Volga region and the southern Urals. The Bolsheviks managed to keep the empire intact, but, at what price? This is a question of great importance. The 'triumphal march' of Soviet power in 1917–18 led to bloody civil war, repression terror and national segregation during the 1920s and 1930s. A very costly price indeed. The main point here is that the activities of the national liberation movements in Russia were forcibly cut short before they could realise their goals and aspirations.

The principle of national territorial or national federal self-determination (with the right to secede) was abandoned under the Soviet system. As Zaki Validi wrote to V. I. Lenin in February 1923: 'The right to self-determination up to secession granted to the peoples of Russia and the East by the Soviet government on November 20, 1917 in the Declaration "To All Laborers of Russia and the East" is made null and void by the Resolution of May 19, 1920'.[6] After the 1920s, national liberation movement leaders went underground in the Soviet Union or fled abroad to join emigré circles. The CPSU's struggle and that of the Soviet system against nationalism and nationalists has not yet received an adequate historical assessment. However it is evident that this unrelenting struggle not only damaged the development of nations and cultures, but also distorted the ideas and slogans of the national movement, the notions of self-determination, autonomy and federation.

The Soviet state formally acknowledged Bashkirian (Bashkort) autonomy in 1920. According to a resolution of the Soviet government of 19 May 1920, 'On the Statehood of the Bashkirian Autonomous Soviet Republic', the majority of 'people's commissariats of the Bashkirian Republic ... are subordinate to the people's commissariats of the RSFSR, whose decrees and instructions are paramount.[7] The doubly federal state (the USSR and the RSFSR) developed a highly centralised political and economic structure. Relations between centre and the republics and provinces became one of the key political problems in the Soviet Union and is yet to be fully investigated. The powerful pressure exerted by the single political party equalised the lives and behaviour of the peoples inhabiting the territory of the Soviet Union, including 54 national republics, provinces and regions, in the interests of creating a new socio-political entity, 'the Soviet people'.

But the situation was not as simple as some portray it. The decades of Soviet rule were characterised by industrial development, technical progress, progress in education, culture, science and many other spheres of civilisation. Most significant was the experience of cooperation between republics, regions and peoples. However these years were also marked by a certain loss of ethnicity, including national cultures and lifestyles. This twofold process, to some degree reflected general social trends all over the world. But in the Soviet Union the process was rigidly enforced and it took only four decades for the unitarian state system to bring about the political and ideological 'unity' of peoples from the Baltic Sea to the Pacific Ocean. The gradual loss of ethnic cultures resulting from forcible assimilation into the Russian culture contained the seeds of the national liberation movements we are witnessing today.

While the economic circumstances and social standing of Russian peasants, workers and intelligentsia did not differ in any way from those of other nationalities, the CPSU ideologists and the leading Russian elite promoted the idea of ethnic subordination when it came to the peoples of the republics. The idea of the 'elder brother' in the concord of nations and the 'progressive' influence of the Russian nation, Russian culture and Russian language were propagated at every level of people's lives and formed the basis of the deethnisation and loss of ethnic culture that took place to varying degrees throughout the Soviet Union, including, paradoxically, Russia itself. During the Second World War and in the postwar period, anti-Semitism was promoted (especially during the campaign against cosmopolitanism), as well as a negative or even hostile attitude towards the repressed nationalities, the exiled peoples of the Volga region, Crimea and the northern Caucasus. The prolonged years of ideological pressure twisted the thinking of a section of the population, who became poisoned by chauvinistic and nationalistic thoughts. The revival of national movements reveals a similar mentality, expressed as Rusophobia, anti-Semitism, dislike of Caucasians and Tatars or antipathy towards German Russians. Interethnic enmity and chauvinistic ideology are evident in the slogans and programmes of numerous politically minded groups. Another aspect of the current reaction of the former ideology is extreme radicalism, which sometimes explodes into armed conflicts. Such are the echoes of the past in modern history.

The revival of national liberation movements

With *perestroika* (restructuring) came the revival of national movements. Ideas that emerged early in the twentieth century but could not be realised are evident today in the goals, slogans and programmes of national cultural societies – the ideas of independence, national states, democratic federalism, and territorial and cultural autonomy.

In the 1990s, due to differences and conflicts between political groups, the desire for independence grew and republic after republic declared its sovereignty. This could have happened early in the twentieth century. The national liberation movements' slogans and goals do not include the idea of national cultural autonomy, especially in territories that have been granted some form of statehood. The reason is obvious: during the 70 years of Soviet rule there existed just one form of national territorial (national federal) self-determination, and public consciousness does not perceive any other way of realising the principle of self-determination. A tragic irony is that, in the majority of republics that have declared independence, the contradictions and problems that have emerged in the sphere of national relations are the same as those which proved the stumbling-block for the Soviet Union.

In all sovereign republics one can observe a tendency towards indivisible unitarian statehood and opposition to the principles of democratic federalism. Despite the constantly declared principle of full equality among all nationalities, 'elder brothers' and the 'titular nations' have become dominant in all the republics, where the ruling political forces do not recognise minorities' right to self-determination and hinder their passage towards territorial sovereignty. Even the idea of cultural autonomy is put to trial in many areas. Nor has the Russian Federation escaped these difficulties and contradictions – conflicts in the northern Caucasus, the middle Volga, the Urals and southern Siberia, aggression towards Caucasians, the revival of anti-Semitism in some regions, new migratory tendencies and local clashes testify to the Russian state's beleaguered position.

It is quite evident that national movements are representing the genuine desire of peoples for the revival and growth of their languages, traditions and cultures while simultaneously striving for influence and power.[8] The mass of contradictions tends to exacerbate the ethnopolitical problems in the territories of the former Soviet Union and the Russian Federation. In the author's opinion the current developments should be viewed as just a fragment of a lengthy and unfinished process. Obviously we must investigate more thoroughly the specific ethnopolitical history of Russia.[9] From this perspective, scholars must search for possible ways of influencing events in order to prevent Russia's disintegration.

Old and new slogans of national movements

From the perspectives of solving the existing contradictions, two extreme tendencies are especially dangerous. They express the interests and aspirations of radicals in national politics who package these tendencies in traditional political slogans. First, unitarians, who represent the interests of 'patriotic' forces, harp on the theme of 'single and indivisible' Russia. The meaning of this slogan is rather vague: 'single' within which frontiers', 'indivisible' in what sense and from whom? Is this a realistic slogan for the third millenium, borrowed as it is from the chauvinists of nineteenth-century tsarist Russia and the totalitarian, centralist ideologies of the twentieth century? Despite the democratic protestations of the advocates of this goal – that authority and responsibility would be shared between the centre and the republics – in reality unitarianism is implied.

There can be only one response to the unitarians after eight years of difficult democratisation: the reestablishment of a unitarian Russian state is unrealistic and would breed violence – besides Bashkortostan, Tatarstan, the Republic of Sakha and the Chechen Republic, the Russian Federation includes seventeen restless republics. Moreover it would be unjustifiable and incomprehensible for Russia, having declared its sovereignty, to attempt to pursue the unrealistic policies of the former Soviet Union towards the republics – policies that were discredited by the disintegration of the Soviet Union.

Second, in some autonomous republics, especially Tatarstan, Bashkortostan, Tuva and Chechnya, social movements have emerged under the banner of total independence and secession from Russia. This is in part a reaction to the extremely stiff and inflexible policies of the Moscow bureaucracy, which has been slow to abandon its role of 'elder brother', and to the aspirations of the unitarians whose ideas are not officially supported, but are exploited in the political struggle. The idea of state independence and secession from Russia occupies the minds of certain social groups not only in the national republics, but also in a number of regions (*oblasts*), whose leaders have revealed their wish for independence and self-sufficiency. This could provoke Russian unitarians to call for the suppression of nationalistic and national separatist movements. During the Russian Federation's constitutional debates heated discussions took place on these ethnopolitical problems, with some proposing equal rights for republics, *oblasts* and *krais* (territories) in the economic and political spheres. Obviously this was encouraged by the federal agreement on the republics' sovereignty. Conversely there is a strong antirepublican mood in the Ural region, where a radical wing of the Russian patriotic movement has gained ground.[10] The idea of a unified politico-administrative structure for the Russian Federation has found support among those who look to the past and call for the restoration of *gubernias*, and attempt to show the advantages of subdividing the country into states, lands and provinces on the Western pattern.

Are these ideas relevant at the end of the twentieth century? The answer can hardly be positive. Unlike the peoples of Transcaucasia and Central Asia, the peoples of the Volga region and the southern Urals have been part of Russia for almost four centuries. Consequently there has been a long experience of cooperation between Turkic, Finno-Ugric and East Slavonic peoples with a common cultural bond, which ensures relative interethnic stability in the Volga–Ural region. Another important factor to take into account is the Bashkorts voluntarily joined the expanding Russian state in 1559.[11]

Despite the complexity of the struggle by Bashkorts and other nations to prevent Russia from constantly violating the treaties that spelt out the conditions of their membership of the Russian state, in the long run their relationship has been productive and played a significant part in the formation of Russia's multinational statehood and the preservation of ethnicity.[12] The principles of national political formations within Russia go far back into the prerevolutionary past but have remained in people's minds. This fact should not be overlooked in the analysis of modern conditions and perspectives of ethno-political development in the Russian Federation.

On the threshold of the third millennium we are entering upon a transitional period which requires compromises from different societies striving for rapprochement with the civilised world, which espouses democratic principles, including human rights and the rights of small ethnic communities. For the sake of stability and progress of all nations, these compromises must be based on the principles of national self-determination, which would safeguard human rights, equality of peoples, and national autonomy.

The Volga–Ural region is multi-ethnic and multi-religious, where 35–75 per cent of the population is non-indigenous; most of them are Russians and others. If extremely radical movements, which espoused mutually antagonistic programs – like Russia's unitarian statehood, or absolute national independence for the indigenous people – were allowed to hold sway in this region, then violent confrontations would erupt between the Russians and indigenous populations. Russia cannot afford to nurture ambitions of unitarian federalism; and indigenous populations cannot afford to secede from the Russian Federation.

The need for a democratic federation

In such conditions, the only positive alternative for Russia and its republics is democratic federalism. This idea was championed by leaders of national movements as early as the beginning of the twentieth century. The principles of democratic federalism envisage (1) a form of government which combines dynamic federal power along with republics' sovereignty; (2) extensive rights for other subjects of the Federation; (3) the principles of political and social plurality of views and (4) the peoples' representation on all levels of state power.

As a system of ruling the country democratic federalism maintains the balance of power between the center, republics, local areas, and also promotes equilibrium for the social and cultural development of all people. Federation, as we see, presents a two-tier political system, where the sovereign subjects of federation and sovereign federal centre are interrelated, but their sovereignties are mutually limited.

We must not forget that the other alternative is a totalitarian federation like the Soviet Union, which was much more centralised than democratic unitary systems. In Russia, considerable changes occurred in the orientations of ethnic groups because of close contacts and higher level of communication. In a high degree, these changes took place in the Volga–Ural region, especially in Bashkortostan, where ethnic and administrative–political frontiers do not coincide.

In the Commonwealth of Independent States (CIS), where radicals prevailed, conflicts emerged and led to local wars. Nowadays, the problem of refugees is urgent, which acquired a catastrophic scale. Paradoxically, the declaration of sovereignty by the CIS countries often followed the ideology of the former Soviet Union, where minorities are denied equal rights. Consequently conflicts developed in Nagorno-Karabakh, Trans-Dniester, Abkhazia and Ossetia. Genuinely democratic federal structures of multinational Soviet Union would have checked the wars, and opened the ways to closer economic and political integration.

The autonomous republics also need political and economic resources for future development and prosperity, which would also ensure Russia's well being. Conditions set forth in the 'Addendum to the Federative Treaty of the Republic of Bashkortostan' are directed towards the creation of such conditions.[13] The Russian Federation's desire to create promptly an economic and financial basis of the federal state is understandable. But its indifference to the needs of the republics in the Russian Federation can grow into dangerous confrontation. A wise policy would call for reasonable increase of federal expenditure, redistribution of resources for social and cultural needs of the centre and the republics, establishing wider possibilities for the revival and independent development of the republics.

Sometimes in Russian 'patriotic' circles, a rhetorical debate is conducted: against whom and which powers is the national liberation movement directed today? Then an answer is rhetorically provided: there is no tsarist Russia 'the jailhouse of peoples', no Soviet Union, and consequently, no centre and periphery. Then the conclusion is drawn: the national liberation movement is directed against Russia and the Russians! This is an erroneous and dangerous thesis. In reality the national movements in the autonomous republics of the Volga–Ural region are directed not against, but mainly towards a certain level of political and economic independence within the Russian Federation. There would not have been 'sovereignty' parades if the notion of autonomy was not so devalued. Indeed there are some negative elements in the indigenous peoples' movements; but they are not necessarily against Russia. They are directed against the bureaucratic system, administrative mentality, syndrome of centralism, the snobbish ideology of 'Russian elder brother' and the conception of people's inequality. The clashes between the Russian and indigenous populations in the Volga–Ural region cannot be ruled out. Two factors which may deteriorate Russian and indigenous peoples' relations, refer to the diversity of the cultural levels of Russian city-dwellers, (whose ancestors settled in big cities) and the indigenous peoples who have not yet quite adapted to city life.

Self-determination and self-development

The concept of 'sovereignty' has found diverse interpretations in mass media. In some central newspapers and magazines, sovereignty is equated with separatism and nationalism (in the negative sense of the word), undermining the unity of Russia and the economic reforms. Sovereignty is thus understood by its opponents as 'self-determination leading to secession.' Indigenous peoples are often reproached that they seek political and economic privileges only because they belong to the so-called 'titular' nation.

It is only fair to mention that some radical national movements include in their programmes the final step of secession. But, the overwhelming majority of the citizens of the republics, including Tatarstan and Bashkortostan, understand sovereignty as a rather high level of political and economic independence of their republics within Russia – this scope of independence is understood in its wider sense, especially by business circles who look upon independence as the ability to conduct external economic activities, which were denied previously. In a certain sense republican sovereignty and democratic centralism do not oppose but complement each other. Consequently, there are no grounds to identify republics' sovereignty with separatism. In Bashkortostan, there are no anti-Russian slogans, no political separatism or plans for the disintegration of Russia.

Sovereignty for the republic is an expression of historical progress of the Bashkort people, their ardent desire to make their motherland prosperous and to improve its ecology. Realistic understanding of sovereignty besides territorial–federal self-determination implies self-development, self-responsibility and revival of lifestyle and behaviour in all levels of the society, including the ethnic identity. The realisation of the republic's sovereignty includes its claims on its own Parliament, government, and other structures of power. Finally, sovereignty implies that every person has the opportunity to attain a high level of self-independence, self-improvement and self-responsibility.

The people of Bashkortostan

In the CIS, including the Russian Federation, a new impulse is galvanising Russians, and the indigenous populations, to address their problems, especially in regard to their language, culture and ethnic territory. Intense discussions are taking place about the rights and interrelations of the 'indigenous' peoples and 'exogenous' Russians. The peculiarities of the current situation may be considered natural and unavoidable. In the process of creating new Russia and sovereign Bashkortostan there is an opportunity to avoid the errors which were committed in the CIS, and to direct the political and social processes into the democratic channel. For Bashkort people, a stabilising level will be reached when federal support becomes available to them to achieve high social, economic and cultural–educational standards. Consequently Bashkorts will be more adapted to urban way of living, and their agriculture will also be highly developed. The Bashkorts and other ethnics of the republic are ready to move in the direction of this development. The fact that Bashkorts live in their historical motherland is deeply rooted in their consciousness, and finds its reflection in their traditionally rich spiritual culture.

The citizens of sovereign Bashkortostan include multinational populations of the republics, including Russians, Ukrainians, Tatars, Chuvashes, Kazakhs, Mordovians, Udmurts, Germans, Latvians, Maris and Jews. They have their specific cultural–linguistic peculiarities, interests and aspirations.

All of them maintain contacts with their maternal ethnic groups in other republics of the Russian Federation, and naturally have the right to this free access and deserve federal support. However, the process of integration of all nations inhabiting Bashkortostan into a single community, which can be entitled 'the people of Bashkortostan' is also natural and appropriate.

This term – the people of Bashkortostan – is being used in the press, and official documents, while the process of the formation of the community has just started. It will develop only if all nationalities of the republic are committed to this type of development. However some programme items and slogans of national movements must be corrected. It will be useful in particular to eliminate from the strategic decision of the 6th All-Bashkirian Congress (1922) any reference to total independence of Bashkortostan. This decision runs counter to the modern world tendencies, and evokes a negative response from the non-Bashkort population of the republic, and heightens their anxiety. Unrealistic are slogans of the Tatar Public Centre (TPC) about the Ufa district's secession from Bashkortostan and the establishment of Idel-Ural state. These slogans evoke a negative response from the Bashkortostan public. Inadequate are the theses in the programmes of the Bashkort National Centre (BNC) about historically conditioned adherence of Bashkorts to the communal way of life. It is well known that long before the 1917 revolution, these principles, which were assisted by communal life, were destroyed and were subsequently fully transformed into *kolkhoz-sovkhoz* forms of the organisation of labour and the collective way of life, which is, in fact, an impersonal usage of the state land.

In the strategic aspect of national development it is appropriate to establish principles of nationally personalised (cultural) autonomy, which in Bashkortostan may be applied to comparatively not very numerous minorities, including Chuvashes, Maris, Mordovians, Udmurts, Germans, Jews, Latvians and others.

The educational, scientific and cultural potential of Bashkortostan

If the parliament, the government of the Republic of Bashkortostan and the leaders of national and public movements are really serious that sovereign Bashkortostan within the Russian democratic federation should undertake economic development, then it is imperative first of all to work out a realistic democratic plan of reforms in education, science and culture before the Republic can hope to join the most civilised countries of the world. This dilemma was faced especially by the Federal Republic of Germany and Japan after the Second World War. Bashkortostan's system of pluralistic education, would have to tackle four requirements of (1) developing a feeling of patriotism nationalities; towards the Republic of Bashkortostan especially in younger generations of all; (2) the feelings of adherence to one's own nationality and (3) simultaneously to the peoples of Bashkortostan and (4) Russia.

Sovereignty of the republic of Bashkortostan imposes its claims on the organisation and structure of scientific education. It is imperative to pass from the Soviet Union's established vertical hierarchies to a horizontal system, which should be the foundation for renewed organisation of science in Bashkortostan. Also, contacts with the scientific centres in the Russian Federation and other states should be preserved and strengthened. The restructuring of science in the republic is a complex process because in a relatively unified political and economic space fundamental science, industrial research, higher educational establishments and their research structures intertwine and make up a certain unity. The main link in this unity is fundamental science, which influences the efficacy of other links of the system. The institution of the Academy of Sciences of Bashkortostan is a breakthrough which benefits the republic and its multinational people.

The reforms in education, science and culture are catalytic factors of development of all republics and nationalities. Changes in social and national orientations take time; but they would lead the way to harmony in the society, and preservation of Russia's unity. The implementation of these reforms would require Bashkortostan to create its own internal political and administrative structure. This structure must take into account specific features of the democratic federal system and create opportunities for cultural development. The renewed administrative–political structure with rights to self-management would enable Bashkortostan to protect the rights of all ethnic groups, including those rights which are registered in international conventions. The renewed administrative system would entail the election of a new generation of politically and socially active people into structures of power. Frequent elections would also eliminate conservative elements, who are entrenched on the regional echelons of power.

Relationship between the centre and the republics of multinational states are never simple. In Russia, they experience an additional complication due to an inevitable transition to horizontal links, which are based on equality and parity. These relations can be harmonious, business-like and civilised, if: (1) the Russian Federation formulated the general principles of its national policy, and espoused democratic principles of statehood; (2) Bashkortostan should clearly relate its national policy, including language policy and the administrative structure and simultaneously declare its policy towards the rights of national minorities; (3) it is appropriate to have a chamber of nationalities in Bashkortostan's legislature, which should determine the share of nationalities' participation in legislative and executive bodies; (4) Bashkortostan should pursue a programme of radical economic reforms in coordination with Russia's programme.

In conclusion, it should be said that this author has expressed his own understanding of the current situation. All references to the future include not only Bashkortostan, but also the Russian Federation. Russian citizens must learn to develop a habit of thinking in the context of world tendencies. Today's world is multinational, and deserves to be preserved and multiplied. The classic view of 'national state's' dominating role comes into clash with modern realities. The notion of 'nation' should evolve from the category of 'ethnicity' (people) to the category of 'citizenship', which stands for mutual tolerance and acceptance of different cultures.

Notes and references

1. Ismail-bey Gasprinskiy, *Russian Muslims* (Oxford, 1985), p. 25.
2. *Program Documents of Muslim Political Parties. 1917–1920* (Oxford, 1985), p. 11.
3. A. Iskhaki, *Idel-Urals*, (London, 1988), p. 49–50.
4. *Program Documents of Muslim Political Parties*, op. cit., p. 86.
5. M. S. Sultan-Galiyev, *The Articles* (Oxford, 1984, p. 38).
6. Obrazovaniye BASSR, *Sbornik dokumentov i materialov* (Ufa, 1959), pp. 487–8.
7. Dialog. Prilozheniye k zhurnalu 'Agidel'. December 1990, p. 3.
8. Yu. G. Kulchik, in *Ethnopoliticheskiye protesessy v Bashkortostane (Informatsionno-analiticheskiy obzor* (Moscow, 1992).
9. The study of Bashkortostan has been facilitated by the publication of the informative, three-volume *Etnopoliticheskaya mozaika of Bashkortostana Ocherki Dokumenty. Khronika* (compiled and edited by M. N. Guboglo): vol. I, *Kontury etnopoliticheskoi situatsii v ocherkakh i zakonodatelnykh aktakh* (Moscow, 1992); vol. 2, *Bashkirskoye natsionalnoye dvizheniye* (Moscow, 1992); vol. 3, *Vektory etnopoliticheskoy situatsii v dokumentakh I materialakh* (Moscow, 1993).
10. P. Tropinin, *Kraya, Oblasti otvergayut ranzhirovaniye Otechestovo* (Ufa, 1993, N 13, May).
11. R. G. Abdulatipov, L. F. Boltenkova and Yu. V. Yarov, *Federatsiya v istorii Rossii* (Moscow, 1992), pp. 35, 139–40.
12. *Izvestiya Bashkortostana*, July 17 1992.

16

The Ethno-Linguistic Situation in the Republic of Bashkortostan

Zinnour Uraksin

Some preliminary observations

The functioning of any language depends on various extra-linguistic factors – the size, composition and density of the population, statehood, the degree of urbanisation, the level of education, the linguistic policies of the state, the degree of national self-awareness – and purely linguistic factors such as the existence of a standard literary language and the degree of its structural perfection, versatility and ability to serve the growing needs of social communication. So far, in the case of the Republic of Bashkortostan all these peculiarities and conditions have been investigated in relation to the indigenous Bashkort nation and not all aspects have been taken into account.

The current linguistic and ethnic situation in Bashkortostan is the result of at least a thousand years of developments in the area. The Bashkorts' historical place of residence has been multi-ethnic and multilingual since the early days, and since the eighth century there has been interaction between Turkic, Aryan and Fenno-Ugric tribes and their languages or dialects.

The Bashkorts were by far the largest population group and by the fifteenth century the non-Bashkort tribes had been assimilated into their number, although their traces can be found in numerous archaeological sites and place names. There is no mention of any military clashes in the early history of the region either in the folklore, legend or historical documents. There is reason to believe that by the start of the sixteenth century Bashkortostan had turned into a relatively monolingual and mono-ethnic land of Bashkorts.

The region's current population structure started to form in the mid sixteenth century after it was annexed to the Russian state, which for more than four centuries vigorously imposed its state management system, economy and culture.[1] One of the major features of Russia's overlordship was the forceful or voluntary resettling of people of various extraction from Russian provinces to the Bashkort lands – by the close of the eighteenth century the newcomers constituted about 58.7 per cent of the region's population.[2] That process continued throughout the next century and by the 1920s the present ethnic composition of the region was in place: Bashkorts 30.1 per cent; Tatars, Mishars and Teptiars 20.9 per cent, Russians 34.4 per cent, Ukrainians 3.08 per cent; Maris 3.36 per cent, Chuvashes 2.9 per cent, Mordvas 1.8 per cent, White Russians 1.17 per cent, Udmurts 0.91 per cent and Letts 0.34 per cent.[3] Thus over the centuries the ethnic composition of Bashkortostan drastically altered to the Bashkorts' disadvantage.

The current demographic and linguistic situation in Bashkortostan

Demographic and sociolinguistic phenomena are interrelated and shifting. This point is supported by the All-Union censuses held every decade in Bashkortostan since 1959. According to the 1989 data, that year the total population stood at 3.943 million, comprising 863 808 Bashkorts (21.9 per cent), 1.546 million Russians (39.3 per cent), 944 507 Tatars (28.4 per cent), 126 638 Chuvashes (3.0 per cent), 109 638 Maris (2.7 per cent), 76 005 Ukrainians (1.9 per cent), 40 745 Mordvas (0.8 per cent), 27 918 Udmurts (0.6 per cent), 17 985 Belorussians (0.4 per cent), 12 104 Germans (0.3 per cent) and 6668 Jews (0.1 per cent).[4]

Thus the largest ethnic group (53.4 per cent) consisted of Turkic peoples (Bashkorts, Tatars, Chuvashes and Kazakhs), followed by Slavic peoples (Russians, Ukrainians and Belorussians – 41.6 per cent). This composition has remained fairly stable, with some minor changes occurring by the end of 1994: the Bashkorts population grew by 4.6 per cent, the Tatar by 1.0 per cent, the Udmurts by 16.5 per cent and the Mordva by 1.5 per cent. There was a slight reduction in the number of Russians, Ukrainians, Germans and Belorussians.[5]

According to the 1989 census the total number of Bashkorts was 1.449 million, 59.6 per cent in Bashkortostan and the rest in the Chelyabinsk region (161 200), the Orenburg region (53 300), Perm (52 300), Sverdlovsk (41 500), the Tyumen region (41 100), Kurgan (17 500), the Samara region (7500), the Saratov region (4080), Tatarstan (19 100), Kazakhstan (41 800), Uzbekistan (34 800), Ukraine

(7400), Tajikistan (6800), Turkmenistan (4600), Kyrgyzstan (4020), Moscow (8400), St Petersburg (3010) and elsewhere.[6]

The peculiarity of the ethnic demographic situation in Bashkortostan is that the Bashkorts occupy third place after the Russians and Tatars. In 1926, 87.6 per cent of the total Bashkort population resided in Bashkortostan, falling to 79.6 per cent in 1939, 68.2 per cent in 1979 and a mere 59.6 per cent in 1979.[7] Up to the 1990s their proportion in the total population of the republic tended to stagnate or fall. The indigenous people accounted for 22.8 per cent of the total population in 1926, 21.2 per cent in 1939, 22.1 per cent in 1959, 23.4 per cent in 1970 and 21.9 per cent in 1989. This reduction was due to Bashkorts migrating in the 1950–1980s to adjoining areas of Russia and Central Asia, as well as the process of assimilation.

The Bashkorts are predominantly rural dwellers. In 1989 42.3 per cent of Bashkorts lived in towns; a substantially lower proportion than Russians and Tatars. Rural Bashkorts live in close proximity with each other, thus creating favourable conditions for the functioning of the Bashkort language. On the other hand the ethnic diversity and residential intermingling in towns, workers' settlements and district centres has an adverse effect on the use of the Bashkort language. As a rule Russian is the language of communication in the work place and in the spheres of trade and transportation, although the closeness of the Bashkort and Tatar languages means that it is possible for the respective speakers to dispense with Russian when communicating with each other. Most Chuvash, Mari and Udmurt speakers have a working knowledge of the Tatar language, and to a lesser extent Bashkort, favouring the functional development of these languages. The two languages are largely underused by the younger generation of Bashkorts and Tatars, who rely heavily on Russian for communication. Even in rural areas there is not a single district with fewer than three nationalities, and five or more nationalities dwell in 36 districts out of the total of 54.[8] This situation necessitates Russian to be employed at events at the district level. Even district Bashkort conventions (*Kurultais*) in many places were held in Russian in 1995–96, causing much disapproval and bewilderment among the participants themselves.

The majority of non-Russian people in Bashkortostan are bilingual in their native language and Russian (89.0 per cent), while the Russian residents are notoriously monolingual, not mastering any of the languages of the people of the republic. In the 1989 census 74.7 per cent of Bashkorts declared Bashkort as their native language.[9] The remaining 25.3 per cent habitually spoke Tatar, and Russian to a lesser degree.

A large number of north–western Bashkorts have gradually switched to Tatar as the language of family communication and school instruction, while maintaining their Bashkort ethnic identity. This process has been going on for centuries, and the prerevolutionary Bashkort language was approximate to the standard Tatar language. The new standard Bashkort language, having been moulded in the 1920s on colloquial and ancient language styles, has not been welcomed by the Bashkorts and has had a vast effect on their national self-consciousness, resulting in part of the Bashkort population gradually transferring themselves to the Tatar nation.

The educational level of the population has also influenced the employment of particular languages – the more persons there are with a higher or college education, the higher the degree to which one or other language is mastered and employed, native languages included. The Bashkorts are lagging behind the Russians and Tatars residing in Bashkortostan as far as this is concerned. According to the 1989 census 0.9 per cent of adult Bashkorts had received higher education and 18.9 per cent a college education; the equivalent figures for Russians and Tatars were 1.02 per cent and 24.6 per cent, and 0.95 per cent and 20.15 per cent respectively.[10]

Trilingualism is also a feature of the Bashkortostan linguistic scene, such as Bashkort–Tatar–Russian, Chuvash–Tatar–Russian, Mari–Tatar–Russian, Udmurt–Tatar–Russian and Chuvash–Bashkort–Russian. Trilingualism manifests itself mainly in the sphere of oral communication.

The functioning of the Bashkort language

Bashkort is one of the Turkic languages of the Russian Federation, second only to Tatar in terms of the number of speakers and its use in certain spheres. It has three forms: written standard (scientifically standardised and regulated by state and public bodies), colloquial standard (less subject to regulations) and dialect, which is constantly influenced by the two other forms.

Written and oral standard Bashkort is used for high school education and in preschool education for Bashkorts. The use of Bashkort for high school education since the 1920s has fluctuated according to the central government's policies. It reached a high in 1960, when Bashkort was the lingua franca in schools (106 000 pupils).[11] Thereafter many schools switched to Russian as the language of instruction, with Bashkort being taught as a subject only.

The democratisation process in Russia prompted an upsurge in Bashkorts national self-consciousness, a return to the national culture and a rebirth of the native language. Despite much difficulty the national school system (Bashkort schools included) started to develop in the 1990s. In Ufa two city gymnasium schools were opened, with most of the subjects being taught in Bashkort. In the academic year 1993/94 there were 825 Bashkort-language schools, rising to 886 in 1995/96, and the number of pupils studying Bashkort rose 1.9 fold.[12] Bashkort as a subject was taught three hours a week in 416 mixed schools and in Russian-language schools at the request of parents.

Higher education in the Bashkort language is provided mainly in the humanities (philology and to a certain extent history and law). Departments of Bashkort letters are functioning at the Bashkort State University, the Bashkort and Sterletamaq Teachers' Training Colleges and the Sibai branch of the Bashkort State Teachers' Training College. The use of Bashkort to teach in schools and colleges will require the training of instructors in the republic's institutes of higher education.

Standard Bashkort is widely employed in the mass media. In 1996 there were nine magazines in Bashkort and three republican newspapers. An international paper entitled *Zaman-Bashkortostan* was printed in Bashkort, Russian, Tatar and Turkish, with an overall print run of 5000. There has been a tendency for the number of newspapers and magazines to grow and the print run to fall. For example circulation of the literary and socio-political magazine *Agithel* was 65 000 in the 1980s, but by 1996 it had fallen to a modest 12 000. The reasons for this are the high production costs and a fall in the number of those able to read Bashkort due to Russian being used as the language of education in the 1960s and 1980s. Bashkort is widely employed in the sphere of culture, for example six professional and scores of peoples' theatres put on plays in Bashkort.

The use of Bashkort in the legislative assembly, other state bodies, industry, transportation, trade, science and business is limited. Russian is the main language in these spheres, and is likely to remain so for a long time. All statutes and presidential decrees are published in both Bashkort and Russian, as are passports, birth and marriage certificates, political slogans, appeals, polling station bulletins and other items of national importance.

While books are printed in Bashkort, including works of fiction, there has been a decrease in the number of titles. Few academic books are issued in Bashkort, reflecting the fact that only a limited number of academics have the ability to write scholarly treaties in the Bashkort language. Also contributing to this is the poor development of Bashkort terminology in science, technology, economics, politics, law and other social sciences.

Popular spoken Bashkort remains in everyday use, but in towns and workers' settlements Russian has taken a large edge over Bashkort. Even in worker and peasant families, parents tend to communicate with their children in Russian, which can be viewed as a result of a decrease in national self-consciousness and a change in the population's cultural and educational bearings.

Many people entertain the hope that the prestige of the native language and its role among the Bashkort people and the republic's social life will grow. This will require the native tongue to acquire state language status in Bashkortostan, a suggestion that was raised during the World Bashkort' Congress in Ufa on 1–2 June 1995, in numerous reports in the press and at public gatherings.

The Bashkort language issue

In the Volga–Ural area the standard Turkic language of the Bashkorts was not recognised by the state until the 1920s. The first move in this direction took place in June 1921, when the Regional Committee of the Communist Party adopted the following resolution at their plenary session: 'Bashkort shall be recognised as a state language on a par with Russian, and the compulsory study of Bashkort will commence in all places of academic and military instruction, starting with Bashkort language and history courses for Soviet functionaries'.[13]

The issue was also discussed at the Second Bashkort Congress of the Soviets on 2 July 1922, and a similar resolution was passed.[14] An official paper, 'Abstracts on the Nationalities Issue', adopted by the Bashkort RCP (Bolshevik) Conference in September 1922, specified the areas where Bashkort should be used: courts of law, state bodies, the press, schools, theatres, clubs and all cultural and educational bodies.[15] On 14 April 1924 the All-Russia Central Executive Committee passed a decree that legal transactions should be conducted in the native language at state national offices in the republics and regions.[16]

These decrees then made Bashkort and Russian languages state languages. Also the constitution of the Bashkort Autonomous Soviet Republic (BASR) was adopted in December 1924. During the 1920s a vast amount of work was done to translate the constitution into reality. The BASR Council of Ministers established the central commission which cooperated with locally functioning cantonal commissions in order to implement the use of Bashkort in various areas of public life.

Regrettably, in the mid 1930s the Soviet Union steered sharply towards unitarianism and its language policy was brought into line with the general policies and ideology of the Communist Party. That is why the constitution adopted by the BASR in 1937 merely made some points of a linguistic nature and did not define the status of the Bashkort language, for example 'Laws passed by the Supreme Council of the BASR shall be published in Bashkort, Russian and Tatar' (Article 24).[17] Likewise, 'Legal and court proceedings in rural districts, towns and settlements with a Bashkort, Russian, Tatar, Mari and Chuvash majority shall be conducted in Bashkort, Russian, Tatar, Mari or Chuvash respectively. In the central courts, law proceedings shall be held in Bashkort, Russian or Tatar. Persons not speaking those languages shall be given full access to an interpreter/ translator and have the right to speak their native language in court' (Article 178).

As can be seen, these two articles did not define the status of the languages in questions, they merely point to the spheres of their employment. The same applied to the constitutions adopted by the BASR Supreme Council on 30 May 1978, which emphasised only two major spheres of usage: 'Statutes of the Bashkort ASSR, resolutions and other bills of the BASR Supreme Council shall be published in Bashkort and Russian' (Article 98).[18] General aspects of the language issue (but not official status) were laid down in the current constitution, which was passed on 24 December 1993 by the Bashkort Supreme Soviet: 'Any propaganda relating to social, racial, national, religious or linguistic supremacy is prohibited' (Article 33)[19] and 'Citizens of the Republic of Bashkortostan have the right to choose their language of communication, the right to use their native language, the right to education and upbringing in their native language' (Article 35).[20]

More specifically, Article 92 stipulates that any elected president of the Republic of Bashkortostan should 'know the Bashkort and Russian languages'.[21] This point caused some protest in oppositional circles and was deemed as discriminating against non-Bashkorts.[22] A special commission, composed of expert linguists, was set up to ensure that this clause was adhered to. The commission sat in session before the 1993 elections to determine the native language proficiency of M. Rahimov and R. Kadirov, who were both running for the presidency (the present writer acted as chairman of this commission). The conduct of the proceedings and the fact-finding activities of the commission did not cause any later complications, as had been feared, and the proceedings were business-like rather than political game playing.

After the present constitution was adopted the press published some critical articles on the undetermined status of the Bashkort language. The situation was resolved with the adoption of 'A Statute on the Languages of the Peoples in the Republic of Bashkortostan', the draft of which had been prepared in 1991 by the History, Language and Literature Research Institute of the Russian Academy of Sciences and was published in Russian and Bashkort.[23] Then another bill was proposed for Bashkort and Russian to be granted state language status. The Republic of Bashkortostan is the only state in the world to further the development of the Bashkort nation and its language. When Bashkortostan was incorporated into the Russian Federation, Russian – the language of interstate and internal communication – also became a state language of the republic. It is suggested that the languages of other nations (such as Tatar, Chuvash, Mari and Ukrainian) be adopted as mass media languages and used in the cultural and educational arenas by representatives of those peoples.

The status of the Russian language in Bashkortostan is not questioned by anyone; however the suggestion that Bashkort be made a state language is resented. Opponents argue that (1) Bashkort is the language of the republic's minority, and (2) it would be imposed on other peoples who constitute the majority of the population.[24] These interrelated arguments can not be substantiated. First, in other republics in Russia where the native peoples are in the minority their languages have been recognised as state languages (Buryat, Khakass, Komi, Tatar, Yakut and so on).[25] Second, the languages of the numerical minority are declared as the state language of their native speakers, that is the Bashkort language for Bashkorts, Chuvash for Chuvashes. This is a defensive measure, not an offensive one because minority languages are in danger of extinction.

The negative attitude towards the study of Bashkort and its recognition as a state language displayed by some persons of Russian and other extraction in Bashkortostan has bewildered the Bashkorts. For the success of any state or republic lies in its being multilingual, and knowledge of Bashkort is a key to cognizance of many Turkic languages and their cultures (Tatar, Kazakh, Kara-kalpaq and Uzbek, which are close to each other and to a certain degree to Turkish). There is also such a thing as elementary respect for each other, and language is a direct road to people's souls and hearts. In Chuvashia and Tatarstan the authorities have authorised the teaching of Chuvash and

Tatar as a subject and no negative stand is taken on those languages in the republics in question.[26]

The Tatar Social Centre in Bashkortostan has proposed that Tatar be instituted as the republic's third state language. As the Tatar language has already been declared an official language in Tatarstan, it can be viewed as functioning as an already accepted state language amongst the Tatar population of Bashkortostan.

President Rahimov of Bashkortostan maintains a reserved and cool policy towards the question of language status, deeming it a secondary matter in peoples' lives, one that should develop naturally rather than as a result of state regulation. That policy has earned him constant criticism and reproaches, both in the press and at Bashkort public gatherings. The longer the issue is left unsettled the more complicated it will become.

The Bashkort script

The Bashkorts have had three scripts during their history: Arabic prior to 1928, Latin from 1928 to 1939 and Cyrillic from 1940 onwards. Little is known about the use of ancient Turkic (runic) writing on the territory of Bashkortostan, but some monuments with runic inscriptions have been unearthed in Tatarstan, Chuvashia and the Orenburg region.

The discarding of the Arabic script after a millenium or so of constant use represented a serious break with the nation's cultural and historical heritage. Until the start of the 1990s there persisted an official view that the Bashkorts had lacked a script and a literary language prior to the October Revolution, but the error of this claim is now officially admitted. The Arabic language and script is being taught only in Bashkort and Tatar institutes of higher education to a very limited number of students.

In the opinion of some linguists and educationalists the script that most adequately reflects the phonetics of the Bashkort language is Latin, and this has been the subject of heated discussion in the press and at various public meetings.[27] Some authors have voiced sharp criticism of scholars who favour adoption of the Latin script and accuse them of having a pro-Turkish cultural and political orientation.[28] There is no doubt that scholars and people of culture in the Turkish Republic are going to great points to propagandise the Latin script to the Turkic peoples of the CIS and Russia, and hold annual international symposia and conferences on the subject. Some of the Turkic republics of the former Soviet Union (Kyrgyzstan, Uzbekistan and Turkmenstan) have already passed decrees on the adoption of this script in the near future.

In Tatarstan, scholars have published an alphabet and textbook for schools based on the Latin script. However, given the present economic crisis in the Russian Federation, the sovereign republics therein are hardly likely to be able to bear the large financial outlay needed for full changeover. Besides, a section of the intelligentsia is still inclined towards maintaining the current Cyrillic script. It may be appropriate to use all three systems (Arabic, Latin and Cyrillic) in the field of education, thus avoiding any sharp confrontations and drastic changeovers. There have been several articles in favour of such a step in the Bashkortostan press.[29]

So the eventual nature of the Bashkort script is still a matter of conjecture and the debate is sure to continue.

The language conflict

Sociolinguists employed at the Russian Academy of Sciences in Moscow, who are largely responsible for the linguistic policies of the Russian Federation, are inclined to believe that the roots of the language conflict lie in the fact that many national republics have declared their native (non-Russian) language as a state language without due legal and psychological preparation and without first creating the necessary conditions.[30]

With regard to the situation in Bashkortostan, some Moscow scholars allege that knowledge of the Bashkort language is being made a criterion for 'getting into the political elite'.[31] This accusation is based on superficial knowledge of the situation or information from biased sources. The biased interpretation of the linguistic situation in Bashkortostan was initiated in the late 1980s by the CPSU secretary for ideology, the notorious Egor Ligachev, who at the CPSU Central Committee plenary meeting in February 1988 came out with a one-sided appraisal of the teaching of native languages in Bashkortostan. His evaluation received widespread support in Ufa, Kazan and Moscow. Even one Yu Rimarenko of Kiev joined in the debate when he wrote on Bashkort 'nationalism',[32] having visited the republic only once and assimilating his 'fresh facts' in toto from an article by A. Khalim in the magazine *Druzhba Narodov*.[33]

Not a single writer on this topic has bothered to raise the following question: what is to become of the 24 per cent of Bashkorts who reside in the north–west of Bashkortostan and have lost their native language by speaking and studying Tatar, while never ceasing to consider themselves as Bashkorts? This is a burning issue and the cause of much discontent amongst Bashkort intellectuals.

Many consider that the way to preserve and develop the Bashkort language is to give it state language status and provide instruction in it to Bashkorts through a system of education and tutoring. Furthermore the role of the Bashkort language in social life should be strengthened since a certain number of Bashkorts are gradually losing their sense of national identity and are growing indifferent to the nation's history and fate. Moreover they have started to acquire spiritual values other than their own.

The issue is not of a matter of conflict as it concerns only Bashkorts-turned-Tatar regaining the use of their mother tongue and returning to the Bashkort fold. There are any number of Bashkorts who consider Russian to be their mother tongue, but no one dares to deny that they are Bashkorts. There could be a gradual overcoming of all these problems by dint of a separate study of the Bashkort language and by making full use of it in the press and the education system.

The Bashkort and the Tatar languages

How close are the Bashkort and Tatar languages? In appraising the degree of relatedness between the Turkic languages one has to adopt a different approach from that used to deal, say, with the Indo-Aryan languages. The latter have diverged greatly from each other, to the point where language lessons are required if their speakers are to converse with each other. Conversely, the Turkic languages have remained close and possess many common features, such as a basic vocabulary and a largely unified grammar. Thus the Kypchaq languages, for instance Bashkort, Tatar, Kazakh, Kara-kalpaq, Balkar, Nogai, Kumyk, Karachai and to a certain extent Uzbek and Kirgiz, are so close to each other as to prevent any major difficulty in conversation. Nonetheless they are distinct languages, not dialects of the same language. Each has its own dialects, for instance Tatar has Middle and Mishar dialects and the vernacular of the Siberian Tatars, with many subdialects, while the Bashkort language has the Eastern, Southern and North–western dialects and scores of subdialects.

The words in the various Turkic languages possess stable common roots and the agglutinative structure has created a common grammatical system. That is why the Orkhon-Yenissei inscriptions dating from the fifth to the seventh centuries AD are comprehensible to the speakers of modern Turkic languages. More than a millenium of Bashkort–Tatar coexistence in the Urals, their cultural similarities and intermarriage between the two peoples have boosted the linguistic closeness, notably at the lexical level (a commonality of up to 90 per cent, but less in the case of dialects and subdialects). However they do differ phonetically, and the Bashkort language occupies a peculiar place among the Turkic languages as far as consonants are concerned, approximating only Turkmen in regard to some sounds.

The Bashkorts also have their own cultural peculiarities: epic poems with an ancient mythological background (*Kubairs*, or legends in verse), folk songs, dances, clothing, musical instruments and other cultural paraphernalia. It is therefore appropriate to suggest that one should take account of the full array of ethnical, historical and cultural phenomena when studying the problems of language kinship.

Notes and references

1. Alton S. Donelly, *The Conquest of Bashkiria 1552–1740* (Ufa, 1995) (translation of the 1968 English edition). pp. 219–263.
2. U. Kh. Rakhmatullin, *The Population of Bashkortostan (XVII–XVIII centuries)* (Moscow: Nauka, 1988), p. 186.
3. B. Kh. Yuldashbayev, *The Bashkirs and Bashkortostan in the XXth century* (Ufa: Ethnostatistics, 1995). p. 27.
4. *Bashkortostan and Bashkirs in the Mirror of Statistics,* compiled by M. Murzabulatoff (Ufa 1995), p. 64.
5. Ibid., p. 106.
6. N. V. Bikbulatoff *The Bashkirs. A Concise Reference Book* (Ufa, 1995), p. 3.
7. Draft state programme 'Rebirth and Development of the Bashkir Nation,' compiled by Z. Uraksin and R. Valiakhmetoff (Ufa, 1995), p. 13.
8. *The Development of Social Functions of Standard Bashkir* (Ufa, 1987), p. 16.
9. *Bashkortostan and Bashkirs in the Mirror of Statistics* (Ufa, 1995), p. 75.
10. Ibid. (the percentages are our own calculations).
11. *The Development of Social Functions of Standard Bashkir* (Ufa, 1987), pp. 46–7.
12. *Vatandash* (Compatriot) magazine, no. 1 (1996), p. 40.
13. 'Formation of the BASR', a collection of papers and materials (Ufa, 1959), p. 611.
14. *Documents of the Soviet Congresses, 1917–1936,* vol. 1 (1959), p. 545.
15. *Resolutions of Regional Bashkir Party Conferences (1917–1940)* (Ufa, 1959), pp. 159–61.
16. A. Yuldashev, 'The Bashkir Language', *Zakonomernosti razvitia literaturnyeh jazykov Narodov SSSR v Sovetskojy epokhu,* 1969, p. 136.
17. The BASR Constitution, adopted and modified by the BASR Supreme Council on 9 October 1953 and 22 June 1954, p. 8.
18. The BASR Constitution, adopted on 30 May 1978 (Ufa, 1984), p. 28.
19. The Constitution of the Republic of Bashkortostan (Ufa, 1994), p. 14.
20. Ibid., p. 15.

21. Ibid., p. 34.
22. R. Khakimov, 'We Demand Impeachment' and R. Kadyrov, 'Face to Face with Totalitarian Machinery', *Economies and US* (newspaper), no. 48, 1993, also see *Otechestvo* (newspaper), no. 32, November 1993.
23. *Ethnopolitical Mosaics of Bashkortostan* (Moscow, 1993); *Bashkortostan* (newspaper), 26 May 1995.
24. I. Petrov, 'Ne mytyom, tak Katanyem', *Otechestvo* (newspaper), no. 4 (1995); V. Osipenko and A. Burakow, 'To Stop another Folly', *Otechestvo*, no. 5 (1995).
25. V. P. Neroznak, 'The Language Reform (1990–1995)' *RAN Bulletin*, vol. 66, no. 1 (1996), p. 4.
26. I. Andreyev, 'Functioning and Development of Chuvash in a Bilingual Medium', *Chuvash National Academy of Sciences Bulletin*, no. 1 (1995), p. 35.
27. Sh. Garifullin, 'In Latin script?' *Leninets*, (newspaper) June 14 1990.
28. R. Sultangareyev, 'People's Fate is No Toy', *Evening Ufa* (newspaper), 18 June 1992, R. Nizamoff, 'Latin to scholars, Cyrillics to the People', *Yanaryu* (newspaper), 3 September 1993.
29. R. Masalim, 'Is Cyrillic the best of the ABCs?', *Zaman-Bashkortostan* (newspaper), 4–10 November 1995. Sh. Garifullin, 'Ctoby bukva zvukom otzyvalas', *Sovetskaya Bashkiria* (newspaper), 13 July 1995.
30. T. Kruchkova, 'Are Linguistic Conflicts in Russia Possible?', *Science in Russia*, no. 3 (1994), p. 54.
31. V. Solntsev and V. Mikhalehenko, 'The Linguistic Situation and Language Policies in the Russian Federation', *Problemy yazykovoi zhizni Rossiyskoi Federatsii* ... 1994, p. 9.
32. Yu. Rimarenko, *Following the Snow Man's Foot-prints* (Moscow, 1989).
33. A. Khalim, 'Yazyk moj-drug mo', *Druzhba Narodov*, no. 6 (1988).

Index

Rakhimov, Bashkortostan's President, 163
Rakhmatullin, U. Kh., 288
Rasulev, Mufti, 161
Rasuly, 160
Rathore, Naim, xiii
Reagan/Bush period, 37
  Reagan, President, 54
realpolitik, 73, 86, 103, 161
Referendum, December 1993, 84
regime sovereignty, 97
regionalism, 122
  regional cooperation, 66
  regional development, 185, 201
  regional instability, 69
  regional and international
    terrorism, 124, 128
  regional stability, 70, 97
relations with Russia, 127
religion and free association, 3
religious nationalism, 31
Republican-dominated 104th
    Congress, 131
reunification of the former Soviet
    Union nations, 234
Reutov, Aleksandr, 25
revival of ethnic Russian culturalism,
    100
Rigveda, 241
Rimarenko, Yu, 286, 289
Risordgimento, 20, 221
River Volga, x
RMU, 164
Robbins, G., 136
Robins, Philip, 57
Rodzianko, 248
Roman civilisation, 2, 208–9
Rorlich, Azade-Ayse, 250
Rostov region, 104
Rothkopt, David, 2, 24
RSFSR, 266
Rubin, Barnett, 80
Rubinstein, Alvin Z., xv, 12–14, 36,
    56, 58, 79
Rudenko, S. I., 164
Rumyantsev, Oleg, former executive
    secretary of the Constitutional
    Committee of the Russian
    Federation, 259–260

Rushd, Ibn, 209
Rusi, Alpo M., 25
Russia, x, xi, xii, 1–5, 8, 9, 11–14, 16,
    17, 19, 20, 29, 30, 32, 33, 35, 39,
    40, 43, 48, 55, 59, 62–5, 67–8, 74,
    78–9, 87–8, 98–9, 105–7, 110,
    113, 122, 124, 127, 132–3, 142–3,
    145, 147–8, 152–4, 169, 172–5,
    178–9, 185–6, 191, 197, 204–5,
    211–13, 226, 233–5, 237, 243–4,
    253, 257, 265–6, 270–3, 275–81,
    287
Russia's Choice, 129
Russia's foreign policy, 126
Russia's Orthodox Church, ix, 118,
    119, 120; clergy, 101; church,
    10, 99, 100, 158, 170, 226
Russia and the Islamic factor,
    struggle for power, 139; Islam's
    weakness in, 162, 163; Islam's
    threat to, 156; Islamic
    community, 118; relations
    with countries of the CIS, the
    Islamic factor, 146
Russia is Our Home Party, 129
Russia's Strategic Rocket Forces, 100
Russia–Tatarstan treaty of February
    1994, 17, 18
Russia-Tatarstan relations, 196
  Bashkortostan's relations with, 233
  Great State in, multinational, 218
  freedom of religion in, 10
  market-oriented economy, 125
  Mongol invasion of, 169
  Muslims in, 127–8; Russian Muslim
    Union (RMU), 163
  neoimperialist ambitions, 124
  policy towards Iran, 69; Russian-
    supplied arms, 70
  policy towards the former Soviet
    republics, 4
  relations with its former empire, 45
  relations with the Gulf nations, 126
  relations with Kazakhstan and
    Central Asia, 153
  relations with the United States, xii
  Spiritual Body of Muslims of, 119
  Tatarstan's treaty with, 188, 192,
    202